ISBN 978-1-331-66093-4
PIBN 10219354

This book is a reproduction of an important historical work. Forgotten Books uses
state-of-the-art technology to digitally reconstruct the work, preserving the original format
whilst repairing imperfections present in the aged copy. In rare cases, an imperfection in
the original, such as a blemish or missing page, may be replicated in our edition. We do,
however, repair the vast majority of imperfections successfully; any imperfections that
remain are intentionally left to preserve the state of such historical works.

1 MONTH OF
FREE
READING

at
www.ForgottenBooks.com

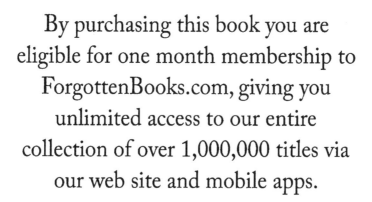

By purchasing this book you are eligible for one month membership to ForgottenBooks.com, giving you unlimited access to our entire collection of over 1,000,000 titles via our web site and mobile apps.

To claim your free month visit:
www.forgottenbooks.com/free219354

Collins's Select Library.

HISTORY

OF

THE REFORMATION

IN THE

SIXTEENTH CENTURY.

BY

J. H. MERLE D'AUBIGNE, D.D.

J'appelle accessoire, l'estat des affaires de ceste vie caduque et transitoire. J'appelle principal, le gouvernement spirituel auquel reluit souverainement la providence de Dieu.—*Theodore de Beze.*

By *accessory*, I mean the state of affairs in this fading and transitory life. By *principal*, I mean the spiritual government in which the providence of God is sovereignly displayed.—*Theodore Beza.*

A NEW TRANSLATION, CONTAINING THE AUTHOR'S LATEST IMPROVEMENTS,

BY

HENRY BEVERIDGE, ESQ., ADVOCATE.

VOL. II.

GLASGOW:

WILLIAM COLLINS, PUBLISHER & QUEEN'S PRINTER.

1862.

CONTENTS.

HISTORY OF THE REFORMATION

SIXTEENTH CENTURY.

BOOK FIFTH.

CHAP. I.

THE DISCUSSION OF LEIPSIC, 1519.

'Luther's Dangers—God saves Luther—The Pope sends a Chamberlain—The Legate's Journey—Briefs of Rome—Circumstances favourable to the Reformation—Miltitz with Spalatin—Tezel's Terror—Caresses of Miltitz—A Recantation demanded—Luther refuses, but offers to be silent—Agreement between Luther and the Nuncio—The Legate's Embrace—Tezel overwhelmed by the Legate—Luther to the Pope—Nature of the Reformation—Luther against Separation—De Vio and Miltitz at Trèves—Luther's cause extends in different countries—Luther's writings the commencement of the Reformation.

DANGERS had gathered round Luther and the Reformation. The doctor of Wittemberg's appeal to a General Council was a new attack on papal authority. By a bull of Pius II, the greater excommunication had been denounced even against emperors who should dare to incur the guilt of such a revolt. Frederick of Saxony, as yet imperfectly confirmed in evangelical doctrine, was prepared to send Luther away from his states;[1] and hence a new message from Leo might have thrown the Reformer among strangers, who would be afraid to compromise themselves by receiving a monk whom Rome had anathematised. And even should the sword of some noble be drawn in his defence, mere knights, unable to cope with the powerful princes of Germany, must soon have succumbed in the perilous enterprise.

But at the moment when all the courtiers of Leo X were urging him to rigorous measures, and when one blow more might have placed his adversary in his hands, the pope suddenly changed his

[1] Letter of the Elector to his envoy at Rome, (L. Op. (L.) xvii, p. 298.)

2   A

course to one of conciliation and apparent mildness.[1] It may be said, no doubt, that he was under a delusion as to the Elector's feelings, and deemed them more decided in Luther's favour than they really were. It may also be admitted that the public voice and the spirit of the age, powers which at this time were altogether new, seemed to throw an impregnable barrier around the Reformer. It may even be supposed, with one of Leo's biographers,[2] that he followed the promptings of his mind and heart which inclined to gentleness and moderation. Still this new mode of action on the part of Rome, at such a moment, is so extraordinary that it is impossible not to recognise in it a higher and mightier hand.

There was then at the Court of Rome a Saxon noble who was chamberlain to the pope and canon of Mentz, Trèves, and Meissen. He had turned his talents to advantage. As he boasted of being, in some degree, allied to the Saxon princes, the Roman courtiers sometimes designated him by the title of Duke of Saxony. In Italy he made an absurd display of his German nobility, while in Germany he aped the manners and polish of the Italians. He was given to wine[3]—a vice which his residence at the Court of Rome had increased. Still the Roman courtiers hoped great things from him. His German extraction—his insinuating address—and his ability in negotiation—all led them to expect that Charles de Miltitz (this was his name) would, by his prudence, succeed in arresting the mighty revolution which was threatening to shake the world.

It was of importance to conceal the true object of the chamberlain's mission, and in this there was no difficulty. Four years before, the pious Elector had applied to the pope for the golden rose. This rose, the fairest of flowers, was emblematic of the body of Jesus Christ, and being annually consecrated by the sovereign pontiff, was presented to one of the first princes in Europe. On this occasion it was resolved to send it to the Elector. Miltitz set out with a commission to examine into the state of affairs, and to gain over the Elector's counsellors, Spalatin and Pfeffinger, for whom he had special letters. Rome hoped that, by securing the favour of the persons about the prince, she would soon become mistress of her formidable adversary.

The new legate, who arrived in Germany in December 1518, was careful as he came along to ascertain the state of public opinion. To his great astonishment he observed, at every place where he stopped, that the majority of the inhabitants were friendly

[1] " Rationem agendi prorsus oppositam inire statuit, (Pallavicini, Hist. Conc. Trid. T. !, p. 51.   [2] Roscoe's Life of Leo X.   [3] Nec ab usu immoderato vini abstinuit, (Pallavicini Hist. Conc. Trid. i, p. 69).

to the Reformation,[1] and spoke of Luther with enthusiasm. For one
person favourable to the pope, there were three favourable to the
Reformer.[2] Luther has preserved an anecdote of the journey—
"What think you of the see (seat) of Rome?" frequently asked
the legate at the mistresses of the inns and their maidservants.
One day, one of these poor women, with great simplicity, replied—
"How can we know what kind of seats you have at Rome, and
whether they are of wood or stone?"[3]

The mere rumour of the new legate's arrival filled the Elector's
court, the university, the town of Wittemberg, and all Saxony,
with suspicion and distrust. "Thank God," wrote Melancthon,
in alarm,[4] "Martin still breathes." It was confidently stated that
the Roman chamberlain had received orders to possess himself of
Luther's person, by force or fraud; and the doctor was advised, on
all hands, to be on his guard against the stratagems of Miltitz.
"His object in coming," said they, "is to seize you and give you
up to the pope. Persons worthy of credit have seen the briefs of
which he is the bearer." "I await the will of God," replied
Luther.[5]

In fact, Miltitz brought letters addressed to the Elector and his
counsellors, to the bishops and to the burgomaster of Wittemberg.
He was also provided with seventy apostolic briefs. Should the
flattery and the favours of Rome attain their object, and Frederick
deliver Luther into her hands, these seventy briefs were to serve as
a kind of passports. He was to produce and post up one of them
in each of the towns through which he had to pass, and hoped he
might thus succeed in dragging his prisoner, without opposition,
all the way to Rome.[6]

The pope seemed to have taken every precaution. The electoral court knew not well what course to take. Violence would
have been resisted, but the difficulty was to oppose the chief of
Christianity, when speaking with so much mildness, and apparently with so much reason. Would it not be the best plan, it was
said, to place Luther somewhere in concealment until the storm
was over? . . . An unexpected event relieved Luther, the Elector,
and the Reformation, from this difficult situation. The aspect of
affairs suddenly changed.

---

[1] "Sciscitatus per viam Miltitzius quanam esset in æstimatione Lutherus....sensit de
eo cum admiratione homines loqui." (Pallavicini, Hist. Concil. Trid. Tom. i, p. 51.)
[2] "Ecce ubi unum pro papa stare inveni, tres pro te contra papam stabant." (L.
Op. Lat. in Præf.) [3] Quid nos scire possumus quales vos Romæ habeatis sellas,
ligneasne an lapideas? (Ibid.) [4] "Martinus noster, Deo gratias, adhuc spirat.
(Corpus Reformatorum. Edidit Bretschneider, I, 61.) [5] Expecto consilium
Dei. (L. Ep. i, p. 191.) [6] Per singula oppida affigeret unum, et ita tutus me per-
duceret Romam. (L. Op. Lat. in Præf.)

On the 12th of January, 1519, Maximilian, the Emperor of Germany, died, and Frederick of Saxony, agreeably to the Germanic constitution, became regent o' the empire. From this time the Elector feared not the schemes of nuncios, while new interests began to engross the court of Rome—interests which, obliging her to be chary of giving offence to Frederick, arrested the blow which Miltitz and De Vio were undoubtedly meditating.

The pope earnestly desired to prevent Charles of Austria, already King of Naples, from ascending the imperial throne. A neighbouring king appeared to him more formidable than a German monk; and in his anxiety to secure the Elector, who might be of essential service to him in the matter, he resolved to give some respite to the monk that he might be the better able to oppose the king Both, however, advanced in spite of him.

In addition to the change thus produced in Leo, there was another circumstance which tended to avert the storm impending over the Reformation. The death of the emperor was immediately followed by political commotions. In the south of the empire the Swabian confederation sought to punish Ulric of Wurtemberg, for his infidelity to it, while in the south, the Bishop of Hildesheim proceeded, sword in hand, to invade the bishopric of Minden, and the territories of the Duke of Brunswick. How could men in power, amid such disturbances, attach any importance to a dispute relating to the remission of sins? But, above all, the reputation for wisdom enjoyed by the Elector, now regent of the empire, and the protection which he gave to the new teachers, were made subservient by Providence to the progress of the Reformation. "The tempest," says Luther, intermitted its fury, and papal excommunication began to fall into contempt. The gospel, under the shade of the Elector's regency, spread far and wide, and in this way great damage was sustained by the papacy."[1]

Moreover, the severest prohibitions were naturally mitigated during an interregnum. In every thing there was more freedom and greater facility of action. Liberty which began to shed its rays on the infant Reformation, rapidly developed the still tender plant, and any one might have been able to predict how favourable political freedom would prove to the progress of evangelical Christianity.

Miltitz, having arrived in Saxony before the death of Maximilian, lost no time in visiting his old friend Spalatin; but no sooner did he begin his complaint against Luther than the chaplain made an attack upon Tezel, acquainting the nuncio with the lies and blas-

---

[1] " Tunc desiit paululum sævire tempestas. . . . ." (L. Op. Lat in Præf.)

phemies of the vender of indulgences, and assuring him that all Germany blamed the Dominican for the division which was rending the Church.

Miltitz was taken by surprise. Instead of accuser he had become the accused. Turning all his wrath upon Tezel, he summoned him to appear at Altenburg and give an account of his conduct.

The Dominican, as great a coward as a bully, and afraid of the people whom he had provoked by his impostures, had ceased his peregrinations over town and country, and was living in retirement in the college of St. Paul. He grew pale on receiving the letter of Miltitz. Even Rome is abandoning, threatening, and condemning him—is insisting on dragging him from the only asylum in which he feels himself in safety, and exposing him to the fury of his enemies ... Tezel refused to obey the nuncio's summons. "Assuredly," wrote he to Miltitz, on the 31st of December, 1518, "I would not regard the fatigues of the journey if I could leave Leipsic without endangering my life; but the Augustin, Martin Luther, has so stirred up men in power, and incensed them against me that I am not in safety any where. A great number of Luther's partizans have conspired my death, and therefore I cannot possibly come to you." [1] There was a striking contrast between the two men, the one of whom was then living in the college of St. Paul at Leipsic, and the other in the cloister of the Augustins at Wittemberg. In presence of danger the servant of God displayed intrepid courage—the servant of men despicable cowardice.

Miltitz had orders, in the first instance, to employ the arms of persuasion; and it was only in the event of failure that he was to produce his seventy briefs, and at the same time endeavour, by all the favours of Rome, to induce the Elector to put down Luther. He accordingly expressed a desire to have an interview with the Reformer. Their common friend, Spalatin, offered his house for this purpose, and Luther left Wittemberg on the 2nd or 3rd of January to repair to Altenburg.

At this interview Miltitz exhausted all the address of a diplomatist and a Roman courtier. The moment Luther arrived the nuncio approached him with great demonstrations of friendship. "O," thought Luther, "how completely his violence is turned into gentleness! This new Saul came into Germany provided with more than seventy apostolic briefs to carry me alive and in chains to murderous Rome, but the Lord has cast him down on the way." [2]

"Dear Martin," said the pope's chamberlain to him in a coaxing

<hr/>

[1] Löscher, ii, 567. [2] Sed per viam a Domino prostratus .... mutavit violentiam in benevolentiam fallacissime simulatam. (L. Ep. i, p. 206.)

tone, "I thought you were an old theologian sitting quietly behind your stove, and stuffed with theological crotchets; but I see that you are still young, and in the full vigour of life.[1] Do you know," continued he in a more serious tone, "that you have stirred up the whole world against the pope and attached it to yourself?"[2] Miltitz was aware that to flatter men's pride is the most effectual mode of seducing them; but he knew not the man with whom he had to do. "Had I an army of twenty-five thousand men," added he, "assuredly I would not undertake to seize you and carry you off to Rome."[3] Rome, notwithstanding of her power, felt herself feeble in presence of a poor monk, and the monk felt strong in presence of Rome. "God," said Luther, "arrests the billows of the ocean at the shore, and arrests them . . . . by the sand."[4]

The nuncio, thinking he had thus prepared the mind of his opponent, continued as follows: "Do you yourself bind up the wound which you have inflicted on the Church, and which you alone can cure." "Beware," added he, letting a few tears fall, "beware of raising a tempest, which would bring ruin on Christendom."[5] He then began gradually to insinuate that a recantation was the only remedy for the evil; but he at the same time softened the offensiveness of the term by giving Luther to understand that he had the highest esteem for him, and by expressing his indignation at Tezel. The net was laid by a skilful hand, and how was it possible to avoid being taken in it? "Had the Archbishop of Mentz spoken thus to me at the outset," said the Reformer afterwards, "this affair would not have made so much noise."[6]

Luther then replied. With calmness, but also with dignity and force, he stated the just grievances of the Church; expressed all the indignation he felt at the Archbishop of Mentz, and nobly complained of the unworthy treatment he had received from Rome, notwithstanding of the purity of his intentions. Miltitz, though he had not expected this firm language, was able, however, to conceal his wrath.

Luther resumed, "I offer to be silent in future as to these matters, and let the affair die out of itself,[7] provided my opponents also are silent; but if they continue to attack me, a petty quarrel will soon beget a serious combat. My armour is quite ready. I will do still more," added he, after a momentary pause, "I will write

---

[1] O Martine, ego credebam et esse senem aliquem theologum, qui post fornacem sedens. . . . . (L. Op. Lat. in Præf.) [2] Qui d orbem totum mihi conjunxerim et papæ abstraxerim. (L. Ep. i, p. 231.) si haberem 25 millia armatorum, non confiderem te posse a me Romam perduci. (L. Op. Lat. in Præf.) [4] L. Op. (W.) xxii.
[5] Profusis lacrymis ipsum oravit, ne tam perniciosam Christiano generi tempestatem cleret. (Pallavicini, i, 52.) [6] Non evasisset res in tantum tumultum. (L. Op. Lat. in Præf.) [7] Und die Sache sich zu Tode bluten.) L. Ep. i, 207.

his Holiness, acknowledging that I have been somewhat too violent, and declaring that it was as a faithful child of the Church I combated harangues which subjected her to mockery and insult from the people. I even consent to publish a document in which I will request all who read my books not to see any thing in them adverse to the Roman Church, but to remain subject to her. Yes: I am disposed to do every thing and bear every thing; but as to retractation never expect it from me."

Luther's decided tone convinced Miltitz that the wisest course was to appear satisfied with the promise which the Reformer had just made, and he merely proposed that an archbishop should be appointed arbiter to decide certain points which might come under discussion. "Be it so," said Luther, " but I am much afraid that the pope will not consent to have a judge. In that case no more will I accept the judgment of the pope, and then the strife will begin anew. The pope will give out the text, and I will make the commentary."

Thus terminated the first interview between Luther and Miltitz. They had a second, in which the truce, or rather peace, was signed. Luther immediately informed the Elector of what had passed. " Most serene prince and very gracious lord," wrote he, " I hasten very humbly to inform your Electoral Highness, that Charles de Miltitz and I have at length agreed, and have terminated the affair by means of the two following articles :—

" 1st, Both parties are forbidden to preach or write, or to do any thing further in reference to the dispute which has arisen.

" 2ndly, Miltitz will immediately acquaint the holy father with the state of matters. His holiness will order an enlightened bishop to enquire into the affair, and specify the erroneous articles which I am required to retract. If I am found to be in error, I will retract willingly, and never more do any thing that may be prejudicial to the honour or the authority of the holy Roman Church."[1]

The agreement being thus made, Miltitz appeared quite delighted. " For a hundred years," exclaimed he, " no affair has given the cardinals and Roman courtiers more anxiety than this. They would have given ten thousand ducats sooner than consent to its longer continuance."[2]

The chamberlain of the pope made a great show of feeling before the monk of Wittemberg. Sometimes he expressed joy, at other times shed tears. This display of sensibility made little impression on the Reformer, but he refrained from showing what he thought of it. " I looked as if I did not understand what was

---

[1] L. Ep. i, 209. [2] " Ab integro jam sæcuio nullum negotium Ecclesiæ contigisse quod majorem illi sollicitudinem incussisset." (Pallavicini, Tom. i, p. 52.)

meant by these crocodile tears,"[1] said he. The crocodile is said to weep when it cannot seize its prey.

Luther having accepted an invitation to supper from Miltitz, the host laid aside the stiffness attributed to his office, while Luther gave full scope to his natural gaiety. It was a joyous repast,[2] and when the parting hour arrived, the legate took the heretical doctor in his arms and kissed him.[3] "A Judas kiss," thought Luther, "I pretended," wrote he to Staupitz, "not to comprehend all these Italian manners."[4]

Was this then to be in truth the kiss of reconciliation between Rome and the dawning Reformation? Miltitz hoped so, and rejoiced at it, for he had a nearer view than the courtiers of Rome of the fearful results which the Reformation might produce in regard to the papacy. If Luther and his opponents are silent, said he to himself, the dispute will be ended, and Rome by availing herself of favourable circumstances will regain all her ancient influence. It thus seemed that the debate was drawing to a close: Rome had stretched out her arms and Luther had apparently thrown himself into them; but the Reformation was the work not of man but of God. The error of Rome consisted in seeing the quarrel of a monk where she ought to have seen an awakening of the Church. The revival of Christendom was not to be arrested by the kisses of a pope's chamberlain.

Miltitz, in fulfilment of the agreement which he had just concluded, proceeded from Altenburg to Leipsic, where Tezel was residing. There was no occasion to shut Tezel's mouth, for, sooner than speak, he would, if it had been possible, have hidden himself in the bowels of the earth; but the nuncio was determined to discharge his wrath upon him. Immediately on his arrival at Leipsic Miltitz summoned the unhappy Tezel before him, loaded him with reproaches, accused him of being the author of the whole mischief, and threatened him with the pope's displeasure.[5] Nor was this all: the agent of the house of Fugger, who was then at Leipsic, was confronted with him. Miltitz laid before the Dominican the accounts of that house, together with papers which he himself had signed, and proved that he had squandered or stolen considerable sums. The poor wretch, who had stickled at nothing in his day of glory, was overwhelmed by the justice of these accusations: despair seized him, his health gave way, and he knew not where to hide his shame. Luther heard of the miserable condition of his old enemy,

---

[1] "Ego dissimulabam has crocodili lacrymas a me intelligi." (L. Ep. i, 216.) [2] "Atque vesperi, me accepto, convivio lætati sumus." (Ibid. 231.) [3] "Sic amice discessimus etiam cum osculo; (Judæ scilicet.)" (Ibid. 216.) [4] Has Italitates. (L. Ep. i, 231.) [5] Verbis minisque pontificiis ita fregit hominem, hactenus terribilem cunctis et imperterritum stentorem. (L. Op. in Præf.)

and was the only person who felt for him. In a letter to Spalatin he says, "I pity Tezel."[1] Nor did he confine himself to such expressions. He had hated not the man but his misconduct, and, at the moment when Rome was pouring out her wrath upon him, wrote him in the most consolatory terms. But all was to no purpose. Tezel, stung by remorse, alarmed at the reproaches of his best friends, and dreading the anger of the pope, not long after died miserably, and as was supposed of a broken heart.[2]

Luther, in fulfilment of his promises to Miltitz, on the 3rd of March wrote the following letter to the pope:—

"Blessed Father! will your Blessedness deign to turn your paternal ears, which are like those of Christ himself, towards your poor sheep and kindly listen to its bleat. What shall I do, Most Holy Father! I am unable to bear the fierceness of your anger, and know not how to escape from it. I am asked to retract, and would hasten to do so could it lead to the end which is proposed by it. But, owing to the persecutions of my enemies, my writings have been circulated far and wide, and are too deeply engraven on men's hearts to be effaced. A recantation would only add to the dishonour of the Church of Rome, and raise an universal cry of accusation against her. Most Holy Father! I declare before God and all his creatures, that I have never wished, and do not now wish, either by force or guile, to attack the authority of the Roman Church or of your Holiness. I acknowledge that there is nothing in heaven or on the earth which ought to be put above this Church, unless it be Jesus Christ the Lord of all."[3]

These words might seem strange and even reprehensible in the mouth of Luther, did we not reflect that the light did not break in upon him all at once, but by slow and progressive steps. They show, and this is very important, that the Reformation was not simply an opposition to the papacy. Its accomplishment was not effected by warring against this or that form, or by means of this or that negative tendency. Opposition to the pope was only one of its secondary features. Its creating principle was a new life, a positive doctrine—"Jesus Christ, the Lord of all and paramount to all—to Rome herself," as Luther says in the conclusion of his letter. To this principle the revolution of the 16th century is truly to be ascribed.

It is probable that at an earlier period a letter from the monk of Wittemberg, positively refusing to retract, would not have been allowed by the pope to pass without animadversion. But Maximilian,

---

[1] Doleo Tetzelium. (L. Ep. i, p. 223.) [2] Sed conscientia indignitate Papæ forte occulruit. (L. Op. in Præf.) [3] Præter unum Jesum Christum Dominum omnium. (L. Ep. i, p. 234.)

was dead, the topic of engrossing interest was the election of his successor, and amid the political intrigues which then agitated the pontifical city, Luther's letter was overlooked.

The Reformer was employing his time to better purpose than his powerful antagonist. While Leo X, engrossed by his interests as a temporal prince, was straining every nerve to prevent a dreaded neighbour from reaching the Imperial throne, Luther was daily growing in knowledge and in faith. He studied the Decretals of the popes, and made discoveries which greatly modified his views. Writing Spalatin he says, "I am reading the Decretals of the popes, and, let me say it in your ear, I know not whether the pope is Antichrist himself or only his apostle;[1] to such a degree in these Decretals is Christ outraged and crucified."

Still he continued to respect the ancient Church of Rome, and had no thought of separating from her. "Let the Roman Church," said he in the explanation which he had promised Miltitz to publish, "be honoured of God above all others. On this point there cannot be a doubt. St. Peter, St. Paul, forty-six popes, and several hundred thousand martyrs, have shed their blood in her bosom, and there vanquished hell and the world, so that the eye of God specially rests upon her. Although every thing about her is now in a very sad condition that is no ground for separating from her. On the contrary the worse things are, the more firmly we should cling to her. Our separation is not the means by which she can be improved. We must not abandon God because there is a devil; nor the children of God who are still at Rome. because the majority are wicked. No sin, no wickedness, can justify us in destroying charity or violating unity; for charity can do all things, and nothing is difficult to unity."[2]

It was not Luther that separated from Rome, but Rome that separated from Luther, and by so doing rejected the ancient catholic faith of which he was then the representative. Nor was it Luther that deprived Rome of her power and compelled her bishop to descend from an usurped throne. The doctrines which he announced, the doctrine of the Apostles, again divinely proclaimed throughout the Church with great force and admirable purity, alone could prevail against a power by which the Church had for ages been enslaved.

These declarations, which Luther published at the end of February, did not fully satisfy Miltitz and De Vio. These two vultures, after both missing their prey, had retired within the ancient walls

---

[1] Nescio an Papa sit Antichristus ipse vel apostolus ejus. (L. Ep. 1, 239.)
[2] L. Op. (L.) xvii, 224.

of Trèves. There, seconded by the Prince-archbishop, they hoped jointly to accomplish the object in which they had failed individually. The two nuncios were aware that nothing more was to be ·expected from Frederick, now invested with supreme power in the empire. They saw that Luther persisted in his refusal of retracta-·tion. The only plan, therefore, was to withdraw the heretical monk from the protection of the Elector, and entice him into their own neighbourhood. If the Reformer were once in Trèves, in a state subject to a prince of the Church, he would be dexterous indeed if he got away without giving full satisfaction to the sovereign pontiff. The scheme was immediately proceeded with. "Luther," ·said Miltitz to the Elector-archbishop of Trèves, "has accepted your Grace as arbiter; call him therefore before you." The Elec-·tor of Trèves accordingly (3rd May) wrote to the Elector of Sax-·ony, and requested him to send Luther. De Vio, and afterwards Miltitz himself, also wrote, announcing that the rose of gold had ·arrived at Augsburg, at the house of Fugger. Now, thought they, ·is the moment to strike the decisive blow.

But things were changed, and neither Frederick nor Luther felt ·alarmed. The Elector, understanding his new position, had no ¹onger any fear of the pope and far less of his servants. The Re-·former, seeing Miltitz and De Vio in concert, had some idea of the fate which awaited him if he complied with their invitation. "Everywhere," says he, " on all hands, and in all ways, they seek my life."[1] Besides, he had requested the pope to decide ; but the pope, engrossed with crowns and intrigues, had given no answer. Luther thus wrote to Miltitz : "How could I undertake the journey, without an order from Rome, amid the troubles which shake the empire ? How could I face so many dangers and subject myself to so much expence, I who am the poorest of men ?"

The Elector of Trèves, a man of wisdom and moderation, and a friend of Frederick, was willing to meet his views. He had no de-·sire, moreover, to involve himself in the affair without being posi-·tively called upon. He therefore agreed with the Elector of Saxony to defer the investigation till the next diet. Two years elapsed ·before this diet assembled at Worms.

While the hand of Providence successfully warded off all the ·dangers which threatened him, Luther was boldly advancing to a result of which he was not himself aware. His reputation was ·extending, the cause of truth was gaining strength, and the num-·ber of the students of Wittemberg, among whom were the most

---

[1] Video ubique, undique, quocumque modo, animam meam quæri. (L. Ep. i, p. 274, 16th May.)

distinguished young men in Germany, rapidly increased. "Our town," wrote Luther, "can scarcely contain all who come to it;" and on another occasion, "The number of students increases out of measure, like a stream overflowing its banks."[1]

But Germany was no longer the only country in which the voice of the Reformer was heard. It had passed the frontiers of the empire, and begun to shake the foundations of the Roman power in the different states of Christendom. Frobenius, the famous printer of Bâle, had published the collected Works of Luther, which were rapidly disposed of. At Bâle even the bishop applauded Luther; and the Cardinal of Sion, after reading his work, exclaimed somewhat ironically, and punning on his name, "O, Luther, thou art a true Luther!" (a true purifier, Lauterer.)

Erasmus was at Louvain when Luther's works arrived in the Netherlands. The prior of the Augustins of Antwerp, who had studied at Wittemberg, and according to the testimony of Erasmus, held true primitive Christianity, and many other Belgians besides, read them with avidity. "But," says the scholar of Rotterdam, "those who sought only their own interest, and entertained the people with old wives' fables, gave full vent to their grovelling fanaticism." "It is not in my power," says Erasmus, in a letter to Luther, "to describe the emotions, the truly tragic scenes, which your writings have produced.[2]

Frobenius sent six hundred copies of the works into France and Spain. They were publicly sold at Paris, and, as far as appears, the doctors of Sorbonne then read them with approbation. "It was time," said several of them, "that those engaged in the study of the Holy Scriptures should speak thus freely." In England the Works were received with still greater eagerness. Spanish merchants at Antwerp caused them to be translated into their native tongue, and sent them into Spain. "Assuredly," says Pallavicini, "these merchants were of Moorish blood."[3]

Calvi, a learned bookseller of Pavia, carried a great number of copies of the works into Italy, and circulated them in all the transalpine towns. This learned man was animated not by a love of gain but a desire to contribute to the revival of piety. The vigour with which Luther maintained the cause of godliness filled him with joy. "All the learned of Italy," exclaimed he, "will concur with me, and we will see you celebrated in stanzas composed by our most distinguished poets."

[1] Sicut aqua inundans. (L. Epp. i. p. 278, 279.)   [2] Nullo sermone consequi queam, quas tragœdias hic excitarint tui libelli. (Erasm. Ep. vi, 4.) I am not able by any words to describe the tragedies which your works have produced here.
[3] Maurorum stirpe prognatis. (Pallav. i, 91.)

Frobenius, in transmitting a copy of the publication to Luther, told him all these gladdening news, and added, " I have disposed of all the copies except ten, and never had so good a return." Other letters also informed Luther of the joy produced by his works. "I am glad," says he, " that the truth gives so much pleasure, although she speaks with little learning, and in a style so barbarous."[1]

Such was the commencement of the revival in the different countries of Europe. In all countries, if we except Switzerland, and even France where the gospel had previously been heard, the arrival of Luther's writings forms the first page in the history of the Reformation. A printer of Bâle diffused these first germs of the truth. At the moment when the Roman pontiff entertained hopes of suppressing the work in Germany, it began in France, the Netherlands, Italy, Spain, England, and Switzerland; and now, even should Rome hew down the original trunk, what would it avail? The seeds are already diffused over every soil.

CHAP. II.

The War seems ended in Germany—Eck Revives the Contest—Debate between Eck and Carlstadt—The Question of the Pope—Luther Replies—Alarm of Luther's Friends—Luther's courage—Truth triumphs single-handed—Refusal of Duke George—Delight of Mosellanus and Fears of Erasmus.

While the combat was only beginning beyond the limits of the empire it seemed to him almost ceased within it. The most blustering soldiers of Rome, the Franciscan monks of Jüterbock, after having imprudently attacked Luther, had, after a vigorous rejoinder from the Reformer, hastened to resume silence. The partisans of the pope were quiet; and Tezel was unfit for service. Luther's friends conjured him not to persist in the contest, and he had promised to comply. The theses were beginning to be forgotten. By this perfidious peace the eloquent tongue of the Reformer was completely paralysed; and the Reformation seemed to be arrested. "But," says Luther afterwards, when speaking of this period, "men were imagining vain things, for the Lord had arisen to judge the nations."[2] " God," says he in another place, " does not lead but urges and hurries me along. I am not my own master. I would fain be at rest, but am precipitated into the midst of tumult and revolution."[3]

---

[1] " In his id gaudeo, quod veritas tam barbare et indocte loquens, adeo placet. (L. Ep. i, 255.) [2] Dominus evigilavit et stat ad judicandos populos. (L. Op. Lat. in Præf.) [3] Deus rapit, pellit, nedum ducit me : non sum compos mei : volo esse quietus et rapior in medios tumultus. (L. Ep. i, 231.)

The person who renewed the contest was Eck the schoolman, Luther's old friend, and the author of the Obelisks. He was sincerely attached to the papacy, but seems to have been devoid of genuine religious sentiment, and to have belonged to a class of men, at all times too numerous, who value learning, and even theology and religion, merely as a means of gaining a name in the world. Vain glory lurks under the priest's cassock as well as the soldier's helmet. Eck had studied the art of disputation according to the scholastic rules, and was an acknowledged master in this species of warfare. While the knights of the middle ages, and the warriors at the period of the Reformation, sought glory in tournaments, the schoolmen sought it in the syllogistic disputations, which were often exhibited in universities. Eck, who was full of himself, stood high in his own opinion, and was proud of his talents, of the popularity of his cause, and the trophies which he had won in eight universities in Hungary, Lombardy, and Germany, eagerly longed for an opportunity of displaying his power and dexterity in debate with the Reformer. He had spared nothing to secure the reputation of being one of the most celebrated scholars of the age. He was ever seeking to stir up new discussions, to produce a sensation, and by means of his exploits procure access to all the enjoyments of life. A tour which he made in Italy had, by his own account. been only a series of triumphs. The most learned of the learned had been constrained to subscribe to his theses. A practised bravado, he fixed his eyes on a new field of battle, where he thought himself secure of victory. That little monk, who had grown up all at once into a giant, that Luther, whom no one had hitherto been able to vanquish, offended his pride, and excited his jealousy.[1] It might be that Eck, in seeking his own glory, might destroy Rome . . . . but scholastic vanity was not to be arrested by any such consideration. Theologians, as well as princes, have repeatedly sacrificed the general interest to their individual glory. Let us attend to the circumstances which gave the doctor of Ingolstadt an opportunity of entering the lists with his troublesome rival.

The zealous but too ardent Carlstadt was still of one mind with Luther—the special bond of union between them being their attachment to the doctrine of grace, and their admiration of St. Augustine. Carlstadt, who was of an enthusiastic temperament, and possessed little prudence, was not a man to be arrested by the address and policy of a Miltitz. In opposition to the Obelisks of Dr.

---

[1] Nihil cupiebat ardentius, quam sui specimen præbere in solemni disputatione cum æmuio. (Pallavicini, Tom. i, p. 60.)

Eck, he had published theses in which he defended Luther and their common faith. Eck had replied, and Carlstadt, determined not to leave him the last word, had rejoined. The combat grew warm. Eck, eager to avail himself of so favourable an opportunity, had thrown down the gauntlet; and the impetuous Carlstadt had taken it up. God employed the passions of these two men to accomplish his designs. Though Luther had taken no part in these debates, he was destined to be the hero of the fight. There are men whom the force of circumstances always brings upon the scene. Leipsic was fixed upon, and hence the origin of the celebrated discussion which bears its name.

Eck cared little about combating with Carlstadt, and even van-quishing him. Luther was the opponent whom he had in view. He accordingly employed every means to bring him into the field; and with this view published thirteen theses,[1] directed against the leading doctrines which had been espoused by the Reformer. The thirteenth was in these terms:—" We deny that the Roman Church was not superior to other Churches before the time of Pope Sylvester; and we acknowledge at all times, that he who has occupied the see of St. Peter and professed his faith,[2] is the suc-cessor of St. Peter and the vicar of Jesus Christ." Sylvester lived in the time of Constantine the Great; and hence Eck, in this thesis, denied that the primacy which Rome enjoyed was conferred on her by that emperor.

Luther, whose consent to remain silent had not been given, without reluctance, was strongly excited when he read these pro-positions. He saw that he was the person aimed at, and felt that he could not, with honour, evade the contest. " This man," said he, " names Carlstadt as his antagonist, and at the same time makes his assault upon me. But God reigns, and knows what result he designs to bring out of this tragedy.[3] The question is not between Dr. Eck and me. God's purpose will be accomplished. Thanks to Eck, this affair, which hitherto has been mere sport, will at length become serious, and give a fatal blow to the tyranny of Rome and the Roman Pontiff."

Rome herself broke the agreement. She did more; when she renewed the signal for battle, she directed it to a point which Luther had not previously attacked. The subject which Dr. Eck singled out for his antagonists was the primacy of the pope. In thus following the dangerous example which Tezel had given, Rome invited the blows of the champion; and if she left her

---

[1] Defensio adversus Echii monomachiam.   [2] L. Op. (L.) xvii, p. 242.
[3] Sed Deus in medio deorum ; ipse novit quid ex ea tragœdia deducere voluerit.
(L. Ep. i, 230, 222.)   [4] 1st vol. p. 402.

mangled members on the arena, she had herself to blame for the punishment inflicted by his mighty arm.

The pontifical supremacy being once overthrown, the whole of the Roman platform fell to pieces. Hence the papacy was in imminent peril; and yet neither Miltitz nor Cajetan took any steps to prevent this new contest. Did they imagine that the Reformation would be vanquished, or were they smitten with that blindness by which the ruin of the mighty is accomplished?

Luther, who, by his long silence, had given an example of rare moderation, boldly met the challenge of his antagonist, whose theses he immediately opposed by counter theses. The last was in these terms:—"The primacy of the Church of Rome is defended by means of miserable decretals of the Roman pontiffs, composed within the last four hundred years; whereas this primacy is contradicted by the authentic history of eleven centuries, the declarations of Holy Scripture, and the canons of the Council of Nice, which is the purest of all Councils."[1]

At the same time Luther thus wrote to the Elector:—"God knows it was my firm determination to be silent; and I rejoiced to see the game at length brought to a close. So faithfully have I observed the paction concluded with the pope's commissioner, that I did not reply to Sylvester Prierias, notwithstanding of the taunts of adversaries and the counsels of friends. But now Dr. Eck attacks me, and not only me, but the whole University of Wittemberg besides. I cannot allow it to be thus covered with obloquy."[2]

At the same time Luther wrote to Carlstadt, "I am unwilling, excellent Andrew, that you should engage in this quarrel, since I am the person aimed at." "I will gladly lay aside my serious labours and enter into the sports of these flatterers of the Roman pontiff."[3] Then apostrophising his adversary with disdain, and calling from Wittemberg to Ingolstadt, he exclaims—"Now, then, my dear Eck, be courageous, and gird thy sword upon thy thigh, thou mighty man.[4] Having failed to please you as mediator, perhaps I will please you better as antagonist. Not that I have any thought of vanquishing you, but after all the trophies which you have gained in Hungary, Lombardy, and Bavaria, (at least if we are to take your account for it,) I will give you an opportunity of acquiring the name of the conqueror of Saxony and Misnia, so that you will be for ever saluted by the glorious title of Augustus."[5]

All Luther's friends did not share his courage, for up to this hour

---

[1] L. Op. (L.) xvii, p. 245.   [2] L. Ep. i, p. 237.   [3] Gaudens et ridens post-habeo istorum mea seria ludo. (Ibid. p. 251.)   [4] Esto vir fortis et accingere gladio tuo super femur tuum, potentissime! (Ibid.)   [5] Ac si voles semper Augustus saluteris in æternum. (Ibid. p. 251.)

none had been able to withstand the sophistry of Dr. Eck. But what alarmed them most was the subject of dispute—the primacy of the pope ! . . . . How does the poor monk of Wittemberg dare to encounter this giant who for ages has crushed all his enemies? The courtiers of the Elector begin to tremble. Spalatin the confidant of the prince, and intimate friend of the Reformer, is full of anxiety. Frederick, too, feels uneasy: even the sword of the Knight of the Holy Sepulchre, with which he had been armed at Jerusalem, would be unequal to this warfare. Luther alone feels no alarm. His thought is, "The Lord will deliver him into my hands." The faith with which he is animated enables him to strengthen his friends. "I beg of you, my dear Spalatin," said he, "not to give yourself up to fear; you know well that if Christ was not with me, all that I have done up to this hour must have been my ruin. Was it not lately written from Italy, to the chancellor of the Duke of Pomerania, that I had upset Rome, and that, not knowing how to appease the tumult, they were purposing to attack me not according to the forms of justice, but by Roman finesse, (the very words used,) that is, I presume, by poison, ambush, and assassination?"

"I restrain myself, and from love to the Elector, and the univer-sity, keep back many things which I would employ against Babylon, were I elsewhere. O ! my poor Spalatin ! it is impossible to speak of Scripture and of the Church without irritating the beast. Never, therefore, hope to see me at rest, at least, until I renounce theology If this work is of God, it will not be terminated before all my friends have forsaken me, as Christ was forsaken by his disciples. Truth will endure single-handed, and triumph in virtue of its own prowess, not mine or yours, or any man's.[1] If I fall, the world will not perish with me. But, wretch that I am, I fear I am not worthy to die in such a cause." "Rome," he again wrote about this time, "Rome is burning with eagerness to destroy me, while I sit quiet and hold her in derision. I am informed that, in the field of Flora at Rome, one Martin Luther has been publicly burned in effigy, after being loaded with execrations. I abide their fury.[2] The whole world," continues he, "is in agitation, heaving to and fro. What will happen? God knows. For my part, I foresee wars and disasters. The Lord have mercy on us."[3]

Luther wrote letter after letter to Duke George,[4] in whose states

[1] Et sola sit veritas, quæ salvet se dexterâ suâ, non meâ, non tuâ, non ullius hominis . . . (L. Ep. i, 261.) And let truth stand alone ; she will save herself by her own right hand—not by yours or mine, or that of any man. . . (L. Ep. i, 261.)
[2] Expecto furorem illorum. (Ibid. 280, 30th May, 1519.)   [3] Totus orbis nutat et movetur, tam corpore quam animâ. (Ibid.) The whole world nods and is shaken both in body and soul.   [4] Ternis literis, a duce Georgio non potui certum obtinere responsum. (Ibid., p. 282.) After three letters, I could not obtain a decided answer from Duke George.

Leipsic is, entreating permission to repair thither and take part in the debate, but received no answer. The grandson of the Bohemian king, Podiebrad, alarmed at Luther's proposition concerning the pope, and afraid of seeing Saxony involved in the wars of which Bohemia had so long been the theatre, was unwilling to grant the doctor's request. Luther, therefore, determined to publish explanations of his thirteenth Thesis. But this treatise, far from persuading Duke George, on the contrary, confirmed him in his resolution. Positively refusing to give the Reformer authority to debate, he merely allowed him to be present as a spectator.[1] This was a great disappointment to Luther. Nevertheless, as he had only one wish, and that was to obey God—he resolved to attend as a spectator, and await the result.

The prince at the same time did every thing in his power to forward the discussion between Eck and Carlstadt. Duke George was devoted to the ancient doctrine; but he was upright and sincere, and friendly to free enquiry, and did not think that an opinion was to be charged with heresy, merely because it displeased the court of Rome. The Elector, moreover, urged his cousin to permit the discussion; and the duke, confirmed by Frederick's statements, ordered it to take place.[2]

Bishop Adolphus of Merseburg, in whose diocese Leipsic is situated, was more alive than Miltitz and Cajetan, to the danger of trusting such important questions to the chances of single combat. Rome could not expose the fruit of the labours of so many ages to such hazard. All the theologians of Leipsic were equally alarmed, and implored their bishop to prevent the discussion. Adolphus accordingly presented most energetic remonstrances to Duke George, who replied with much good sense.[3] "I am surprised at seeing a bishop so terrified at the ancient and laudable custom of our fathers in examining doubtful questions as to matters of faith. If your theologians refuse to defend their doctrines, the money given to them would be far better employed in the maintenance of aged women and young children who would be able at least to spin and sing."

This letter had little effect on the bishop and his theologians. There is in error a secret consciousness which makes it dread enquiry even when making loud professions of being favourable to it. After an imprudent advance it makes a cowardly retreat. Truth did not give the challenge, but firmly stood its ground. Error gave it, and ran off. Moreover, the prosperity of the university of

---

[1] Ita ut non disputator, sed spectator futurus Lipsiam ingrederer. (L. Op. in Præf.)
[2] Principis nostri verbo firmatus. (L. Ep. 1, 255.)   [3] Scheinder, Lips. Chr. iv, 168.

Wittemberg, excited the jealousy of that of Leipsic. The monks and priests inveighed from the pulpits of that city, urging the people to shun the new heretics, slandering Luther, and painting him, as well as his friends, in the blackest colours, in order to stir up the fanaticism of the populace against the Reformers.[1] Tezel, who was still alive, awoke to cry from the depth of his retreat,— " It is the devil that is forcing on this contest."[2]

All the professors of Leipsic, however, did not participate in these apprehensions. Some belonged to the indifferent class, consisting of persons who are always ready to laugh at the faults of both parties. Of this class was the Greek professor Peter Mosellanus, who cared very little for John Eck, Carlstadt, and Martin Luther, but anticipated great amusement from the strife. Writing to his friend Erasmus, he says, "John Eck, who is the most illustrious of pen gladiators and rhapsodists, and like the Socrates of Aristophanes, contemns even the gods, is to have a turn in debate with Andrew Carlstadt. The battle will end in uproar, and there will be laughter in it for ten Democratuses."[3]

The timid Erasmus, on the contrary, was frightened at the idea of a combat, and his prudence, ever ready to take alarm, would fain have prevented this discussion. In a letter to Melancthon, he says, " If you will be advised by Erasmus, you will be more anxious to promote the advancement of sound literature than to attack the enemies of it.[4] My belief is that, in this way, our progress will be greater. Above all, while engaged in this struggle, let us not forget that victory must be obtained, not only by eloquence, but also by moderation and meekness." Neither the alarms of priests, nor the prudence of pacificators, could now prevent the combat. The parties made ready their weapons.

CHAP. III.

Arrival of Eck and the Wittembergers — Amsdorf—The Students — Carlstadt's accident—Placard—Eck and Luther—Pleissenburg—Shall Judges be appointed ? —Luther objects.

At the time when the Electors met at Frankfort to give an emperor to Germany, (June, 1519,) theologians met at Leipsic for an act

---

[1] Theologi interim me proscindunt . . . populum Lipsiæ inclamant. (L. Ep. i, 255.) The theologians, in the meantime, inveigh against me, . . . and declaim to the people of Leipsic.   [2] Das walt der Teufel. (L. Ep. i, 255.)   [3] Seckend., p. 201.
[4] Malim te plus operæ sumere in asserendis bonis literis, quam in sectandis harum hostibus. (Corpus Ref. ed. Bretschneider, i, 73, 22nd April, 1519.)

which, though unnoticed by the world, was destined to be not less important in its results.

Eck was the first who arrived at the place of rendezvous. On the 21st June he entered Leipsic in company with Poliander, a young man whom he had brought from Ingolstadt to report the debate. All kinds of honours were paid to the scholastic doctor, who, on the Fête Dieu, paraded the town in full canonicals, and at the head of a numerous procession. There was a general eagerness to see him. According to his own account, all the inhabitants were in his favour. "Nevertheless," adds he, "a rumour was current in the town that I was to be worsted in the encounter."

The day after the fête, viz., Friday, 24th June, (St. John's Day,) the Wittembergers arrived. Carlstadt, Eck's destined opponent, came first in a chariot by himself. Next, in an open carriage, came Duke Barnim of Pomerania, who was then studying at Wittemberg under the direction of a tutor, and had been elected rector of the University. On each side of him sat the two great theologians, the fathers of the Reformation, Melancthon and Luther. Melancthon had been unwilling to quit his friend. He had said to Spalatin, "Martin, the soldier of the Lord, has stirred up this fetid marsh.[1] I cannot think of the shameful conduct of the pope's theologians without indignation. Be firm, and adhere to us." Luther himself had expressed a desire that his Achates, as he has been called, should accompany him.

John Lange, vicar of the Augustins, some doctors in law, several masters of arts, two licentiates in theology, and other ecclesiastics, among whom Nicolas Amsdorf was conspicuous, closed the rear. Amsdorf, the member of a noble family in Saxony, disregarding the brilliant career which his birth might have opened to him, had devoted himself to theology. The theses on indulgences having brought him to the knowledge of the truth, he had forthwith made a bold profession of the faith.[2] Vigorous in intellect and vehement in temper, Amsdorf often pushed on Luther, by nature abundantly ardent, to acts which were perhaps imprudent. Born to high rank, he was not overawed by the great, and occasionally addressed them with a freedom bordering on rudeness. "The gospel of Jesus Christ," said he one day in an assembly of nobles, "belongs to the poor and afflicted, and not to you princes, lords, and courtiers, whose lives are passed in luxury and joy."[3]

But we have not yet mentioned the whole train from Wittem-

1 Martinus, Domini miles, hanc camarinam movit. (Corp. Ref. i, p. 82.)
2 Nec cum carne et sanguine diu contulit, sed statim palam ad alios fidei confessionem constanter edidit. (M. Adami. Vita Amsdorf.) Nor did he confer with flesh and blood, but forthwith made a public and firm profession of his faith.
3 Weisman. Hist. Eccl. i, p. 1444.

berg. A large body of students accompanied their teachers. Eck affirms that the number amounted to two hundred. Armed with pikes and halberds, they walked beside the carriages of the doctors ready to defend them, and proud of their cause.

Such was the order in which the body of Reformers entered Leipsic. Just as they passed the Grimma gate, which is in front of St. Paul's cemetery, one of the wheels of Carlstadt's carriage broke down. The archdeacon, who, with great self-complacency, was enjoying the solemn entry, tumbled into the mire. He was not hurt, but was obliged to proceed to his lodgings on foot. Luther's chariot, which was immediately behind Carlstadt's, moved rapidly forward, and delivered the Reformer safe and sound. The inhabitants of Leipsic, who had assembled to witness the entry of the Wittemberg champions, considered the accident as a bad omen for Carlstadt ; and the inference was soon current over the town, viz., that he would be defeated in the combat, but that Luther would come off victorious.[1]

Adolphus of Merseberg did not remain idle. As soon as he learned the approach of Luther and Carlstadt, and even before they had lighted from their carriages, he caused a notice to be posted up on all the church-doors forbidding the discussion under pain of excommunication. Duke George, astonished at his presumption, ordered the town council to tear down the bishop's placard, and imprison the individual which had been employed to put it up.[2] The Duke George, who had come in person to Leipsic, attended by all his court—among others by Jerôme Emser, with whom Luther spent the famous evening at Dresden, sent the disputants the usual presents. "The duke," boasted Eck, "presented me with a fine stag, and gave Carlstadt only a roebuck."[4]

Eck was no sooner informed of Luther's arrival than he called upon him—" What !" said he, " it is said that you refuse to debate with me."

Luther.—" How can I when the duke forbids me?"

Eck.—" If I cannot debate with you, I am not anxious to have any thing to do with Carlstadt. It was for you I came here." Then, after a short pause, he added—" If I obtain the duke's permission, will you take the field?"

Luther (*joyfully*).—" Obtain it, and we shall debate."

Eck forthwith repaired to the duke, and tried to dissipate his fears, representing to him that he was certain of victory, and that the authority of the pope, so far from suffering by the discussion, would

---

[1] Seb. Fröschel vom Priesterthum. Wittemb., 1585, in Præf.   [2] L. Op. (L.) xvii, p. 245.   [3] First vol., p. 172.   [4] Seckend. p. 190.   [5] Si tecum non licet dis. putare, neque cum Carlstatio volo : propter te enim huc veni. (L. Op. in Præf.)

come out of it more glorious. "We must strike at the head. If Luther stands erect, so do all his adherents—if he falls, they all fall." George granted permission.

The duke had caused a large hall to be prepared in his palace of Pleissenburg. Two desks had been erected opposite to each other, tables arranged for the notaries who were to take down the discussion in writing, and benches for the spectators. The desks and benches were covered with rich tapestry. At the doctor of Wittemberg's desk was suspended the protrait of St. Martin, after whom he was named; and at that of Dr Eck, the portrait of the knight of St. George. "We shall see," said the arrogant Eck, with his eye on the emblem, "whether I do not, with my steed, trample down my enemies." Every thing bespoke the importance which was attached to the combat.

On 25th June, the parties met in the castle to arrange the order of proceeding. Eck, who had more confidence in his declamation and gesture than in his arguments, exclaimed, "We will debate freely, off hand, and the notaries will not take down our words in writing.

Carlstadt.—"The agreement was, that the discussion should be written down, published, and submitted to the judgment of all men."

Eck.—"To write down every thing is to wear out the spirit of the disputants, and protract the battle. In that case there can be no hope of the vivacity requisite in an animated debate. Do not lay an arrest on the flow of eloquence."[1]

Dr. Eck's friends supported his proposal, but Carlstadt persisted in his objection, and Eck was obliged to yield.

Eck.—"Be it so, let there be writing; but, at all events, the debate, when taken down by the notaries, is not to be published before it has been submitted to the decision of judges."

Luther.—"The truth of Dr. Eck and the Eckians fears the light."

Eck.—"There must be judges."

Luther.—"And what judges?"

Eck.—"After the debate is over we will agree upon them."

The object of the partisans of Rome was evident. If the theologians of Wittemberg accepted judges, their cause was lost. It was obvious beforehand who the persons were whom their opponents would suggest; and yet the Reformers, if they refused them, would be covered with obloquy, as it would be circulated every where that they were afraid of submitting to impartial judges.

[1] Melancth. Op. i. p. 139. (Koethe ed.)

The judges whom the Reformers desired were not individuals whose opinion was already declared, but the whole of Christendom. Their appeal was made to the general voice. It mattered little who condemned them, if, in pleading their cause in presence of the Christian world, they succeeded in bringing some individuals to the light. "Luther," says a Roman historian, "demanded all the faithful for judges—in other words, demanded a tribunal so numerous that there could be no urn large enough to hold its votes."[1]

The meeting broke up. "See their stratagem," said Luther and his friends to each other. "They would to a certainty ask to have the pope or the universities for judges."

In fact, the theologians of Rome, next morning, sent one of their party to Luther, with a proposal that the judge should be . . . . the pope! . . . . "The pope!" said Luther, "how could I accept him?" "Beware," exclaimed all his friends, "of accepting conditions so unjust." Eck and his friends having consulted anew, gave up the pope, and proposed certain universities. "Don't take from us the liberty which you have already granted us," replied Luther. "We cannot yield this point," resumed Eck. "Then," exclaimed Luther, "I don't debate."[2]

They again parted, and what had just passed was talked of over the whole town. The Romans kept crying every where, "Luther won't debate—he refuses to accept of any judge!" Commenting on, and torturing his words, they endeavoured to represent them in the most unfavourable light. "What! truly? he will not debate?" say the best friends of the Reformer, and hasten to him to express their alarm. "You decline the contest," exclaim they. "Your refusal will bring eternal disgrace on your university and your cause." This was to attack Luther in his most tender point. "Very well," replied he, his heart filled with indignation, "I accept the terms which are imposed on me; but I reserve a right of appeal, and I decline the Court of Rome."[3]

---

[1] "Aiebat, ad universos mortales pertinebat judicium, hoc est ad tribunal cujus colligendis calculis nulla urna satis capax." (Pallavicini, T. i, p. 55.)
[2] L. Op. (L. xvii, p. 245.)   [3] Ibid., p. 246.

CHAP. IV.

The Procession—Mass—Mosellanus—Veni, Sancte Spiritus!—Portraits of Luther and Carlstadt—Doctor Eck—Carlstadt's Books — Merit of Congruity—Natural Powers—Scholastic distinction—Point where Rome and the Reformation separate —Grace gives man freedom—Carlstadt's Note-Book—Commotion in the auditory —Melancthon during the debate—Manœuvres of Eck—Luther Preaches— The Citizens of Leipsic—Quarrels of Students and quarrels of Teachers.

The 27th of June was the day fixed for the commencement of the discussion. In the morning the parties met in the hall of the university, and thereafter walked in procession to the Church of St. Thomas, where high mass was celebrated by the order and at the expence of the duke. After service, those present proceeded to the ducal castle. At their head walked Duke George, and the Duke of Pomerania; next came counts, abbots, knights, and other persons of distinction; and, lastly, the doctors of the two parties. A guard composed of seventy-six citizens, carrying halberds, accompanied the procession, with colours flying, and drums beating, and halted at the castle gate.

On the arrival at the palace, each took his place in the hall where the debate was to take place—Duke George, the hereditary Prince John, Prince George of Anhalt, a boy of twelve, and the Duke of Pomerania, occupying the seats allotted to them.

Mosellanus, by order of the duke, mounted a pulpit, to remind the theologians of the manner in which the discussion was to be carried on. "If you begin to quarrel," said the orator to them, "what difference will there be between a theological disputant and a swaggering duellist? What is victory here but just to recall a brother from his error? .... Each, it would seem, should be more desirous to be conquered than to conquer."[1]

At the conclusion of the address, sacred music echoed along the aisles of the Pleissenberg, the whole assembly knelt down, and the ancient hymn of invocation to the Holy Spirit, "Veni, Sancte Spiritus," was sung. Solemn hour in the annals of the Reformation! The invocation was thrice repeated; and, while the solemn chant was pealing, the defenders of the ancient, and the champions of the new doctrines, the men of the Church of the middle ages, and those desirous of re-establishing the Church of the apostles, mingling together without distinction, in lowly attitude bent their faces to the ground. The ancient tie of one single communion still

[1] Seckend., p. 209.

united all these different minds, and the same prayer still proceeded· from all these lips as if a single heart had dictated it.

These were the last moments of external lifeless unity for which a new spiritual living unity was about to be substituted. The Holy Spirit was invoked in behalf of the Church, and the Holy Spirit was about to answer by a revival of Christendom.

When the hymn and prayer were finished, the assembly rose up. The discussion should have now commenced; but, as the hour of noon had arrived, there was an adjournment of two hours.

The leading personages who proposed to attend the debate, having dined with the duke, returned with him after dinner to the castle hall, which was filled with spectators. Meetings of this description were the public assemblies in which the representatives of the age discussed questions of general and engrossing interest. The orators were soon at their post. That a better idea may be formed of them, we will give their portraits as drawn by one of the most impartial witnesses of the debate.

"Martin Luther is of middle size; and so emaciated by hard study that one might almost count his bones. He is in the vigour of life, and his voice is clear and sonorous. His learning and knowledge of the Holy Scriptures are beyond compare: he has the whole word of God at command.[1] In addition to this he has great store of arguments and ideas. It were perhaps to be wished that he had a little more judgment in arranging his materials. In conversation he is candid and courteous; there is nothing stoical or haughty about him ; he has the art of accommodating himself to every individual. His address is pleasing, and replete with good humour. He displays firmness, and is never discomposed by the menaces of his adversaries, be they what they may. One is, in a manner, compelled to believe that, in the great things which he has done, God must have assisted him. He is blamed, however, for being more sarcastic in his rejoinders than becomes a theologian, especially when he announces new religious ideas.

" Carlstadt is of smaller stature; his complexion is dark and sallow, his voice disagreeable, his memory less retentive, and his· temper more easily ruffled than Luther's. Still however he possesses, though in an inferior degree, the same qualities which distinguish his friend.

" Eck is tall and broad shouldered. He has a strong and truly German voice, and such excellent lungs that he would be well· heard on the stage, or would make an admirable town-crier. His·

---

[1] Seine Gelehrsamkeit aber und Verstand in heiliger Schrift ist unvergleichlich, so-dass er fast alles im Griff hat. (Mosellanus in Seckend., 206.)

accent is rather coarse than elegant, and he has none of the gracefulness so much lauded by Cicero and Quintilian. His mouth, his eyes, and his whole features, suggest the idea of a soldier or a butcher, rather than a theologian.[1] His memory is excellent, and were his intellect equal to it he would be faultless. But he is slow of comprehension, and wants judgment, without which all other gifts are useless. Hence, when he debates, he piles up, without selection or discernment, passages from the Bible, quotations from the Fathers, and arguments of all descriptions. His assurance, moreover, is unbounded. When he finds himself in a difficulty he darts off from the matter in hand, and pounces upon another; sometimes, even, he adopts the view of his antagonist, and changing the form of expression, most dexterously charges him with the very absurdity which he himself was defending."

Such, according to Mosellanus, were the men who drew the eyes of the crowds who were then thronging into the great hall of Pleissenburg.

The discussion was opened by Eck and Carlstadt.

Eck, for some moments, fixed his eyes on the books which lay on the little table in front of his opponent's desk, and seemed to give him uneasiness: they were the Bible and the Fathers. "I decline the discussion," exclaimed he suddenly, "if you are allowed to bring books with you." A theologian have recourse to his books in discussion! The astonishment of Dr. Eck was still more astonishing. "It is merely a fig leaf which this Adam is employing to hide his shame," said Luther. " Did Augustine consult no books in combating the Manichees?"[2] No matter! Eck's partisans made a great noise. Carlstadt remonstrated. "The man is altogether devoid of memory," said Eck. At last it was decided, agreeably to the desire of the chancellor of Ingolstadt, that each disputant should have the use only of his memory and his tongue. " Thus then," said several, "the object in this debate will not be to discover truth, but to show off the eloquence and memory of the disputants."

The discussion lasted seventeen days; but as it is impossible to give the whole of it, we must, as a historian says, imitate painters who, in representing a battle, place the most distinguished exploits in front, and leave the others in the back ground.[3]

The subject of discussion between Eck and Carlstadt was important. " Before conversion," said Carlstadt, " the will of man is incapable of doing good; every good work comes entirely and

---

[1] Das Maul, Augen, und ganze Gesicht, presentirt che einen Fleischer oder Soldaten, als einen Theologum. (Mosellanus in Seckend., 206.) [2] Prætexit tamen et hic Adam ille folium fici pulcherrimum. (L. Epp. i, p. 294.) " Here, however, this Adam too weaved for himself a most beautiful fig-leaf." [3] Pallavicini, i, 66.

exclusively from God, who gives first the will to do, and afterwards the ability to perform." This truth is proclaimed by the Scriptures, which say, "*It is God which worketh in you, both to will and to do of his good pleasure*,"[1] and by Augustine, who, in disputing with the Pelagians, delivers it in almost the very same terms. Every work in which there is neither love to God nor obedience to his will, is, in his sight, devoid of the only quality which could render it truly good, even should it be in other respects dictated by the most honourable human motives. Now there is in man a natural enmity to God—an enmity which he is utterly unable to suppress. He has not the power to do so—he even wants the will. If ever, therefore, it is to be suppressed, it must be by the power of God.

This is the doctrine of free will, so much declaimed against in the world, and yet so simple. It had been the doctrine of the church. But the schoolmen had explained it in a manner which caused it to be misunderstood. "No doubt," said they, "the natural will of man cannot do any thing which is truly pleasing to God; but it can do much to render man more capable and more worthy of receiving divine grace. These preparatives they termed merit of congruity;[2] "because," as St. Thomas expressed it, "it is congruous for God to bestow peculiar favour on those who make a good use of their will." In regard, again, to the conversion which man must undergo, it is no doubt true that, according to the schoolmen, the grace of God behoved to accomplish it, but still without excluding his natural powers. "These powers," said they, "have not been annihilated by sin; sin only puts an obstacle in the way of their development; but as soon as this obstacle is removed (and this, according to them, was what the grace of God had to do,) these powers begin again to act." To use one of their favourite comparisons—"the bird whose legs are tied does not thereby lose either its powers, or forget the art of flying, though it must be loosed by some other hand before it can be able again to use its wings." "The same," said they, "is the case with man."[3]

Such was the question discussed between Eck and Carlstadt. At first Eck seemed to deny Carlstadt's propositions out and out, but feeling the difficulty of maintaining his ground, said, "I grant that the will has not power to do a good work, but receives it from God." "Confess then," rejoined Carlstadt, overjoyed at obtaining such a concession, "that every good work comes entirely from God." "Every good work comes indeed from God," replied the schoolman subtlely, "but not entirely." "There," exclaimed Me-

---

[1] Philippians, ii, 13.   [2] Meritum congruum.   [3] Planck, i, p. 176.

lancthon, "goes a discovery well worthy of theological science."
" An apple," added Eck, " is all produced by the sun, but not
altogether, and without the co-operation of the tree." [1] Assuredly
no man ever thought of maintaining that an apple is all produced
by the sun.

" Very well," said his opponents, going still deeper into this
delicate question, so important in philosophy and in religion, "let us
consider how God acts on man, and how man conducts himself
when so acted on. " I acknowledge," said Eck, " that in conversion the first impulse comes from God, and that the human will is
entirely passive." [2] So far the disputants were agreed. "I acknowledge," said Carlstadt, on his part, " that after this first action
on the part of God, something must come from man, something
which St. Paul calls *the will*, and which the fathers designate by
consent." Here again both parties were agreed—but at this point
the separation began. " This consent of man," said Eck, " comes
partly from our natural will, and partly from the grace of God." [3]
" No," said Carlstadt, " this will in man is entirely created by
God." [4] Hereupon Eck began to express astonishment and indignation at words so well fitted to impress man with a sense of his
utter nothingness. " Your doctrine," exclaims he, " makes man a
stone or a block, incapable of any counter action . . . ." " What,"
replied the Reformers, "does not the faculty of receiving the powers
which God produces in him (a faculty which we admit that he possesses) sufficiently distinguish him from a stone and a block?" " But,"
resumed their antagonist, " by denying man all natural power, you
contradict experience." " We deny not," was the reply, " that
man possesses certain powers, and has in him a faculty of reflect-
ing, meditating, and choosing. We only consider these powers
and faculties as mere instruments, incapable of doing any thing
that is good until the hand of God sets them in motion. They
are like the saw in the hands of the sawyer." [5]

The great question of liberty was here debated, and it was easy
to demonstrate that the doctrine of the Reformers did not divest
man of the liberty of a moral agent or make him a passive machine.
The liberty of a moral agent consists in the power of acting con-

---

[1] Quanquam totum opus Dei sit, non tamen *totaliter* a Deo esse, quemadmodum
totum pomum efficitur a sole, sed non a sole *totaliter* et sine plantæ efficentiâ. (Pallavicini, Tom. i, p. 53.) Although the *whole* work is of God, it is not *wholly* of God—just
as the *whole* apple is produced by the sun, but not *wholly* by the sun, and without the
co-operation of the plant. [2] "Motionem seu inspirationem prevenientem esse
a solo Deo ; et ibi liberum arbitrium habet se passive." Preventing motion, or inspiration, is from God, and therein free-will is passive. [3] Partim a Deo, partim a
libero arbitrio. [4] Consentit homo, se consensus est donum Dei. Consentire
non est agere." Man consents ; but consent is the gift of God. Consent is not action.
[5] Ut serra in manu hominis trahentia.

formably to his choice. Every action done without external constraint, and in consequence of the determination of the mind itself, is a free action. The mind is determined by motives, but we constantly see that the same motives act differently on different minds. Many do not act conformably to the motives which their judgment approves. This inefficiency of motives is attributable to the obstacles which they meet with in the corruption of the understanding and the heart. Now, God, by giving a new heart and a new spirit, removes those obstacles, and thereby so far from depriving man of freedom, on the contrary, removes what prevented him from acting freely, and in obedience to the dictates of his conscience. In the language of the gospel it renders him "free indeed." (John, viii, 36.)

A slight incident for a short time interrupted the debate. Carlstadt (this is Eck's account[1]) had prepared different heads of argument; and, as is done by many of the orators of our day, read what he had written. Eck saw in this only a school boy's tactics, and objected. Carlstadt embarrassed, and fearing he might be taken at a disadvantage if deprived of his note-book, insisted on retaining it. "Ah!" said the scholastic doctor, quite proud of the advantage which he thought he had over him, "his memory is shorter than mine." The point having been submitted to arbiters, it was decided that quotations from the Fathers might be read, but that in other respects the discussion should be extempore.

This first part of the discussion often met with interruption from the audience. They ruffed and screamed. Any proposition offensive to the ears of the majority instantly aroused their clamour, and then, as in our day, it was necessary to call to order. The disputants also occasionally allowed themselves to be carried away in the heat of discussion.

Melancthon sat near Luther, and attracted almost equal attention. He was of short stature, and would scarcely have been thought more than eighteen. Luther, who was a whole head taller, seemed to be united to him by the closest friendship; they came in, went out, and walked together. "To look at Melancthon," says a Swiss theologian,[2] who studied at Wittemberg, "one would think him a mere boy, but in judgment, learning, and talent he is a giant. It is difficult to comprehend how so much wisdom and genius can be contained within so puny a body." Between the sittings, Melancthon conferred with Carlstadt and Luther. He assisted them in preparing for the debate, and suggested arguments drawn from the stores of his vast erudition; but during the discus-

---

[1] Seckendorf, p. 192.   [2] John Kessler, afterwards reformer of St. Gall.

sion he remained quietly seated among the spectators, giving close attention to every thing that was said by the theologians.[1] Occasionally, however, he came to the aid of Carlstadt.[2] When the latter was on the point of giving way under the powerful declamation of the chancellor of Ingolstadt, the young professor whispered a word in his ear, or slipt a paper to him on which he had noted down the answer. Eck on one occasion perceived this, and indignant that this grammarian, as he called him, should presume to intermeddle with the discussion, turned towards him, and haughtily said, "Be silent, Philip, keep to your own studies, and give me no disturbance." Perhaps Eck had already a presentiment of the formidable adversary he was afterwards to encounter in this young man. Luther was offended at the rude insult given to his friend; "The judgment of Philip," said he, "weighs more with me than that of a thousand doctor Ecks."

The calm Melancthon easily discerned the weak points of this discussion. "We can only be surprised," says he with the wisdom and grace conspicuous in all his words, "when we think of the violence which was brought to the discussion of such subjects. How could any advantage be derived from it? The Spirit of God loves retreat and silence: there dwell those whose hearts he penetrates. The bride of Christ does not stand in streets and public places, but conducts the Bridegroom into her mother's house."[3]

Both parties claimed the victory. Eck employed all his address to make it appear that he had gained it. As the points of divergence almost met, he often exclaimed that he had brought over his opponent to his opinion, or like a new Proteus, as Luther calls him, turning suddenly round, he stated Carlstadt's own opinion in different words, and then asked, with an air of triumph, if he did not feel constrained to yield. The unskilful, who were unable to detect the sophist's manœuvre, applauded and triumphed with him. . . . . In several respects the match was unequal. Carlstadt was slow, and sometimes left his opponent's objections unanswered till next day. Eck, on the contrary, was master of his subject, and could lay his hand at once on whatever he required. He came forward with a haughty air, mounted his desk with a firm step, and when there, stamped with his foot, moved backwards and forwards, made the ceiling ring with his powerful voice, gave some sort of reply to every argument, and astonished the audience with his memory and adroitness. Still Eck, without perceiving it, conceded much more in the discussion than he had

---

[1] Lipsicæ pugnæ otiosus spectator in reliquo volgo sedi. (Corpus Reformatorum, i, 112.) At Leipsic I sat among the crowd as an idle spectator.   [2] Tace tu, Philippe, ac tua studia cura, ne me perturba. (Ibid., i, 149.)   [3] Melancth. Op., p. 134.

intended. His partizans shouted and laughed at each of his turns, "but," says Luther, "I strongly suspect they only made a show of laughing, and were exceedingly vexed at heart when they saw their chief, who had commenced with so much bravado, quit his standard, abandon his army, and become a shameless deserter."[1]

Three or four days after the discussion had commenced, it was interrupted by the feast of St. Peter and St. Paul.

The Duke of Pomerania requested Luther to preach before him, on the occasion, in his chapel. Luther gladly complied. The chapel was soon filled, and crowds still arriving, it became necessary to remove to the great hall of the castle, where the discussion was held. Luther preached from the text of the day, on the grace of God, and the power of Peter, and gave a popular exposition of the views which he was wont to maintain before a learned audience. Christianity causes the light of truth to penetrate alike into the highest and the humblest intellects, and is in this way distinguished from all other religions, and from all philosophical systems. The theologians of Leipsic, who had been present at the sermon, hastened to acquaint Eck with the expressions which had offended them. "These subtile errors," exclaimed they, "must be answered, must be publicly refuted." This was just what Eck wished. All the churches were open to him, and on four successive occasions he mounted the pulpit to declaim against Luther and his sermon. Luther's friends were indignant, and demanded that the theologian of Wittemberg should be heard in his turn. But they demanded in vain. The pulpits were open to the enemies of evangelical truth, but shut against those who proclaimed it. "I kept silence," says Luther, "and was obliged to submit to attacks, insults, and calumnies, without being able to exculpate and defend myself."[2]

The ecclesiastics were not the only persons who displayed hostility to the evangelical doctrine: the citizens of Leipsic were in this respect of one mind with their clergy, and yielded themselves up with blind fanaticism to the falsehoods and animosities which were industriously propagated. The principal inhabitants did not visit either Luther or Carlstadt. They left them unnoticed when they met them in the street, and tried to prejudice the duke against them. On the other hand they visited and gave daily entertainments to the doctor of Ingolstadt, who enjoyed their good cheer, and learnedly discussed the comparative merits of Saxony and Bavarian beer. His manners, somewhat free, did not indicate a

---

[1] Relictis signis, desertorem exercitus et transfugam factum. (L. Ep. I, 295.)
[2] Mich verklagen, schelten und schmæhen . . . . (L. Op. (L.) xvii, p. 247.)

very strict morality.[1] The only thing offered to Luther was the customary present of wine to the disputants. Moreover, even those who wished him well were anxious that others should not know it; several Nicodemites visited him by night or in secret. There were only two who did themselves honour by publicly declaring their friendship. These were Dr. Auerback, whom we have already met at Augsburg, and Dr. Pistor, junior.

The greatest excitement prevailed in the town. The two parties formed, as it were, two hostile camps, and sometimes came to blows. In taverns, frequent quarrels took place between the students of Leipsic and Wittemberg. It was openly averred, even at meetings of the clergy, that Luther carried about with him a devil, confined in a little box. " Whether the devil is in a box, or only under his frock," said Eck, maliciously, " I know not ; but most assuredly he is in one or other of them."

During the discussion several doctors of both parties lodged with the printer Herbipolis; and the dispute ran so high that the host was obliged to station a town-officer at the top of the table with a halbert to keep the peace, and prevent the guests from coming to blows. One day Baumgartner, a vender of indulgences, had a scuffle with a gentleman, a friend of Luther, and fell into such a rage that he dropt down dead. Fröschel, who gives the account, says, " I was one of those who carried him to the grave."[2] The general agitation which prevailed was thus manifested. Then, as now, the discourses of the desk were re-echoed in the drawing-room and in the streets.

Duke George, though very decidedly in favour of Eck, did not betray so much passion as his subjects. He invited Eck, Luther, and Carlstadt to dine together with him. He even asked Luther to pay him a visit in private, but soon showed how strongly he was prejudiced against him. " By your book on the Lord's Prayer," said the duke to him, with bitterness, " you have led many consciences astray. There are persons who complain of not having been able to say one *pater* for more than four days."

1 Eck to Haven and Bourkard, 1st July, 1519. (Walch., xv, p. 1456.)
2 Löscher, iii, 278.

CHAP. V.

Hierarchy and Rationalism—Two Peasants' Sons—Eck and Luther begin—The head of the Church—The primacy of Rome—Equality of Bishops—Peter the Foundation—Christ the Foundation—Eck insinuates that Luther is a Hussite—Luther on the doctrine of Huss—Agitation in the audience—Pleasantry of Dr. Eck—The Word alone—The Court Fool—Luther at Mass—Saying of the Duke—Purgatory— Close of the Discussion.

On the 4th of July the debate between Eck and Luther commenced. Every thing announced that it would be keener, more decisive, and more interesting than that which had just been concluded, and during which the audience had gradually thinned away. The two antagonists descended into the arena, resolved not to lay down their arms till victory should declare in favour of one of them. All were in eager expectation, for the subject to be debated was the primacy of the pope. Christianity has two great adversaries : hierarchism and rationalism. Rationalism, as applied to the doctrine of man's natural powers, had been attacked by the Reformation in the former branch of the Leipsic discussion. Hierarchism, viewed with reference to what is at once its apex, and its base, viz., the doctrine of the pope, was now to be considered. On the one side appeared Eck boasting of the debates in which he had been engaged, as a general boasts of his battles.[1] On the other side stood Luther, to whom the contest seemed to promise only persecution and obloquy, but who came forward with a good conscience, a firm resolution to sacrifice everything for the cause of truth, and a confident expectation founded on faith in God and the deliverance which he affords. New convictions had sunk deep into his mind; as yet they were not arranged into a system, but in the heat of debate they flashed forth like lightning. Grave and intrepid, he manifested a decision which set all trammels at defiance. His features bore marks of the storms which had raged within his soul, and of the courage with which he was prepared to face new tempests. Two peasants' sons, representatives of the two systems which still divide Christendom, were on the eve of a contest, the issue of which would go far to decide the future destiny of the State and the Church.

[1] Faciebat hoc Eccius quia certam sibi gloriam propositam cernebat, propter propositionem meam, in qua negabam Papam esse jure divino caput Ecclesiæ ; hic patuit ei campus magnus. (L. Op. in Præf.) Eccius did so because he anticipated certain victory, in consequence of my proposition, in which I denied that the pope was *jure divino* head of the church ; here he had a wide field in which to expatiate.

C   2

At seven in the morning the two antagonists were in their desks, in the midst of a numerous and attentive assembly.

Luther rose and, in the exercise of a necessary precaution, modestly said:—

" In the name of the Lord! Amen. I declare, that the respect which I feel for the Sovereign Pontiff would have disposed me to avoid this discussion had the excellent Dr. Eck left me any alternative."

Eck.—" In thy name, dear Jesus! before I descend into the arena I protest in your presence, mighty lords, that whatever I shall say is under correction of the first of all sees, and the master who occupies it."

After a momentary pause, Eck continued—"There is in the church of God a primacy derived from Jesus Christ himself. The church militant is an image of the church triumphant. But the latter is a monarchical hierarchy, rising step by step up to the sole head, who is God, and, accordingly, Christ has established the same gradation upon earth. What kind of monster should the Church be if she were without a head!"[1] . . . .

Luther, (turning towards the audience).—" The doctor is correct in saying that the universal Church must have a head. If there is any one here who maintains the contrary, let him stand up? the remark does not at all apply to me."

Eck.—" If the Church militant has never been without a monarch, I should like to know who that monarch is, if he is not the pontiff of Rome?"

Luther.—" The head of the Church militant is not a man, but Jesus Christ himself. This I believe on the testimony of God." " *Christ,*" says the Scripture, " *must reign until he has put* ALL HIS ENEMIES *under his feet.*"[2] We cannot therefore listen to those who would confine Christ to the Church triumphant in heaven. His reign is a reign of faith. We cannot see our Head, and yet we have him."[3]

Eck, not admitting that he was beaten, had recourse to other arguments, and resumed, "According to St. Cyprian, sacerdotal unity is derived from Rome."[4]

Luther.—" Granted in regard to the Western Church. But is not the Church of Rome herself a descendant of the Church of Jerusalem, which is properly the mother and nurse of all the churches?"[5]

[1] " Nam quod monstrum esset, Ecclesiam esse acephalam!" (L. Op. Lat. i, p. 243.) [2] 1 Cor. xv, 25. [3] " Prorsus audiendi non sunt qui Christum extra Ecclesiam militantem tendunt in triumphantem, cum sit regnum fidei. Caput nostrum non videmus; tamen habemus." (L. Op. Lat. i, p. 243.) [4] " Unde sacerdotalis unitas exorta est. (Ibid.) [5] Hæc est matrix propriæ omnium ecclesiarum. (Ibid 244.)

Eck.—"St. Jerome declares, that unless an extraordinary power, superior to all other powers, is given to the pope, churches will have as many schisms as pontiffs."[1]

Luther.—" *Granted,* that is to say, this power might, by human authority, be attributed to the Roman pontiff, provided all the faithful consent to it.[2]   And, in like manner, I, for my part, deny not that if all the faithful throughout the world were to concur in acknowledging the bishop, either of Rome, or of Paris, or of Magdeburg, as prime and sovereign pontiff, it would be necessary to acknowledge him as such in deference to this universal consent of the Church.   The thing, however, never has been, and never will be seen.   Even in our own day does not the Greek Church refuse her assent to Rome ?"

At this period Luther was quite ready to acknowledge the pope as first magistrate of the Church, elected by her own free choice ; but he denied that he was of divine institution.   At a later period he denied that subjection was due to him in any respect, and this denial he owed to the discussion at Leipsic.   Eck had come upon ground which he did not know so thoroughly as Luther.   The latter, it is true, could not maintain his thesis, that the papacy had not been in existence for more than four centuries.   Eck quoted authorities of an earlier date, and these Luther was unable to obviate, criticism not having yet attacked the spurious decretals.   But the nearer the discussion was brought to primitive times, the more Luther's strength increased.   Eck appealed to the Fathers.   Luther quoted the Fathers in reply, and all the hearers were struck with his superiority to his rival.

" That my exposition," said he, " is that of St. Jerome, I prove by St. Jerome's own Epistle to Evagrius, in which he says, "Every bishop, whether at Rome, or Eugubium, or Constantinople, or Rhegium, or Alexandria, or Tanis, has the same merit, and the same priesthood.[3]   The power of riches, and the humiliation of poverty, constitute the only precedence or inferiority among bishops."

From the writings of the Fathers, Luther passed to the decrees of Councils which regard the bishop of Rome as only a first among equals.[4]

" We read," says he, " in the decree of the Council of Africa," " The bishop of the first see must not be called either prince of the the pontiffs, or sovereign pontiff, or any other similar name, but only bishop of the first see.   Were the supremacy of the bishop

---

[1] Cui si non exors quædam et ab omnibus eminens detur potestas.   (Ibid. 243.)
[2] *Detur,* inquit, hoc est jure humano, posset fieri, consentientibus, cæteris omnibus fidelibus.   (L. Op. Lat. i, p. 244.)   [3] " Ejusdem meriti et ejusdem sacerdotii est." (L. Op. Lat. i, p. 244.)   [4] Primus inter pares.

of Rome of divine institution, would not these words be heretical?"

Eck replied by one of those subtile distinctions which were so familiar to him.

"The bishop of Rome, if you will so have it, is not universal bishop, but bishop of the universal church." [1]

Luther.—"I am quite willing to leave this reply unanswered: let our hearers judge for themselves."

"Assuredly," said he, afterwards, "the gloss is worthy of a theologian, and well fitted to satisfy a disputant thirsting for glory. My expensive sojourn in Leipsic has not been for nothing, since I have learned that the pope, though not indeed the universal bishop, is the bishop of the universal church." [2]

Eck.—"Very well, I come to the essential point. The venerable doctor calls upon me to prove that the primacy of the church of Rome is of divine institution—I prove it by these words of Christ: ' *Thou art Peter, and on this rock I will build my Church.*' St. Augustine, in one of his epistles, has thus expounded the passage, ' Thou art Peter, and upon this rock, that is to say, on this Peter, I will build my Church.' It is true, Augustine has elsewhere said that, by this rock must be understood Christ himself, but he never retracted his former exposition."

Luther.—"If the reverend doctor would attack me, he should first reconcile these contrary statements of Augustine. It is undeniable that St. Augustine has again and again said that the rock was Christ, and he may perhaps have once said that it was Peter himself. But even should St. Augustine and all the Fathers say that the apostle is the rock of which Christ speaks, I would combat their view on the authority of an apostle, in other words, divine authority; [3] for it is written, ' *No other foundation can any man lay than that is laid, namely, Jesus Christ.*' [4] Peter himself calls Christ, ' *the chief and corner stone on which we are built up a spiritual house.*' " [5]

Eck.—"I am astonished at the humility and modesty with which the reverend doctor undertakes single-handed to combat so many distinguished Fathers, and to know better than sovereign pontiffs, councils, doctors, and universities. . . . It would, certainly, be astonishing that God should have concealed the truth from so many saints and martyrs . . . and not revealed it until the advent of the reverend father!"

---

[1] Non episcopus universalis, sed universalis Ecclesiæ episcopus. (Ibid. 246.)
[2] Ego glorior me tot expensis non frustra . . . . (L. Ep. i, 299.)   [3] " Resistam eis ego unus, auctoritate apostoli, id est iure divino." (L. Op. Lat. i, p. 237.)
[4] 1 Cor. iii, 11.   [5] 1 Peter, ii, 4, 5.

Luther.—" The Fathers are not against me. The distinguished doctors, St. Augustine, and St. Ambrose, speak as I do. '*Super isto articulo fidei, fundata est ecclesia,*'[1] says St. Ambrose, when explaining what must be understood by the rock on which the church is built. Let my opponent then bridle his tongue. To express himself as he does is to stir up strife, not to discuss like a true doctor."

Eck had not expected that his opponent would possess so much knowledge of the subject, and be able to disentangle himself from the labyrinth in which he tried to bewilder him. " The reverend doctor," said he, " has entered the lists after carefully studying his subject. Your highnesses will excuse me for not presenting them with such exact researches. I came to debate and not to make a book." Eck was astonished, but not beaten. Having no more arguments to give, he had recourse to a mean and despicable artifice, which, if it did not vanquish his opponent, would at least subject him to great embarrassment. If the charge of being a Bohemian, a heretic, a Hussite fastens upon Luther, he is vanquished, for the Bohemians were detested in the Church. The scene of discussion was not far from the frontiers of Bohemia. Saxony, which, immediately after the condemnation of John Huss by the Council of Constance, had been subjected to all the horrors of a long and ruinous war, was proud of the resistance which she had then given to the Hussites. The university of Leipsic had been founded to oppose their tenets, and the discussion was in presence of nobles, princes, and citizens, whose fathers had fallen in that celebrated struggle. To make out that Luther was at one with Huss was almost like giving him the finishing blow, and this was the stratagem to which the doctor of Ingolstadt had recourse. "From primitive times downwards," says he, "it was acknowledged by all good Christians, that the Church of Rome holds its primacy of Jesus Christ himself and not of man. I must confess, however, that the Bohemians, while obstinately defending their errors, attacked this doctrine. The venerable father must pardon me if I am an enemy of the Bohemians, because they are the enemies of the Church, and if the present discussion has reminded me of these heretics; for, ... according to my weak judgment, ... the conclusions to which the doctor has come are all in favour of their errors. It is even affirmed that the Hussites loudly boast of this."[2]

Eck had calculated well. All his partizans received the insinuation with acclamation, and an expression of applause was general

---

[1] On this article of faith the Church is founded. (L. Op. Lat. i, p. 254.)
[2] Et, ut fama est, de hoc plurimum gratulantur. (L. Op. Lat. i, p. 260.)

throughout the audience. " These slanders," said the Reformer at a later period. " tickled their fancy much more agreeably than the discussion itself."

Luther.—"I love not a schism and I never shall. Since the Bohemians, of their own authority, separate from our unity, they do wrong even were divine authority decisive in favour of their doctrine; for at the head of all divine authority is charity and the unity of the Spirit." [1]

It was at the morning sitting, on the 5th July, that Luther thus expressed himself. Shortly after, the meeting adjourned for dinner. Luther felt uneasy. Had he not gone too far in thus condemning the Christians of Bohemia? Have they not maintained the doctrine which Luther is maintaining at this hour? He sees all the difficulty of the step before him. Will he declare against the Council which condemned John Huss, or will he abjure the grand idea of an universal Christian Church, an idea deeply imprinted on his mind? Resolute Luther hesitated not. " I must do my duty come what may." Accordingly, when the assembly again met at two o'clock, he rose and said firmly :—

" Certain of the tenets of John Huss and the Bohemians are perfectly orthodox. This much is certain. For instance, ' That there is only one universal church,' and again, ' That it is not necessary to salvation to believe the Roman Church superior to others.' Whether Wickliffe or Huss has said so I care not . . . . It is the truth."

This declaration of Luther produced an immense sensation in the audience. The abhorred names of Huss and Wickliffe pronounced with eulogium by a monk in the heart of a Catholic assembly ! . . . A general murmur was heard. Duke George himself felt as much alarmed, as if he had actually seen the standard of civil war, which had so long desolated the states of his maternal ancestors, unfurled in Saxony. Unable to conceal his emotion, he struck his thigh, shook his head, and exclaimed, loud enough to be heard by the whole assembly, " The man is mad !" [2] The whole audience was extremely excited. They rose to their feet, and every one kept talking to his neighbour. Those who had fallen asleep, awoke. Luther's opponents expressed their exultation, while his friends were greatly embarrassed. Several persons, who till then had listened to him with pleasure, began to doubt his orthodoxy. The impression produced upon the mind of the duke by this declara-

---

[1] " Nunquam mihi placuit, nec in æternum placebit quodcumque schisma . . . Cum supremum jus divinum sit charitas et unitas Spiritus (Ibid.)
[2] Das walt die Sucht!

tion was never effaced; from this moment he looked upon the Reformer with an unfavourable eye, and became his enemy.[1]

Luther was not intimidated by this explosion of disapprobation One of his leading arguments was, that the Greeks had never recognised the pope, and yet had never been declared heretics; that the Greek Church had subsisted, was subsisting, and would subsist without the pope, and was a Church of Christ as much as the Church of Rome. Eck, on the contrary, boldly affirmed that the Christian Church and the Roman Church were one and the same; that the Greeks and Orientals, by abandoning the Church, had also abandoned Christian faith, and unquestionably were heretics. "What!" exclaimed Luther, "Are not Gregory of Nanzianzen, Basil the Great, Epiphanius, Chrysostom, and an immense number of other Greek bishops in bliss? and yet they did not believe that the Church of Rome was superior to other churches! .... It is not in the power of the pontiff of Rome to make new articles of faith. The Christian believer has no other authority than the Holy Scriptures—they alone constitute *divine law*. I pray the illustrious doctor to admit that the pontiffs of Rome were men, and have the goodness not to make gods of them." [2]

Eck had recourse to one of those witticisms which at small cost give a little air of triumph to the person employing them.

"The reverend father," says he, "not being well versed in the culinary art, makes an odd mixture of Greek saints and heretics, so that the perfume of holiness in the one disguises the poison in the other.[3]

Luther—(hastily interrupting Eck.)—"The worthy doctor is impertinent. I do not hold that there is any communion between Christ and Belial."

Luther had taken a large step in advance. In 1516, and 1517, he had only attacked the discourses of the venders of indulgences, and had respected the decrees of the popes. At a later period he had rejected these decrees, but had appealed from them to a council. Now he had discarded this last authority also, declaring that no council can establish a new article of faith, or claim to be infallible. Thus all human authorities had successively fallen before him. The sand brought along by the rain and the floods had disappeared;

---

[1] Nam adhuc erat Dux Georgius mihi non inimicus, quod sciebam certo. (L. Op. in Præf.) For I was well assured that Duke George was not yet my enemy.

[2] Nec potest fidelis Christianus cogi ultra Sacram Scripturam, quæ est proprie jus divinum. (L. Op. Lat. i, 252.) Nor can a Christian believer be forced beyond the Sacred Scripture, which is properly divine law. [3] At Rev. Pater, *artis coquinariæ* minus instructus, commiscet sanctos græcos cum schismaticis et hæreticis, ut fuco sanctitatis Patrum, hæreticorum tueatur perfidiam." (Ibid.) But the Rev. Father, imperfectly skilled in the *culinary art*, confounds Greek saints with schismatics and heretics, that by the sanctity of the Fathers he may disguise the perfidy of the heretics.

and now, for building up the ruins of the Lord's house, there remained only the eternal rock of the Word of God. " Venerable father !" said Eck to him, " if you believe that a council, lawfully assembled, can err, you are to me only a heathen man and a publican."

Such were the discussions between the two doctors. The audience were attentive but occasionally began to flag, and hence were pleased with any incident which enlivened the scene and gave them a momentary relaxation. The gravest matters have their comic interludes; and so it was at Leipsic.

Duke George, according to the custom of the time, had a court fool, to whom some wags said, " Luther maintains that a court fool may marry. Eck maintains the contrary." On this the fool took a great dislike to Eck, and, every time he came into the hall with the servants of Duke George, eyed the theologian with a menacing air. The chancellor of Ingolstadt, not disdaining to descend to pleasantry, one day shut one eye, (the fool was blind of one,) and with the other began to squint at the poor creature, who, in a perfect rage, let fly a volley of abuse. " The whole assembly," says Peiffer, " burst into laughter." This amusing incident somewhat relieved their minds from the stretch on which they had been kept.[1]

At the same time, both in the town and in the churches scenes occurred which showed how much the partisans of Rome were horrified at Luther's bold assertions. An outcry was raised against him, especially in the convents attached to the pope.

Luther had one day walked into the church of the Dominicans, before high mass. The only persons present were some monks, saying low mass at the side altars. No sooner was it told in the cloister that the heretic Luther was in the church than the monks came down in all haste, laid hold of the *ostensorium*, and carrying it into the tabernacle shut it up, carefully watching it, lest the holy sacrament should be profaned by the heretical eye of the Augustin of Wittemberg. At the same time, those who were saying mass hastily gathered up their articles, quitted the altar, ran across the church, and took refuge in the sacristy, " just," says a historian, " as if the devil had been at their heels."

The discussion became the general subject of conversation. In the inns, at the university, and the court, every one gave his opinion. Duke George, whatever his irritation may have been, did not obstinately shut his ears against conviction. One day, when Eck and Luther were dining with him, he interrupted their conversa-

<hr />

[1] L. Op. (W.) xv, 1440.—2 Löscher, iii, p. 281.

tion, saying, " Let the pope be pope, whether by divine or human law; at all events he is pope."[1] Luther was much pleased with the expression. " The prince," says he, " never would have uttered it, if my arguments had not made some impression on him."

The discussion on the primacy of the pope had lasted during five days. On the 8th of July, the doctrine of purgatory was discussed, and occupied two days. Luther was still a believer in the existence of purgatory; but he denied that the doctrine, as held by the school-men and his opponent, was taught either in the Scriptures or by the Fathers. " Our Doctor Eck," said he, referring to the superficial knowledge of his opponent, " has to-day run over the Holy Scriptures almost without touching them, just as an insect skims the water."

On the 11th July indulgences were discussed. " It was mere sport and burlesque," says Luther. " Indulgences gave way at once, and Eck was almost entirely of my opinion." [2] Eck himself said, " Had I not disputed with Doctor Martin on the primacy of the pope, I could almost agree with him."[3]

The discussion afterwards turned on repentance, absolution by the priest, and satisfactions. Eck, as usual, quoted the school-men, the dominicans, and the canons of the pope. Luther closed the discussion with these words:—

" The reverend doctor flees before the Holy Scriptures, as the devil does before the cross. For my part, with all due deference to the Fathers, I prefer the authority of Scripture, and recommend it to our judges." [4]

This closed the debate between Eck and Luther, but Carlstadt and the doctor of Ingolstadt continued for two days longer to discuss the subject of human merit and good works. On the 16th July, the whole proceeding, after having lasted twenty days, was closed by a discourse from the rector of Leipsic. The moment the discourse was finished, thrilling music burst forth, and the whole concluded with the *Te Deum.*

But, during this solemn chant, the feelings of the audience no longer were what they had been during the *Veni Spiritus.* The presentiments which several persons had expressed seemed to be actually realised. The blows struck by the champions of the two systems had made a large wound in the papacy.

[1] Ita ut ipse Dux Georgius inter prandendum, ad Eccium et me dicat: " Sive sit jure-humano, sive sit jure divino, papa; ipse est papa." (L. Op. in Præf.)
[2] L. Op. (L.) xvii, 246. [3] So wollt'er fast einig mit mir gewest seyn. (Ibid.)
[4] Videtur fugere a facie Scripturarum, sicut diabolus crucem. Quare, salvis reverentiis Patrum, præfero ego auctoritatem Scripturæ, quod commendo judicibus futuris. (L. Op. Lat. i, p. 291.)

CHAP. VI.

These theological discussions, to which the worldly-minded of the present day would not devote a few short moments, had been attended and listened to with eagerness, during twenty days—lay-men, knights, and princes, taking a deep interest in them to the last. Duke Barnim, and Duke George, seemed particularly atten-tive, whereas some of the theologians of Leipsic, friends of Dr. Eck, slept, as an eye-witness expresses it, "quite soundly." It was even necessary to awake them on the adjournments, that they might not lose their dinner.

Luther was the first to quit Leipsic, and next Carlstadt. Eck remained several days after they were gone.

No formal decision was given on the points discussed.[1] Every one spoke as he thought. "There was at Leipsic," says Luther, "loss of time, and no investigation of truth. During the two years in which we have been examining the doctrines of our opponents, we have counted all their bones. Eck, on the contrary, has hardly skimmed the surface;[2] but he cried more in one hour than we did in two long years."

Eck, when writing privately to his friends, admitted his defeat to a certain extent, though he was at no loss for an explanation. "The Wittembergers," wrote he to Hochstraten on the 24th July,[3] "defeated me on several points—first, because they brought books with them—secondly, because they took down the debate in writ-ing, and examined it at home at their leisure—and thirdly, because they were more numerous. Two doctors, (Carlstadt and Luther,) Lange, vicar of the Augustins, two licentiates, Amsdorff, and a very arrogant nephew of Reuchlin, (Melancthon,) three doctors of law, and several masters of arts, lent their assistance both in public and private, whereas I stood alone, having nothing but a good

---

[1] "Ad exitum certaminis, uti solet, nulla prodiit decisio." (Pallavicini, i, 65.) As usual no decision was given on the conclusion of the debate.

[2] "Totam istam conclusionum cohortem multo acrius et validius nostri Wittember-genses . . . oppugnaverunt et ita examinaverunt ut ossa eorum numerare licuerit, quas Eccius vix in facie cutis leviter perstrinxit." (L. Ep. i, 291.) This whole host of conclusions our Wittembergers boldly and vigorously assailed, and so exposed that all their bones might have been counted, whereas Eck scarcely pierced their skin.

[3] "Verum in multis me obruerunt." (Corpus Reform. i, 83.)

·cause for my companion." Eck forgot Emser, and all the doctors
·of Leipsic.

Though these concessions escaped Eck in familiar correspondence,
he acted otherwise in public. The doctor of Ingolstadt, and the
theologians of Leipsic, made a great noise with what they called
·*their victory*. They everywhere set false reports in circulation,
while all the tongues of the party reiterated their expressions of
·self-complacency. "Eck goes about triumphing," [1] wrote Luther.
There were disputes, however, in the camp of Rome, in regard to
the laurels. "Had we not come to the help of Eck," said the
·theologians of Leipsic, "the illustrious doctor would have been
·overthrown." "The theologians of Leipsic," said Eck on his part,
"are well enough, but I had hoped too much from them—I did the
whole myself." "You see," said Luther to Spalatin, "how they
are chanting a new Iliad, and a new Æneid. They are kind enough
·to make me a Hector or a Turnus, ·vhile Eck is their Achilles, or
Æneas. Their only doubt is whether the victory was gained by
·the arms of Eck, or by those of Leipsic. All I can say to throw
light on the matter is, that Eck uniformly kept bawling, and the
Leipsickers as uniformly held their peace." [2]

"Eck," says the elegant, clever, and sagacious Mosellanus "has
triumphed in the estimation of those who do not understand the
·subject, and who have grown old in poring over the schoolmen;
but, in the estimation of all men of learning, intellect, and moderation, Luther and Carlstadt are the victors." [3]

The Leipsic discussion, however, was not destined to vanish into
·smoke. Every work which is devoutly performed bears fruit.
The words of Luther had penetrated the minds of his hearers with
irresistible force. Several of those who had daily thronged the
·castle hall were subdued by the truth, whose leading conquests
·were made among her most decided opponents. Even Poliander,
·the secretary, familiar friend and disciple of Eck, was gained to
·the Reformation, and began, in 1522, to preach the gospel at
Leipsic. John Camerarius, professor of Hebrew, one of the keenest opponents of the Reformation, impressed by the words of the
·mighty teacher, began to examine the Holy Scriptures more
·thoroughly; and, shortly after throwing up his situation, came to
Wittemberg to study at the feet of Luther. He was afterwards
·pastor at Frankfort and Dresden.

Among those who had taken their place on the seats reserved

---

[1] Eccius triumphat ubique.' (L. Ep. i, 290.)   [2] "Novam quamdam Iliada et
Æneida illos cantare . . . . (L. Ep. i, p. 305.)   [3] "Lutheri Sieg sey um so viel
weniger berühmt, weil der Gelehrten, Verstandigen, und derer die sich selbst nicht
·hoch rühmen, wenig seyen. (Seckendorff, 207.)

for the Court, and accompanied Duke George, was George of
Anhalt, a young prince, twelve years of age, of a famuy which had
distinguished itself in the wars against the Saracens. At this time
he was studying at Leipsic with his tutor. Great ardour for
science, and a strong attachment to truth, had already become the
characteristics of the illustrious young prince. He was often heard
to repeat the words of Solomon, *falsehood ill becomes a prince*. The
Leipsic discussion inspired this child with serious reflection, and
with a decided leaning to Luther.[1] Some time after a bishopric
was offered to him. His brother, and all his family, with the view
of raising him to high honour in the Church, urged him to accept
it, but he resolutely declined. His pious mother, who was secretly
favourable to Luther, having died, he became possessed of all the
Reformer's writings. He was constant and fervent in prayer to
God, to incline his heart to the truth ; and, often in the solitude
of his chamber, exclaimed, with tears, " *Deal mercifully with thy
servant, and teach me thy statutes.*"[2]   His prayers were heard.
Carried forward by his convictions, he fearlessly joined the ranks
of the friends of the gospel. In vain did his guardians, and particularly Duke George, besiege him with entreaties and remonstrances. He remained inflexible, and the Duke, half convinced
by his pupil's reasons, exclaimed, " I cannot answer him; still,
however, I will keep by my Church—I am too old a dog to be
trained." We will afterwards see in this amiable prince one of the
finest characters of the Reformation, one who himself preached the
word of life to his subjects, and to whom the saying of Dion re-
specting the emperor Marcus Antoninus, has been applied, " He
was through life consistent with himself, he was a good man, a
man free from guile."[3]

But Luther's words met with an enthusiastic reception, especially
from the students. They felt the difference between the spirit and
life of the doctor of Wittemberg, and the sophistical distinctions,
and vain speculations, of the chancellor of Ingolstadt. They saw
Luther founding upon the word of God, and they saw Dr. Eck
founding only on human traditions. The effect was soon visible.
The classes of the university of Leipsic almost emptied after the
discussion. One circumstance partly contributed to this. The
plague threatened to make its appearance—but there were many
other universities—for example, Erfurt, or Ingolstadt, to which
the students might have repaired. The force of truth drew them
to Wittemberg, where the number of the students was doubled.[4]

[1] L. Op. (W.) xv, p. 1440.   [2] . . . . A Deo petivit, flecti pectus suum ad veritatem,
ac lacrymans sæpe hæc verba repetivit . . . . (M. Adami. Vita Georgii Anhalt, p. 248.)
[3] Ὁμοίως διὰ πάντων ἐγίνετο, ἀγαθὸς δὲ ἦν, καὶ οὐδὲν πρὸς ποίησιν εἶχιν.
(Ibid. 255.)   [4] Peifer Histor. Lipsiensis. 356.

Among those who removed from the one university to the other was a youth of sixteen, of a melancholy air, who spoke little, and often amid the conversation and games of his fellow-students seemed absorbed by his own thoughts.[1] His parents at first thought him of weak intellect, but they soon found him so apt to learn, and so completely engrossed by his studies, that they conceived high hopes of him. His integrity, his candour, his modesty, and his piety, made him a general favourite, and Mosellanus singled him out as a model to all the university. He was called Gaspard Cruciger, and was originally from Leipsic. This new student of Wittemberg was afterwards the friend of Melancthon, and the assistant of Luther in the translation of the Bible.

The Leipsic discussion produced results still more important, in as much as the theologian of the Reformation then received his call. Modest and silent, Melancthon had been present at the discussion almost without taking any part in it. Till then his attention had been engrossed by literature, but the discussion gave him a new impulse, and gained him over to theology. Henceforth his science did homage to the word of God. He received the evangelical truth with the simplicity of a child. His audience heard him expound the doctrines of salvation with a grace and clearness by which all were charmed. He boldly advanced in this, which was to him a new career; "for," said he, "Christ will never leave his people."[2] From this moment the two friends walked side by side, contending for liberty and truth, the one with the energy of St. Paul, and the other with the meekness of St. John. Luther has admirably expressed the difference of their calling:—
"I was born," said he, "to enter the field of battle, and contend with factions and demons. Hence, my writings breathe war and tempest. I must root up the trunks, remove the thorns and the brambles, and fill up the marshes and pools. I am the sturdy wood-cutter who must clear the passage and level the ground; but master Philip advances calmly and softly; he digs and plants, sows, and waters joyously, in accordance with the gifts which God has, with so liberal a hand, bestowed upon him."[3]

If Melancthon, the quiet sower, was called to the work by the discussion of Leipsic, Luther, the hardy wood-cutter, felt his arm strengthened, and his courage still more inflamed by it. The mightiest result of this discussion was produced in Luther himself. "Scholastic theology," said he, "sunk entirely in my estimation, under the triumphant presidency of Dr. Eck." In regard

[1] Et cogitabundus et sæpe in medios sodalitios quasi peregrinante animo. (Melch. Adami, Vita Crucigeri. p. 193.) [2] Christus suis non deerit. (Corp. Reform. i, 104.) [3] L. Op. (W.) xiv, 290.

to the reformer, the veil which the School and the Church had
hung up in front of the sanctuary was rent from top to bottom.
Constrained to engage in new enquiries, he arrived at unexpected
discoveries. With equal astonishment and indignation he saw the
evil in all its magnitude. While poring over the annals of the
Church, he discovered that the supremacy of Rome had no other
origin than ambition on the one hand, and credulous ignorance on
the other. The narrow point of view under which he had hitherto
looked at the Church was succeeded by one both clearer and
wider. In the Christians of Greece and the East he recognised
true members of the Catholic Church; and, instead of a visible
head, seated on the banks of the Tiber, he adored, as sole Head of
his people, that invisible and eternal Redeemer, who, according to
his promise, is always, and in all parts of the world, in the midst of
those who believe in his name. The Latin Church Luther no longer
regarded as the universal Church. The narrow barriers of Rome
were thrown down; and he shouted for joy when he saw the
glorious domain of Jesus Christ stretching far beyond them.
Henceforth he felt that he could be a member of the Church of
Christ without belonging to the Church of the pope. In particular, the writings of John Huss made a strong impression on him.
To his great surprise, he discovered in them the doctrine of St.
Paul and St. Augustine, the doctrine to which he had himself
arrived, after so many struggles. "I believed," said he, "and,
without knowing it, taught all the doctrines of John Huss.[1] So
did Staupitz. In short, without suspecting it, we are all Hussites,
as are also St. Paul and St. Augustine. I am confounded at it,
and know not what to think. . . . . O what dreadful judgments
have not men merited from God! Evangelical truth, when unfolded,
and published more than a century ago, was condemned, burned,
and suppressed. . . . . Woe! Woe to the earth!"

Luther disengaged himself from the papacy, regarding it with
decided aversion and holy indignation. All the witnesses, who in
every age had risen up against Rome came successively before
him to testify against her, and unveil some of her abuses or errors.
"O darkness!" exclaimed he.

He was not allowed to be silent as to these sad discoveries.
The pride of his adversaries, their pretended triumph, and the
efforts which they made to extinguish the light, fixed his decision.
He advanced in the path in which God was leading him, without
any uneasiness as to the result. Luther has fixed upon this as the

---

[1] Ego imprudens hucusque omnia Johannis Huss et docui, et tenui . . . (L. Ep. ii,
p. 452.)

moment of his emancipation from the papal yoke—"Learn by me," said he, "how difficult it is to disencumber oneself of errors which the whole world confirms by its example, and which, from long habit, have become a second nature.[1] For seven years I had been reading, and, with great zeal, publicly expounding the Holy Scriptures, so that I had them almost entirely by heart.[2] I had also all the rudiments of knowledge and faith in the Lord Jesus Christ,—that is to say, I knew that we were not justified and saved by our works, but by faith in Christ: and I even maintained openly, that the pope is not head of the Christian Church by divine authority. And yet . . . . I could not see the inference, viz.—that certainly and necessarily the pope is of the devil. For whatever is not of God must, of necessity, be of the devil."[3] Further on, Luther adds—"I no longer vent my indignation against those who are still attached to the pope, since I myself, after reading the Holy Scriptures so carefully, and for so many years, still clung to the pope with so much obstinacy."[4]

Such were the true results of the discussion of Leipsic—results far more important than the discussion itself, and resembling those first successes which discipline an army and inflame its courage.

CHAP. VII.

Eck attacks Melancthon— Melancthon's defence— Interpretation ot Scripture— Luther's firmness—The Bohemian Brethren—Emser—Staupitz.

Eck abandoned himself to all the intoxication of what he would fain have passed off as a victory. He kept tearing at Luther, and heaped accusation upon accusation [5] against him. He also wrote to Frederick. Like a skilful general, he wished to take advantage of the confusion which always succeeds a battle, in order to obtain important concessions from the prince. Preparatory to the steps which he meant to take against his opponent personally, he invoked the flames against his writings, even those of them which he had not read. Imploring the Elector to convene a provincial council, the coarse-minded doctor exclaimed, "Let us exterminate all this vermin before they multiply out of measure."[6]

---

[1] Quam difficile sit eluctari et emergere ex erroribus, totius orbis, exemplo firmatis- . ⁄ . . (L. Op. Lat. in Præf.)   [2] Per septem annos, ita ut memoriter pene omnia- tenerem. . . . (Ibid.)   [3] Quod enim ex Deo non est, necesse est ex diabolo esse. (Ibid.)   [4] Cum ego tot annis sacra legens diligentissime, tamen ita hæsi tenaciter. (Ibid.)   [5] Proscidit, post abitum nostrum, Martinum inhumanissime. (Melancthon Corp- Refor. i, 106.)   [6] Ehe das Ungeziffer uberhand nehme. (L. Op. (L.) xvii, 271.)

Luther was not the only person against whom he vented his rage. He had the imprudence to call Melancthon into the field. Melancthon, who was in terms of the greatest intimacy with the excellent Œcolampadius, gave him an account of the discussion, and spoke of Eck in eulogistic terms.[1] Nevertheless, the pride of the chancellor of Ingolstadt was offended, and he immediately took up the pen against this "grammarian of Wittemberg, who, it is true," said he, "was not ignorant of Latin and Greek, but had dared to publish a letter in which he had insulted him, Dr. Eck."[2]

Melancthon replied. It is his first theological writing, and displays the exquisite urbanity which characterised this excellent man. Laying down the fundamental principles of Hermeneutics, he shows that the Holy Scriptures ought not to be explained according to the Fathers, but the Fathers according to the Holy Scriptures. "How often," says he, "did not Jerome commit mistakes, how often Augustine, how often Ambrose; how often do they differ in opinion, how often do they retract their own errors; . . . . there is only one volume inspired by the Spirit of heaven—pure and true throughout."[3]

"Luther," it is said, "does not follow some ambiguous expositions of the ancients, and why should he follow them? When he expounds the passage of St. Matthew, "*Thou art Peter, and upon this rock I will build my Church,*" he agrees with Origen, who by himself alone is worth a host; with Augustine in his homily, and Ambrose in his sixth book on St. Luke, to say nothing of others. What, then, you will say, do the Fathers contradict each other? Is it surprising that they should?[4] I believe in the Fathers, because I believe in the Holy Scriptures. The meaning of Scripture is one, and simple, like heavenly truth herself. We arrive at it by comparing different passages together; we deduce it from the thread and connection of the discourse.[5] There is a philosophy enjoined us in regard to the Book of God, and it is to employ it as the touch-stone by which all the opinions and maxims of men must be tried."[6]

It was a long time since these great truths had been so elegantly expounded. The Word of God was restored to its proper place, and the Fathers to theirs. The simple method by which we ascer-

---

[1] Eccius ob varias et insignes ingenii dotes. . . . (L. Op. Lat. i, p. 337.) [2] Ausus est grammaticus Wittembergensis, Græce et Latine sane non indoctus, epistolam edere. . . . (L. Op. Lat. i, p. 338.) [3] Una est Scriptura, cœlestis Spiritus, pura, et per omnia verax. (Contra Eckium Defensio, Corp. Refor. i, p. 115.) [4] Quid igitur ! Ipsi secum pugnant! quid mirum ? (Contra Eckium Defensio, Corp. Refor., i, p. 115.) [5] Quem collatis Scripturis e filo ductuque orationis licet assequi. (Ibid. 114.) [6] Ut hominum sententias, decretaque, ad ipsas, ceu ad Lydium lapidem exigamus. (Ibid. p. 115) By it (Scripture), as by a Lydian stone, let us test the decisions and opinions of men.

tain the meaning of Scripture was distinctly traced. The Word had precedence over all the difficulties and the expositions of the School. Melancthon furnished the answer to those who, like Dr. Eck, would envelope this subject in the mists of a remote' antiquity. The feeble *grammarian* had risen up, and the broad and sturdy shoulders of the scholastic gladiator had bent under the first pressure of his arm.

The weaker Eck was, the more noise he made, as if his rhodomontades and accusations were to secure the victory which he had failed to obtain in debate. The monks and all the partisans of Rome re-echoing his clamour, Germany rang with invectives against Luther, who, however, remained passive. "The more I see my name covered with opprobrium," said he in finishing the expositions which he published, on the propositions of Leipsic, "the prouder I feel; the truth, in other words, Christ, must increase, but I must decrease. The voice of the Bridegroom and the bride delights me more than all this clamour dismays me. Men are not the authors of my sufferings, and I have no hatred against them. It is Satan, the prince of evil, who would terrify me. But he who is in us is greater than he who is in the world. The judgment of our contemporaries is bad; that of posterity will be better." [1]

If the Leipsic discussion multiplied Luther's enemies in Germany, it also increased the number of his friends abroad; "What Huss was formerly in Bohemia, you, O Martin, are now in Saxony," wrote the brothers of Bohemia to him; "wherefore pray and be strong in the Lord."

About this time war was declared between Luther and Emser, now a professor of Leipsic. The latter addressed a letter to Dr. Zach, a zealous Roman Catholic of Prague, in which his professed object was to disabuse the Hussites of the idea that Luther was of their party. Luther could not doubt that under the semblance of defending him, the learned Leipsicker's real purpose was to fasten on him a suspicion of adhering to the Bohemian heresy, and he resolved to tear aside the veil under which his old Dresden host was endeavouring to shroud his enmity. With this view he published a letter addressed to the " goat Emser," Emser's arms being a goat. Luther concludes with a sentiment which well delineates his own character, " To love all, but fear none." [2]

While new friends and new enemies thus appeared, old friends seemed to draw off from Luther. Staupitz, who had been the means of bringing the Reformer out of the obscurity of the cloister of

---

[1] "Præsens male judicat ætas ; judicium melius posteritatis erit." (L. Op. Lat. i, 310.)
[2] L. Op. Lat. i, 252.

Erfurt, began to show him some degree of coolness. Luther was rising too high for Staupitz to follow him.—" You abandon me," wrote Luther to him. " The whole day I have been exceedingly grieved on your account, like a child just weaned and weeping for its mother.[1] Last night," continues the Reformer, " I dreamed of you, you were keeping aloof from me, and I was sobbing and shedding tears; then you gave me your hand, and told me to dry up my tears, for you would return to me."

The pacificator, Miltitz, wished to make a new attempt at conciliation. But what hold can be had on men while still under the excitement of the contest? His endeavours led to no result. He brought the famous rose of gold, but the Elector did not even take the trouble to receive it in person.[2] Frederick knew the artifices of Rome, and was not to be imposed upon.[3]

CHAP. VIII.

Epistle to the Galatians—Christ for us—Blindness of Luther's Adversaries—First Ideas on the Supper—Is the Sacrament Sufficient without Faith?—Luther a Bohemian—Eck attacked—Eck sets out for Rome.

Far from drawing back, Luther uniformly continued to advance, and at this time struck one of his severest blows at error, by publishing his first commentary on the Epistle to the Galatians.[4] It is true, the second commentary was superior to the first; but still the first contained a forcible exposition of the doctrine of justification by faith. Every expression of the new apostle was full of life; and God employed him to imbue the hearts of the people with divine knowledge. "Christ gave himself for our sins," said Luther to his contemporaries.[5] " It was not silver or gold that he gave for us; nor was it a man or angels. He gave himself—himself, out of whom there is no true greatness; and this incomparable treasure he gave .... for our sins. Where, now, are those who proudly boast of the powers of our will? where are the lessons of moral philosophy? where the power and strength of the law? Our sins being so great that they cannot possibly be taken away without an immense ransom, shall we pretend to acquire righteousness by the energy

[1] Ego super te, sicut ablactatus super matre sua, tristissimus hac die fui. (Ep. i, p. 342.)
[2] Rosam quam vocant auream nullo honore dignatus est ; imo pro ridicula habuit. (L. Op. Lat. in Præf.) What is called the golden rose he held in no estimation, nay, he held it in derision.   [3] Intellexit princeps artes Romanæ curiæ et eos (legatos) digne tractare novit. (Ibid.) The prince understood the arts of the Roman Court, and knew what treatment was due to them (the legates).   [4] 3rd September, 1519.
[5] L. Op. (L.) x, 461.

of our will, by the power of the law, and the doctrines of men? What will all these cunning devices, all these illusions, avail us? Ah! we will only cover our iniquities with a spurious righteousness and convert ourselves into hypocrites, whom no worldly power can save."

But while Luther thus proves that man's only salvation is in Christ, he also shows how this salvation changes his nature, and enables him to abound in good works. "The man," says he, " who has truly heard the word of Christ, and keeps it, is immediately clothed with the spirit of charity. If thou lovest him who has made thee a present of twenty florins, or done thee some service, or in some way given thee a proof of his affection, how much more oughtest thou to love him, who, on thy account, has given not silver or gold, but himself, received so many wounds, endured a bloody sweat, and even died for thee; in one word, who, in paying for all thy sins, has annihilated death, and secured for thee a Father full of love in heaven! . . . If thou lovest him not, thy heart has not listened to the things which he has done; thou hast not believed them; for faith works by love." "This epistle," said Luther, in speaking of the Epistle to the Galatians, "is my epistle —I am married to it."

His opponents caused him to proceed at a quicker pace than he would otherwise have done. At this time Eck instigated the Franciscans of Juterbock to make a new attack upon him; and Luther, in his reply,[1] not satisfied with repeating what he had already taught, attacked errors which he had recently discovered. "I would fain know," says he, "in what part of Scripture the power of canonising saints has been given to the popes; and also what the necessity, or even the utility is, of canonising them?" . . . . "However," adds he, ironically, "let them canonise as they will."[2]

These new attacks of Luther remained unanswered. The blindness of his enemies was as favourable to him as his own courage. They passionately defended secondary matters, and said not a word when they saw the foundations of Roman doctrine shaking under his hand. While they were eagerly defending some outworks, their intrepid adversary penetrated into the heart of the citadel, and there boldly planted the standard of truth; and hence their astonishment, when they saw the fortress sapped, blazing, and falling to pieces amid the flames, at the moment when they thought it impregnable, and were hurling defiance at their assailants. Thus it is that great changes are accomplished.

---

[1] Defensio contra malignum Eccii judicium. (Lat. i, p 356.)
[2] Canoniset quisque quantum volet. (Ibid. p. 367.)

The sacrament of the Lord's supper began, at this time, to engage Luther's attention. He looked for it in the mass, but in vain. One day, shortly after his return from Leipsic, he mounted the pulpit. Let us mark his words, for they are the first which he pronounced, on a subject which afterwards divided the Church and the Reformation into two parties. " In the holy sacrament of the altar," says he, " there are three things which it is necessary to know; the sign, which must be external, visible, and under a corporal form; the thing signified, which is internal, spiritual, and within the mind; and faith, which avails itself of both." [1] Had the definitions not been pushed farther, unity would not have been destroyed.

Luther continues. " It were good that the Church should, by a general council, decree that both kinds shall be distributed to all the faithful; not, however, on the ground that one kind is insufficient, for faith by itself would be sufficient." These bold words pleased his audience, though some were astonished and offended, and exclaimed, " This is false and scandalous." [2]

The preacher continues. " There is no union closer, deeper, or more inseparable than that between food and the body which is nourished by it. In the sacrament, Christ unites himself to us so closely that he acts in us as if he were identified with us. Our sins attack him. His righteousness defends us."

But Luther, not deeming it enough to expound the truth, attacks one of the most fundamental errors of Rome. [3] The Roman Church pretends that the sacrament operates by itself, independently of the disposition of him who receives it. Nothing can be more convenient than such an opinion, since to it, both the eagerness with which the sacrament is sought, and the profits of the clergy are to be ascribed. Luther attacks this doctrine, [4] and maintains its opposite [5]—viz., that faith and a right disposition of heart are indispensable.

This energetic protestation was destined to overthrow ancient superstitions; but, strange to say, it attracted no attention. Rome overlooked what might have made her scream in agony, and impetuously attacked the unimportant observation which Luther threw out at the commencement of his discourse, concerning communion in two kinds. The discourse having been published in

---

[1] L. Op. (L.) xvii, p. 272.　　　Ibid. p. 281.　　　[3] " Si quis dixerit per ipsa novæ legis sacramenta *ex opere operato* non conferri gratiam, sed solam fidem divinæ promissionis, ad gratiam consequendam sufficere, anathema sit." (Council of Trent, Sess. 7, can. 8.) If any man says that grace is not bestowed through the Sacraments of the New Covenant, by the mere act, (*ex opere operato*,) but that faith alone in the divine promise is sufficient to obtain grace, let him be anathema.
[4] Known by the name of *opus operatum*, the work performed.
[5] That of the *opus operantis*, the work of the performer, the communicant.

December, a general cry of heresy was raised. "It·is just the doctrine of Prague unadulterated," was the exclamation at the Court of Dresden, where the sermon arrived during the Christmas festivals. "It is written, moreover, in German, in·order to make it accessible to the common people."[1] The devotion of the prince was troubled, and on the third day of the festival he wrote to his cousin Frederick. "Since the publication of this discourse, the number of persons who receive the sacrament in two kinds has received an increase of 6000. Your Luther, from being a professor of Wittemberg, is on the eve of becoming a bishop of Prague, and an arch-heretic." . . . The cry was, "he was born in Bohemia, of Bohemian parents, he was brought up at Prague, and trained in the writings of Wickliffe."

Luther judged it right to contradict these rumours in a writing in which he gravely detailed his parentage. "I was born at Eisleben," said he, "and was baptised in St. Peter's church. The nearest town to Bohemia in which I have ever been, is Dresden."[2]

The letter of Duke George did not prejudice the Elector against Luther, for a few days after he invited him to a splendid entertainment which he gave to the Spanish ambassador, and at which Luther valiantly combated the minister of Charles.[3] The Elector's chaplain had, by his master's order, requested Luther to use moderation in defending his cause. "Excessive folly displeases man," replied Luther to Spalatin, "but excessive wisdom displeases God. The gospel cannot be defended without tumult and scandal. The word of God is sword, war, ruin, scandal, destruction, poison;"[4] and, hence, as Amos expresses it, "it presents itself like a bear in the path, and a lioness in the forest. I ask ·nothing, I demand nothing. There is one greater than I who asks and demands. Whether he stands or falls, I am neither · gainer nor loser."[5]

It was obvious that faith and courage were about to become more necessary to Luther than ever. Eck was forming projects of revenge. Instead of the laurels which he had counted on gaining, he had become a laughing-stock to all men of intellect throughout the nation. Cutting satires were published against him. Eck was cut to the very heart by "An Epistle of Ignorant Canons," written by Œcolompadius, and a complaint against him probably by the

---

[1] L. Op. (L.) xvii, p. 281.   [2] L. Op. (L.) xvii, p. 281.   [3] Cæterum ego natus sum in Eisleben. . . . . (L. Ep. i, p. 389.)   [4] Cum quo heri ego et Philippus certavimus, splendide invitati. (Ibid. p. 396.)   With whom Philip and I had a debate yesterday at a splendid entertainment.   [5] Verbum Dei gladius est, bellum est, ruina est, scandalum est, perditio est, venenum est. . . . . . (L. Ep. i, p. 417.)
[6] Ego nihil quæro ; est qui quærat. Stet ergo, sive cadat ; ego nihil lucror, aut amitto. (Ibid. p. 418.)

excellent Pirckheimer of Nuremberg, exhibiting a combination of sarcasm and dignity of which the 'Provincial Letters' of Pascal alone can give some idea.

Luther expressed his dissatisfaction with some of these writings. " It is better," said he, " to attack openly than to keep barking behind a hedge." [1]

How greatly the chancellor of Ingolstadt had miscalculated! His countrymen abandon him, and he prepares for a journey beyond the Alps, to invoke the aid of strangers. Wherever he goes he vents his threatenings against Luther, Melancthon, Carlstadt, and the Elector himself. " From the haughtiness of his expressions," says the doctor of Wittemberg, " one would say he imagines himself to be God Almighty." [2] Inflamed with rage, and thirsting for vengeance, Eck, having in February, 1520, published a work on the primacy of St. Peter,—a work devoid of sound criticism, in which he maintained that this apostle, the first of the popes, resided for twenty-five years at Rome—set out for Italy in order to receive the reward of his pretended triumphs, and to forge at Rome. near the papal capitol, thunders mightier than the frail scholastic arms which had given way in his hands.

Luther was aware of all the dangers to which the journey of his antagonist would expose him—but he feared not. Spalatin, alarmed, urged him to make proposals of peace. " No," replied Luther, " so long as he clamours, I cannot decline the contest. I commit the whole affair to God, and leave my bark to the winds and waves. It is the battle of the Lord. How can it be imagined that Christ will advance his cause by peace? Did he not combat even unto death, and have not all the martyrs since done the same? " [3]

Such was the position of the two combatants of Leipsic, at the commencement of the year 1520. The one was stirring up the whole papacy to strike a blow at his rival, who, on his part, waited for war as calmly as if he had been waiting for peace. The year on which we are entering will see the bursting of the storm.

[1] Melior est aperta criminatio, quam iste sub sepe morsus. (Ibid. p. 423.)
[2] Deum crederes omnipotentem loqui. (L. Ep. i, p. 380.)   [3] Cogor rem Deo committere, data flatibus et fluctibus nave. Bellum Domini est. . . . (Ibid. p. 425.)

BOOK SIXTH.

CHAP. I.

Character of Maximilian—The Competitors for the Empire—Charles—Francis I—Inclination of the Germans—The Crown offered to Frederick—Charles is Elected.

A NEW character was going to appear upon the stage. God saw meet to place the monk of Wittemberg in presence of the most powerful monarch who had appeared in Christendom since Charlemagne. He chose a prince, in the fervid vigour of youth, to whom every thing presaged a reign of long duration—a prince whose sceptre extended over a considerable portion both of the old and the new world; so that, according to a celebrated expression, the sun never set on his vast dominions—and opposed him to this humble Reformation, which began with the anguish and sighs of a poor monk, in the obscure cell of a convent at Erfurt. The history of this monarch and his reign seems to have been destined to give a great lesson to the world. It was to show the nothingness of all "the power of man," when it presumes to contend with "the weakness of God." Had a prince, friendly to Luther, been called to the empire, the success of the Reformation would have been attributed to his protection. Had even an emperor opposed to the new doctrine, but feeble, occupied the throne, the triumphant success of the work would have been accounted for by the feebleness of the monarch. But it was the proud conqueror of Pavia who behoved to humble his pride before the power of the Divine Word, that all the world might see how he, who had found it easy to drag Francis I a captive to Madrid, was compelled to lower his sword before the son of a poor miner.

The Emperor Maximilian was dead, and the electors had met at Frankfort to give him a successor. In the circumstances in which Europe was placed, this election was of vast importance, and was regarded with deep interest by all Christendom. Maximilian had not been a great prince; but his memory was dear to the people, who took a pleasure in remembering his presence of mind and good-humoured affability. Luther often talked of him to his friends, and one day related the following anecdote.

A beggar had kept running after him asking charity, and addressing him as his *brother;* "for," said he, "we are both descended from the same father, Adam. I am poor," continued he, "but you are rich, and it is your duty to assist me." At these words the emperor turned round and said to him—"Hold, there's a penny: go to your other brothers, and if each gives you as much, you will soon be richer than I am."[1]

The person about to be called to the empire was not a good-natured Maximilian. Times were to undergo a change; ambitious potentates were competing for the imperial throne of the West; the reins of the empire were to be seized by an energetic hand; profound peace was to be succeeded by long and bloody wars.

At the assembly of Frankfort, three kings aspired to the crown of the Cæsars. A youthful prince, grandson of the last emperor, born at the opening of the century, and consequently nineteen years of age, first presented himself. He was named Charles, and was born at Ghent. His paternal grandmother, Mary, daughter of Charles the Bold, had left him Flanders and the rich States of Burgundy. His mother, Joan, daughter of Ferdinand of Arragon and Isabella of Castile, and wife of Philip, son of the Emperor Maximilian, had transmitted to him the united kingdoms of Spain, Naples, and Sicily, to which Christopher Columbus had added a new world, while the recent death of his grandfather put him in possession of the hereditary States of Austria. This young prince, who was endowed with great talents. To a turn for military exercises (in which the dukes of Burgundy had long been distinguished)—to the finesse and penetration of the Italians—to the reverence for existing institutions which still characterises the house of Austria, and promised the papacy a firm defender, he joined a thorough knowledge of public affairs, acquired under the direction of Chièvres, having from fifteen years of age taken part in all the deliberations of his cabinet.[2] These diversified qualities were, in a manner, shrouded under Spanish reserve and taciturnity. In personal appearance he was tall in stature, and had somewhat of a melancholy air. "He is pious and tranquil," said Luther, "and I believe does not speak as much in a year as I do in a day."[3] Had the character of Charles been formed under the influence of freedom and Christianity, he would perhaps have been one of the most admirable princes on record; but politics engrossed his life, and stifled his great and good qualities.

Not contented with all the sceptres which he grasped in his hand, young Charles aspired to the imperial dignity. "It is like a sunbeam, which throws lustre on the house which it illumines," said several, "but put forth the hand to lay hold of it and you will find nothing." Charles, on the contrary, saw in it the pinnacle of all earthly grandeur, and a means of acquiring a magic influence over the spirit of the nations.

Francis I was the second of the competitors. The young paladins of the court of this chivalric king were incessantly representing to him that he was entitled, like Charlemagne, to be the emperor of all the West, and reviving the exploits of the ancient knights, to attack the crescent which was menacing the empire, discomfit the infidels, and recover the holy sepulchre.

"It is necessary," said the ambassadors of Francis to the electors, "it is necessary to prove to the Dukes of Austria, that the imperial crown is not hereditary. Besides, in existing circumstances, Germany has need not of a young man of nineteen, but of a prince who, to an experienced judgment, joins talents which have already been recognised. Francis will unite the arms of France and Lombardy to those of Germany, and make war on the Mussulmans. Sovereign of the duchy of Milan, he is already a member of the imperial body." These arguments, the French ambassadors supported by four hundred thousand crowns, which they distributed in purchasing votes and in festivities, by which they endeavoured to gain over their guests.

The third competitor was Henry VIII, who, jealous of the influence which the choice of the electors might give to Francis or Charles, also entered the lists, but soon left his powerful rivals sole disputants for the crown.

The electors were not disposed to favour either. Their subjects thought they would have in Francis a foreign master, and a master who might deprive the electors themselves of their independence, as he had lately deprived the nobles of his own dominions. As to Charles, it was an ancient rule with the electors not to choose a prince who was already playing an important part in the empire. The pope shared in these fears. He wished neither the king of Naples, who was his neighbour, nor the king of France, whose enterprising spirit filled him with alarm; "Choose rather some one from amongst yourselves," was his message to the electors. The elector of Trèves proposed Frederick of Saxony, and the imperial crown was laid at the feet of Luther's friend.

This choice would have obtained the approbation of all Germany.

Frederick's wisdom, and affection for his people, were well known. During the revolt of Erfurt, he had been urged to take the town by assault, and refused, in order to spare blood. " But it will not cost five men." "A single man would be too many," replied the prince.[1] The triumph of the Reformation seemed on the eve of being secured by the election of its protector. Ought not Frederick to have regarded the offer of the electors as a call from God himself? Who could have presided better over the destinies of the empire than a prince of so much wisdom? Who could have been stronger to oppose the Turks than an emperor strong in faith? The refusal of the Elector of Saxony, so much lauded by historians, was perhaps a fault. For the contests which afterwards tore Germany to pieces he is perhaps partly to blame. But it is difficult to say whether Frederick deserves censure for his want of faith or honour for his humility. He thought that even the safety of the empire made it his duty to refuse the crown.[2] " To save Germany," said this modest and disinterested prince, " an emperor more powerful than I is requisite."

The legate of Rome seeing that the choice would fall upon Charles, intimated that the pope withdrew his objections; and on the 28th of June, the grandson of Maximilian was elected. "God," said Frederick afterwards, "gave him to us in mercy and in anger."[3] The Spanish envoys sent a present of thirty thousand gold florins to the Elector of Saxony, as a mark of their master's gratitude; but the prince refused it, and charged his ministers not to accept of any present. At the same time he secured the German liberties by an engagement, to which the envoys of Charles took an oath in his name. The circumstances in which the latter prince encircled his head with the imperial crown seemed still better fitted than the oath to secure the Germanic liberties, and the success of the Reformation. The young prince was jealous of the laurels which his rival, Francis I, had gained at Marignan. The struggle was to be continued in Italy, and in the meantime the Reformation would doubtless be made secure. Charles left Spain in May, 1520, and was crowned on the 22nd of October, at Aix-la-Chapelle.

[1] L. Op. (W.) xxii, p. 1858. [2] " Is vero heroïca plane moderatione animi magni-fice repudiavit . . . . (Pallavicini, i, p. 79.) With a moderation amounting to heroism he nobly declined it. [3] L. Op. (W.) xxii, p. 188).

CHAP. II.

Luther writes to the Emperor—Luther's dangers—Instructions of Frederick to the court of Rome—Luther's sentiments—Melancthon's fears—The German nobles favourable to the Reformation—Schaumburg—Seckingen—Ulric de Hütten—Luther's Confidence—Luther's Greater Freedom—Faith the source of Works—What Faith gives—Luther judging his own writings.

Luther had foreseen that the cause of the Reformation would soon be brought before the new emperor; and, when Charles was still at Madrid, addressed a letter to him, in which he said, " If the cause which I defend is worthy of being presented before the heavenly Majesty, it cannot be unworthy of engaging the attention of a prince of this world. O, Charles! prince of the kings of the earth, I cast myself as a suppliant at the feet of your most serene majesty, and beseech you to deign to take under the shadow of your wings, not me, but the very cause of eternal truth, for the defence of which God has entrusted you with the sword." [1] The young king of Spain threw aside this odd letter from a German monk, and returned no answer.

While Luther was turning in vain toward Madrid, the storm seemed gathering around him. Fanaticism was rekindled in Germany. Hochstraten, indefatigable in his efforts at persecution, had extracted certain theses from Luther's writings, and obtained their condemnation by the universities of Cologne and Louvain. That of Erfurt, which had always had a grudge at Luther, for having given Wittemberg the preference, was on the eve of following their example. But the doctor, having been informed of it, wrote Lange, in terms so energetic that the theologians of Erfurt took fright, and said nothing. Still, however, there was enough to inflame the minds of men in the condemnation pronounced by Cologne and Louvain. More than this; the priests of Misnia who had espoused Emser's quarrel said openly (such is Melancthon's statement) that there would be no sin in killing Luther. [2] " The time is come," said Luther, " when men think they will do Jesus Christ service by putting us to death." The murderous language of the priests did not fail of its effect.

" One day," says a biographer, " when Luther was in front of the Augustin convent, a stranger, with a pistol hid under his arm,

---

[1] Causam ipsam veritatis . . . . (L. Ep. i, p. 392. 15th Jan., 1520)
[2] " Ut sine peccato esse eum censebant qui me interfecerit." (L. Ep. i, p. 383.)

accosted him, and said, Why do you walk about thus quite alone?"
" I am in the hands of God," replied Luther; " He is my strength
and my shield." " Thereupon," adds the biographer, "the stranger
grew pale, and fled trembling." [1] About the same time Serra-
Longa, the orator of the conference of Augsburg, wrote to the
Elector, " Let not Luther find any asylum in the states of your
highness, but, repulsed by all, let him be stoned to death in the
face of heaven. This would please me more than a gift of ten
thousand crowns." [2]

But the sound of the gathering storm was heard, especially in
the direction of Rome. Valentine Teutleben, a noble of Thuringia,
vicar of the Archbishop of Mentz, and a zealous partisan of the
papacy, was the representative of the Elector of Saxony at Rome.
Teutleben, ashamed of the protection which his master gave to the
heretical monk, could not bear to see his mission paralysed by this
imprudent conduct; and imagined that, by alarming the Elector,
he would induce him to abandon the rebel theologian. Writing to
his master, he said, " I am not listened to, because of the protection which you give to Luther." But the Romans were mistaken
if they thought they could frighten sage Frederick. He knew that
the will of God and the movements of the people were more irresistible than the decrees of the papal chancery. He ordered his
envoy to hint to the pope that, far from defending Luther, he had
always left him to defend himself, that he had moreover told him
to quit Saxony and the university, that the doctor had declared
his readiness to obey, and would not now be in the electoral states
had not the legate, Charles de Miltitz, begged the prince to keep
him near himself, from a fear that in other countries he would
act with still less restraint than in Saxony.[3] Frederick did still
more; he tried to enlighten Rome. " Germany," continues he, in
his letter, " now possesses a great number of learned men distinguished for scholarship and science ; the laity themselves begin
to cultivate their understanding, and to love the Holy Scriptures.
Hence, there is great reason to fear that, if the equitable proposals of Doctor Luther are not accepted, peace will never be re-
established. The doctrine of Luther has struck its roots deep in
many hearts. If, instead of refuting it by passages from the Bible,
an attempt is made to crush him by the thunders of ecclesiastical
power, great scandal will be given, and pernicious and dreadful
outbreaks will ensue." [4]

---

[1] Was kann mir ein Mensch thun ? (Keith, L. Umstände, p. 89.)   [2] Tenze.
Hist. Ber. ii, p. 168.   [3] Da er viel freyer und sicherer schreiben und handeln
möchte was er wollte. . . . (L. Op. (L.) xvii, p. 298.)   [4] Schreckliche, grausame,
schädliche und verderbliche Emporungen erregen. (Ibid.)

The Elector, having full confidence in Luther, caused Teutleben's letter to be communicated to him, and also another letter from ·cardinal St. George. The Reformer was moved on reading them. He at once saw all the dangers by which he was surrounded, and for an instant his heart sank. But it was in such moments as these that his faith displayed its full power. Often, when feeble -and ready to fall into despondency, he rallied again, and seemed ·greater amid the raging of the storm. He would fain have been ·delivered from all these trials; but, aware of the price that must have been paid for repose, he spurned it with indignation. "Be ·silent!" said he, "I am disposed to be so, if I am allowed—that is to say, if others are silent. If any one envies my situation he is welcome to it. If any one is desirous to destroy my writings, let him burn them. I am ready to remain quiet, provided gospel truth is not compelled to be quiet also.[1] I ask not a cardinal's hat; I ask neither gold, nor aught that Rome esteems. There is nothing which I will not concede, provided Christians are not excluded from the way of salvation.[2] All their threatenings do not terrify—all their promises cannot seduce me."

Animated by these sentiments, Luther soon resumed his war-like temperament, preferring the Christian combat to the calmness of solitude. One night was sufficient to revive his desire of over-throwing Rome. "My part is taken," wrote he next day. "I despise the fury of Rome, and I despise her favour. No more re-conciliation, nor more communication with her for ever.[3] Let her condemn and burn my writings! I, in my turn, will condemn and publicly burn the pontifical law, that nest of all heresies. The moderation which I have shown up to this hour has been useless, and I have done with it!"

His friends were far from feeling equally tranquil. Great alarm prevailed at Wittemberg. "We are waiting in extreme anxiety," said Melancthon. "I would sooner die than be separated from Luther.[4] Unless God come to our assistance we perish." Writing a month later, in his anxiety, he says, "Our Luther still lives, and God grant he long may; for the Roman sycophants are using every mean to destroy him. Pray for the life of him who is sole vindicator of sound theology."[5]

These prayers were not in vain. The warnings which the Elector had given Rome, through his envoy, were not without

---

[1] Semper quiescere paratus, modo veritatem evangelicam non jubeant quiescere. (L. Ep. i, p. 462.)   [2] Si salutis viam Christianis permittant esse liberam, hoc unum peto ab illis, ac praeterea nihil. . . (Ibid.)   [3] Nolo eis reconciliari nec communicare in perpetuum. . . (Ibid. p. 466, 10th July, 1520.)   [4] Emori malim, quam ab hoc viro avelli. (Corp. Reform. pp. 160, 163.   [5] Martinus noster spirat, atque utinam diu. . . (Corpus Refor. i, pp. 190, 208.)

foundation. The word of Luther had been every where heard, in cottages, and convents, at the firesides of the citizens, in the castles of nobles, in academies, and in the palaces of kings. He had said to Duke John of Saxony, " Let my life only have contributed to the salvation of a single individual, and I will willingly consent that all my books perish." [1] Not a single individual, but a great multitude, had found light in the writings of the humble doctor; and hence, in all quarters, there were men ready to protect him. The sword which was to attack him was on the anvil of the Vatican; but there were heroes in Germany who would interpose their bodies as his buckler. At the moment when the bishops were waxing wroth, when princes were silent, when the people were awaiting the result, and when the thunder was already grumbling on the seven hills, God raised up the German nobility, and placed them as a rampart around his servant.

At this time Sylvester of Schaumburg, one of the most powerful nobles of Franconia, sent his son to Wittemberg with a letter for the Reformer, in which he said, " Your life is exposed to danger. If the support of electors, princes, or magistrates fails you, I beg you to beware of going into Bohemia, where, of old, very learned men had much to suffer; come rather to me; God willing, I shall soon have collected more than a hundred gentlemen, and with their help, will be able to keep you free from harm." [2]

Francis of Seckingen, the hero of his age, whose intrepid courage we have already seen,[3] loved the Reformer, because he found that he was worthy of love, and also because he was hated by the monks.[4] " My person, my property, and services, all that I possess," wrote he to him, " is at your disposal. Your wish is to maintain Christian truth, and in that I am ready to assist you." [5] Harmuth of Cronberg, spoke in similar terms. Ulric von Hütten, the poet and valiant knight of the sixteenth century, ceased not to speak in commendation of Luther. But how great the contrast between these two men! Hütten wrote to the Reformer—" We must have swords, bows, javelins, and bullets, to destroy the fury of the devil." Luther, on receiving these letters, exclaimed—" I have no wish that men should have recourse to arms and carnage in order to defend the gospel. It was by the Word the world was overcome, by the Word the Church has been saved, and by the Word will she be re-established." " I despise not his offers," said he on receiving the above letter from Schaumburg, " but still I

---

[1] L. Op. (L.) xvii, p. 392.   [2] " Denn Ich, und hundert von Adel, die Ich (ob Gott will) aufbringen will, euch redlich anhalten." . . . . . (L. Op. (L.) xvii, p. 381.)
   [3] Equitum Germaniæ rarum decus ;" " the pink of German knights," says Melancthon on this occasion. (Corp. Reform. i, p. 201.)   [4] Et ob id invisus illis (Ibid. p. 132.)   [5] (Ibid.)

wish to lean on none but Christ."[1] So spake not the pontiffs of Rome when they waded in the blood of the Vaudois and Albigenses. Hütten was sensible of the difference between his cause and Luther's, and accordingly wrote with noble frankness : " I am occupied with the things of man, but you, rising to a far greater height, give yourself wholly to those of God."[2] After thus writing, he set out to try, if possible, to gain over Ferdinand and Charles V to the truth.[3]

Thus, on the one hand, Luther's enemies assail him, and on the other, his friends rise up to defend him. " My bark," says he, " floats here and there at the pleasure of the winds, . . . hope and fear reign by turns, but what matters it ?"[4] Still his mind was not uninfluenced by the marks of sympathy which he received. " The Lord reigns," said he, " and so visibly as to be almost palpable."[5] Luther saw that he was no longer alone; his words had proved faithful, and the thought inspired him with new courage. Now that he has other defenders prepared to brave the fury of Rome, he will no longer be kept back by the fear of compromising the Elector. He becomes more free, and, if possible, more decided. This is an important period in the development of Luther's mind. Writing at this time to the Elector's chaplain, he says, " Rome must be made aware, that though she should succeed, by her menaces, in exiling me from Wittemberg, she will only damage her cause. Those who are ready to defend me against the thunders of the papacy are to be found not in Bohemia, but in the heart of Germany. If I have not yet done to my enemies all that I am preparing for them, they must ascribe it neither to my moderation nor to their tyranny, but to my fear of compromising the name of the Elector, and the prosperity of the university of Wittemberg. Now, that I have no longer any such fears, I will rush with new impetuosity on Rome and her courtiers."[6]

Still Luther's hope was not placed on the great. He had often been urged to dedicate a book to Duke John, the Elector's brother, but had never done it. " I fear," he had said, " that the suggestion comes from himself. The Holy Scriptures must be subservient only to the glory of God's name."[7] Luther afterwards laid aside his suspicions, and dedicated his discourse on good works to Duke

---

[1] "Nolo nisi Christo protectore niti." (L. Ep. i, p. 148.)   [2] Mea humana sunt; tu perfectior, jam totus ex divinis pendes. (L. Op. Lat. ii, p. 175.   [3] Viam facturus libertati (cod. Bavar veritati) per maximos principes. (Corp. Reform. i, p. 201.) To make a way for liberty (in the Bavarian MS. " truth,") by means of the greatest princes.   [4] " Ita fluctuat navis mea ; nunc spes, nunc timor regnat." (L. Ep. i, p. 443.)   [5] " Dominus regnat, ut palpare possimus." Ibid. p. 451.)
   [6] " Sævius in Romanenses grassaturus. . . (L. Ep. i, p. 465.)   [7] " Scripturam sacram nolim alicujus nomini nisi Dei servire." (Ibid. p. 431.) I would not have sacred Scripture subservient to any name but that of God.

John, a discourse in which he gives a forcible exposition of the doctrine of justification by faith, a mighty doctrine, whose power he rates far higher than the sword of Hütten, the army of Seckingen, or the protection of dukes and electors.

"The first, the noblest, the sublimest of all works," says he, "is faith in Jesus Christ.[1] From this work all other works should proceed; they are all the vassals of faith, and from it alone derive their efficacy.

"If a man's own heart assures him, that what he is doing is agreeable to God, the work is good should it be merely the lifting up of a straw, but in the absence of this assurance the work is not good, though it should be the raising of the dead. A pagan, a Jew, a Turk, a sinner, can do all other works, but to trust firmly in the Lord, and feel assured of pleasing him, are works of which none are capable but the Christian strengthened by grace.

"A Christian, who has faith in God, acts, at all times, with freedom and gladness, whereas, the man who is not at one with God is full of cares, and is detained in thraldom; he anxiously asks how many works he ought to do, he runs up and down interrogating this man and that man, and, nowhere finding any peace, does everything with dissatisfaction and fear.

"Hence, I have always extolled faith. But it is otherwise in the world: there the essential point is to have many works, works great and high, and of all dimensions, while it is a matter of indifference whether or not faith animates them. Thus men build their peace, not on the good pleasure of God, but on their own merits, that is to say, on the sand. . . . . (Matt. vii, 27.)

"To preach faith is, it is said, to prevent good works; but though a single man should have in himself the powers of all men, or even of all creatures,[2] the mere obligation of living by faith would be a task too great for him ever to accomplish. If I say to a sick person, be in health and you will have the use of your members—will it be said that I forbid him to use his members? Must not health precede labour? The same holds true in the preaching of faith; it must be before works, in order that works themselves may exist.

"Where then, you will ask, is this faith found, and how is it received? This, indeed, is the most important of all questions. Faith comes solely from Jesus Christ, who is promised, and given gratuitously.

---

[1] Das erste und höchste, alleredelste . . . gute Werck ist der Glaube in Christum. . . . . (L. Op. (L.) xvii, p. 394.)   [2] Wenn ein Mensch tausend, oder alle Menschen, oder alle Creaturen wäre. (L. Op. (L.) p. 398.) "Were one man a thousand, or all men, or all creatures."

"O, man! represent Christ to thyself, and consider how in him God manifests his mercy to thee without being anticipated by any merit on thy part.[1] In this image of his grace receive the faith and assurance that all thy sins are forgiven thee. Works cannot produce it. It flows from the blood, the wounds, and the death of Christ, whence it wells up in the heart. Christ is the rock out of which come milk and honey. (Deut., xxxii.)

Not being able to give an account of all Luther's works, we have quoted some short fragments of this discourse on good works, on account of the opinion which the Reformer himself had of it. "It is in my judgment," said he, "the best work that I have published." He immediately subjoins this profound observation. "But I know that when any thing I write pleases myself, the infection of this bad leaven prevents it from pleasing others."[2] Melancthon, in sending a copy of this discourse to a friend, thus expressed himself, "Of all Greek and Latin authors none has come nearer the spirit of St. Paul than Luther."[3]

CHAP. III.

The Papacy Attacked—Appeal to the Nobility—The Three Walls—All Christians are Priests—The Magistrate's duty to Correct the Clergy—Abuses of Rome—Ruin of Italy—Dangers of Germany—The Pope—The Legates—The Monks—The Marriage of Priests—Celibacy—Festivals—The Bohemians—Charity—The Universities—The Empire—The Emperor must retake Rome—A Book not Published—Luther's Modesty—Success of the Address.

But the substitution of a system of meritorious works for the idea of grace and amnesty was not the only evil existing in the Church. A domineering power had risen up among the humble pastors of Christ's flock. Luther must attack this usurped authority. A vague and distant rumour of Eck's intrigues and success at Rome awakened a warlike spirit in the Reformer, who, amid all his turmoil, had calmly studied the origin, progress, and usurpations of the papacy. His discoveries having filled him with surprise, he no longer hesitated to communicate them and strike the blow which was destined, like the rod of Moses of old, to awaken a whole nation out of a lethargy, the result of long bondage. Even before Rome had time to publish her formidable bull, he published

[1] Siehe, also musst du Christum in dich bilden, und sehen wie in Ihm Gott—seine Barmherzigkeit dir fürhält und arbeut. (Ibid. p. 401.)
[2] "Erit meo judicio omnium quæ ediderim, optimum : quanquam scio quæ mihi mea placent, hoc ipso fermento infecta, non solere aliis placere." (L. Ep. i, p. 431.)
[3] "Quo ad Pauli spiritum nemo proprius accessit. (Corp. Refor. i, p. 202)

2   e

his declaration of war. "The time of silence," exclaims he, "is past; the time for speaking has arrived. The mysteries of Antichrist must at length be unveiled." On the 24th June, 1502, he published his famous '*Appeal to his Imperial Majesty, and the Christian Nobility of Germany, on the Reformation of Christianity.*'[1] This work was the signal of the attack which was at once to complete the rupture and decide the victory.

"It is not from presumption," says he, at the outset of this Treatise, "that I, who am only one of the people, undertake to address your lordships. The misery and oppression endured at this moment by all the States of Christendom, and more especially by Germany,. wring from me a cry of distress. I must call for aid ; I must see whether God will not give his Spirit to some one of our countrymen, and stretch out a hand to our unhappy nation. God has given us a young and generous prince, (the Emperor Charles V,)[2] and thus filled our hearts with high hopes. But we too must, on our own part, do all we can.

"Now, the first thing necessary is, not to confide in our own great strength, or our own high wisdom. When any work otherwise good is begun in self-confidence, God casts it down, and destroys it. Frederick I, Frederick II, and many other emperors besides,. before whom the world trembled, have been trampled upon by the popes, because they trusted more to their own strength than to God. They could not but fall. In this war we have to combat the powers of hell, and our mode of conducting it must be to expect nothing from the strength of human weapons—to trust humbly in the Lord, and look still more to the distress of Christendom than to the crimes of the wicked. It may be that, by a different procedure, the work would begin under more favourable appearances, but suddenly in the heat of the contest confusion would arise, bad men would cause fearful disaster, and the world would be deluged with blood. The greater the power, the greater the danger, when things are not done in the fear of the Lord."

After this exordium, Luther continues:—

"The Romans, to guard against every species of reformation, have surrounded themselves with three walls. When attacked by the temporal power, they denied its jurisdiction over them, and maintained the superiority of the spiritual power. When tested by Scripture, they replied, that none could interpret it but the pope. When threatened with a council, they again replied, that none but the pope could convene it.

---

[1] I. Op. (L.) xvii, 457-504.   [2] Gott hat uns ein junges edles Blut zum Haupt gegeben. (Ibid., p. 457.)

" They have thus carried off from us the three rods destined to chastise them, and abandoned themselves to all sorts of wickedness. But now may God be our help, and give us one of the trumpets which threw down the walls of Jericho. Let us blow down the walls of paper and straw which the Romans have built around them, and lift up the rods which punish the wicked, by bringing the wiles of the devil to the light of day."

Luther next commences the attack, and shakes to the foundation that papal monarchy which had for ages united the nations of the West into one body under the sceptre of the Roman bishop. There is no sacerdotal caste in Christianity. This truth, of which the Church was so early robbed, he vigorously expounds in the following terms :—

" It has been said that the pope, the bishops, the priests, and all those who people convents, form the spiritual or ecclesiastical estate; and that princes, nobles, citizens, and peasants, form the secular or lay estate. This is a specious tale. But let no man be alarmed. All Christians belong to the spiritual estate, and the only difference between them is in the functions which they fulfil. We have all but one baptism, but one faith, and these constitute the spiritual man. Unction, tonsure, ordination, consecration, given by the pope or by a bishop, may make a hypocrite, but can never make a spiritual man. We are all consecrated priests by baptism, as St. Peter says, ' You are a royal priesthood;' although all do not actually perform the offices of kings and priests, because no one can assume what is common to all, without the common consent. But if this consecration of God did not belong to us, the unction of the pope could not make a single priest. If ten brothers, the sons of one king, and possessing equal claims to his inheritance, should choose one of their number to administer for them, they would all be kings, and yet only one of them would be the administrator of their common power. So it is in the Church. Were several pious laymen banished to a desert, and were they, from not having among them a priest consecrated by a bishop, to agree in selecting one of their number, whether married or not, he would be as truly a priest, as if all the bishops of the world had consecrated him. In this way were Augustine, Ambrose, and Cyprian elected.

" Hence it follows that laymen and priests, princes and bishops, or, as we have said, ecclesiastics and laics, have nothing to distinguish them but their functions. They have all the same condition, but they have not all the same work to perform.

" This being so, why should not the magistrate correct the

clergy? The secular power was appointed by God for the punishment of the wicked and the protection of the good, and must be left free to act throughout Christendom without respect of persons, be they pope, bishops, priests, monks, or nuns. St. Paul says to all Christians, ' *Let every soul,*' (and consequently the pope also,) ' *be subject to the higher powers; for they bear not the sword in vain.*' " [1]

Luther, after throwing down the other two walls in the same way, takes a review of all the abuses of Rome. With an eloquence of a truly popular description he exposes evils which had, for ages, been notorious. Never had a nobler remonstrance been heard. The assembly which Luther addresses is the Church, the power whose abuses he attacks is that papacy which had for ages been the oppressor of all nations, and the Reformation for which he calls aloud is destined to exercise its powerful influence on Christendom, all over the world, and so long as man shall exist upon it.

He begins with the pope. " It is monstrous," says he, " to see him who calls himself the vicar of Jesus Christ displaying a magnificence, unequalled by that of any emperor. Is this the way in which he proves his resemblance to lowly Jesus, or humble Peter? He is, it is said, the lord of the world. But Christ, whose vicar he boasts to be, has said, ' *My kingdom is not of this world.*' Can the power of a vicegerent exceed that of his prince? . . . ."

Luther proceeds to depict the consequences of the papal domination. " Do you know of what use the cardinals are? I will tell you. Italy and Germany have many convents, foundations, and benefices, richly endowed. How could their revenues be brought to Rome? . . . Cardinals were created; then, on them, cloisters and prelacies were bestowed, and at this hour . . . . . Italy is almost a desert—the convents are destroyed—the bishopricks devoured—the towns in decay—the inhabitants corrupted—worship dying out, and preaching abolished. . . . . Why? Because all the revenues of the churches go to Rome. Never would the Turk himself have so ruined Italy."

Luther next turns to his countrymen.

" And now that they have thus sucked the blood of their own country, they come into Germany. They begin gently, but let us be on our guard. Germany will soon become like Italy. We have already some cardinals. Their thought is—before the rustic Germans comprehend our design they will have neither bishoprick, nor convent, nor benefice, nor penny, nor farthing. Antichrist must possess the treasures of the earth. Thirty or forty cardinals will be elected in a single day; to one will be given Bamberg, to

[1] Πᾶσα ψυχή. Rom. xiii. 1, 4.

another the duchy of Wurtzburg, and rich benefices will be annexed until the churches and cities are laid desolate. And then the pope will say, ' I am the vicar of Christ, and the pastor of his flocks. Let the Germans be resigned.' "

Luther's indignation rises.

" How do we Germans submit to such robbery and concussion on the part of the pope ? If France has successfully resisted, why do we allow ourselves to be thus sported with and insulted ? Ah! if they deprived us of nothing but our goods. But they ravage churches, plunder the sheep of Christ, abolish the worship and suppress the word of God."

Luther then exposes the devices of Rome to obtain money and secure the revenues of Germany. Annats, palliums, commendams, administrations, expected favours, incorporations, reservations, etc., all pass in review. Then he says, " Let us endeavour to put a stop to this desolation and misery. If we would march against the Turks—let us begin with the worst species of them. If we hang pickpockets, and behead robbers, let us not allow Roman avarice to escape—avarice, which is the greatest of all thieves and robbers, and that too in the name of St. Peter and Jesus Christ. Who can endure it ? Who can be silent ? Is not all that the pope possesses stolen ? He neither purchased it nor inherited it from St. Peter, nor acquired it by the sweat of his own brow. Where then did he get it ?"

Luther proposes remedies for all these evils, and energetically arouses the German nobility to put an end to Roman depredation. He next comes to the reform of the pope himself. " Is it not ridiculous," says he, " that the pope should pretend to be the lawful heir of the empire ? Who gave it to him ? Was it Jesus Christ, when he said, ' *The kings of the earth exercise lordship over them, but it shall not be so with you*' (Luke, xxii, 25, 26). How can he govern an empire, and at the same time preach, pray, study, and take care of the poor ? Jesus Christ forbade his disciples to carry with them gold or clothes, because the office of the ministry cannot be performed without freedom from every other care ; yet the pope would govern the empire, and at the same time remain pope." . .

Luther continues to strip the sovereign pontiff of his spoils. " Let the pope renounce every species of title to the kingdom of Naples and Sicily. He has no more right to it than I have. His possession of Bologna, Imola, Ravenna, Romagna, Marche d'Ancona, etc., is unjust and contrary to the commands of Jesus Christ. '*No man*,' says St. Paul, ' *who goeth a warfare entangleth himself with the affairs of this life*,' (2 Tim., ii, 2). And the pope, who pretends to take the lead in the war of the gospel, entangles himself more with the affairs of this life than any emperor or king. He must be disencumbered of all this toil. The emperor should put a bible and a prayer book into the hands of the pope, that the pope may leave kings to govern, and devote himself to preaching and prayer." [1]

Luther is as averse to the pope's ecclesiastical power in Germany as to his temporal power in Italy. " The first thing necessary is to banish from all the countries of Germany, the legates of the pope, and the pretended blessings which they sell us at the weight of gold, and which are sheer imposture. They take our money— and why? For legalising ill gotten gain, for loosing oaths, and teaching us to break faith, to sin, and go direct to hell. . . . Hearest thou, O, pope ! not pope most holy, but pope most sinful. . . . May God, from his place in heaven, cast down thy throne into the infernal abyss !"

The Christian tribune pursues his course. After citing the pope to his bar, he cites all the abuses in the train of the papacy, and endeavours to sweep away from the Church all the rubbish by which it is encumbered. He begins with the monks.

" And now I come to a lazy band which promises much, but performs little. Be not angry, dear Sirs, my intention is good; what I have to say is a truth at once sweet and bitter; viz., that it is no longer necessary to build cloisters for mendicant monks. Good God ! we have only too many of them, and would they were all suppressed. . . . To wander vagabond over the country never has done, and never will do good."

The marriage of ecclesiastics comes next in course. It is the first occasion on which Luther speaks of it.

" Into what a state have the clergy fallen, and how many priests are burdened with women and children and remorse, while no one comes to their assistance? Let the pope and the bishops run their course, and let those who will, go to perdition; all very well! but I am resolved to unburden my conscience and open my mouth freely, however pope, bishops, and others may be offended! . . . . I say, then, that according to the institution of Jesus Christ and the apostles, every town ought to have a pastor or bishop, and that this pastor may have a wife, as St. Paul writes to Timothy, " *Let the bishop be the husband of one wife*," (1 Tim. iii. 2,) and as is still practised in the Greek Church. But the devil has persuaded the pope, as St. Paul tells Timothy (1 Tim. iv, 1-3), to forbid the

---

[1] Ihm die Blblien und Betbücher dafür anzeigen . . . . und er predige und bete.
(L. Op. xvii, p. 472.)

clergy to marry. And hence, evils so numerous, that it is impossible to give them in detail. What is to be done? How are we to
save the many pastors who are blameworthy only in this, that
they live with a female, to whom they wish with all their heart to
be lawfully united? Ah! let them save their conscience! let them
take this woman in lawful wedlock, and live decently with her, not
troubling themselves whether it pleases or displeases the pope.
The salvation of your soul is of greater moment than arbitrary and
tyrannical laws, laws not imposed by the Lord."

In this way the Reformation sought to restore purity of morals
within the Church. The Reformer continues:—

" Let feast-days be abolished, and let Sunday only be kept, or
if it is deemed proper to keep the great Christian festivals, let them
be celebrated in the morning, and let the remainder of the day be
a working-day as usual. For by the ordinary mode of spending
them in drinking and gaming and committing all sorts of sins, or in
mere idleness, God is offended on festivals much more than on
other days."

He afterwards attacks the dedications of Churches, (which he
describes as mere taverns,) and after them fasts and fraternities. He
desires not only to suppress abuses, but also to put an end to
schisms. "It is time," says he, "to take the case of the Bohemians into serious consideration, that hatred and envy may cease,
and union be again established." He proposes excellent methods
of conciliation, and adds—" In this way must heretics be refuted
by Scripture, as the ancient fathers did, and not subdued by fire.
On a contrary system, executioners would be the most learned of
all doctors. Oh! would to God that each party among us would
shake hands with each other in fraternal humility, rather than
harden ourselves in the idea of our power and right! Charity is
more necessary than the Roman papacy. I have now done what
was in my power. If the pope or his people oppose it, they will
have to give an account. The pope should be ready to renounce
the popedom, and all his wealth, and all his honours, if he could
thereby save a single soul. But he would see the universe go to
destruction sooner than yield a hair-breadth of his usurped power.[1]
I am clear of these things."

Luther next comes to universities and schools.

" I much fear the universities will become wide gates to hell, if
due care is not taken to explain the Holy Scriptures, and engrave
it on the hearts of the students. My advice to every person is,
not to place his child where the Scripture does not reign para-

---

[1] Nun liess er ehe dei Welt untergehen, ehe er ein Haarbreit seiner vermessenen
Gewalt liesse abbrechen. (L. Op. (L.) xvii, p. 483.)

mount. Every institution in which the studies carried on lead to a relaxed consideration of the Word of God must prove corrupting;[1] a weighty sentiment, which governments, literary men, and parents in all ages would do well to ponder."

Towards the end of his address he returns to the empire and the emperor.

"The popes," says he, "unable to lead the ancient masters of the Roman empire at will, resolved on wresting their title and their empire from them and giving it to us Germans. This they accomplished, and we have become bondmen to the pope. For the pope has possessed himself of Rome, and bound the emperor by oath never to reside in it; and the consequence is, that the emperor is the emperor of Rome without having Rome. We have the name; the pope has the country and its cities. We have the title and the insignia of empire; the pope its treasury, power, privileges, and freedom. The pope eats the fruit, and we amuse ourselves with the husk. In this way our simplicity has always been abused by the pride and tyranny of the Romans.

"But now, may God who has given us such an empire, be our aid! Let us act conformably to our name, our title, our insignia; let us save our freedom, and give the Romans to know that, through their hands it was committed to us by God. They boast of having given us an empire. Very well! let us take what belongs to us. Let the pope surrender Rome, and every part of the empire that he possesses. Let him put an end to his taxes and extortions. Let him restore our liberty, our power, our wealth, our honour, our soul, and our body. Let the empire be all that an empire ought to be; and let the sword of princes no longer be compelled to lower itself before the hypocritical pretensions of a pope."

In these words there is not only energy and eloquence, but also sound argument. Never did orator so speak to the nobility of the empire, and to the emperor himself. Far from being surprised that so many German states revolted from Rome we should rather wonder that all Germany did not proceed to the banks of the Tiber, and there resume that imperial power, the insignia of which the popes had imprudently placed on the head of their chief.

Luther thus concludes his intrepid address.

"I presume, however, that I have struck too high a note, proposed many things that will appear impossible, and been somewhat too severe on the many errors which I have attacked. But what can I do? Better that the world be offended with me than God! . . . . The utmost which it can take from me

[1] Es muss verderben, alles was nicht Gottes Wort ohn Unterlass treibt. (L. Op. L. xvii, p. 186.)

is life. I have often offered to make peace with my opponents, but, through their instrumentality God has always obliged me to speak out against them. I have still a chant upon Rome in reserve, and if they have an itching ear, I will sing it to them at full pitch. Rome! do ye understand me?" . . It is probable that Luther here refers to a treatise on the papacy which he was preparing for publication, but which never was published. Rector Burkhard, writing at this time to Spengler, says, " There is, moreover, a short tract, *De Execranda Venere Romanorum*, but it is kept in reserve." The title of the work seems to intimate something which would have given great offence, and it is pleasing to think that Luther had moderation not to publish it.

" If my cause is just," continues he, " it must be condemned on the earth, and justified only by Christ in heaven. Therefore, let pope, bishops, priests, monks, doctors, come forward, display all their zeal, and give full vent to their fury. Assuredly they are just the people who ought to persecute the truth, as in all ages they have persecuted it."

Where did this monk obtain this clear knowledge of public affairs, which even the states of the empire often find it so difficult to unravel? Whence did this German derive this courage which enables him to hold up his head among his countrymen who had been enslaved for so many ages, and deal such severe blows to the papacy? By what mysterious energy is he animated? Does it not seem that he must have heard the words which God addressed to one of ancient times; " Lo! I have strengthened thy face against their faces, I have made thy forehead like a diamond, and harder than flint; be not then afraid because of them"?

This exhortation, being addressed to the German nobility, was soon in the hands of all those for whom it was intended. It spread over Germany with inconceivable rapidity. Luther's friends trembled, while Staupitz, and those who wished to follow gentle methods, thought the blow too severe. " In our days," replied Luther, " whatever is treated calmly falls into oblivion, and nobody cares for it." [1] At the same time, he displayed extraordinary simplicity and humility. He was unconscious of his own powers. " I know not," writes he, " what to say of myself; perhaps I am the precursor of Philip (Melancthon). Like Elias, I am preparing the way for him, in spirit and in power, that he may one day trouble Israel, and the house of Ahab." [2] But there was no occasion to wait for any other than he who had appeared. The house of Ahab

---

[1] Quæ nostro sæculo quiete tractantur, mox cadere in oblivionem . . . . (L. Ep: i,. p. 479.)   [2] Ibid. p. 478.

·was already shaken. The *Address to the German Nobility* was published on the 26th of June, 1520, and, in a short time, 4000 copies were sold, a number at that period unprecedented. The astonishment was universal, and the whole people were in commotion. The vigour, spirit, perspicuity, and noble boldness by which it was ·pervaded, made it truly a work for the people, who felt that one who spoke in such terms truly loved them. The confused views which many wise men entertained were enlightened. All became aware of the usurpations of Rome. At Wittemberg, no man had .any doubt whatever, that the pope was Antichrist. Even the Elector's court, with all its timidity and circumspection, did not ·disapprove of the Reformer, but only awaited the issue. The nobility and the people did not even wait. The nation was awa- ·kened, and, at the voice of Luther, adopted his cause, and rallied around his standard. Nothing could have been more advantageous ·to the Reformer than this publication. In palaces, in castles, in ·the dwellings of the citizens, and even in cottages, all are now ·prepared, and made proof, as it were, against the sentence of con- ·demnation which is about to fall upon the prophet of the people. All Germany is on fire, and the bull, come when it may, never ·will extinguish the conflagration.

CHAP. IV.

·Preparations at Rome—Motives to resist the Papacy—Eck at Rome—Eck gains the Day—The Pope is the World—God produces the Separation—A Swiss Priest pleads for Luther—The Roman Consistory—Preamble of the Bull—Condemnation of Luther.

At Rome every thing necessary for the condemnation of the ·defender of the liberty of the Church was prepared. Men had long ·lived there in arrogant security. The monks of Rome had long ac- ·cused Leo X of devoting himself to luxury and pleasure, and of spending his whole time in hunting, theatricals, and music,[1] while ·the Church was crumbling to pieces. At last, through the clamour · of Dr. Eck, who had come from Leipsic to invoke the power of the Vatican, the pope, the cardinals, the monks, all Rome awoke and · bestirred themselves to save the papacy.

Rome, in fact, was obliged to adopt the severest measures. The · gauntlet had been thrown down, and the combat was destined to

---

1 Sopra tutto musico eccellentissimo, e quando el canta con qualche uno, li fa donar cento e più ducati. . . (Zorsi. MS. C.) And above all a most excellent musician, and · any person with whom he sings he presents with a hundred ducats.

be mortal. Luther attacked not the abuses of the Roman pontificate, but the pontificate itself. At his bidding, the pope was humbly to descend from his throne, and again become a simple pastor, or bishop, on the banks of the Tiber. All the dignitaries of the Roman hierarchy were required to renounce their riches and worldly glory, and again become elders or deacons of the churches of Italy. All the splendour and power which had for ages dazzled the West behoved to vanish away and give place to the humble and simple worship of the primitive Christians. These things God could have done, and will one day do, but they were not to be expected from men. Even should a pope have been disinterested enough, and bold enough to attempt the overthrow of the ancient and sumptuous edifice of the Romish Church, thousands of priests and bishops would have rushed forward to its support. The pope had received power under the express condition of maintaining whatever was entrusted to him. Rome deemed herself appointed of God to govern the Church; and no wonder, therefore, that she was prepared with this view to adopt the most decisive measures. And yet, at the outset, she did show hesitation. Several cardinals and the pope himself, were averse to severe proceedings. Leo had too much sagacity not to be aware that a decision, the enforcement of which depended on the very dubious inclinations of the civil power, might seriously compromise the authority of the Church. He saw, moreover, that the violent methods already resorted to had only increased the evil. " Is it impossible to gain this Saxon monk?" asked the politicians of Rome. "Would all the power of the Church, and all the wiles of Italy, be ineffectual for this purpose? Negotiation must still be attempted."

Eck accordingly encountered formidable obstacles. He neglected nothing to prevent what he termed impious concessions. Going up and down Rome, he gave vent to his rage, and cried for vengeance. The fanatical faction of the monks having immediately leagued with him he felt strong in this alliance, and proceeded with new courage to importune the pope and the cardinals. According to him all attempts at conciliation were useless. " The idea of it," said he, " is only the vain dream of those who slumber at a distance from the scene. But he knew the danger; for he had wrestled with the audacious monk. The thing necessary was to amputate the gangrened limb, and so prevent the disease from attacking the whole body. The blustering disputant of Leipsic solves objections one after another, and endeavours, but finds it difficult to persuade the pope.[1] He wishes to save Rome in spite of herself.

[1] Sarpi. Hist. of Council of Trent.

Sparing no exertion, he spent whole hours in deliberation in the
cabinet of the pontiff,[1] and made application both to the court and,
the cloisters, to the people and the Church. " Eck is calling to the
depth of depths against me," said Luther, " and setting on fire the
forests of Lebanon."[2]   At length he succeeded.   The fanatics in
the councils of the papacy vanquished the politicians.   Leo gave
way, and Luther's condemnation was resolved.   Eck began again
to breathe, and his pride felt gratified by the thought that his own
efforts had procured the ruin of his heretical rival, and thereby
saved the church. " It was well," said he, "that I came to Rome
at this time, for little was known of Luther's errors.   It will one
day be seen how much I have done in this cause."[3]

No one exerted himself so much in seconding Dr. Eck as the
master of the sacred palace, Sylvester Mazzolini De Priorio, who
had just published a work, in which he maintained, that not only
to the pope alone appertained the infallible decision of all debate-
able points, but also that papal ascendancy was the fifth monarchy
of Daniel, and the only true monarchy; that the pope was the
prince of all ecclesiastical, and the father of all secular princes,
the chief of the world, and even in substance the world itself.[4]   In
another writing he affirmed, that the pope is as much superior to
the emperor as gold is to lead;[5] that the pope can appoint and
depose emperors and electors, establish and annul positive rights;
and that the emperor, with all the laws and all the nations of
Christendom, cannot decide the smallest matter contrary to the
pope's will.   Such was the voice which came forth from the palace
of the sovereign pontiff, such the monstrous fiction which, in union
with scholastic dogmas, aimed at suppressing reviving truth.   Had
this fiction not been unmasked, as it has been, and that even by
learned members of the Catholic Church, there would have been
neither true history nor true religion.   The papacy is not merely a
lie in regard to the Bible. it is also a lie in regard to the annals
of nations.   And hence the Reformation, by destroying its fas-
cinating power, has emancipated not only the Church, but also
kings and nations.   The Reformation has been described as a
political work, and in this secondary sense it truly was so.

Thus God sent a spirit of delusion on the doctors of Rome.

1 Stetimus nuper, papa, duo cardinales . . . . et ego per quinque horas in delibera-
tione . . . . (Eckii Epistola, 3 Maii. L. Op. Lat. ii, p. 48.)   The pope, two cardinals,
and I lately remained five hours in deliberation.   2 Impetraturus abyssos-
abyssorum. . . . succensurus saltum Libani . . . . (L. Ep. i, p. 421, 429.)
3 Bonum fuit me venisse hoc tempore Romam . . . . (Epist. Eckii.)
4 Caput orbis et consequenter orbis totus in virtute (De juridica et irrefragabili
veritate Romanæ Ecclesiæ. Bibl. Max. xix, cap. iv.)   5 Papa est imperatore
major dignitate plus quam aurum plombo. (De Papa et ejus potestate, p. 371.)

The separation between truth and error must now be accom‑ plished, and it is to error that the task is assigned. Had a compromise been entered into, it must have been at the expense of truth; for to mutilate truth in the slightest degree is to pave the way for her complete annihilation. Like the insect, which is said to die on the loss of one of its antennæ, she must be complete in all her parts, in order to display the energy which enables her to gain great and advantageous victories, and propagate herself through coming ages. To mingle any portion of error with truth is to throw a grain of poison into a large dish of food. The grain suffices to change its whole nature, and death ensues slowly, it may be; but yet surely. Those who defend the doctrine of Christ against the attacks of its adversaries keep as jealous an eye on its farthest outposts as on the citadel itself, for the moment the enemy gains any footing at all he is on the highway to conquest. The Roman pontiff determined at the period of which we now treat to rend the Church; and the fragment which remained in his hand, how splendid soever it may be, in vain endeavours under pompous ornaments to hide the deleterious principle by which it is attacked. It is only where the word of God is, that there is life. Luther, however great his courage was, would probably have been silent had Rome been so and made some faint show of concession. But God did not leave the Reformation to depend on a weak human heart. Luther was under the guidance of a clearer intellect than his own. The pope·was the instrument in the hand of Provi‑ dence to sever every tie between the past and the future, and launch the Reformer on a new, unknown, and to him uncertain career, and the difficult avenues to which he would, if left to him‑ self, have been unable to find. The papal bull was a writing of divorce sent from Rome to the pure Church of Jesus Christ, as personified in him who was then her humble but faithful represen‑ tative. And the Church accepted the writing on the understand‑ ing that she was thenceforth to depend on none but her heavenly Head.

While at Rome, Luther's condemnation was urged forward with so much violence, a humble priest, dwelling in one of the humble towns of Helvetia, and who had never had any correspondence with the Reformer, was deeply moved when he thought of the blow which was aimed at him; while even the friends of the Wit‑ temberg doctor trembled in silence, this mountaineer of Switzer‑ land resolved to employ every means to stay the formidable bull. His name was Ulrick Zwingle. William des Faucons, who was secretary to the papal Legate in Switzerland, and managed the affairs of Rome during the Legate's absence, was his friend, and a few days before had said to him, " while I live you may calculate· on obtaining from me everything that a true friend can be expected to give." The Helvetian priest, trusting to this declaration, repaired to the Roman embassy. This, at least, may be inferred from one of his letters. For himself, he had no fear of the dangers to which evangelical faith exposed him, knowing that a disciple of Jesus Christ must always be ready to sacrifice his life ; " All I ask of Christ for myself," said he to a friend to whom he was unbosoming his solicitude on Luther's account, " all I ask is to be able to bear like a man whatever evils await me. I am a vessel of clay in his hands. Let him break or let him strengthen me as seemeth to him good."[1] But the Swiss evangelist had fears for the Christian Church, should this formidable blow reach the Reformer, and he endeavoured to persuade the representative of Rome to enlighten the pope, and employ all the means in his power to prevent him from launching an excommunication at Luther.[2] " The dignity of the holy see itself," said he to him, " is here at stake, for if matters are brought to such a point, Germany, in the height of her enthusiasm for the gospel, and for its preacher, will despise the pope and his anathemas."[3] The efforts of Zwingle were in vain. It appears, indeed, that when he was making them, the blow had been already struck. Such was the first occasion on which the paths of the Saxon doctor and the Swiss priest met. The latter we will again meet with in the course of this history, and will see him gradually expanding and growing until he obtain a high standing in the Church of the Lord.

After Luther's condemnation was at last resolved upon, new difficulties arose in the Consistory. The theologians wished to proceed at once to fulmination, whereas the lawyers were for beginning with a citation, asking their theological colleagues, " Was not Adam first cited ? '*Adam, where art thou?*' said the Lord. It was the same with Cain, the question asked at him was, ' where is thy brother, Abel?' " These strange arguments, drawn from Scripture, the canonists strengthened by appealing to the principles of the law of nature. " The certainty of a crime," said they, " cannot deprive the criminal of his right of defence."[4] It is pleasing to find a sense of justice still existing in a Roman consistory. But these scruples did not suit the theologians, who,

---

[1] Hoc unum Christum obtestans, ut masculo omnia pectore ferre donet, et me figulinum suum rumpat aut firmet, ut illi placitum sit. (Zwinglii Epistolæ, curant. Schulero et Schulthessio, p. 144.) [2] Ut pontificem admoneat, ne excommunicationem ferat. (Ibid.) [3] Nam si teratur, auguror Germanos cum excommunicatione pontificem quoque contempturos. (Zwinglii Epistolæ, curant. Schulero et Schulthessio, p. 144.) [4] Sarpi Hist. of the Council of Trent, i, p. 12.

hurried on by passion, thought only of proceeding to business with despatch. It was at length agreed that the doctrine of Luther should be immediately condemned, and that a period of sixty days should be granted to him and his adherents; after which, provided they did not retract, they should all be, *ipso facto*, excommunicated. De Vio, who had returned from Germany in ill health, was carried to the meeting, that he might not lose this little triumph, which carried with it some degree of consolation. Having been defeated at Augsburg, he longed to be able at Rome to condemn the invincible monk, before whom his knowledge, finesse, and authority had proved unavailing. Luther not being there to reply, De Vio felt himself strong. A last conference, which Eck attended, was held in presence of the pope himself, in his villa at Malliano. On the 15th of June the sacred college resolved on condemnation, and approved of the famous bull.

"Arise, O Lord!" said the Roman pontiff, speaking at this solemn moment as vicar of God and head of the Church, "arise and be judge in thy own cause. Remember the insults daily offered to thee by infatuated men. Arise, O Peter, remember thy holy Roman Church, the mother of all churches, and mistress of the faith! Arise, O Paul, for here is a new Porphyry, who is attacking thy doctrines and the holy popes our predecessors! Arise, in fine, assembly of all the saints, holy Church of God, and intercede with the Almighty!" [1]

The pope afterwards quotes as pernicious, scandalous, and poisonous, forty-one propositions in which Luther had expounded the holy doctrine of the gospel. Among these propositions we find the following:—

"To deny that sin remains in an infant after baptism, is to trample St. Paul and our Lord Jesus Christ under foot."

"A new life is the best and noblest penance."

"To burn heretics is contrary to the will of the Holy Spirit, etc."

The moment this Bull is published," continued the pope, "it will be the duty of the bishops to make careful search for the writings of Martin Luther, which contain these errors, and to burn them publicly and solemnly in presence of the clergy and laity. In regard to Martin himself, good God! what have we not done! Imitating the goodness of the Almighty, we are ready, even yet, to receive him into the bosom of the Church, and we give him sixty days to transmit his retractation to us in a writing sealed by two prelates; or, what will be more agreeable to us, to come to

[1] L. Op. (ﾚﾑ) xvii, p. 305, and Op. Lat. i, p. 82.

Rome in person, that no doubt may be entertained as to his submission. Meanwhile, and from this moment, he must cease to preach, teach, or write, and must deliver his works to the flames. If, in the space of sixty days, he do not retract, we, by these presents, condemn him and his adherents as public and absolute heretics." The pope afterwards pronounces a multiplicity of excommunications, maledictions, and interdicts against Luther and all his adherents, with injunctions to seize their persons and send them to Rome.[1] It is easy to conjecture what the fate of these noble confessors of the gospel would have been in the dungeons of the papacy.

A thunder storm was thus gathering over the head of Luther. Some had been able to persuade themselves, after Reuchlin's affair, that the Court at Rome would not again make common cause with the Dominicans and the Inquisitors. These, however, were again in the ascendant, and the old alliance was solemnly renewed. The Bull was published, and for ages the mouth of Rome had never pronounced a sentence of condemnation without following it up with a death blow. This murderous message was about to issue from the seven hills, and attack the Saxon monk in his cloister. The moment was well chosen. There were good grounds for supposing that the new emperor, who, for many reasons, was anxious to obtain the friendship of the pope, would hasten to merit it by the sacrifice of an obscure monk. Leo X, the cardinals, and all Rome, were exulting in the belief that their enemy was already in their power.

CHAP. V.

Wittemberg—Melancthon—His Marriage—Catharine—Domestic Life—Beneficence —Good Humour—Christ and Antiquity—Labour—Love of Letters—His Mother —Outbreak among the Students.

While the inhabitants of the eternal city were thus agitated more tranquil events were occurring at Wittemberg, where Melancthon was shedding a soft but brilliant light. From 1500 to 2000 hearers, who had flocked from Germany, England, the Netherlands, France, Italy, Hungary, and Greece, often assembled around him. He was twenty-four years of age, and had not taken

---

[1] Sub prædictis pœnis, præfatum Lutherum, complices adhærentes, receptatores et fautores, personaliter capiant et ad nos mittant. (Bulla Leonis, loc. cit.)

orders. Every house in Wittemberg was open to this learned and amiable young professor. Foreign universities, in particular Ingolstadt, were desirous to gain him, and his Wittemberg friends wished to get him married, and thereby retain him among them. Luther, though he concurred in wishing that his dear Philip should have a female companion, declared openly that he would give no counsel in the matter. The task was undertaken by others. The young doctor was a frequent visitor of Burgomaster Krapp. The burgomaster was of an ancient family, and had a daughter named Catharine, remarkable for the mildness of her dispositions, and her great sensibility. Melancthon was urged to ask her in marriage; but the young scholar was buried among his books, and could talk of nothing else. His Greek authors and his New Testament were all his delight. He combated the arguments of his friends; but at length his consent was obtained, and all the arrangements having been made by others, Catharine became his wife. He received her with great coolness,[1] and said, with a sigh, "God has willed it; so I must renounce my studies and my delights, to follow the wishes of my friends." [2] Still he appreciated the good qualities of Catharine. "The disposition and education of the girl," said he, are such as I might have asked God to give her, δεξιᾷ ὁ Θεὸς τεκμαίροιτο. [3] She certainly deserved a better husband." The matter was settled in August. The espousals took place on the 25th of September, and the marriage was celebrated in the end of November. Old John Luther and his wife came with their daughters to Wittemberg on the occasion.[4] Many learned and distinguished persons were also present.

The young bride was as warm in her affection as the young professor was cold. Ever full of anxiety for her husband, Catharine took the alarm the moment she saw him threatened with even the semblance of danger. If Melancthon proposed to take any step which might compromise him, she urged and entreated him to abandon it. "On one of these occasions," wrote Melancthon, " I was obliged to yield to her weakness. . . . . It is our lot." How much unfaithfulness in the Church has had a similar origin. To the influence of Catharine ought, perhaps, to be attributed the timidity and fears with which her husband has often been reproached. Catharine was as fond a mother as a wife. She gave liberally to the poor. "O God, leave me not in my old age, when my hair shall begin to turn grey!" Such was the frequent prayer

[1] Uxor enim datur mihi non dico quam frigenti. (Corp. Ref. i, p. 211.)
[2] Ego meis studiis, mea me voluptate fraudo. (Ibid., i, p. 265.) [3] May God by his right hand give a happy issue. (Corp. Ref. i, p. 212.)
[4] Parentes mei cum sororibus nuptias honorarunt Philippi. (Ep. i, ɲ. 528.)

ƒ

of this pious and timorous soul. Melancthon was soon won by the affection of his wife. When he had tasted the pleasures of domestic society he felt how sweet they were, for he was of a nature to feel them. His happiest moments were beside his Catharine and her children. A French traveller having one day found the "preceptor of Germany" rocking his infant with one hand, and with a book in the other, started back in surprise; but Melancthon, without being discomposed, so warmly explained to him the value of children in the sight of God, that the stranger left the house, (to use his own words,) "wiser than he had entered it."

The marriage of Melancthon gave a domestic hearth to the Reformation. There was, thenceforth, in Wittemberg, a family whose house was open to all those whom the principle of a new life now animated. The concourse of strangers was immense.[1] Melancthon was waited on for a thousand different affairs, and his rule was never to deny himself to any body.[2] The young professor was particularly skilful in concealing his own good deeds. If he had no more money he secretly carried his silver plate to some merchant, never hesitating to part with it, provided he had the means of assisting those who were in distress. "Hence," says his friend, Camerarius, "it would have been impossible for him to provide for his own wants and those of his family had not a divine and hidden blessing from time to time furnished him with the means." He carried his good nature to an extreme. He had some antique medals of gold and silver, which were extremely curious. One day when showing them to a stranger who was visiting him, Melancthon said, "Take any one of them you wish." "I wish them all," replied the stranger. "I confess," says Philip, "I was at first offended at the selfishness of the request; however I gave them to him.[3] Melancthon's writings had a savour of antiquity. This, however, did not prevent them from exhaling the sweet savour of Christ, while it gave them an inexpressible charm. There is not one of his letters to his friends which does not contain some very apt allusion to Homer, Plato, Cicero, and Pliny, while Christ is always brought forward as his master and his God. Spalatin had asked him for an explanation of our Saviour's words—" *Without me ye can do nothing,*" (John, xv, 5). Melancthon refers him to Luther —" *Cur agam gestum'spectante Roscio?* as Cicero expresses it;"[4] and then continues, "This passage means that we must be ab-

---

1 Videres in ædibus illis perpetuo accedentes et introeuntes et discedentes atque exeuntes aliquos. (Camerar. Vita Melancth. p. 40.)   In that house you would constantly see persons approaching and entering, or coming out and going away.

2 Ea domus disciplina erat, ut nihil cuiquam negaretur. (Ibid.)

3 Sed dedisse nihilominus illos. (Camerar. Vita Melancth. p. 43.) 4 Why should I play a part and Roscius be a looker on? (Corp. Ref. Ep. April 13, 1520.)

sorbed by Christ, so that it is no longer we that act, but Christ that liveth in us. As in his person the Divine has been incorporated with the human nature, so must man be incorporated with Jesus Christ by faith."

The distinguished scholar's habit was to go to bed shortly after supper, and get up to his studies at two or three in the morning.[2] During these early hours his best works were composed. His manuscripts usually lay on his table exposed to the view of all who came and went, so that several were stolen. When he had a party of his friends, he asked one or other of them, before they sat down to table, to read some short composition in prose or verse. During his journeys he was always accompanied by some young persons with whom he conversed in a manner at once instructive and amusing. If the conversation flagged, each of them had to repeat in his turn some passage taken from the ancient poets. He often had recourse to irony, but always tempered it with great gentleness. "He stings and cuts," said he of himself, "but still without doing any harm."

The acquisition of knowledge was his ruling passion. The aim of his life was to diffuse literature and instruction. Let us not forget, that with him the first place in literature was given to the Holy Scriptures, and only a secondary place to the ancient classics. "My sole object," said he, "is the defence of literature; we must, by our example, inspire youth with an admiration of literature, and make them love it for itself, and not for the pecuniary profit which it may be made to yield. The downfall of literature involves the destruction of all that is good—of religion and morals—of things human and divine.[3] . . . . The better a man is, the more ardently does he exert himself in favour of learning, for he knows that the most pernicious of all pests is ignorance."

Some time after his marriage, Melancthon went to Bretten, in the Palatinate, accompanied by Camerarius and other friends, to pay a visit to his affectionate mother. On coming in sight of his native town, he dismounted from his horse, threw himself on his knees, and thanked God for permitting him to see it again. Margaret, on embracing her son, almost fainted with joy. She would have had him reside at Bretten, and earnestly entreated him to continue in the faith of his fathers. On this head, Melancthon excused himself, but with great tenderness, that he might not give offence to the conscientious feelings of his mother; he had great difficulty in parting with her, and whenever a traveller brought

<hr/>

1 Surgebat mox aut non longo intervallo post mediam noctem. (Camerar, p. 56)
2 Religionem, mores, humana divinaque omnia labefactat literarum inscitia. (Corp. Ref. i, 207. July 22, 1520.)

him news of his native town, he rejoiced, to use his own expression, as if he had renewed the joys of his childhood. Such was the character of one of the greatest instruments employed in the religious revolution of the sixteenth century.

The domestic calmness and studious activity of Wittemberg was, however, disturbed by a commotion, the consequence of a rupture which took place between the students a id the citizens. The Rector betrayed great weakness. One may suppose how deeply Melancthon was grieved when he saw these disciples of literature committing such excesses. Luther felt indignant, and had no idea of trying to gain them over by a false condescension. The disgrace which these disorders brought upon the university stung him to the heart.[1] Having mounted the pulpit, he inveighed in strong terms against these commotions, calling upon both parties to submit to the authorities.[2] His discourse produced great irritation; "Satan," says he, "unable to attack us from without, is trying to do us mischief from within. Him I fear not, but I fear lest the wrath of God be kindled against us for not having duly received his word. During the three last years I have been thrice exposed to great danger. In 1518, at Augsburg; in 1519, at Leipsic; and now, in 1520, at Wittemberg. It is neither by wisdom nor by arms that the renovation of the Church will be accomplished, but by humble prayers, and by an intrepid faith which puts Jesus Christ on our side.[3] O, my friend! unite your prayers to mine, that the evil spirit may not be able, by means of this small spark, to kindle a vast conflagration."

___

CHAP. VI.

The Gospel in Italy—Discourse on the Mass—The Babylonish Captivity of the Church—Baptism—Abolition of Vows—Progress of the Reformation.

But fiercer combats awaited Luther. Rome was brandishing the sword with which she had resolved to attack the gospel. Her threatened sentence, however, so far from dispiriting the Reformer increased his courage. The blows of this arrogant power gave him little concern. He will himself give more formidable blows, and thereby neutralize those of his adversaries. While Transalpine consistories are fulminating their anathemas against him, he will, with the sword of the gospel, pierce to the very heart of the Italian states. Luther having been informed, by letters from Venice, of

___

[1] Urit me ista confusio academiæ nostræ. L. Ep. i, p. 467.)   [2] Commendans potestatem magistratuum. (Ibid.)   [3] . . . . Nec prudentia nec armis, sed humili oratione et forti fide, quibus obtineamus Christum pro nobis. (Ibid. p. 463.'

the favourable reception which had been given to his opinions, felt an ardent desire to carry the gospel over the Alps. Evangelists must be found to transport it. " I wish," said he, " that we had living books, I mean preachers,[1] and that we could multiply them, and afford them protection in all quarters, in order that they might convey the knowledge of holy things to the people. The prince could not do a work more worthy of him. Were the inhabitants of Italy to receive the truth our cause would be unassailable." It does not appear that this project of Luther was realised. It is true that, at a later period, evangelists, even Calvin himself, sojourned for a while in Italy, but at this time the design was not followed out. He had applied to one of the great ones of the earth. Had he made his appeal to men low in station, but full of zeal for the kingdom of God, the result might have been very different. The idea at this period was, that every thing behoved to be done by governments. The association of private individuals, by which so much is now accomplished in Christendom, was almost unknown.

If Luther did not succeed in his plans of spreading the truth in a distant country, he was only the more zealous in proclaiming it himself. At this time his discourse, 'On the Holy Mass,'[2] was delivered at Wittemberg. In it he inveighed against the numerous sects of the Romish Church, and justly reproached it with its want of unity. " The multiplicity of spiritual laws," said he, " has filled the world with sects and divisions. Priests, monks, and laics, have shown more hatred of each other than subsists between Christians and Turks. What do I say? Priests are mortal enemies of priests, and monks of monks. Each is attached to his particular sect, and despises all others. There is an end of Christian love and unity." He then attacks the idea that the mass is a sacrifice, and has any efficacy in itself. " The best thing in every sacrament, and consequently in the Supper, is the word and promises of God. Without faith in this word, and these promises, the sacrament is dead; a body without a soul, a flagon without wine, a purse without money, a type without an antitype, the letter without the spirit, a casket without its diamond, a scabbard without its sword."

Luther's voice, however, was not confined to Wittemberg; and if he failed to procure missionaries to carry his instructions to distant lands, God provided him with a missionary of a new description. The art of printing supplied the place of evangelists. The press was destined to make a breach in the Roman fortress. Luther

[1] Si vivos libros, hoc est concionatores possemus multiplicare. . . (L. Ep. i, p. 491.)
[2] L. Op. (L.) xvii, p. 490.

had prepared a mine, the explosion of which shook the Roman edifice to its very foundations. This was his famous treatise on the *Babylonish Captivity of the Church*, which appeared 6th October, 1520.[1] Never had man displayed such courage in st ch critical circumstances.

In this writing he first enumerates, with a kind of ironical pride, all the advantages for which he is indebted to his enemies.

"Whether I will or not," says he, "I daily become more learned, spurred on as I am by so many celebrated masters. Two years ago I attacked indulgences, but with so much fear and indecision, that I am now ashamed of it. But, after all, the mode of attack is not to be wondered at, for I had nobody who would help me to roll the stone." He returns thanks to Prierio, Eck, Emser, and his other opponents, and continues—"I denied that the papacy was of God, but I granted that it had the authority of man. Now, after reading all the subtleties by which these sparks prop up their idol, I know that the papacy is only the kingdom of Babylon, and the tyranny of the great hunter Nimrod. I therefore beg all my friends, and all booksellers, to burn the books which I wrote on this subject, and to substitute for them the single proposition—'*The papacy is a general chace, by command of the Roman pontiff, for the purpose of running down and destroying souls.*'"[2]

Luther afterwards attacks the prevailing errors on the sacraments, on monastic vows, etc. The seven sacraments of the Church he reduces to three—viz., baptism, penitence, and the Lord's supper. He then proceeds to baptism, and when discussing it dwells especially on the excellence of faith, and makes a vigorous attack upon Rome. "God," says he, "has preserved this single sacrament to us clear of human traditions. God has said, '*Whoso believeth*, and is *baptized*, shall be saved.' This divine promise must take precedence of all works however splendid, of all vows, all satisfactions, all indulgences, all that man has devised. On this promise, if we receive it in faith, all our salvation depends. If we believe, our heart is strengthened by the divine promise, and though all else should abandon the believer, this promise will not abandon him. With it he will resist the adversary who assaults his soul, and will meet death though pitiless, and even the judgment of God himself. In all trials his comfort will be to say, 'God is faithful to his promises, and these were pledged to me in baptism; if God be for me, who can be against me?' Oh, how rich the Christian, the baptized! Nothing can destroy him but his own refusal to believe."

[1] L. Op. Lat. ii, 63, and Leip. xvii, p. 511.   [2] "Papatus est robusta venatio Romani Episcopi." The papacy is a vigorous hunt by the Roman bishop.

"It may be that, to my observations on the necessity of faith will be opposed the baptism of little children. But as the Word of God is powerful to change even the heart of the wicked, though neither less deaf, nor less impotent than a little child; so the prayer of the Church, to which all things are possible, changes the little child by means of the faith which God is pleased to pour into its soul, and so cleanses and renews it." [1]

After explaining the doctrine of baptism, Luther employs it as a weapon against the papacy. In fact, if the Christian finds complete salvation in the renewal which accompanies the baptism of faith, what need has he of the prescriptions of Rome?

" Wherefore," says Luther, " I declare that neither the pope, nor the bishop, nor any man whatever, is entitled to impose the smallest burden on a Christian—at least without his consent. Whatsoever is done otherwise is done tyrannically.[2] We are free of all men. The vow which we made in baptism is sufficient by itself alone, and is more than all we could ever accomplish.[3] Therefore, all other vows may be abolished. Let every one who enters the priesthood, or a religious order, consider well that the works of a monk or a priest, how difficult soever they may be, are, in the view of God, in no respect superior to those of a peasant labouring in the field, or a woman attending to the duties of her house.[4] God estimates all these things by the rule of faith. And it often happens that the simple labour of a man-servant, or a maid-servant, is more agreeable to God than the fastings and works of a monk, these being deficient in faith. . . . . The Christian people is the people of God led away into captivity, to Babylon, and there robbed of their baptism."

Such were the weapons by which the religious revolution whose history we are tracing was accomplished. First, the necessity of faith was established, and then the reformers used it as a hammer to break superstition in pieces. They attacked error with that divine power which removes mountains. These, and many similar passages of Luther circulated in towns, convents, and the country, were the leaven which leavened the whole lump.

[1] " Sicut enim verbum Dei potens est dum sonat, etiam impii cor immutare, quod non minus est surdum et incapax quam ullus parvulus, ita per orationem Ecclesiæ offerentis et credentis parvulus, fide infusa mutatur, mundatur, et renovatur." (L. Op. Lat. ii, p. 77.)   [2] " Dico itaque, neque papa, neque episcopus, neque uilus hominum habet jus unius syllabæ constituendæ super Christianum hominem, nisi id fiat ejusdem consensu ; quidquid aliter fit, tyrannico spiritu fit." (Ibid. p. 77.)

[3] " Generali edicto tollere vota . . . . abunde enim vovimus in baptismo, et plus quam possimus implere." (Ibid. p. 78.) There ought to be a general edict abolishing vows . . . . for in baptism we vow enough, and more than we can perform.

[4] " Opera quantum libet sacra et ardua religiosorum et sacerdotum, in oculis Dei prorsus nihil distare ab operibus rustici in agro laborantis aut mulieris in domo sua curantis. (ibid.)

The conclusion of this famous production on the captivity of
Babylon is in the following terms:—
" I learn that a new papal excommunication has been prepared
against me. If so, the present book may be regarded as part of
my future recantation. In proof of my obedience, the rest will soon
follow, and the whole will, with the help of Christ, form a collection, the like to which Rome never saw or heard before."

CHAP. VII.

New Negotiations—Miltitz and the Augustins of Eisleben—Deputation to Luther
—Miltitz and the Elector—Conference at Lichtemberg—Luther's Letter to the
Pope—Book Presented to the Pope—Union of the Believer with Christ—Freedom
and Bondage.

After this publication, all hope of reconciliation between the
pope and Luther must have vanished. Persons of the least possible discernment must have been struck with the incompatibility
of the Reformer's belief with the doctrine of the Church; and yet,
at this very moment, new negotiations were about to commence.
In the end of August, 1520, five weeks before the publication of the
' Captivity of Babylon,' the general Chapter of the Augustins had
assembled at Eisleben. At this meeting, the venerable Staupitz
resigned his office of vicar-general of his order, and Winceslas
Link, he who accompanied Luther to Augsburg, was invested with
it. Suddenly, in the middle of the Chapter, arrived the indefatigable Miltitz, burning with eagerness to reconcile Luther and the
pope.[1] His avarice, and, above all, his jealousy and hatred, were
interested. Eck and his swaggering had galled him; he knew that
the doctor of Ingolstadt had spoken disparagingly of him at Rome,
and there was nothing he would not have sacrificed in order to
defeat the designs of this troublesome rival by means of a speedily
concluded peace. The interest of religion gave him no concern.
One day, by his own account, he was dining with the bishop of
Leipsic. After the guests had drunk very freely, a new work
of Luther's was brought in. On being opened and read, the bishop
flew into a passion, and the official swore, but Miltitz laughed with
all his heart.[2] The Reformation was treated by Miltitz as a man
of the world, and by Eck as a theologian.

Aroused by the arrival of Dr. Eck, Miltitz addressed the Chapter
of the Augustins, in a discourse which he delivered with a very

[1] Nondum tot pressus difficultatibus animum desponderat Miltitius .... dignus
profecto non mediocri laude. (Pallavicini, i, p. 68.)   [2] Der Bischof entrustet,
der Official gefluchet, et aber gelachet habe. (Seckend. p. 266.)

marked Italian accent,[1] thinking thus to overawe his countrymen.
"The whole Augustin order is compromised by this affair." said
he. "Show me some method of silencing Luther."[2] "We have
nothing to do with the doctor," replied the Fathers, "and we know
not what counsel to give you." They founded doubtless on what
Staupitz had done at Augsburg, when he loosed Luther from his
vows of obedience to the order. Miltitz insisted, "Let a deputation from this venerable Chapter wait upon Luther, and soli-
cit him to write a letter to the pope, assuring him that he has
never plotted in any respect against his person.[3] That will be
sufficient to terminate the affair." The Chapter gave their consent,
and assigned the task of conferring with Luther, no doubt at the
nuncio's request, to the ex-vicar-general, Staupitz, and his successor
Link. The deputation forthwith set out for Wittemberg with a
letter from Miltitz to the doctor filled with expressions of the
highest respect. "There is no time to be lost," said he, "the
thunder already hovering over the head of the Reformer, will soon
burst, and then all is over."

Neither Luther nor the deputies, who concurred in his opinions,[4]
hoped any thing from a letter to the pope. That however was a
reason for not refusing to write it, as it would only be a mere
matter of form, and might serve to bring out Luther's rights.
"This Italian of Saxony (Miltitz), "thought Luther," in making
this demand has doubtless his own particular interest in view. Very
well, be it so, I will write, as I can with truth, that I have never
objected to the pope personally. I will even endeavour to guard
against severity in attacking the see of Rome. Still it shall have
its sprinkling of salt."[5]

Luther having shortly after been informed of the arrival of the
bull in Germany, declared to Spalatin, on the 3rd of October, that
he would not write the pope, and, on the 6th of the same month,
published his book on the ' *Captivity of Babylon*.' Miltitz did not
even yet despair of success. His eagerness to humble Eck made
him believe an impossibility. On the 2nd of October, he had
written the Elector, in high spirits. "Every thing will go well,
but, for the love of God, delay no longer to order payment of the
pension which I have had from you and your brother for some
years. I must have money in order to make new friends at Rome.
Write the pope, and do homage to the young cardinals, the relatives of his holiness, with gold and silver pieces, from the mint of

---

[1] Orationem habuit Italica pronuntiatione vestitam. (L. Ep. i, p. 483.)
[2] Petens consilium super me compescendo. (Ibid.) [3] Nihil me in personam
suam fuisse molitum. (L. Ep. i, p. 484.) [4] Quibus omnibus causa mea non
displicet. (Ibid. p. 486.) [5] Aspergetur tamen sale suo. (Ibid.)

your electoral highness, and add some for me also, for I was robbed
of those which you gave me." [1]

Even after Luther was acquainted with the bull, the intriguing
Miltitz was not discouraged, and requested a conference with
Luther at Lichtemberg. The Elector ordered Luther to repair
thither.[2] But his friends, and especially the affectionate Melancthon, opposed it.[3] " What, thought they, at the moment when a
bull has appeared ordering Luther to be seized and carried off
to Rome, to accept a conference with the pope's nuncio in a retired
spot! Is it not evident that, because Dr. Eck from having too
openly proclaimed his hatred is not able to approach the Reformer,
the wily chamberlain has been employed to ensnare Luther in his
nets?"

These fears could not deter the doctor of Wittemberg. The
prince has commanded, and he will obey. " I am setting out for
Lichtemberg," wrote he, to the chaplain on the 11th of October,
"pray for me." His friends would not quit him. The same day,
towards evening, Luther entered Lichtemberg on horse-back, amid
thirty horsemen, one of whom was Melancthon. The papal nuncio
arrived almost at the same time with only four attendants.[4] Was
this modest escort a stratagem to throw Luther and his friends off
their guard?

Miltitz urged Luther with the most pressing solicitations,
assuring him that the blame would be thrown upon Eck and his
foolish boastings,[5] and that every thing would terminate to the
satisfaction of both parties. " Very well," replied Luther, " I
offer henceforth to keep silence, provided my opponents keep it
also. For the sake of peace I will do every thing that it is possible
for me to do." [6]

Miltitz was delighted; and accompanying Luther as far as Wittemberg, the Reformer and the papal nuncio walked arm in arm
into this town which Dr. Eck was now approaching, holding men-
acingly in his hand the formidable bull which was to overthrow the
Reformation. " We will bring the matter to a happy conclusion,"
wrote Miltitz forthwith to the Elector; " Thank the pope for his
rose, and at the same time send forty or fifty florins to Cardinal
Quatuor Sanctorum." [7]

Luther felt bound to keep his promise of writing the pope.
Before bidding Rome an eternal adieu, he wished once more to tell

[1] Den Pabsts Nepoten, zwei oder drei Churfürstliche Gold und Silberstücke, zu
verehren. . . . Seckend. p. 267.)   [2] Sicut princeps ordinavit. (L. Ep. i, p. 455.)
[3] Invito praeceptore (Melancthon) nescio quanta metuente. (Ibid.)   [4] Jener
von mehr als dreissig, dieser aber kaum mit vier Pferden begleitet. (Seckend. p. 268.)
[5] Totum pondus in Eccium versurus. (ibid.)   [6] Ut nihil videar omittere
quod in me ad pacem quoquo modo facere possit. (Ibid.)   [7] Seckend, p. 268.

her important and salutary truths. Some perhaps will regard his letter only as a piece of irony—a bitter and insulting satire—but this were to mistake the sentiments by which he was actuated. He sincerely believed that Rome was to blame for all the evils of Christendom ; and in this view his words are not insults, but solemn warnings. The more he loved Leo, and the more he loved the Church of Christ, the more he desired to unfold the full magnitude of the disease. The energy of his expressions is proportioned to the energy of his feelings. The crisis has arrived, and he seems like a prophet walking round the city for the last time, upbraiding it for all its abominations, denouncing the judgments of the Almighty, and crying aloud, " Still some days of respite." The letter s as follows :—

" To the Most Holy Father in God, Leo X, Pope at Rome, Salvation in Christ Jesus our Lord. Amen.

" From amid the fearful war which I have been waging for three years with disorderly men, I cannot help looking to you, O Leo, Most Holy Father in God. And although the folly of your impious flatterers has compelled me to appeal from your judgment to a future council, my heart is not turned away from your Holiness, and I have not ceased to pray God earnestly and with profound sighs, to grant prosperity to yourself and your pontificate.[1]

" It is true I have attacked some antichristian doctrines, and have inflicted a deep wound on my adversaries because of their impiety. Of this I repent not, as I have here Christ for an example. Of what use is salt if it have lost its savour. or the edge of a sword if it will not cut ?[2] Cursed be he who does the work of the Lord negligently. Most excellent Leo, far from having conceived any bad thoughts with regard to you, my wish is that you may enjoy the most precious blessings throughout eternity. One thing only I have done : I have maintained the word of truth. I am ready to yield to all in every thing ; but, as to this word, I will not, I cannot, abandon it.[3] He who thinks differently on this subject is in error.

" It is true that I have attacked the Court of Rome; but neither yourself nor any man living can deny that there is greater corruption in it than was in Sodom and Gomorrah, and that the impiety which prevails makes cure hopeless. Yes; I have been horrified on seeing how, under your name, the poor followers of Christ were deceived. I have opposed this, and will oppose it

---

[1] Ut non totis viribus. sedulis atque quantum in me fuit gemebundis precibus apud Deum quæsierim. (L. Ep. i, p. 498.)   [2] Quid proderit sal, si non mordeat ? Quid os gladii, si non cædat ? (Ibid. 499.)   [3] Verbum deserere et negure nec possum, nec volo. (Ibid.)

still, not that I imagine it possible, in spite of the opposition of flatterers, to accomplish any thing in this Babylon, which is confusion itself; but I owe it to my brethren to endeavour, if possible, to remove some of them from these dreadful evils.

" You know it; Rome has for many years been inundating the world with whatever could destroy both soul and body. The Church of Rome, formerly the first in holiness, has become a den of robbers, a place of prostitution, a kingdom of death and hell;[1] so that Antichrist himself, were he to appear, would be unable to increase the amount of wickedness. All this is as clear as day.

" And yet, O Leo, you yourself are like a lamb in the midst of wolves—a Daniel in the lions' den. But single-handed, what can you oppose to these monsters? There may be three or four cardinals who to knowledge add virtue. But what are these against so many? You should perish by poison even before you could try any remedy. It is all over with the Court at Rome—the wrath of God has overtaken and will consume it.[2] It hates counsel—it fears reform—it will not moderate the fury of its ungodliness; and hence it may be justly said of it as of its mother—*We would have healed Babylon, but she is not healed; forsake her.*[3] It belonged to you and your cardinals to apply the remedy; but the patient laughs at the doctor, and the horse refuses to feel the bit. . . . .

" Cherishing the deepest affection for you, most excellent Leo, I have always regretted that, formed as you are for a better age, you were raised to the pontificate in these times. Rome is not worthy of you, and those who resemble you; the only chief whom she deserves to have is Satan himself, and hence, the truth is, that in this Babylon he is more king than you are. Would to God, that, laying aside this glory which your enemies so much extol, you would exchange it for a modest pastoral office, or live on your paternal inheritance. Rome's glory is of a kind fit only for Iscariots. . . .

O, my dear Leo, of what use are you in this Roman court, unless it be to allow the most execrable men to use your name and your authority in ruining fortunes, destroying souls, multiplying crimes, oppressing faith, truth, and the whole Church of God ? O Leo, Leo, you are the most unfortunate of men, and you sit upon the most dangerous of thrones. I tell you the truth because I wish your good.

" Is it not true, that, under the vast expanse of heaven there is nothing more corrupt, more hateful, than the Roman Court? In

---

[1] Facta est . . . . spelunca latronum licentiosissima, lupanar omnium impudentissimum, regnum peccati, mortis et inferni. . .(ibid. p. 500.)
[2] Actum est de Romana curia : pervenit in eam ira Dei usque in finem. . . . (L. Ep. 1, p. 500.)   [3] Jeremiah, li, 9.   [4] Olim janua cœli, nunc patens quoddam os inferni et tale os, quod urgente ira Dei, obstrui non potest. . . . (L. Ep. i, p. 501.)

vice and corruption it infinitely exceeds the Turks. Once the gate of heaven, it has become the mouth of hell—a wide mouth which the wrath of God keeps open, so that, on seeing so many unhappy beings thrown headlong into it, I was obliged to lift my voice, as in a tempest, in order that, at least, some might be saved from the fearful abyss. Such, O Leo, my father, was the reason why I inveighed against this death-giving see. Far from attacking your person, I thought I was labouring for your safety, when I valiantly assaulted this prison, or rather this hell in which you are confined. To do all sorts of evil to the Court of Rome were to discharge your own duty; to cover it with shame is to honour Christ; in one word, to be a Christian is to be anything but a Roman.

" Meanwhile, seeing that in succouring the see of Rome, I was losing my labour and my pains, I sent her a letter of divorce I said to her, ' Adieu, Rome! *He that is unjust, let him be unjust still, and he that is filthy, let him be filthy still;'* [1] and devoted myself to the tranquil and solitary study of the sacred volume. Then Satan opened his eyes and awoke his servant, John Eck, a great enemy of Jesus Christ, in order that he might oblige me again to descend into the arena. Eck's wish was to establish the primacy not of Peter but of himself, and, for that purpose, to lead vanquished Luther in triumph. The blame of all the obloquy which has been cast on the see of Rome rests with him."

Luther narrates his intercourse with De Vio, Miltitz, and Eck, and then continues.

" Now, then, I come to you, O Most Holy Father, and, prostrated at your feet, pray you, if possible, to put a curb on the enemies of the truth. But I cannot retract my doctrine. I cannot permit rules of interpretation to be imposed on the Holy Scriptures. The Word of God, the source whence all freedom springs, must be left free. [2]

" O, Leo, my father! listen not to those flattering Sirens who tell you that you are not a mere man, but a demi-god, and can ordain what you please. You are the servant of servants, and the seat which you occupy is of all others the most dangerous, and the most unhappy. Give credit not to those who exalt, but to those who humble you. Perhaps I am too bold in giving advice to so high a majesty, whose duty it is to instruct all men. But I see the dangers which surround you at Rome, I see you driven hither and thither, tossed as it were upon the billows of a raging sea. Charity urges me, and I cannot resist sending forth a warning cry.

[1] Rev. xxii, 11.　　[2] Leges interpretandi verbi Dei non patior, cum oporteat verbum Dei esse non alligatum, quod libertatem docet. (L. Ep. i, p. 504.)

"Not to appear empty handed before your Holiness, I present you with a little book, which has appeared under your name, and which will make you aware of the subjects to which I will be able to devote myself, if your flatterers permit me. It is a small matter as regards the size of the volume, but a great one in regard to its contents, for it comprehends a summary of the Christian life. I am poor, and have nothing else to offer; besides, you have no want of any thing but spiritual gifts. I commend myself to your Holiness. May the Lord keep you for ever and ever, amen."[1]

The little book with which Luther did homage to the pope was his 'Treatise on the liberty of the Christian;' in which he demonstrates without any polemical discussion, how the Christian, without infringing on the liberty which faith has given him, may submit to every external ordinance in a spirit of freedom and love. Two truths form the basis of the whole discourse, viz., The Christian is free—all things are his : The Christian is a servant subject to all in every thing. By faith he is free, by love he is subject.

At first he explains the power of faith to make the Christian free. "Faith unites the soul with Christ, as a bride with the bridegroom. Every thing that Christ has becomes the property of the believer, every thing that the believer has becomes the property of Christ. Christ possesses all blessings, even eternal salvation, and these are thenceforth the property of the believer. The believer possesses all vices and all sins, and these become, thenceforth. the property of Christ. A happy exchange now takes place. Christ who is God and man, Christ who has never sinned, and whose holiness is invincible, Christ, the Omnipotent and Eternal, appropriating to himself by his wedding ring—that is to say, by faith, all the sins of the believer; these sins are swallowed up in him and annihilated; for no sin can exist in presence of his infinite righteousness. Thus, by means of faith, the soul is delivered from all sins, and invested with the eternal righteousness of Jesus Christ the bridegroom. O happy union! Jesus Christ the rich, the noble, the holy bridegroom, takes in marriage this poor, guilty, contemned bride, delivers her from all evil, and decks her in the richest robes. . . Christ, a King, and Priest, shares this honour and glory with all Christians. The Christian is a king, and consequently possesses all things. He is a priest, and consequently possesses God. And it is faith, not works, which procures him this honour. The Christian is free from all things, and above all things—faith giving him every thing in abundance."

In the second part of the treatise Luther presents the truth in its other point of view. "Although the Christian has thus been made free, he voluntarily becomes a servant that he may act towards his brethren as God has acted towards him through Jesus Christ. I desire," said he, " freely, joyfully, and gratuitously, to serve a Father who hath thus shed upon me all the riches of his goodness. I wish to become every thing to my neighbour, as Christ has become every thing to me." . . . . "From faith," continues ` Luther, "flows love to God, and from love a life full of liberty, charity, and joy. O how noble and elevated a life the life of the Christian is! But, alas, none know it and none preach it. By faith the Christian rises even to God: by love he descends to man; still, however, remaining always in God. This is true liberty, a liberty as far above every other species of liberty as the heavens are above the earth."

Such was the treatise which accompanied Luther's letter to Leo X.

CHAP. VIII.

The Bull in Germany—Eck's Reception—The Bull at Wittemberg—Interposition. of Zuinglius.

While the Reformer was thus addressing the Roman pontiff for the last time, the bull which anathematised him was already in the hands of the Germanic Church, and at Luther's own door. It would seem that no doubt was entertained at Rome as to the success of the measure which had thus been adopted against the Reformation. The pope had charged two high functionaries of his court, Carracioli and Aleander, to be the bearers of it to the Archbishop of Mentz who was requested to see to its execution. But Eck himself appeared in Saxony as the herald and executor of the great pontifical work. No man knew better than the doctor of Ingolstadt how formidable the blows were which Luther had struck. Alive to the danger he had stretched forth his hand to sustain the tottering edifice of Rome. In his own estimation he was the Atlas, destined to support the ancient Roman world on his robust shoulders, when on the point of falling to pieces. Proud of the success of his journey to Rome; proud of the charge which he had received from the sovereign pontiff; proud to appear in Germany with the new title of protonotary and pontifical nuncio; proud of the bull which he held in his hand, and which contained the condemnation of his indomitable rival, he regarded his present mission as a triumph more splendid than all the victories which he had gained in Hungary, Bavaria, Lombardy, and Saxony, and from which he had previously derived so much renown. But this pride was soon to be humbled. The pope, in entrusting the publication of the bull to Eck, had committed a blunder which was destined to neutralise its effect. The proud distinction conferred on a man who did not hold high rank in the Church gave offence to sensitive and jealous spirits. The bishops, accustomed to receive the bulls directly from the pope, were offended at the publication of this one in their dioceses by an upstart nuncio. The nation who had hooted the pretended conqueror of Leipsic at the moment of his flight into Italy, were equally astonished and indignant when they saw him repass the Alps, decked in the insignia of pontifical nuncio, and with the power of crushing whomsoever he chose. The sentence brought by his implacable adversary, Luther regarded as an act of personal revenge. " He regarded it, says Pallavicini, " as the perfidious poniard of a mortal enemy, and not as the legitimate act of a Roman lictor."[1] It was generally viewed as less the bull of the sovereign pontiff, than of Dr. Eck. In this way, the blow was obstructed and weakened before-hand by the very person at whose instigation it was struck.

The chancellor of Ingolstadt had hastened back to Saxony, which, as having been the scene of battle, he was desirous should also be the scene of his victory. Having arrived he published the bull at Meissen, Merseburg, and Brandenburg towards the end of September. But in the first of these towns it was posted up in a place where nobody could read it; and the bishops of those three sees were in no haste to publish it. Even Duke George, Eck's great patron, prohibited the Council of Leipsic from making it public, before receiving orders from the Bishop of Merseburg, and these orders did not arrive till the following year. " These are only difficulties of form," said John Eck to himself at first, for every thing else seemed to smile upon him. Duke George sent him a golden cup and some ducats. Even Miltitz, who had hastened to Leipsic, on learning that his rival had arrived, invited him to dinner. The two legates were boon companions; and Miltitz thought he could not have a better opportunity of sounding Eck than over their wine. " After he had drunk pretty freely, he began," says the pope's chamberlain, " to boast in grand style— he displayed his bull, and told how he meant to bring that droll fellow Martin to his senses."[2] But the Ingolstadt doctor soon had

----

[1] Non tanquam a securi legitimi lictoris, sed e telo infensissimi hostis. . . . (Pallavicini, i, p. 74.)   [2] Nachdem (writes Miltitz) er nun tapfer getrunken hatte, fieng er gleich an trefflich von seiner ordre zu prahlen, etc. (Seckend., p. 288.)

Occasion to observe that the wind was veering. The course of a year had produced a great change in Leipsic.[1] On St. Michael's day some students posted up placards, in ten different places, containing a severe attack on the new nuncio, who, in amazement, took refuge in the cloister of St. Paul, where Tetzel had previously found his asylum, and declining every visit, induced the rector to call his youthful opponents to account. By this poor Eck gained little. The students composed a song upon him, and sang it in the streets. Eck must have heard it in his prison. On this all his courage failed him, and the redoubtable champion trembled in every limb. Every day brought him threatening letters. One hundred and fifty students, who had arrived from Wittemberg, spoke out boldly against the papal envoy. For once the poor apostolical nuncio could hold out no longer. "I would not have them kill him," said Luther, "though I wish his designs to fail."[2] Eck, quitting his retreat at night, clandestinely escaped from Leipsic to go and hide himself at Coburg. Miltitz, who gives the account, triumphed more than the Reformer. His triumph, however, was not of long duration. All the chamberlain's projects of conciliation failed, and he came at last to a miserable end. One day, when drunk, he fell into the Rhine at Mentz, and was drowned.

Eck gradually recovered courage. Repairing to Erfurt, whose theologians had on more than one occasion betrayed their jealousy of Luther, he insisted on having his bull published in this town, but the students seized the copies, tore them to pieces, and threw them into the river, saying, "since it is a bull, let it swim."[3] "Now," said Luther, on being informed of this, "the pope's paper is a true bull." Eck durst not make his appearance at Wittemberg; but he sent the bull to the rector with a threat, that if it was not conformed to, he would destroy the university. At the same time he wrote Duke John, Frederick's brother, and co-regent, "Do not take what I do in bad part, I am acting in behalf of the faith, and it costs me many cares, great labour, and much money."[4]

The bishop of Brandenburg, supposing him inclined, was not entitled to act at Wittemberg in his capacity of ordinary, the university being protected by its privileges. Luther and Carlstadt, who were condemned by the bull, were asked to take part in the meetings which were held to deliberate on its contents. The rector

---

[1] Longe aliam faciem et mentem Lipsiæ eum invenire quam sperasset . . . . (L. Ep. i, p. 492.)   [2] Nollem eum occidi, quanquam optem ejus consilia irrita fieri. (Ibid.)
[3] A studiosis discerpta et in aquam projecta, dicentibus: Bulla est, in aquam natet! (L. Ep. i, p. 526.)   [4] Mit viel Mühe, Arbeit, und Kosten. (L. Op. (L.) xvii, p. 317.)

declared that, as he had not received a letter from the pope along
with the -bull, he declined to publish it. The university had-
already acquired greater authority in the surrounding countries.
than the sovereign pontiff himself. Its declaration served as a
model to the government of the Elector; and thus the spirit which
was in Luther triumphed over the bull of Rome.

While the German mind was thus strongly agitated by this‹
affair, a grave voice was heard in another quarter of Europe. An
individual, foreseeing the immense rent which the papal bull was
about to make in the Church. came forward to give a solemn,
warning, and to defend the Reformer. It was that of the Swiss,
priest, of whom we have already spoken, viz., Ulrich Zuinglius,
who, though not united to Luther by any friendly tie, published a
treatise full of wisdom and dignity, the first of his numerous,
writings.[1] A kind of fraternal affection seemed to draw him towards the doctor of Wittemberg. "The piety of the pontiff,"
said he, "requires that he shall joyfully sacrifice whatever is
dearest to him for the glory of Christ his King, and for the public
peace of the Church. Nothing is more injurious to his dignity ›
than to defend it by pensions or terror. Even before the writings
of Luther were read, he had been calumniated to the people as a
heretic, a schismatic, and as Antichrist himself. Not one gave him
warning, none refuted him. He called for a discussion; but all
he could get was a sentence of condemnation. The bull which is
published displeases even those who honour the majesty of the pope.
For it is everywhere regarded as an expression of the impotent
hatred of some monks, and not of the mildness of a pontiff, who
ought to be the vicar of a Saviour full of love. All acknowledge that
the true doctrine of the gospel of Jesus Christ has greatly degenerated, and that a public and thorough reformation of laws and
manners is required.[2] Consider all men of learning and virtue—the
more sincere they are, the stronger is their attachment to evangelical
truth, and the less their dissatisfaction with Luther's writings.[3]
There is not one who does not acknowledge that he has derived
benefit from these books, though he may have met with passages
which he was unable to approve. Let men of sound doctrine and
acknowledged probity be selected. Let three princes above all
suspicion—the emperor Charles, the King of England, and the
king of Hungary—name the judges. Let these judges read

[1] Consilium cujusdam ex animo cupientis esse consultum et pontificis dignitati, et
Christianæ religionis tranquillitati. (Zuinglii Opera, curant. Schulero et Schulthessio,
iii, p. 1-5.) [2] Multum degenerasse ab illa sincera Christi evangelica doctrina,
adeo ut nemo non fateatur opus esse publica aliqua et insigni legum ac morum instau-
ratione. (Ibid, p. 3. [3] Nemo non fatetur se ex illius libris factum esse meliorem.
Ibid., p. 4.)

Luther's writings. Let them hear his defence, and then let their decision, whatever it be, be confirmed. Νικησατω ἡ του Χριστου παιδεια και αληθεια."[1] This proposal, which came from the country of the Swiss, led to no result. It was necessary that the great divorce should take place. It was necessary that Christendom should be rent in twain. Her very wounds were destined to be the cure of her diseases.

CHAP. IX.

Luther Examines himself in the presence of God—Luther's opinion of the Bull—A neutral Family—Luther on the Bull, and against the Bull of Antichrist—The Pope prohibits Faith—Effects of the Bull—The faggot pile of Louvain.

But what signified all this resistance by students, rectors, and priests. If the mighty arm of Charles V is joined to the mighty arm of the pope, will they not crush these scholars and grammarians? Will any one be able to resist the combined power of the pontiff of Christendom and of the emperor of the West? The blow has been struck. Luther is excommunicated, and the gospel seems lost. At this solemn moment the Reformer does not disguise to himself the magnitude of the danger to which he is exposed; but he looks upward, and prepares to receive, as from the hand of the Lord himself, a blow which seems destined to annihilate him. He retires within himself, and meditates at the footstool of the throne of God. "What the result is to be," says he, "I know not, and I am not anxious to know; certain as I am that He who sits in heaven has from all eternity foreseen the beginning, the progress, and the end of this affair. Wherever the blow is to strike, I am without fear. The leaf of a tree falls not without our Father's will. How much less shall we fall. It is a small matter to die for the Word, since this Word which became incarnate and that for us has itself first died. If we die with it, we shall rise again with it; and, passing along the same road by which it passed, will arrive where it has arrived, and remain with it throughout eternity."[2] Sometimes, however, Luther could not restrain the contempt which he felt for the manœuvres of his enemies. On these occasions he displays his characteristic combination of sublimity and sarcasm. "I know nothing of Eck," says he, "except that he arrived with a long

[1] Let the teaching and truth of Christ prevail. [2] Parum est nos pro verbo mori, cum ipsum incarnatum pro nobis prius mortuum sit. . . . (L. Ep. i, p. 490.)

beard, a long bull, and a long purse. . . . . But I will laugh at his bull."[1]

On the third of October he was made acquainted with the papal letter. "At length," says he, "this Roman bull has arrived. I despise it, and defy it as impious, false, and in all respects worthy of Eck. It is Christ himself who is condemned. It gives no reasons; it merely cites me, not to be heard, but simply to sing a palinode. I will treat it as spurious, though I have no doubt it is genuine. O, if Charles V were a man, and would, for the love of Christ, attack these demons![2] I rejoice in having to endure some hardships for the best of causes. I already feel more liberty in my heart; for at length I know that the pope is Antichrist, and that his see is that of Satan himself."

It was not in Saxony merely that the thunders of Rome had produced alarm. A quiet family of Swabia, a neutral family, saw its peace suddenly broken up. Bilibald Pirckheimer, of Nuremberg, one of the most distinguished men of his age, having early lost his beloved wife Crescentia, was united in the closest affection with his two young sisters, Charitas, abbess of St. Clair, and Clara, a nun of the same convent. These two pious females served God in solitude, and divided their time between study, the care of the poor, and preparation for eternity. Bilibald, who was a statesman, relaxed from public affairs by maintaining a correspondence with them. They were learned, read Latin, and studied the Fathers; but their favourite volume was the Holy Scriptures. They had never had any other teacher than their brother. The letters of Charitas are written in a delicate and amiable spirit. Tenderly attached to Bilibald she took alarm at the least danger which threatened him. Pirckheimer, to dissipate the fears of this timid spirit, wrote a dialogue between Charitas and Veritas, (Charity and Truth), in which Veritas tries to strengthen Charitas.[3] Nothing can be more touching, or better fitted to solace a tender and agonised heart.

What must have been the terror of Charitas when the rumour spread that in the papal bull Bilibald's name was posted up beside that of Luther, on the doors of cathedrals? In fact, Eck, pushed on by blind fury, had associated with Luther six of the most distinguished men of Germany, viz., Carlstadt, Feldkirchen, and Egranus, (who gave themselves very little concern about it,) and Adelman, Pirckheimer, and his friend Spengler, whose public functions made them particularly alive to the insult. There was great agitation in

<hr />

[1] Venisse eum barbatum, bullatum, nummatum . . . Ridebo et ego bullam sive ampullam. (L. Ep. i, p. 488.) [2] Utinam Carolus vir esset, et pro Christo hos Satanas aggrederetur. (Ibid., p. 494.) [3] Pirckheimeri Op. Francof.

the Convent of St. Clair. How shall the disgrace of Bilibald be borne? Nothing affects relatives more deeply than such trials. In vain did the city of Nuremberg, the Bishop of Bamberg, and even the dukes of Bavaria interfere in behalf of Spengler and Pirckheimer; these noble-minded men were obliged to humble themselves before Dr. Eck, who made them feel all the importance of a Roman protonotary, and obliged them to write a letter to the pope, declaring that they adhered to the doctrines of Luther only in so far as they were conformable to Christian faith. At the same time Adelman, with whom Eck had once had a scuffle on rising up from table after a discussion on the great question which then occupied all minds, was required to appear before the bishop of Augsburg and purge himself on oath of all participation in the Lutheran heresy. Still, however, anger and revenge had proved bad counsellors to Eck. The names of Bilibald and his friends damaged the bull. The character of these eminent men and their extensive connections increased the general irritation.

Luther at first pretended to doubt the authenticity of the bull. " I learn," says he in the first work which he published after it, " that Eck has brought from Rome a new bull, which resembles him so much, is so stuffed with falsehood and error, that it might well be named *Doctor Eck*. He gives out that it is the work of the pope, whereas it is only a work of lies." After explaining his reasons for doubting its genuineness, Luther thus concludes, " I must with my own eyes see the lead, the seal, the tape, the conclusion, the signature of the bull—every part of it, in short, or I will not estimate all this clamour at the weight of a straw." [1]

But no man doubted, not even Luther himself, that the bull was the pope's. Germany waited to see what the Reformer would do. Would he stand firm? All eyes were fixed on Wittemberg. Luther did not keep his contemporaries long in suspense. On the 4th of November, 1520, he replied with a discharge of thunder, by publishing his treatise ' *Against the Bull of Antichrist*.'

" What errors, what impostures," said he, " have crept in among the poor people under the cloak of the Church, and the pretended infallibility of the pope ! how many souls have thus been lost ! how much blood shed !, what murders committed ! what kingdoms ruined !

Further on he ironically says, " I know very well how to distinguish between art and malice, and set very little value on a malice which has no art. To burn books is so easy a matter that even children can do it; how much more the Holy Father and his

[1] Oder nicht ein Haarbreit geben ... L. Op. (L.) xvii, p 343.

doctors.[1] It would become them to show greater ability than is re-quisite merely to burn books. . . . Besides, let them destroy my works! I desire nothing more; for all I wished was to guide men to the Bible, that they might thereafter lay aside all my writ-ings.[2] Good God! if we had the knowledge of Scripture, what need would there be for my writings? . . . . I am free by the grace of God, and bulls neither solace nor frighten me. My strength and consolation are where neither men nor devils can assail them."

Luther's tenth proposition, condemned by the pope, was in the fol-lowing terms: "No man's sins are pardoned, if, when the priest absolves him, he does not believe that they are pardoned." The pope in condemning it denied that faith was necessary in the Sacra-ment. " They maintain," exclaims Luther, "that we ought not to believe that our sins are pardoned when we are absolved by the priest. What then are we to do? Listen now, O! Christians, to a new arrival from Rome. Condemnation is pronounced against this article of faith which we profess when we say ' I believe in the Holy Ghost, the Holy Catholic Church, and the forgiveness of sins.' Did I know that the pope had really given this bull at Rome," (he did not doubt it,) " and that it was not the invention of the arch-liar, Eck, I would cry aloud to all Christians that they ought to hold the pope as the true Antichrist spoken of in Scrip-ture. And if he would not desist from proscribing the faith of the Church, . . . then let the temporal sword resist him even sooner than the Turk! . . . For the Turks allow belief, but the pope forbids it."

While Luther was speaking thus forcibly, his perils were increas-ing. The scheme of his enemies was to drive him out of Wittem-berg. If Luther and Wittemberg are separated, both will be des-troyed. A single stroke would thus disencumber Rome of both the heretical doctor and the heretical university. Duke George, the bishop of Merseburg, and the theologians of Leipsic were labouring underhand at this work.[3] Luther on being apprised of it said, " I leave this affair in the hands of God."[4] These proceedings were not without result: Adrian, professor of Hebrew at Wittemberg, suddenly turned against the doctor. It required great firmness in the faith to withstand the shock given by the Roman bull. There are characters which follow the truth only a certain distance, and such was Adrian. Frightened at the condemnation he quitted Wittemberg, and repaired to Leipsic to be near Dr. Eck.

1 So ist Bucher verbrennen so leicht, dass es auch Kinder können, schweig denn der heilige Vater Pabst. . . (L. Op. (L.) xvii, p. 324.)   2 . . . In Biblien zu fuhren dass man deiselben Verstand erlangte, und denn meine Buchlein verschwinden liess. (Ibid.)   Ut Wittemberga pellerer. (L. Ep. i, p. 519.)   4 Id quod in manum Dei refero. (Ibid. p. 520.)

The bull began to be executed. The voice of the pontiff of Christendom was not an empty sound. Long had fire and sword taught subjection to it. Faggot piles.were prepared at his bidding, and everything indicated that a dreadful catastrophe was to put an end to the audacious revolt of the Augustin monk. In October, 1520, all the copies of Luther's works in the shops of the booksellers at Ingolstadt were seized, and put under seal. The Archbishop-Elector of Mentz, moderate as he was, had to banish Ulric of Hütten from his court, and imprison his printer. The papal nuncios having laid siege to the young Emperor, Charles declared that he would protect the ancient religion;[1] and in some of his hereditary possessions scaffolds were erected, on which the writings of the heretic were reduced to ashes. Princes of the Church and magistrates were present at these *auto-da-fe*. Alcander was quite elated with his success. "The pope," said he, in imitation of Prierio, "may dethrone kings! He may, if he chooses, say to the emperor, Thou art only a tanner! He knows well how to bring one or two miserable grammarians to their senses. We will dispose, moreover, of Duke Frederick also." To hear the proud nuncio, one would have said that the pile of Mentz which consumed Luther's books was "le commencement de la fin" (*the beginning of the end.*) These flames, it was said at Rome, will carry terror into every quarter. Such, in truth, was the effect on many superstitious and timid spirits; but even in the hereditary states of Charles, where alone it was ventured to execute the bull, the people, and even the grandees, often answered these pontifical demonstrations with derision, or expressions of indignation. "Luther," said the doctors of Louvain, on presenting themselves before Margaret, Regent of the Netherlands, "Luther is subverting the Christian faith." "Who is this Luther?" asked the Princess. "An ignorant monk." "Well, then," replied she, "do you, who are learned, and in such numbers, write against him. The world will credit a multitude of learned men sooner than an isolated, ignorant monk." The doctors of Louvain preferred an easier method. They caused a vast pile to be erected at their own expense. The place of execution was covered with spectators, and students and burghers were seen hastening through the crowd, their arms filled with large volumes, which they threw into the flames. Their zeal edified the monks and doctors; but the trick was afterwards discovered. Instead of the writings of Luther, they had thrown into the fire the *Sermones discipuli*, *Tartaret*, and other scholastic and popish books.[2]

[1] A ministris pontificiis mature præoccupatus, declaravit se velle veterem fidem tutari. . . . . Pallavicini, p. 80.　　[2] Seckend. p. 289,

The Count of Nassau, Viceroy of Holland, when the Dominicans were soliciting the favour of burning the doctor's books, said
to them, " Go and preach the gospel as purely as Luther, and you
will have nobody to complain of." At a festival, attended by the
leading princes of the empire, the Reformer having become the
subject of conversation, the Baron of Ravenstein said, aloud, "In
the space of four centuries, only one Christian man has dared to
lift his head, and the pope is wishing to put him to death."[1]

Luther, conscious of the power of his cause, remained tranquil
amid the tumult which the bull had excited.[2] "Did you not
urge me so keenly," said he to Spalatin, " I would be silent, well
knowing that, by the power and counsel of God, this work must be
accomplished."[3] The timid man was anxious for speech, the
strong man wished to be silent. It was because Luther discerned
a power not visible to the eyes of his friend. " Be of good
courage," continues the Reformer; " Christ began these things,
and Christ will accomplish them, though I should be put to flight
or put to death. Jesus Christ is present here, and more powerful
is He who is in us, than he who is in the world."[4]

CHAP. X.

Decisive steps by the Reformer—Luther's Appeal to a General Council—Struggle at
close quarters—The Bull burned by Luther—Meaning of this bold act—Luther
in the Academic Chair—Luther against the Pope—New Work by Melancthon—
How Luther encourages his Friends—Progress of the Contest—Melancthon's
Opinion of the timid—Luther's Work on the Bible—Doctrine of Grace—Luther's
Recantation.

But duty obliged him to speak, in order to manifest the truth
to the world. Rome has struck, and he will make it known how
he receives the blow. The pope has put him under the ban of
the Church, and he will put the pope under the ban of Christendom. Up to this hour the pope's word has been omnipotent.
Luther will oppose word to word, and the world will know which
is the more powerful of the two. " I am desirous," said he, " to
set my conscience at rest, by making men aware of the danger to
which they are exposed."[5] At the same time he prepares to renew
his appeal to an universal council. An appeal from the pope to

------

[1] Es ist in 400 Jahren ein christlicher mann aufgestanden, den will der Pabst todt
.aben. (Seckend. p. 288.)   [2] " In bullosis illis tumultibus." (L. Ep.
p. 519.) In those bull tumults.   [3] " Rem totam Deo committerem."
Ibid, 521.) I would commit the whole affair to God.   [4] " Christus ista
)œpit, ista perficiet, etiam me sive extincto, sive fugato." (Ibid., p. 526.)   [5] " Ut
neam conscientiam redimam." (Ibid., p. 522.) That I may redeem my conscience.

a council was a crime, and hence the mode in which Luther attempts to justify himself is a new act of hostility to papal authority.

On the morning of the 17th November, a notary and five witnesses, of whom Cruciger was one, met at ten o'clock, in one of the halls of the Augustin convent in which the doctor resided. There the public officer, Sarctor of Eisleben, having seated himself to draw up the minute of his protest, the Reformer, in presence of the witnesses, says, with a solemn tone:

"Considering that a general Council of the Christian Church is above the pope, especially in all that concerns the faith;

"Considering that the power of the pope is not above, but beneath Scripture, and that he has no right to worry the sheep of Christ, and throw them into the wolf's mouth:

"I, Martin Luther, Augustin, doctor of the Holy Scriptures at Wittemberg, do, by this writing, appeal for myself, and for all who shall adhere to me, from the most holy Pope Leo, to a future universal Christian Council.

"I appeal from the said Pope Leo, *first*, as an unjust, rash, tyrannical judge, who condemns me without hearing me, and without explaining the grounds of his judgment; *secondly*, as a heretic, a strayed, obdurate apostate, condemned by the Holy Scriptures, inasmuch as he ordains me to deny that Christian faith is necessary in the use of the sacraments;[1] *thirdly*, as an enemy, an antichrist, an adversary, a tyrant of the Holy Scripture,[2] who dares to oppose his own words to all the words of God; *fourthly*, as a despiser, a calumniator, a blasphemer of the holy Christian Church and a free Council, inasmuch as he pretends that a Council is nothing in itself.

"Wherefore, I most humbly supplicate the most serene, most illustrious, excellent, generous, noble, brave, sage, and prudent lords, Charles, the Roman emperor, the electors, princes, counts, barons, knights, gentlemen, counsellors, towns, and commonalties, throughout Germany, to adhere to my protestation, and join me in resisting the antichristian conduct of the pope, for the glory of God, the defence of the Church, and of Christian doctrine,.and the maintenance of free councils in Christendom. Let them do so, and Christ our Lord will richly recompence them by his eternal grace. But if there are any who despise my prayer, and continue to obey that impious man, the pope, rather than God,[3] I, by these presents, shake myself free of the responsibility. Having faith-

---

[1] "Ab erronco, indurato, per Scripturas sanctas damnato, hæretico et apostatu." (L. Op. Lat. ii, p. 50.) See also (L. Op. (L.) xvii, p. 332.) The German copy has a few paragraphs that are not in the Latin.   [2] "Oppressore, totius sacræ Scripturæ." (Ibid.)   [3] Et papæ, impio homini, plus quam Deo obediant. (Ibid.)

fully warned their consciences, I leave them, as well as the pope, and all his adherents, to the sovereign judgment of God."

Such is Luther's deed of divorce, such his answer to the papal bull. There is great seriousness in this declaration. The accusations which he brings against the pope are very grave, and are not made in a spirit of levity. This protestation spread over Germany, and was sent to the leading courts of Christendom.

Though the step which Luther had just taken seemed the very height of daring, he had a still bolder step in reserve. The monk of Wittemberg will do all that the pope dares to do. The son of the Medicis, and the son of the miner of Mansfeld, have descended into the lists, and in this mortal struggle, which shakes the world, not a blow is given by the one which is not returned by the other. On the 10th December, a notice appeared on the walls of Wittemberg, inviting the professors and students to meet at nine o'clock in the morning, at the east gate, near the holy cross. A great number of teachers and pupils assembled, and Luther, walking at their head, led the procession to the appointed spot. How many faggot piles has Rome kindled in the course of ages! Luther desires to make a better application of the great Roman principle. He only wishes to rid himself of some old papers, and the fire, he thinks, is the fit instrument for that. A scaffold had been prepared. One of the oldest masters of arts applied the torch. At the moment when the flames rose, the redoubted Augustin, dressed in his frock, was seen to approach the pile, holding in his hands the Canon Law, the Decretals, the Clementines, the Extravagants of the popes, some writings of Eck and Emser, and the papal bull. The Decretals having first been consumed, Luther held up the bull, and saying, " Since thou hast grieved the Lord's Anointed, let the eternal fire grieve and consume thee," threw it into the flames. Never was war declared with more energy and resolution. Luther quietly took the road back to the town, and the crowd of doctors, professors, and students, after a loud cheer, returned with him to Wittemberg. "The Decretals," said Luther, "resemble a body with a head as soft as that of a maiden, limbs as full of violence as those of a lion, and a tail with as many wiles as a serpent. In all the papal laws, there is not one word to teach us who Jesus Christ is.[1] My enemies," continues he, " have been able, by burning my books, to injure the truth in the minds of the common people, and therefore I have burnt their books in my turn. A serious struggle has now commenced. Hitherto I have only had child's play with the pope. I began the work in the name of God; it will be terminated without me and by his power. If they burn my books, in which, to speak without vain-glory, there is more of the gospel than in all the books of the pope, I am entitled, *a fortiori*, to burn theirs, in which there is nothing good."

Had Luther commenced the Reformation in this way, such a proceeding would doubtless have led to fatal results. Fanaticism would have been able to lay hold of it, and throw the Church into a course of disorder and violence. But the Reformer's grave exposition of Scripture had formed a prelude to his work. The foundations had been wisely laid, and now the mighty stroke which he had just given would not only expose him to no hazard, but even accelerate the hour when Christendom would be delivered from her chains.

Thus solemnly did Luther declare his separation from the pope and his church. After his letter to Leo he might think this neces-sary. He accepted the excommunication which Rome had pro-nounced. It made the Christian world aware that there was now mortal war beween him and the pope. On reaching the shore, he burnt his ships, and left himself no alternative but that of advanc-ing to the combat.

Luther had returned to Wittemberg. Next day the academic hall was fuller than usual. Men's minds were excited. A feeling of solemnity prevailed throughout the audience, in expectation of an address from the doctor. He commented on the Psalms, a task which he had commenced in March of the previous year. Having finished his lecture, he paused a few moments, and then said firmly, " Be on your guard against the laws and statutes of the pope. I have burned the Decretals, but it is only child's play. It is time, and more than time, to burn the pope. I mean, he instant-ly resumed, the see of Rome, with all its doctrines and abomina-tions." Then, assuming a more solemn tone, he said, " If you do not, with all your heart, combat the impious government of the pope, you cannot be saved. Whoever takes pleasure in the religion and worship of the papacy will be eternally lost in the life to come."[1]

" If we reject it," added he, " we may expect all kinds of dan-gers and even the loss of life. But it is far better to run such risks in the world than to be silent ! As long as I live I will warn my brethren of the sore and plague of Babylon, lest several who are with us fall back with the others into the abyss of hell."

It is scarcely possible to imagine the effect produced upon the audience by language, the energy of which still makes us wonder.

[1] " Muss ewig in jenem Leben verlohren seyn." L. Op. (L.) xvii, p. 333.

" None of us," adds the candid student to whom we owe the fact,
" at least, if he be not a block without intelligence, ('as,' adds
he in a parenthesis, 'all the papists are,')—none of us doubts that
it contains the simple truth. It is evident to all the faithful, that
Dr. Luther is an angel of the living God, called to feed the long
bewildered sheep of Christ with the divine Word." [1]

This discourse, and the act which crowned it, mark an important epoch in the Reformation. The Leipsic discussion had detached Luther inwardly from the pope. But the moment when he
burned the bull was that in which he declared, in the most expressive manner, his entire separation from the bishop of Rome and
his church, and his attachment to the Church universal, as founded
by the apostles of Jesus Christ. After three centuries the fire
which he kindled at the East gate is still burning.

" The pope," said he, " has three crowns, and they are these: the
first is against God, for he condemns religion,—the *second* against
the emperor, for he condemns the secular power,—and the *third*
against society, for he condemns marriage." [2]   When he was reproached with inveighing too violently against the papacy, he replied, " Ah! I wish every thing I testify against him were a clap
of thunder, and every one of my words were a thunderbolt." [3]

This firmness of Luther was communicated to his friends and
countrymen. A whole nation rallied round him. The university
of Wittemberg in particular always became more attached to the
hero to whom it owed its importance and renown. Carlstadt
raised his voice against " the raging lion of Florence," who tore
divine and human laws to pieces, and trampled under foot the
principles of eternal truth. At this time Melancthon also addressed
the States of the empire in a writing characterised by his usual
elegance and wisdom. It was a reply to a treatise attributed to
Emser, but published under the name of Rhadinus, a Roman theologian. Luther himself spoke not more forcibly, and yet there
is a grace in Melancthon's words which gives them access to the
heart.

After showing, by passages of Scripture, that the pope is not
superior to other bishops; " What prevents us," says he to the
States of the empire, " from depriving the pope of the privilege
which we have given him? [4]   It matters little to Luther that our
riches, *i. e.* the treasures of Europe, are sent to Rome. But what
causes his grief and ours is, that the laws of the pontiffs, and the
reign of the pope, not only endanger the souls of men but utterly

1 Lutherum esse Dei viventis angelum qui palabundas Christi oves pascat. (L. Op.
Lat. ii, p. 123.)   2 L. Op. (W.) xxii, p. 1313.   3 Und ein jeglich Wort eine
Donneraxt wäre. (Ibid. p. 1350.)   4 " Quid obstat quominus papæ quod dedi-
mus jus adimamus?" (Corp. Reform. L. i, p. 337.)

destroy them. Every man can judge for himself, whether or not it suits him to give his money for the maintenance of Roman luxury, but to judge of the things of religion, and of sacred mysteries, is beyond the reach of the vulgar. Here, then, Luther implores your faith and zeal, and all pious men implore with him, some with loud voice and others with groans and sighs. Remember, princes of the Christian people, that you are Christians, and rescue the sad wrecks of Christianity from the tyranny of Antichrist. You are deceived by those who pretend that you have no authority over priests. The same spirit which animated Jehu against the priests of Baal urges you, in imitation of that ancient example, to abolish the Roman superstition—a superstition far more horrible than the idolatry of Baal."[1] So spoke mild Melancthon to the princes of Germany.

Some cries of alarm were heard among the friends of the Reformation. Timid spirits inclined to excessive moderation—Staupitz in particular, expressed the keenest anguish. " Till now," said Luther to him, " the whole affair has been mere sport. You yourself have said, ' did God not do these things it is impossible they jould by done.' The tumult becomes more and more tumultuous l and I do not think it will be quelled before the last day."[2] Such was Luther's mode of encouraging the timid. The tumult has existed for three centuries and is not quelled !

" The papacy," continued he, " is not now what it was yesterday and the day before. Let it excommunicate and burn my writings; . . . . . let it kill me! it cannot arrest what is going forward. Something wonderful is at the door.[3] I burnt the bull in great trembling, but now I experience more joy from it than from any action of my life."[4]

We stop involuntarily and delight to read in the great soul of Luther all that the future is preparing. " O ! my father," says he to Staupitz in concluding, " pray for the word of God and for me. I am heaved on the billows, and as it were whirled upon them."[5]

War is thus declared on all sides. The combatants have thrown away their scabbards. The Word of God has resumed its rights, and deposes him who had gone the length of usurping God's place. Society is shaken throughout. No period is without egotistical men, who would willingly leave human society in error and corruption, but wise men, even the timid among them, think differently.

---

[1] Ut extinguaris illam multo tetriorem Baalis idololatriâ Romanam superstitionem. (Corp. Ref. i, p. 337.)   [2] Tumultus egregiè tumultuatur, ut nisi extremo die sedari mihi posse non videatur. (L. Ep. i, p. 541.)   [3] Omninò aliquid portenti præ foribus est. (Ibid. p. 542.)   Strange presage of the future !   [4] . . . primum trepidus et orans, sed nunc lætior quam ullo totius vitæ meæ facto. (Ibid.) . . . . at first trembling and praying, but now more joyful than at any action of my whole life.

[5] Ego fluctibus his rapior et volvor. (Ibid.)

" We know well," says the mild and moderate Melancthon, " that.' statesmen have a horror at every thing like innovation; and it must be confessed, that in the sad confusion called human life, discord, even that which arises from the best of causes, is always accompanied with evil. Still it is necessary that in the Church the Word of God take precedence of every thing human.[1] God denounces. eternal wrath against those who strive to extinguish the truth ; and therefore, it was a duty incumbent on Luther—a Christian duty which he could not evade—to rebuke the pernicious errors which' disorderly men were circulating with inconceivable effrontery. If ' discord engenders many evils, (to my great grief I see it does, adds ' sage Philip,) it is the fault of those who at the beginning circulated errors, and of those who, filled with diabolic hatred, are seeking at present to maintain them."

All, however, were not of the same opinion. Luther was loaded with reproaches ; the storm burst upon him from all sides. " He is quite alone," said some—" He teaches novelties," said others.

" Who knows," replied Luther, in accordance with the virtue given him from on high,—" who knows if God has not chosen me, and called me,[2] and if they ought not to fear that in despising me they may be despising God himself? . . . Moses was alone on coming out of Egypt—Elijah alone in the time of King Ahab— Isaiah alone in Jerusalem—Ezekiel alone at Babylon. . . . God never chose for a prophet either the high priest or any other great personage. He usually chose persons who were low and despised, —on one occasion he even chose a shepherd, (Amos). At all times the saints have had to rebuke the great—kings, princes, priests, the learned—at the risk of their lives. And under the New Dispensation has it not been the same? Ambrose in his day was alone ; after him Jerome was alone ; later still Augustine was alone. . . . . I do not say that I am a prophet,[3] but I say they ought to fear just because I am alone and they are many. One thing I am sure of—the Word of God is with me and is not with them.

" It is said also," continues he, " that I advance novelties, and that it is impossible to believe that all other doctors have for so long a period been mistaken.

" No, I do not preach novelties. But I say that all Christian doctrines have disappeared, even among those who ought to have preserved them; I mean bishops and the learned. I doubt not,

---

[1] Sed tamen in Ecclesiâ necesse est anteferri mandatum Dei omnibus rebus humanis. (Melancth. Vit. Lutheri.) [2] Wer weiss ob mich Gott dazu berufen und erwaehlt hat. Fundamental principle of the articles condemned by the papal bull. (L. Op. (L.) xvii, p. 338.) [3] " Ich sage nicht dass Ich ein Prophet sey." (L. Op. (L.) xvii, p. 338.)

however, that the truth has remained in some hearts, should it even have been in infants in the cradle.[1] Poor peasants, mere babes, now understand Jesus Christ better than the pope, the bishops, and the doctors.

" I am accused of rejecting the holy doctors of the Church. I reject them not: but since all those doctors try to prove their writings by Holy Scripture, it must be clearer and more certain than they are. Who thinks of proving an obscure discourse by one still more obscure? Thus, then, necessity constrains us to re-cur to the Bible, as all the doctors do, and to ask it to decide upon their writings; for the Bible is lord and master.

" But it is said men in power persecute him. And is it not clear from Scripture that persecutors are usually in the wrong, and the persecuted in the right; that the majority are always in favour of falsehood, and the minority in favour of truth? The truth has, at all times, caused clamour."[2]

Luther afterwards reviews the propositions condemned in the bull as heretical, and demonstrates their truth, by proofs drawn from Holy Scripture. With what force, in particular, does he now maintain the doctrine of grace !

" What," says he, " will nature be able, before and without grace, to hate sin, avoid it, and repent of it; while that, even since grace is come, this nature loves sin, seeks it, desires it, and ceases not to combat grace, and to be irritated against it; a fact for which all the saints continually do groan ! . . . . . It is as if it were said that a large tree, which I am unable to bend by exerting my utmost strength, bends of itself on my letting it go; or that a tor-rent, which walls and dykes cannot arrest, is arrested the instant I leave it to itself. . . . No, it is not by considering sin and its conse-quences that we attain to repentance, but by contemplating Jesus Christ, his wounds, and boundless love.[3] The knowledge of sin must result from repentance, and not repentance from the know-ledge of sin. Knowledge is the fruit, repentance is the tree. With us the fruit grows upon the tree, but it would seem that, in the states of the holy father, the tree grows upon the fruit."

The courageous doctor, though he protests, also retracts some of his propositions. Surprise will cease when his mode of doing it is known. After quoting the four propositions on indulgences, con-demned by the bull,[4] he simply adds,

" In honour of the holy and learned bull I retract all that I

---

[1] " Und sollten's eitel Kinder in der Wiege seyn." (Ibid, p. 339.) [2] Wahrheit hat alle-zeit rumort. (Ibid., p. 140.) [3] Man soll zuvor Christum in seine Wunden sehen, und aus denselben, seine Liebe gegen uns. (Ibid., p. 351.) [4] 19 to 22 (Ibid., p. 363.)

have ever taught touching indulgences. If my books have been justly burned, it must certainly be because I conceded something to the pope in the doctrine of indulgences; wherefore, I myself condemn them to the fire."

He also retracts in regard to John Huss. " I say now, not that *some* articles, but *all* the articles of John Huss, are Christian throughout. The pope, in condemning Huss, condemned the gospel. I have done five times more than he, and yet I much fear have not done enough. Huss merely says, that a wicked pope is not a member of Christendom; but I, were St. Peter himself sitting to-day at Rome, would deny that he was pope by the appointment of God."

CHAP. XL

Coronation of Charles V.—The Nuncio Aleander—Will Luther's Books be burnt ?—Aleander and the Emperor—The Nuncios and the Elector—The Son of Duke John pleads for Luther—Luther's calmness—The Elector protects Luther—Reply of the Nuncios—Erasmus at Cologne — Erasmus with the Elector—Declaration of Erasmus—Advice of Erasmus—System of Charles V.

The powerful words of the Reformer penetrated all minds, and contributed to their emancipation. The sparks of light which each word threw out were communicated to the whole nation. But a great question remained to be solved. Would the prince, in whose states Luther dwelt, favour the execution of the bull, or would he oppose it ? The reply seemed doubtful. At that time the Elector and all the princes of the empire were at Aix-la-Chapelle where the crown of Charlemagne was placed upon the head of the youngest but most powerful monarch of Christendom. Unprecedented pomp and magnificence were displayed in the ceremony. Charles V, Frederick, the princes, ministers, and ambassadors, immediately after repaired to Cologne. Aix-la-Chapelle, where the plague was raging, seemed to.empty itself into this ancient town on the banks of the Rhine.

Among the crowd of strangers who pressed into the city were the two papal nuncios, Marino Carraccioli and Jerome Aleander. Carraccioli, who had previously executed a mission to Maximilian, was appointed to congratulate the new emperor, and confer with him on matters of state. But Rome had become aware that, in order to succeed in extinguishing the Reformation, it was necessary to send into Germany a nuncio specially entrusted with the task, and with a character, address, and activity fitted to accomplish it. Aleander had been selected.[1] This man, who was afterwards decorated with the cardinals' purple, seems to have been of rather an ancient family, and not of Jewish parentage as has been said. The guilty Borgia called him to Rome to be secretary to his son, the Cesar, before whose murderous sword all Rome trembled.[2] "Like master like servant," says a historian, who thus compares Aleander to Alexander VI. This judgment seems too severe. After the death of Borgia, Aleander devoted himself to study with new ardour. His skill in Greek, Hebrew, Chaldee, and Arabic, gave him the reputation of being the most learned man of his age. He threw his whole soul into whatever he undertook. The zeal with which he studied languages was not a whit stronger than that which he displayed in persecuting the Reformation. Leo X took him into his service. Protestant historians speak of his epicurean habits—Roman historians of the integrity of his life.[3] He seems to have been fond of luxury, show, and amusement. "Aleander," says his old friend Erasmus, " lived in Venice, in high office, but in low epicureanism." He is admitted to have been violent in temper, prompt in action, full of ardour, indefatigable, imperious, and devoted to the pope. Eck is the blustering, intrepid champion of the school,—Aleander the proud ambassador of the arrogant court of the pontiffs. He seemed formed to be a nuncio.

Rome had made every preparation to destroy the monk of Wittemberg. The duty of assisting at the coronation of the emperor, as representative of the pope, was to Aleander only a secondary mission, fitted to facilitate his task by the respect which it secured to him. The essential part of his commission was to dispose Charles to crush the growing Reformation.[4] In putting the bull into the hands of the emperor, the nuncio had thus addressed him :—" The pope, who has succeeded with so many great princes, will have little difficulty in bringing three grammarians to order." By these he meant Luther, Melancthon, and Erasmus. Erasmus was present at this audience.

No sooner had Aleander arrived at Cologne, than he proceeded in concert with Carracioli, to put everything in train for burning Luther's heretical writings throughout the empire, but more especially under the eyes of the princes of Germany who were then

---

[1] Studium flagrantissimum religionis, ardor idolis : \ . incredibile quanta solertia (Pallavicini, i, p. 84.)   [2] Capello, Venetian ambassador at Rome, in 1500, says of him, " Tutta Roma trema di esso ducha non li faza amazzar " . . . (Relatione M.S. Archives of Vienna, extracted by Ranke.)   [3] Er wird übei als ein gebohrner Jude und schaendlicher Epicurer beschrieben. (Seckend. 288.)—Integritas vitæ qua prænoscebatur . . . (Pallavicini, i, p. 84.)   [4] " Cui tota sollicitudo insisteret. nascentis hæresis evellendæ." (Pallavicini, i, p. 83.)   Whose whole anxiety was directed to the extirpation of the growing heresy.

assembled. Charles V had already consented to its being done in his hereditary states. The minds of men were greatly agitated. "Such measures," it was said to the ministers of Charles, and to the nuncios themselves, "far from curing the evil, will only make it worse. Do you imagine that the doctrine of Luther exists only in the books which you throw into the flames? It is written where you cannot reach it—on the hearts of the population.[1] If you will employ force, it must be that of innumerable swords, drawn to massacre an immense multitude.[2] Some billets of wood, collected for the purpose of consuming some bits of paper, will do nothing; such weapons become not the dignity either of the emperor or the pontiff." The nuncio defended his faggot piles. " These flames," said he, "are a sentence of condemnation written in gigantic letters, and understood alike by those who are near, and those who are at a distance, by the learned and the ignorant, by those even who cannot read."

But, in reality the nuncio's efforts were directed not against papers and books, but Luther himself. "These flames," resumed he, " are not sufficient to purify the infected air of Germany.[3] If they deter the simple, they do not correct the wicked. The thing wanted is an edict from the emperor against Luther's head."[4]

Aleander did not find the emperor so complying on the subject of the Reformer's person as on that of his books.

"Having just ascended the throne," said he to Aleander, " I cannot, without the advice of my counsellors, and the consent of the princes, strike such a blow at an immense faction, surrounded by such powerful defenders. Let us first know what our father, the Elector of Saxony, thinks of the affair; after that, we shall see what answer to give to the pope."[5] On the Elector, therefore, the nuncios proceeded to try their wiles, and the power of their eloquence.

On the first Sunday of November, after Frederick had attended mass in the convent of the Cordeliers, Carracioli and Aleander requested an audience. He received them in the presence of the Bishop of Trent, and several of his counsellors. Carracioli first presented the papal brief. Milder than Aleander, he thought it best to gain the Elector by flattery, and began to laud him and his ancestors. " In you," said he, " we hope for the salvation of the Roman Church and the Roman empire."

But the impetuous Aleander, wishing to come to the point,

1 " Altiusque insculptam in mentibus universæ fere Germaniæ." (Pallavicini, i, p. 88.)
2 " In vi innumerabilium gladiorum qui infinitum populum trucidarent." (Ibid.)
3 " Non satis ad expurgandam aërem Germaniæ jam tabificum." (Ibid., p. 89.)
4 Cæsaris edictum in caput .'. . Lutheri. (Ibid.)   5 " Audiamus antea hac in re patrem nostrum Fredericum." (L. Op. Lat., ii, p. 117)

came briskly forward, and interrupted his colleague, who modestly gave way to him.[1] "It is to me," said he, "and Eck, that Martin's affair has been entrusted. See the immense perils to which this man exposes the Christian commonwealth. If a remedy is not speedily applied, the empire is destroyed. What ruined the Greeks if it was not their abandonment of the pope? You cannot remain united to Luther without separating from Jesus Christ.[2] In the name of his Holiness, I ask of you two things: *first*, to burn the writings of Luther; *secondly*, to punish him according to his demerits, or at least to give him up a prisoner to the pope.[3] The emperor, and all the princes of the empire have declared their readiness to accede to our demands; you alone still hesitate. . . . ."

Frederick replied, by the intervention of the Bishop of Trent, "This affair is too grave to be decided on the spur of the moment. We will acquaint you with our resolution."

Frederick's position was difficult. What course will he adopt? On the one side are the emperor, the princes of the empire, and the chief pontiff of Christendom, from whose authority the Elector has as yet no thought of withdrawing; on the other, a monk, a feeble monk; for his person is all that is asked. The reign of the emperor has just commenced, and will discord be thrown into the empire by Frederick, the oldest and the wisest of all the princes of Germany? Besides, can he renounce that piety which led him as far as the sepulchre of Christ? . . . .

Other voices were then heard. John Frederick, son of Duke John, and nephew of Frederick, the pupil of Spalatin, a young prince, seventeen years of age, who afterwards wore the electoral crown, and whose reign was marked by great misfortunes, had been inspired with a heartfelt love of the truth, and was strongly attached to Luther.[4] When he saw him struck with the anathemas of Rome, he embraced his cause with the warmth of a young Christian and a young prince. He wrote to the doctor, he wrote also to his uncle, soliciting him to protect Luther against his enemies. At the same time, Spalatin, though indeed he was often very desponding, Pontanus, and the other counsellors who were with the Elector at Cologne, represented to him that he could not abandon the Reformer.[5]

Amid the general agitation, only one man remained tranquil—

" Cui ita loquenti de improviso sese addit Aleander . . ." (L. Op. Lat., ii, p. 117.)
[2] Non posse cum Luthero conjungi, quin sejungeretur a Christo. (Pallavicini, p. 86.)
[3] Ut de eo supplicium sumeret, vel captum pontifici transmitteret. (L. Op. Lat. ii, p. 117.) [4] . . . Sonderliche Gunst und Gnade zu mir unwürdiglich und den grossen Willen und Lust zer der heiligen göttlichen Wahrheit . . . (L. Ep. i, p. 548, to John Frederick, 30th October, 1520.) • [5] " Assiduo flabello ministrorum, illi jugiter suadentium ne Lutherum desereret." (Pallavicini, i, p. 86.)

that man was Luther. While others were trying to save him by
the influence of the great, the monk, in his cloister at Wittemberg,
thought that the great stood more in need of being saved by him.
Writing to Spalatin, he says, "If the gospel was of a nature to be
propagated or maintained by the power of the world, God would not
have entrusted it to fishermen.[1] To defend the gospel appertains
not to the princes and pontiffs of this world. They have enough
to do to shelter themselves from the judgments of the Lord and his
Anointed. If I speak, I do it in order that they may obtain the
knowledge of the divine word, and be saved by it."

Luther's expectation was not to be deceived. The faith which
a convent of Wittemberg contained exercised its influence in the
palaces of Cologne. The heart of Frederick, shaken perhaps for an
instant, became gradually stronger. He was indignant that the
pope, notwithstanding of urgent entreaties to investigate the matter in Germany, had condemned it at Rome, on the demand of the
Reformer's personal enemy; and that in his absence that enemy
should have dared to publish in Saxony a bull which threatened
the existence of the university and the peace of his people. Besides, the Elector was convinced that Luther had been wronged.
He shuddered at the thought of delivering an innocent man into the
cruel hands of his enemies. Justice, rather than the pope, such was
the rule he adopted. He resolved not to yield to Rome. On the
4th November, when the Roman nuncios were in his presence with
the Bishop of Trent, his counsellors announced to them, on the part
of the Elector, that he was much grieved to see how Doctor Eck
had taken the opportunity of his absence to involve in condemnation several persons not adverted to in the bull; that it might be
that, since his departure, an immense number of the learned and
the ignorant, the clergy and the laity, had united in adhering to
the cause and the appeal of Luther;[2] that neither his Imperial
Majesty, nor any person, had shown him that the writings of
Luther had been refuted, and that the only thing now necessary
was to throw them into the fire, that he moreover demanded a safe
conduct for Doctor Luther, to enable him to appear before learned,
pious, and important judges.

After this declaration, Aleander, Carracioli, and their suite,
retired to deliberate. It was the first time the Elector had publicly
declared his intentions with regard to the Reformer. The nuncios
had anticipated a very different result. "Now," thought they,

---

[1] Evangelium si tale esset, quod potentatibus mundi aut propagaretur aut servare
tur, non illud piscatoribus Deus demandasset. (L. Ep. i, p. 521.)   [2] "Ut
ingens vis populi, doctorum et rudium, sacrorum et profanorum, sese conjunx-
erint . . . ." (L. Op. Lat., ii, p. 116)   [3] "Quo audito, Marinus et Aleander
seorsim cum suis locuti sunt." (Ibid., p. 117.)

" that the Elector, by persisting in playing his part of impartiality, would expose himself to dangers, the full extent of which cannot be foreseen, he will not hesitate to sacrifice the monk." So Rome had reasoned. But her schemes were destined to fail before a power to which she had not adverted—the love of justice and truth.

When again before the Elector's counsellors, " I would fain know," said the imperious Aleander, " what the Elector would think were one of his subjects to choose the King of France or some other foreign prince for judge ?" Seeing at length that the Saxon counsellors were not to be shaken, he said, " We will execute the bull; we will prosecute and burn the writings of Luther. As to his person," added he, affecting a disdainful indifference, " the pope has no anxiety to dip his hand in the blood of the wretch."

News of the reply which the Elector had given to the nuncios having reached Wittemberg, Luther's friends were overjoyed. Melancthon and Amsdorff, in particular, cherished the most flattering hopes. " The German nobility," said Melancthon, " will shape their course by the example of a prince whom they follow in every thing as their Nestor. If Homer called his hero ' *the wall of the Greeks*,' why should not Frederick be called ' *the wall of the Germans ?* ' "[1]

Erasmus, the oracle of courts, the torch of the schools, the light of the world, was then at Cologne, having been invited thither by several princes who wished to consult him. At the period of the Reformation, Erasmus was at the head of the true middle (*juste milieu*) party, at least he thought he was, but erroneously; for when truth and error are in presence of each other, the right side is not the middle. He was the chief of that philosophical and university party, which had for ages aspired to correct Rome, without being able to do so; he was the representative of human wisdom ; but this wisdom was too weak to repress the arrogance of the papacy. The wisdom of God was necessary—that wisdom which the world often calls folly, but at the bidding of which mountains are crushed. Erasmus was unwilling either to throw himself into the arms of Luther, or to seat himself at the feet of the pope. He hesitated, and often vibrated between these two powers, sometimes attracted towards Luther, and then suddenly repelled towards the pope. He had declared for Luther in a letter to the Archbishop of Mentz, in which he had said. " The last spark of Christian piety seems ready to be extinguished. It is this that has moved Luther's heart; he cares neither for money nor honour."[2] The publication of this letter by the

· 1 Homerica adpellatione murum Germaniæ. (Corp. Ref. i, p. 272.)
ᵱ.2 " Et futurum erat . . . . ut tandem prorsus extingueretur illa scintilla Christianæ pietatis : hæc moverunt animum Lutheri . . . . qui nec honores ambit nec pecuniam cupit." (Erasm. Ep. Londini, 1642. p. 586.)

imprudent Ulric von Hütten, subjected Erasmus to so much annoy-
ance that he resolved to act with more prudence in future. Besides,
he was accused of being in concert with Luther whose unguarded
speeches moreover offended him. " Almost all good people," said
he, " are for Luther, but I see that we are on the high way to a
revolt. I would not have my name coupled with his. It hurts me
and does him no good."[2] " Be it so," replied Luther, " since it
pains you, I promise never to mention your name, nor that of any
of your friends." Such was the man to whom both the enemies
and the friends of the Reformer applied.

The Elector, aware that the opinion of a man so much respected
as Erasmus would carry great weight, invited the illustrious Dutch-
man to come to him. Erasmus complied. This was on the 5th of
December. The friends of Luther saw this step not without secret
apprehension. The Elector was sitting before the fire, with Spalatin beside him, when Erasmus was introduced. " What think you
of Luther ? " immediately asked Frederick. The prudent Erasmus,
surprised at the direct question, at first tried to evade it. He
twisted his mouth, bit his lips, and said nothing. Then the Elector,
opening his eyes (says Spalatin,) as he was wont to do when speaking to persons from whom he wished a precise answer, looked pier-
cingly at Erasmus,[3] who, not knowing how to disembarrass himself,
at last said, half in jest, " Luther has committed two great faults ;
he has attacked the pope's crown and the monks' belly." The
Elector smiled, but gave Erasmus to understand that he was in
earnest. Then Erasmus, laying aside his reserve, said, " The
source of all this dispute is the hatred of the monks against letters,
and the fear they have of seeing an end put to their tyranny.[4] What
have they put in operation against Luther? Clamour, cabal, hatred,
libels. The more virtuous, and the more attached to the doctrines of
the gospel a man is, the less is he opposed to Luther.[5] The harshness
of the bull has excited the indignation of all good men, and nobody
has been able to discover in it the meekness of a vicar of Jesus
Christ.[6] Out of so many universities two only have attacked Luther,
and even these have only condemned, not convicted him. Let not
people deceive themselves ; the danger is greater than some suppose. Things difficult and arduous are at hand.[7] . . . To begin

---

[1] Pavent vero ferme boni omnes. (Corp. Ref. i, p. 205.)   [2] Er will von mir
ungenennt seyn. (L. Ep. i, p. 525.) Nam ca res me gravat et Lutherum non sublevat.
(Corp. Ref. i, p. 206.)   [3] Da sperret auch wahrlich mein gnädister
Herr seine Augen nur wohl auf . . . (Spalatin Hist. MS. in Seckend. p. 291.)
[4] Lutherus peccavit in duobus, nempe quod tetigit coronam pontificis et ventres
monachorum, (See 1st vol.)   [5] Cum optimus quisque et evangelicæ doctrinæ
proximus dicatur, minime offensus Luthero. (Axiomata Erasmi in L. Op. Lat. ii, p.
115.)   [6] Bullæ sævitia probos omnes offendit ut indigna mitissimo Christi
vicario. (Ibid.)   [7] Urgent ardua negotia. . . . (Ibid.)

the reign of Charles with an act so hateful as the imprisonment of Luther would be of sad augury. The world is thirsting for evangelical truth.[1] Let us beware of culpably resisting it. Let the affair be examined by grave men of sound judgment ; this would be more accordant with the dignity of the pope himself." Thus spoke Erasmus to the Elector. The reader will perhaps be astonished at his frankness ; but Erasmus knew to whom he was speaking. Spalatin was delighted, and going out with Erasmus, accompanied him as far as the house of the Count of Nuenar, provost of Cologne, where the illustrious scholar was residing. Erasmus, in a fit of frankness, went into his room, took up the pen and wrote down the substance of what he had said to the Elector, and gave it to Spalatin. But fear of Aleander soon took possession of the timid Erasmus, the courage which he had felt in the presence of the Elector and his chaplain vanished, and he begged Spalatin to send back his too bold writing lest it should fall into the hands of the terrible nuncio. It was too late.

The Elector, feeling strong in the opinion of Erasmus, spoke in more decided terms to the emperor. Erasmus himself strove in nocturnal conferences,[2] like Nicodemus of old, to persuade the counsellors of Charles that it was necessary to remit the whole affair to impartial judges. Perhaps he had some hope of being named arbiter in this cause which threatened to divide the Christian world. His vanity would have been flattered by the office. But, at the same time, not to lose himself at Rome, he wrote the most submissive letters to Leo, who replied in kind terms, and thereby put poor Aleander to the torture.[3] From love to the pope, he could have sharply rebuked the pope. Erasmus communicated the pontiff's letters because they added to his credit. The nuncio made a complaint at Rome : " Pretend," was the answer, " that you do not observe the naughtiness of that man. Prudence requires it : it is necessary to leave the door open for repentance."[4]

Charles V himself embraced a vacillating system, which consisted in flattering both the pope and the Elector, and in seeming to incline alternately towards the one or the other according to the wants of the moment. One of his ministers, whom he had sent to Rome on certain Spanish matters, had arrived at the very time when Eck was loudly prosecuting Luther's condemnation. The wily ambassador instantly saw the advantages which his master might derive from the Saxon monk, and on the 12th May, 1520, wrote

---

[1] Mundus sitit veritatem evangelicam. (Axiomata Erasmi in L. Op. Lat. ii, p. 115.)
[2] Sollicitatis per nocturnos congressus. (Pallavicini, p. 87.) [3] Quæ male torquebant Aleandrum. (Ibid.) [4] Prudentis erat consilii hominis pravitatem dissimulare. (Ibid, p. 88.)

the emperor, who was still in Spain : " Your Majesty should go
into Germany, and there show some favour to one Martin Luther,
who is at the Court of Saxony, and, by his discourses, is giving
much uneasiness to the Court of Rome."[1]   Such, at the outset, was
the light in which Charles viewed the matter.   His object was not
to know on which side truth or error lay, or to ascertain what the
great interest of Germany demanded.   What does policy require,
and by what means can the pope be induced to support the emperor?   This was the whole question, and at Rome was well
known to be so.   The ministers of Charles gave Aleander a hint
of the plan which their master meant to follow.   " The emperor,"
said they, " will act towards the pope as the pope acts towards the
emperor: for he cares not to increase the power of his rivals, and
in particular of the king of France."[2] At these words the imperious
nuncio gave vent to his indignation :   " What !" replied he,
" even should the pope abandon the emperor must the emperor
abandon religion?   If Charles means thus to take his revenge . . .
let him tremble !   This unprincipled course will turn against himself."   The imperial diplomatists were not moved by the menaces
of the nuncio.

CHAP. XII.

Luther on Confession—True absolution—Antichrist—Rally around Luther—Satires
—Ulric von Hutten—Lucas Cranach—The Carnival at Wittemberg—Staupitz
intimidated—Luther's Labours—Luther's Humility—Progress of the Reformation.

If the legates of Rome failed with the mighty of the world, the
inferior agents of the papacy succeeded in producing disturbance
among the weak.   The militia of Rome had heard the command
of their chief.   Fanatical priests employed the bull in alarming
consciences, and honest but ill informed ecclesiastics regarded it as
a sacred duty to act conformably to the instructions of the pope.
Luther had begun his struggle against Rome in the confessional,[3]
and in the confessional Rome gave battle to the adherents of the
Reformer.   The bull, though openly contemned by the nation, became powerful in these solitary tribunals.   " Have you read the
writings of Luther," demanded the confessors, " do you possess
them? do you regard them as sound or as heretical? "   If the pen-

---

[1] Despatches of Manuel Llorente, i, p. 388.
[2] Pallav. p. 91.

itent hesitated to pronounce the anathema, the priest refused him absolution. Several consciences were troubled. The people were strongly agitated. This skilful manœuvre promised to restore to the papal yoke whole districts already gained to the gospel. Rome congratulated herself on having, in the thirteenth century, erected a tribunal destined to bring the free consciences of Christians under subjection to the priests.[1] While it continues in force her reign is not ended.

Luther became aware of these circumstances. Single handed what will he do to defeat the manœuvre? The Word—the Word uttered loudly and boldly: such is his weapon. The Word will search out these alarmed consciences, these frightened souls, and strengthen them. A powerful impulse was required, and Luther's voice was heard addressing penitents with heroic boldness, and a noble disregard of all secondary considerations. " When you are asked," says he, " whether or not you approve my books, answer ' You are a confessor, and not an inquisitor or a gaoler. My duty is to confess what my conscience dictates; yours not to probe and discover the secrets of my heart. Give me absolution, and thereafter dispute with Luther, the pope, and whomsoever you please ; but do not connect the sacrament of peace with strife and combat.' If the confessor will not yield, then," continues Luther, " I would rather dispense with his absolution. Give yourself no uneasiness ; if man will not absolve you God will absolve you. Rejoice in that you are absolved by God himself, and present yourself without fear at the sacrament of the altar. The priest will have to account at the final judgment for the absolution which he shall have refused you. They may indeed refuse us the sacrament, but they cannot deprive us of the strength and grace which God has attached to it.— God has placed salvation neither in their will nor in their power but in our faith. Leave their sacrament, altar, priest, church : the Word of God condemned in the bull is more than all these things. The soul can dispense with the sacrament, but cannot live without the Word. Christ, the true Bishop, will himself undertake to nourish you spiritually."[2]

Thus, Luther's voice found its way into families, and alarmed consciences, imparting to them courage and faith. But it was not enough for him merely to defend himself; he felt it his duty to attack and return blow for blow. Ambrose Catherin, a Roman theologian, had written against him. [3]" I will stir up the bile of the

---

[1] In 1215, by the fourth Lateran Council, under Innocent III.
Christus selber speisen. (L. Op. lxvii, p. 563.)
(L. Ep. i, p. 570.)

[2] Und wird dich der rechte Bischof
[3] Italicæ bestiæ bilem movebo.

Italian beast," said Luther ; and he kept his word. In his reply, he proved by the revelations of Daniel and St. John, by the epistles of St. Paul, St. Peter, and St. Jude, that the reign of Antichrist, predicted and described in the Bible, was the papacy. " I know for certain," says he, in conclusion, " that our Lord Jesus Christ lives and reigns. Strong in this assurance, I would not fear several thousands of popes. May God at length visit you according to his infinite power, and cause the day of the glorious advent of his Son to shine, that day in which he will destroy the wicked. And let all the people say, Amen !"[1]

And all the people did say, Amen ! A holy fear took possession of men's souls. They saw Antichrist seated on the pontifical throne. This new idea, an idea which derived great force from the prophetical description, being thrown by Luther into the midst of his age, gave Rome a dreadful shock. Faith in the divine Word was substituted for that, which, till then the Church alone had obtained, and the power of the pope, which had long been adored by the people, became the object of their hatred and terror.

Germany replied to the papal bull by surrounding Luther with acclamation. The plague was in Wittemberg, and yet arrivals of new students daily took place, while from four to six hundred pupils regularly took their seats in the academic halls at the feet of Luther and Melancthon. The church of the convent and the town church were too small for the crowds eager to hear the words of the Reformer. The prior of the Augustins was in terror lest these churches should give way under the pressure of the audience.[2] But the movement was not confined within the walls of Wittemberg : it extended over Germany. Letters full of consolation and faith, from princes, noble and learned men, reached Luther from all quarters. He showed the chaplain more than thirty of them.[3]

One day the Margrave of Brandenburg, with several other princes, arrived at Wittemberg to visit Luther. " They wished to see the man," [4] said the Margrave. In fact all wished *to see the man*, whose word alarmed the pope, and caused the pontiff of the West to totter on his throne.

The enthusiasm of Luther's friends increased from day to day. "Unparalleled folly of Emser!"—exclaimed Melancthon—"to presume to measure weapons with our Hercules, overlooking the finger of God in the actions of Luther,[5] as the king of Egypt overlooked it in the hand of Moses." The mild Melancthon found strong expressions to excite those who seemed to him to retrograde or remain stationary. " Luther has stood up for the truth," wrote he to John Hess, " and yet you keep silence. He still breathes, he still prospers, though Leo is indignant and roars with rage. Remember, it is impossible for Roman impiety to approve of the gospel.[1] How should this unhappy age be without its Judases, Caiaphases, Pilates, and Herods? Arm yourself then with the power of the Word of God against such adversaries."

All the writings of Luther, his Lord's Prayer, and especially a new edition of the German theology, were eagerly devoured. Reading societies were formed, for the purpose of procuring his works, for the use of the members. Friends made new impressions of them, and circulated them by means of hawkers. They were also recommended from pulpits. A German church was demanded, one in which no dignity should in future be conferred on any one who was not able to preach to the people in German, and the German bishops of which should every where oppose the papal power. Moreover, cutting satires directed against the leading Ultra-Montanists were circulated throughout the provinces of the empire. The opposition united all its forces around this new doctrine, which give it precisely what it wanted, by justifying it in regard to religion. The greater part of the lawyers, weary of the quirks of the Ecclesiastical tribunals, attached themselves to the Reformation, but its cause was keenly embraced above all by the Humanists. Ulric von Hütten was indefatigable. He wrote letters to Luther, to the legates, and the leading men of Germany. " I tell you, and tell you again, O Marinus!" said he to the legate, Carracioli, in one of his publications, " the mists with which you blinded us are cleared away—the gospel is preached—the truth proclaimed —the absurdities of Rome treated with contempt—your ordinances languish and die—liberty begins." [2]

Not contenting himself with prose, Hütten had recourse to verse also. He published his Cry on the Burning by Luther.[3] Appealing to Jesus Christ, he prayed him to consume, with the brightness of his countenance, those who dared to deny his power. He began, moreover, to write in German. " Hitherto," said he, " I have

[1] " Non posse Evangelium Romanæ impietati probari. (Ibid. p. 280.) [2] " Ablata illa est a vobis inducta olim nostris oculis caligo, prædicatur Evangelium . . spes est libertatis . . . (Ulric ab Hütten Eques Mar. Carrac. L. Op. Lat. ii, p. 176.)
[3] " Quo tu oculos, pie Christe, tuos, frontisque severæ
Tende supercilium, teque esse ostende neganti
Qui te contemnunt igitur, mediumque tonanti
Ostendunt digitum, tandem iis te ostende potentem.
Te videat ferus ille Leo, te tota malorum
Sentiat inluvies, scelerataque Roma tremiscat,
Ultorem scelerum discant te vivere saltem,
Qui regnare negant " . . . (In Incendium Lutheranum Exclamatio Ulrichi Hütteni Equitis Mar. Carrac. L. Op. Lat. ii, p. 176.)

written in Latin, a language which all could not comprehend, but now I address myself to my country." His German ryhmes laid open and enabled the people to read the shameful and voluminous record of the sins of the Roman Court. But Hütten was unwilling to confine himself to mere words; he was impatient to bring his sword into the struggle, for he thought that by the swords and halberds of the many valiant warriors, of which Germany was proud, the vengeance of God was to be accomplished. Luther opposed his infatuated projects. "I would not," said he, "that men should fight for the gospel by violence and carnage. I have written so to Hütten.[1]

. , The celebrated painter, Lucas Cranach, published, under the title of the *Passions of Christ and Antichrist*, engravings which represented, on the one hand, the splendour and magnificence of the pope, and on the other, the humility and sufferings of the Redeemer. Luther wrote the inscriptions. These engravings, executed with great spirit, produced an astonishing effect. The people withdrew from a church which appeared so opposed to the spirit of its Founder. "This work," said Luther, "is excellent for the laity."[2]

Several, in opposing the Papacy, had recourse to arms which ill accorded with the holiness of the Christian life. Emser, in replying to Luther's tract, entitled, 'To the Goat Emser,' had published one entitled, 'To the Bull of Wittemberg.' The name was not ill chosen. But at Magdeburg, Emser's book was hung on the gallows, with this inscription, "The book is worthy of the place;" and a rod was placed beside it, to indicate the punishment which the author deserved.[3] At Doeblin, there was written under the Papal bull, in derision of its impotent thunders, "The nest is here, but the birds are flown."[4]

At Wittemberg, the students, taking advantage of the carnival, clothed one of their number in a dress resembling that of the pope, and paraded him through the streets "pompously, but rather too ludicrously," says Luther.[5] On arriving at the public square they went down to the banks of the river, and some of them, feigning a sudden attack, seemed to wish to throw the pope into the water; but the pope, having no liking for such a bath, took to his heels. His cardinals, bishops, and familiars, followed his example, dispersing over all the quarters of the town, while the students continued to pursue them. There was not a corner of Wittem-

---

[1] Nollem vi et cæde pro Evangelio certari; ita scripsi ad hominem. (L. Ep. i, p. 243.)   [2] Bonus est pro laicis liber. (L. Ep. i, p. 571.) It would be worth while to make a new impression of this work; I found a copy of it in the library of Zurich.   [3] Publico infamiæ loco affixus. (Ibid. p. 560.)   [4] Das Nest ist hie: die Vogel sind ausgeflogen. (Ibid. p. 570.)   [5] Nimis ludicre Papam personatum circumvenerunt sublimem et pompaticum . . . . (Ibid. p. 561.)

berg where some Roman dignitary did not flee before the shouts and laughter of the inhabitants, who were all in motion.[1] "The enemy of Christ," says Luther, "who sports both with kings and with Christ himself, well deserves to be thus sported with." In this we think him in error. Truth is too beautiful, and ought never to be made to walk through the mire. She ought to fight without such auxiliaries as songs, caricatures, and carnival frolics. It may be that without these popular demonstrations, her success would be less apparent, but it would be more pure, and consequently more durable. Be this as it may, the imprudent and passionate conduct of the Court of Rome had excited universal antipathy, and the bull by which the Papacy thought to stifle every thing was itself the cause of general revolt.

Still the Reformer's whole course was not one of exultation and triumph. Behind the car in which he was drawn by his zealous countrymen, transported with admiration, there was not wanting the slave appointed to remind him of his frailty. Some of his friends seemed disposed to call a halt. Staupitz, whom he called his father, seemed shaken. The pope had accused him, and Staupitz had declared his readiness to submit to the judgment of his Holiness. "I fear," said Luther to him, "that in accepting the pope for judge, you will seem to throw off me and the doctrines which I have maintained. If Christ loves you, he will constrain you to retract your letter. Christ is condemned, spoiled, blasphemed; it is time not to fear, but to cry aloud.[2] Wherefore, while you exhort me to humility, I exhort you to pride; for you have too much humility, just as I have too much of its opposite. I shall be called proud and avaricious, an adulterer, a murderer, an anti-pope, a man guilty of all crimes. It matters not, so long as they cannot accuse me of having kept an impious silence at the moment when the Lord was grieved, and said 'I looked on my right hand, and beheld but there was no man that would know me.' (Ps. cxlii, 4.) The word of Jesus Christ is not a word of peace, but a sword. If you will not follow Jesus Christ, I will walk alone, advance alone, and gain the day."[3]

Thus Luther, like the commander of an army, kept an eye on the whole field of battle, and while he urged fresh troops forward into the thickest of the fight, marked those who appeared faint-hearted and recalled them to their post. His exhortations were every-where heard. His letters rapidly succeeded each other. Three

---

[1] . . . Fugitivum cum Cardinalibus, Episcopis, famulisque suis, in diversas partes oppidi disperserunt et insecuti sunt. (Ibid. 17th Feb. 1521.) [2] Non enim hic tempus timendi sed clamandi. (L. Ep. i, p. 557.) [3] Quod si tu non vis sequi sine me ire et rapi. (Ibid. p. 558.) But if you will not follow, allow me to go and hurry on.

presses were constantly employed in multiplying his writings.[1] His words had free course among the people, strengthened consciences which the confessionals had alarmed, raised up those ready to faint in convents, and maintained the rights of truth in the palaces of princes.

"Amid the tempests which assail me," wrote he to the Elector, "I always hoped I would one day find peace. But I now see it was only a man's thought. Day after day the wave is rising, and I already stand in the midst of the ocean. The tempest breaks loose with fearful roar.[2] With one hand I grasp the sword, and with the other build up the walls of Sion.[3] Her ancient links are snapt asunder, broken by the hand which darted the thunders of excommunication against her." "Excommunicated by the bull," says he, "I am loosed from the authority of the pope and monastic laws. With joy I embrace the deliverance. But I lay aside neither the habit of the order nor the convent."[4] And yet, amidst all this agitation, he never loses sight of the dangers by which his own soul is beset during the strife. He feels the necessity of keeping a watch upon himself. "You do well to pray for me," wrote he to Pellican, who was living at Bâle. "I cannot devote enough of time to holy exercises. My life is a cross. You do well to exhort me to modesty. I feel the want of it; but I am not my own master: I know not what spirit rules me. I wish ill to nobody;[5] but my enemies press me with such fury that I am not sufficiently on my guard against the seductions of Satan. Pray then for me."

Thus both the Reformer and the Reformation hastened on in the direction in which God called them. The movement extended. Men who might have been expected to be most faithful to the hierarchy began to be shaken. "Even those," says Eck, ingenuously enough, "who hold of the pope the best benefices and the richest canonries remain mute as fishes. Several among them even extol Luther as a man filled with the Spirit of God, and call the defenders of the pope sophists and flatterers."[6] The Church, apparently great in power, supported by the treasures, the powers and the armies of the world, but in reality emaciated and enfeebled, without love to God, without Christian life, without enthusiasm for the truth, found herself in presence of men, simple, but bold, men who, knowing that God is with those who combat for His Word, had no doubt of victory? Every age has experienced how powerful an

[1] "Cum tria prela solus ego occupare cogar." (L. Ep. i, p. 558.)   [2] "Videns rem tumultuosissimo tumultu tumultuantem." (ibid. p. 546.)   [3] Una manu gladium apprehendens et altera murum ædificaturus. (Ibid., p. 565.)
[4] Ab ordinis et Papæ legibus solutus . . . . quod gaudeo et amplector. (Ibid., p. 568.)
[5] . . . . Compos mei non sum, rapior nescio quo spiritu, cum nemini me male velle conscius sim. (Ibid., p. 555.)   [6] Reynald. Epist. J. Eckii ad Cardinal Contarenum.

idea is in penetrating the masses, in arousing nations, and, if need be, hurrying thousands to the field of battle and to death ; but if such is the influence of a human idea, what must be the power of an idea sent down from heaven when God opens the door of the human heart. The world has not often seen such a power in operation. It did see it, however, in the first days of Christianity and in those of the Reformation; and it will see it in days yet to come. Men who disdained the world's wealth, and grandeur, and were contented to lead a life of pain and poverty, began to move in behalf of the holiest thing upon the earth—the doctrine of faith and of grace. In this heaving of society, all the religious elements were brought into operation, and the fire of enthusiasm hurried men boldly for-forward into a new life an epoch of renovation which had just open-ed so majestically, and towards which Providence was hastening the nations.

BOOK SEVENTH.

THE DIET OF WORMS.

1521. (JANUARY—MAY,)

CHAP. I.

·Conquests by the Word of God—The Diet of Worms—Difficulties—Charles demanus Luther—The Elector to Charles—State of Men's minds—Aleander's Alarm—The Elector sets out without Luther—Aleander awakens Rome—Excommunication of the Pope, and Communion with Christ—Fulmination of the Bull—Luther's motives in the Reformation.

THE Reformation, which commenced with the struggles of an humble soul in the cell of a convent at Erfurt, had never ceased to advance. An obscure individual, with the Word of life in his hand, had stood erect in presence of worldly grandeur, and made it tremble. This Word he had opposed, first, to Tezel and his numerous host, and these avaricious merchants, after a momentary resistance, had taken flight. Next, he had opposed it to the legate of Rome at Augsburg, and the legate, paralysed, had allowed his prey to escape. At a later period he had opposed it to the champions of learning in the halls of Leipsic, and the astonished theologians had seen their syllogistic weapons broken to pieces in their hands. At last he had opposed it to the pope, who, disturbed in his sleep, had risen up upon his throne, and thundered at the troublesome monk; but the whole power of the head of Christendom this Word had paralysed. The Word had still a last struggle to maintain. It behoved to triumph over the emperor of the West, over the kings and princes of the earth, and then, victorious over all the powers of the world, take its place in the Church to reign in it as the pure Word of God.

The whole kingdom was agitated. Princes and nobles, knights and citizens, clergy and laity, town and country, all were engrossed. A mighty religious revolution, of which God himself was the prime mover, but which was also deeply rooted in the minds of the people, was threatening to overthrow the long venerated head of the Roman hierarchy. A new generation, of a grave, profound, active, and energetic spirit, filled the universities, towns, courts, and castles, the rural districts, and not unfrequently cloisters also. The feeling that a great social transformation was at hand animated all minds with holy enthusiasm. In what relation will the new emperor stand to this movement of the age, and what will be the issue of the mighty impulse, by which all feel that they are borne along?

A solemn Diet was about to be opened. It was the first imperial assembly over which the youthful Charles was to preside. Nuremberg, where, in virtue of the Golden Bull, it ought to have been held, being desolated by the plague, it had been summoned to meet at Worms, on the 6th of January, 1521.[1] Never had a Diet been attended by so many princes. All desired to be present at this first act of the government of the young emperor, and to make a display of their power. Among others, the young Landgrave, Philip of Hesse, who was afterwards to play so important a part in the Reformation, arrived at Worms in the middle of January, with six hundred cavaliers, among them men of renowned valour.

But there was a still more powerful motive which induced the electors, dukes, archbishops, landgraves, margraves, bishops, barons, and lords of the empire, as well as the deputies of towns, and the ambassadors of the kings of Christendom, at this moment, to throng the roads leading to Worms with their brilliant equipages. It had been announced that the Diet would be occupied with the nomination of a council of regency to govern the empire during the absence of Charles, with the jurisdiction of the imperial chamber, and other important questions. But the public attention was particularly directed to another matter, which the emperor had also mentioned in his letter convening the Diet, viz., the Reformation. The great interests of politics trembled before the cause of the Monk of Wittemberg. This cause was the principal subject of conversation among all personages who arrived at Worms.

Every thing announced that the Diet would be difficult and stormy. Charles, scarcely twenty years of age, pale and sickly, yet as skilful as any one in the graceful management of his horse and in breaking a lance, of a character imperfectly developed, and with a grave and melancholy but still benevolent expression of countenance, gave no proof as yet of distinguished talent, and seemed not to have adopted a decided course. The able and active William of Croi, Lord of Chievres, who was his grand chamberlain, his governor, and prime minister, and possessed absolute authority

[1] Sleidan, vol. i, p. 80.

at the court, died at Worms. Numerous ambitious projects were· competing with each other. Many passions were in collision. The· Spaniards and Belgians were eager to insinuate themselves into the counsels of the young prince. The nuncios multiplied their· intrigues, while the princes of Germany spoke out boldly. A struggle might have been foreseen, yet a struggle in which the principal part would be performed by the secret movements of factions.[1]

Charles opened the Diet on the 28th of January, 1521, being the festival of Charlemagne. He had a high idea of the importance of the imperial dignity. In his opening address he said, that no monarchy could be compared to the Roman empire, to which of old almost the whole world had been subject; that, unhappily, the empire was now only the shadow of what it had been; but that he hoped, by means of his kingdoms and powerful alliances, to re-establish it in its ancient glory.

But numerous difficulties immediately presented themslves to the young emperor. How will he act, placed, as he is, between the papal nuncio and the Elector to whom he owes his crown? How can he avoid dissatisfying Aleander or Frederick? The former· urged the emperor to execute the papal bull, and the latter begged· him to undertake nothing against the monk without giving him a· hearing. Wishing to please these two opposite parties, the young prince, during a sojourn at Oppenhem, had written to the Elector to bring Luther to the Diet, assuring him that no injustice would be done him, that he would meet with no violence, and that learned men would confer with him.

This letter of Charles, accompanied by letters from Chievres· and the Count of Nassau, threw the Elector into great perplexity·, An alliance with the pope might at any instant become necessary to the young and ambitious emperor, and in that case it was all over with Luther   Frederick, by taking the Reformer to Worms, was perhaps taking him to the scaffold; and yet the orders of Charles were express. The Elector ordered Spalatin to acquaint Luther with the letters which he had received. "The enemy," said the chaplain to him, "is putting every thing in operation to hasten on the affair."[1]

Luther's friends trembled, but he trembled not. He was then in very feeble health; no matter. "If I cannot go to Worms in health," replied he to the Elector, "I will make myself be carried;· since the emperor calls me, I cannot doubt but it is a call from God himself. If they mean to employ violence against me, as is probable, (for assuredly it is not with a view to their own instruc-

[1] Es gieng aber auf diesem Reichstag gar schlüpferig zu . . . (Seckend. p. 326.)
[2] Adversarios omnia moliri ad maturandum id negotii. (L. Ep. i, p. 534.)

tion that they make me appear,) I leave the matter in the hands of the Lord. He who preserved the three young men in the furnace, still lives and reigns. If He is not pleased to save me, my life is but a small matter; only let us not allow the gospel to be exposed to the derision of the wicked, and let us shed our blood for it sooner than permit them to triumph. Whether would my life or my death contribute most to the general safety? It is not for us to decide. Let us only pray to God that our young emperor may not commence his reign with dipping his hands in my blood; I would far rather perish by the sword of the Romans. You know what judgments befel the emperor Sigismund after the murder of John Huss. Expect every thing of me—save flight and recantation;[1] I cannot fly, still less can I recant."

Before receiving this letter from Luther, the Elector had taken his resolution. As he was advancing in the knowledge of the gospel, he began to be more decided in his measures. Seeing that the conference of Worms could not have a happy result, he wrote to the emperor. "It seems to me difficult to bring Luther with me to Worms; relieve me from the task. Besides, I have never wished to take his doctrine under my protection, but only to prevent him from being condemned without a hearing. The Legates without waiting for your orders, have proceeded to take a step insulting both to Luther and to me, and I much fear, that in this way they have hurried him on to an imprudent act which might expose him to great danger were he to appear at the Diet." The Elector alluded to the pile which had consumed the Papal bull.

But the rumour of Luther's journey to Worms had already spread. Men eager for novelty rejoiced at it. The emperor's courtiers were alarmed, but no one felt so indignant as the papal legate. Aleander on his journey had seen how deep an impression the gospel which Luther preached had made on all classes of society. Literary men, lawyers, nobles, the lower clergy, the regular orders, and the people, were gained to the Reformation.[2] These friends of the new doctrine carried their heads erect, and were bold in their language, while fear and terror froze the partizans of Rome. The papacy still stood, but its props were shaking. A noise of devastation was already heard, somewhat resembling the creaking which takes place at the time when a mountain begins to slip.[3]

Aleander, during his journey to Worms, was sadly annoyed. When he had to dine or sleep, neither literary men nor nobles

[1] Omnia de me præsumas præter fugam et palinodiam. . . . (L. Ep. i, p. 536.)
[2] Multitudo . . turba paperum, nobilium . . . grammatici causidici . . . inferiores ecclesiastici . . factio multorum regulaiium. . . (Pallavicini, i, p. 93.) 2 Hæc omnes conditiones petulanter grassantium . . metuin cuilibet incutiebant. .
(Ibid., p. 93.)

nor priests, even among the supposed friends of the pope, durst
receive him, and the proud nuncio was obliged to seek an asylum
in taverns of the lowest class.[1] He was thus in terror, and
had no doubt that his life was in great danger. In this way he
arrived at Worms; and, thenceforth, to his Roman fanaticism
was added resentment for the personal injuries which he had
received. He immediately put every means in operation to prevent the audacious compearance of the redoubtable Luther.
"Would it not be scandalous," said he, "to see laics re-investi-
gating a cause which the pope had already condemned?" Nothing
alarms a Roman courtier so much as an investigation; and, moreover, an investigation to take place in Germany, and not at Rome.
How humiliating even should Luther's condemnation be unanimously decided! And it was not even certain that such would be
the result. Will not the powerful word of Luther, which has
already done such havoc, involve many princes and nobles in inevitable ruin? Aleander, when before Charles, insisted, implored,
threatened, and spoke out as nuncio of the head of the Church.[2]
Charles yielded; and wrote to the Elector that the time granted to
Luther having already elapsed, the monk was under papal excommunication; and that therefore unless he were willing to retract
his writings, Frederick must leave him at Wittemberg. Frederick
had already quitted Saxony without Luther. "I pray the Lord to
be favourable to our Elector," were the words of Melancthon on seeing him depart; "on him our hopes of the restoration of Christendom
repose. His enemies dare every thing, και παντα λιθον κινησομενους; [3]
but God will bring to nought the counsel of Ahithophel. As for
us, let us do our part in the combat by our lessons and our prayers."
Luther was deeply grieved at being prohibited to appear at Worms.[4]

Aleander did not consider it enough that Luther should not come
to Worms—he wished him to be condemned. Returning incessantly to the charge before the princes, prelates, and different
members of the Diet, he accused the Augustin monk not only of
disobedience and heresy, but also of sedition, rebellion, impiety,
and blasphemy. The very accent in which he spoke betrayed the
passions by which he was actuated; so that men exclaimed, it is
hatred and love of vengeance, rather than zeal and piety, that
excite him.[5] However frequent, however vehement his discourses
were, he made no converts.[6]

1 Nominem nactus qui auderet ipsum excipere ad vilia sordidaque hospitia ægre
divertit. (Pallavicini. i, p. 93.)   2 Legati Romani nolunt ut audiatur homo hæreticus. Minantur multa. (Zw. Ep. p. 157.)   3 There is not a stone which
they will not move. (Corp. Ref., i, p. 279. 24th Jan.)   4 Cum dolore legi novissimas
Caroli litteras. (L. Ep. i, p. 542.)   5 Magis invidiâ et vindictæ libidine quam
zelo pietatis. (Historia Johnnis Cochlœi de actis et scriptis Martini Lutheri. *Parisus,*
1565, p. 27, verso. Cochlœus was all his life one of Luther's greatest enemies. We will
soon see him appear.)   6 Vehementibus suis orationibus parum promovit. (Ibid.)

Some pointed out to him that the papal bull had condemned Luther only conditionally; others did not altogether conceal the joy which they felt at seeing Roman pride humbled. The ministers of the emperor, on the one hand, and the ecclesiastical electors, on the other, affected great coldness—the former to make the pope more sensible how necessary it was for him to league with their master, the latter in order to induce him to pay better for their favour. A conviction of Luther's innocence prevailed in the assembly, and Aleander could not restrain his indignation.

But the coldness of the Diet did not try the patience of the legate so much as the coldness of Rome. Rome, which had so long refused to take a serious view of the quarrel of the drunk German, had no idea that a bull of the sovereign pontiff could prove insufficient to make him humble and submissive. She had accordingly resumed her wonted security,[1] no longer sending either bull or purses of money. But how was it possible without money to succeed in such a business?[2] Rome must be awakened, and Aleander gives the alarm. Writing to the Cardinal de Medicis, he says, ".Germany is detaching herself from Rome, and the princes are detaching themselves from the pope. A few delays more—a few more attempts at compromise and the matter is past hope. Money! money! or Germany is lost."[3]

.' At this cry Rome awakes: the servants of the papacy, laying aside their torpor, hastily forge their dreaded thunder at the Vatican. The pope issues a new bull;[4] and the excommunication with which till then the heretical doctor had been merely threatened, is in distinct terms pronounced against him and all his adherents. Rome herself, breaking the last thread which still attached him to her church, gave Luther greater freedom, and thereby greater power. Thundered at by the pope, he, with new affection, took refuge in Christ. Driven from the external temple, he felt more strongly that he was himself a temple inhabited by God.

. " It is a glorious thing," said he, "that we sinners, in believing on Jesus Christ, and eating his flesh, have him within us with all his strength, power, wisdom and justice, according as it is written, *.He who believeth in me, dwelleth in me and I in him.*' Admirable dwelling! marvellous tabernacle! far superior to that of Moses, and all magnificently adorned within with superb tapestry, veils of purple, and furniture of gold, while.without, as on the tabernacle which God ordered to be constructed in the wilderness of Sinai, is seen

[1] Negligens quædam securitas Romam pervaserat. (Pallavicini, i, p. 94)
[2] Nec-pecunia ad varios pro eadem sumptus. (Ibid.) [3] "Periculum denique amittendæ Germaniæ ex parcimonia monetæ cujusdam. (Ibid.) In fine the danger of losing Germany from niggardliness in withholding a sum of money.
[4] Decet Romanum Pontificem, etc. (Roman. Bullarium.)

only a rough covering of beavers' skins or goats' hair.[1] Christians often stumble, and in external appearance are all feebleness and disgrace. But no matter: within this infirmity and folly dwells secretly a power which the world cannot know, but which overcomes the world; for Christ remaineth in them. I have sometimes seen Christians walking with a halt, and in great weakness ; but when the hour of combat or appearance at the world's bar arrived, Christ of a sudden acted within them, and they became so strong and resolute that the devil in dismay fled before them." [2]

In regard to Luther, such an hour was about to peal, and Christ, in whose communion he dwelt, was not to forsake him. Meanwhile Rome naturally rejected him. The Reformer, and all his partisans, whatever their rank and power, were anathematised, and deprived personally, as well as in their descendants, of all their dignities and effects. Every faithful Christian as he loved his soul's salvation was ordered to shun the sight of the accursed crew. Wherever heresy had been introduced, the priests were, on Sundays and festivals, at the hour when the churches were best filled, solemnly to publish the excommunication. They were to carry away the vessels and ornaments of the altar, and lay the cross upon the ground; twelve priests, with torches in their hands, were to kindle them and dash them down with violence, and extinguish them by trampling them with their feet ; then the bishop was to publish the condemnation of the impious men ; all the bells were to be rung ; the bishops and priests were to pronounce anathemas and maledictions, and preach forcibly against Luther and his adherents.

Twenty-two days had elapsed since the excommunication had been published at Rome, and it was perhaps not yet known in Germany, when Luther, learning that there was again some talk of calling him to Worms, addressed the Elector in a letter written in such terms that Frederick might communicate it to the Diet. Luther wished to correct the erroneous impression of the princes, and frankly explain to this august tribunal the true nature of a cause which was so much misapprehended. "I rejoice with all my heart, most serene lord," said he, "that his imperial majesty means to bring this affair under consideration. I call Jesus Christ to witness that it is the cause of Germany, of the Catholic Church, of the Christian world, and of God himself, ... and not of any single man, and more especially such a man as I.[3] I am ready to repair to Worms, provided I have a safe-conduct, and learned, pious, and

[1] Exodus, xxvi, 7, 14.   [2] So regete sich der Christus, dass sie so fest wurden dass der Teufel fliechen musste. (L. Op. ix, p. 613, on John, vi.)   [3] "Causam, quæ, Christo teste, Dei, Christiani orbis, Ecclesiæ Catholicæ, et totius Germaniæ Nationis, et non unius, et privati est hominis . . . . (L. Ep. i, p. 551.)

impartial judges. I am ready to answer, ... for it is not in a spirit of rashness, or with a view to personal advantage, that I have taught the doctrine with which I am reproached; I have done it in obedience to my conscience, and to the oath which, as doctor, I took to the Holy Scriptures; I have done it for the glory of God, the safety of the Christian Church, the good of the German nation, and the extirpation of many superstitions, abuses, and evils, disgrace, tyranny, blasphemy, and impiety."

This declaration, in the solemn circumstances in which Luther made it, is deserving of our attention. We here see the motives which influenced him, and the primary causes which led to the renovation of Christian society. These were something more than monkish jealousy or a wish to marry.

CHAP. II.

A Foreign Prince—Advice of Politicians—Conference between the Confessor and the Elector's Chancellor—Uselessness of these Manœuvres— Aleander's activity —Luther's Sayings—Charles gives in to the Pope.

But all this was of no importance in the eyes of politicians. How high soever the idea which Charles entertained of the imperial dignity, it was not in Germany that his interests and policy centred. He was always a Duke of Burgundy, who, to several sceptres, added the first crown of Christendom. Strange! at the moment of her thorough transformation, Germany selected for her head a foreign prince in whose eyes her wants and tendencies were only of secondary importance. The religious movement, it is true, was not indifferent to the young emperor; but it was important in his eyes only in so far as it menaced the pope. War between Charles and France was inevitable, and its chief seat was necessarily to be in Italy. An alliance with the pope thus became every day more necessary to the schemes of Charles. He would fain have either detached Frederick from Luther, or satisfied the pope without offending Frederick. Several of those about him manifested, in regard to the affairs of the Augustin monk, that cold disdain which politicians usually affect when religion is in question. " Let us avoid extremes," said they. " Let us trammel Luther by negotiations, and reduce him to silence by some kind of concession. The true course is to stifle the embers, not stir them up. If the monk is caught in the net, we have gained the day. By accepting a compromise he will be interdicted and undone. For appearance some external reforms will be devised ; the Elector will be satisfied ; the pope will be gained, and affairs will resume their ordinary course."

Such was the project of the confidential counsellors of the emperor. The doctors of Wittemberg seem to have divined this new policy. " They are trying in secret to gain men's minds," said Melancthon, " and are working in darkness."[1]   John Glapio, the confessor of Charles V,—a man of rank, a skilful courtier, and an intriguing monk,—undertook the execution of the project.   Glapio possessed the entire confidence of Charles, who (in accordance with Spanish manners) left to him almost entirely the management of matters relating to religion. As soon as Charles was appointed emperor, Leo X had assiduously endeavoured to gain Glapio by favours to which the confessor was strongly alive.[2]   There was no way in which he could make a better return to the pope's kindness than by reducing heresy to silence, and he accordingly set about the task.[3]

One of the Elector's counsellors was Chancellor Gregory Bruck, or Pontanus, a man of great intelligence, decision, and courage, who knew more of theology than all the doctors, and whose wisdom was a match for the wiles of the monks at the emperor's court. Glapio, aware of the influence of the chancellor, asked an interview with him ; and coming up to him as if he had been the friend of the Reformer, said to him, with an expression of good will, " I was delighted when, on reading the first productions of Luther, I found him a vigorous stock, which had pushed forth noble branches, and which gave promise to the Church of the most precious fruits. Several before him, it is true, made the same discoveries : still none but he has had the noble courage to publish the truth without fear.   But when I read his book on the *Captivity of Babylon*, I felt as if beaten and bruised from head to foot." " I don't believe," added the monk, " that Luther acknowledges himself to be the author. I do not find in it either his style or his science. . . . . . " After some discussion, the confessor continued, " Introduce me to the Elector, and I will, in your presence, explain to him the errors of Luther."

The chancellor replied, " That the business of the Diet did not leave any leisure to his Highness, who, moreover, did not meddle with the affair." The monk was vexed when his request was denied. " By the way," said the chancellor, " as you say there is no evil without a remedy, will you explain yourself ? "

[1] " Clanculum tentent et experiantur . . . " (Corp. Reform. i, p. 281, 3rd Feb.)·
[2] " Benignis officiis recens a Pontifice delinitus." (Pallavicini, i, p. 90.)
[3] " Et sane in eo toto negotio singulare probitatis ardorisque specimen dedit." (Ibid.)· And assuredly in the whole business he gave singular proof of probity and zeal.

Assuming a confidential air, the confessor replied: "The emperor earnestly desires to see such a man as Luther reconciled to the Church, for his books (before the publication of his treatise, 'On the Captivity of Babylon,') rather pleased his Majesty.[1] . . . . It must doubtless have been Luther's rage at the bull which dictated that work. Let him declare that he did not wish to disturb the peace of the Church, and the learned of all nations will rally around him. . . . . . Procure me an audience of his Highness."

The chancellor waited upon Frederick. The Elector being well aware that any kind of recantation was impossible replied, " Tell the confessor that I cannot comply with his request, but do you continue the conference."

Glapio received this message with great demonstrations of respect ; and changing the attack, said, " Let the Elector name some confidential persons to deliberate on this affair."

Chancellor.—" The Elector does not profess to defend the cause of Luther."

Confessor.—" Very well, do you at least discuss it with me. . . . Jesus Christ is my witness, that all I do is from love to the Church, and to Luther who has opened so many hearts to the truth."[2]

The chancellor having refused to undertake what was the Reformer's own task, was preparing to retire.

" Stay !" said the monk to him.

Chancellor.—" What then is to be done ?"

Confessor.—" Let Luther deny that he is the author of the Captivity of Babylon."

Chancellor.—" But the papal bull condemns all his other works."

Confessor.—" It is because of his obstinacy. If he retracts his book, the pope, in the plenitude of his power, can easily restore him to favour. What hopes may we not cherish now that we have so excellent an emperor ! . . . ."

Perceiving that these words made some impression on the chancellor, the monk hastened to add—" Luther always insists on arguing from the Bible. The Bible ! . . . it is like wax, and may be stretched and bent at pleasure. I undertake to find in the Bible opinions still more extraordinary than those of Luther. He is mistaken when he converts all the sayings of Jesus into commandments." Then, wishing to work also on the fears of the chancellor, he added, " What would happen if to-day or to-morrow the Emperor were to try the effect of arms? . . . . Think of it." He then allowed Pontanus to retire.

---

[1] " Es haben dessen Bücher Ihro Majestät . . . um et was gefallen. . . . " (Archives Weimar. Seckend. p. 315.) [2] Der andern das Herts zu vielem Guten eroffnet . . (Secken. p. 315.)

The confessor prepared new snares. "After living ten years with him," said Erasmus, "we should not know him."

"What an excellent book that of Luther's on 'Christian Liberty,'" said he to the chancellor when he saw him a few days after—"what wisdom! what talent! what intellect! it is just the style in which a true scholar ought to write. Let unexceptionable persons be chosen on either side, and let the pope and Luther refer to their judgment. No doubt Luther has the best of it on several articles.[1] I will speak to the emperor himself on the subject. Believe me, I do not say these things to you on my own suggestion. I have told the emperor that God will chastise him, as well as all the princes, if the Church, which is the spouse of Jesus Christ, is not washed from all the stains by which she is polluted. I have added that God himself had raised up Luther, and had ordered him to rebuke men sharply, using him as a rod to punish the sins of the world."[2]

The chancellor hearing these words, (they convey the impressions of the time, and show what was then thought of Luther even by his opponents,) thought it right to express his astonishment that more respect was not shown to his master. "Deliberations on this subject," said he, "are daily carried on before the emperor, and the Elector is not invited to them. It seems strange that the emperor, who owes him some gratitude, excludes him from his counsels."

Confessor.—"I have been present only once at these deliberations, and I have heard the emperor resist the solicitations of the nuncios. Five years hence it will be seen how much Charles shall have done for the reformation of the Church."

"The Elector," replied Pontanus, "is ignorant of the emperor's intentions: He should be invited that he may hear them stated."

The confessor answered with a deep sigh,[4] "I call God to witness how ardently I desire to see the Reformation of Christendom accomplished."

To lengthen out the affair, and meanwhile keep Luther's mouth shut, was all that Glapio had in view. At all events, Luther must not come to Worms. A dead man returning from the other world, and appearing in the midst of the Diet, would not have alarmed the nuncios, and monks, and whole host of the pope, so much as the sight of the Wittemberg doctor.

"How many days does it take to come from Wittemberg to

---

[1] Es sey nicht zu zweifeln dass Lutherus in vielen Artickeln werde den Sieg davon tragen . . . . (Seckend., p. 319.)　[2] Dass Gott diesen Mann gesandt, ... dass er eine Geissel seye um der Sünden willen. (Weimar Archiv.—Seckend., p. 320.)
[4] Glapio that hierauf einen tiefen Seufzer, un rufte Gott zum Zeugen. . . . (Seckend. p. 321.)

— Worms ?" asked the monk at the chancellor, affecting an air of indifference ; then begging Pontanus to present his very humble respects to the Elector, he departed.

Such were the manœuvres of the courtiers. The firmness of Pontanus outwitted them. This upright man was immovable as a rock in all negotiations. Moreover, the Roman monks fell into the very snares which they were laying for their enemies. "The Christian," says Luther, in his figurative language, "is like a bird fastened near a trap. The wolves and foxes go round and round, and make a dart upon it to devour it, but fall into the pit and perish, while the timid bird remains alive. Thus holy angels guard us, and devouring wolves, hypocrites, and persecutors, cannot do us any harm."[1] Not only were the confessor's artifices unavailing, but, moreover, his admissions confirmed Frederick in the belief that Luther was in the right, and that it was his duty to defend him.

The hearts of men became every day more inclined towards the gospel. A prior of the Dominicans proposed that the emperor, the kings of France, Spain, England, Portugal, Hungary, and Poland, the pope, and the electors, should name representatives by whom the matter should be decided. "Never," said he, "has reference been made to the pope alone."[2] The general feeling became such, that it seemed impossible to condemn Luther without a hearing and regular conviction.[3]

Aleander became uneasy, and displayed more than wonted energy. It is no longer merely against the Elector and Luther that he has to contend. He is horrified at the secret negotiations of the confessor, the proposition of the prior, the consent of Charles' ministers, and the extreme coldness of Roman piety among the most devoted friends of the pope, "so that one would have thought," says Pallavicini, "that a torrent of ice had passed over them."[4] He had at length received gold and silver from Rome, and held in his hand energetic briefs addressed to the most powerful personages in the empire.[5] Afraid that his prey might escape, he felt that now was the time to strike a decisive blow. He despatched the briefs, showered gold and silver with liberal hand, dealt out the most enticing promises, "and provided," says the Cardinal historian, "with this triple weapon, he strove anew to turn the wavering assembly of the electors in favour of the pope."[6] He laboured

[1] L. Op. (W.) xxii, 1655.)   [2] Und niemals dem Papst allein geglaubt. (Seck., p. 323.)   [3] Spalatinus scribit tantum favoris Evangelio esse istic, ut me inauditum et inconvictum damnari non speret. (L. Ep. i, p. 556, 9th Feb.) Spalatin writes that the gospel is so much in favour there that he hopes I cannot be condemned unheard and unconvicted.   [4] Hinc aqua manabat, quæ successæ pictatis æstum restinguebat. (Pallavicini, i, p. 96.) Hence flowed water which extinguished the flame of piety.   [5] Mandata, pecuniæ ac diplomata. (Ibid. p. 95.)   [6] Triplici hac industria nunc Aleander.   . (Ibid.)

above all to encircle the emperor with his snares. Availing himself of the differences between the Belgian and the Spanish ministers, he laid close siege to the prince. All the friends of Rome,
awakened by his voice, urged young Charles with solicitations.
" Every day," wrote the Elector to his brother John, " deliberations are held against Luther : the demand is that he be put under
the ban of the pope and the emperor ; in all sorts of ways attempts
are made to hurt him. Those who parade about with their red
hats, the Romans with all their sect, labour in the task with indefatigable zeal." [1]

In fact, Aleander urged the condemnation of the Reformer with
a violence which Luther terms "marvellous fury." [2] The apostate-
nuncio,[3] as Luther calls him, hurried by passion beyond the bounds
of prudence, one day exclaimed, "If you mean, O Germans, to
shake off the yoke of Roman obedience, we will act so, that,
setting the one against the other, as an exterminating sword, you
will all perish in your own blood." [4] " Such," adds the Reformer,
" is the pope's method of feeding the sheep of Christ."

Luther himself spoke a very different language. He made no
demand of a personal nature. " Luther is ready," said Melancthon, " to purchase the glory and advancement of the gospel with
his life." [5] But he trembled at the thought of the disasters of
which his death might be the signal. He saw a people led astray,
and perhaps avenging his martyrdom in the blood of his enemies,
especially the priests. He recoiled from the fearful responsibility.
" God," said he, " arrests the fury of his enemies ; but should it
break forth, ... a storm will burst upon the priests similar to
that which ravaged Bohemia. . . . . I am clear of it ; for I have
earnestly besought the German nobility to arrest the Romans by
wisdom, and not by the sword.[6] To war upon priests, a body
without courage and strength, is to war upon women and children."

Charles did not withstand the solicitations of the nuncio. His
Belgian and Spanish devotion had been developed by his preceptor
Adrian, who afterwards occupied the pontifical throne. The pope
had addressed a brief to him imploring him to give legal effect to the
bull by an imperial edict. " In vain," said he to him, " shall God
have invested you with the sword of supreme power if you do not
employ it both against infidels, and also against heretics, who are far
worse than infidels." One day, accordingly, in the beginning of

<hr>

[1] Das thun die in rothen Hüten prangen. (Seck., 364.)   [2] Miro furore Papistæ
moliuntur mihi mala. . . . . (L. Ep. i, p. 556.)   [3] Nuntius *apostaticus* (a play on
the word *apostolicus*) agit summis viribus. (Ibid., p. 569.)   [4] Ut mutuis cædibus
aosumpti vestro cruore pereatis. (Ibid., p. 556.)   [5] Libenter etiam morte sua
Evangelii gloriam et profectum emerit. (Corp. Ref. i, p. 285.)   [6] Non ferro, sed
consiliis et edictis. (L. Ep. i, p. 563.)

February, at the moment when every thing was ready at Worms for a brilliant tournament, and after the emperor's tent had actually been erected, the princes who were preparing to attend the fête were summoned to repair to the imperial palace. There the papal bull was read to them, and they were presented with a stringent edict enjoining the execution of it. "If you have any thing better to propose," added the emperor in the usual form, "I am ready to hear you."

Animated debates then began in the diet. "The monk," wrote the deputy of one of the German free towns, "gives us a great deal to do. Some would like to crucify him, and I don't think that he will escape : the only thing to be feared is that he may rise again on the third day." The emperor had thought he would be able to publish his edict without opposition on the part of the States, but it was not so. Men's minds were not prepared, and it was necessary to gain the Diet. "Convince this assembly," said the young monarch to the nuncio. This was just what Alean-der desired, and he received a promise of being admitted to the Diet on the 13th February.

CHAP. III.

Aleander admitted to the Diet—Aleander's Address—Luther accused—Rome defended —Appeal to Charles against Luther—Effect of the Nuncio's Address.

The nuncio prepared for the solemn audience. The task was important, but Aleander was worthy of it. The ambassador of the sovereign pontiff was surrounded with all the splendour of his office ; he was moreover one of the most eloquent men of his age. The friends of the Reformation looked forward to the sitting not without fear. The Elector, under the pretext of indisposition, kept away, but he ordered some of his counsellors to attend and give heed to the nuncio's address.

On the appointed day, Aleander proceeded to the hall of the as-sembled princes. Men's minds were excited ; several thought of Annas or Caiaphas repairing to Pilate's judgment hall to demand the life of him who was "*perverting the nation.*"[1] At the moment when the nuncio was about to step across the threshold, the officer of the Diet (says Pallavicini,) came briskly up to him, took him by the breast, and shoved him back."[2] "He was a Lutheran at heart," adds the Roman historian. If the story is true, it doubt-less betrays strange passion in the officer, but at the same time, gives an idea of the powerful influence which Luther's doctrine

[1] Luke, xxiii, 2.　　[2] "Pugnis ejus pectori admotis repulerit. (Pallavicini, i, p. 112.)

had produced even on the doorkeepers of the Imperial Council.
Proud Aleander, haughtily drawing himself up, moved on and
entered the hall. Never had Rome been called to make her apo-
logy before so august an assembly. The nuncio placed before him
the judicial documents which he judged necessary, the works of
Luther, and the papal bulls. Silence being called, he spoke as ·
follows :—

" Most august emperor!—most puissant princes!—most excellent
deputies! I come before you to maintain a cause for which my
heart burns with the most ardent affection. The subject is the
preservation on my master's head of that tiara which is reverenced
by all, the maintenance of that papal throne, for which I am ready
to give my body to the flames, could the monster who has engendered the growing heresy be consumed by the same pile, and
mingle his ashes with mine.[1]

" No! the disagreement between Luther and Rome turns not
on the interests of the pope. Luther's books are before me, and
any man with eyes in his head may perceive that the holy doctrines of the Church are the object of his attack. He teaches
that those only communicate worthily whose consciences are filled
with sadness and confusion for their sins, and that there is no
justification in baptism, without faith in the promise of which baptism is the pledge.[2] He denies the necessity of our works to obtain
celestial glory. He denies that we have liberty and power to observe natural and divine law. He affirms that we sin necessarily in
all our actions. Did ever the arsenal of hell send forth arrows better
fitted to loose the reins of modesty? . . . He preaches the abolition
of religious vows. Can more sacrilegious impiety be imagined? . . .
What desolation will not be seen in the world when those who
ought to be the leaven of the people shall have thrown aside
their sacred vestments, abandoned the temples which re-echoed
with their holy hymns, and plunged into adultery, incest, and
dissoluteness! . . .

" Shall I enumerate all the crimes of this audacious monk? He
sins against the dead, for he denies purgatory; he sins against
heaven, for he says, he would not believe an angel from heaven;
he sins against the Church, for he pretends that all Christians are

[1] " Dummodo mecum una monstrum nascentis hæresis arderet." (Pallavicini, i, p.
97.) Seckendorff, and after him several Protestant historians, insist that Pallavicini
himself composed the address which he puts in the mouth of Aleander. It is true
the Cardinal historian states, that he gave it the form in which it appears ; but he
intimates the sources from which he drew it, particularly the letters of Aleander
deposited in the archives of the Vatican. (Acta Wormatiæ, fol. 66 and 99.) I think,
therefore, that to reject it altogether would betray partiality. I have collected som
additional passages of the speech from other sources, Protestant and Romish. . .
[2] " Baptismum neminem justificare, sed fidem in verbum promissionis cui additur
Baptismus." (Cochlœus, Act. Luth. 28.) That no man is justified by baptism, but
only by faith, in the word of the promise to which baptism is annexed.

priests ; he sins against the saints, for he despises their venerable writings ; he sins against the councils, for he terms that of Constance an assembly of demons ; he sins against the world, for he forbids the punishment of death to be inflicted on any one who has not committed a mortal sin.[1] Some say he is a pious man . . . I have no wish to attack his life, I would only remind this assembly that the devil deceives men by semblances of truth."

Aleander having spoken of the condemnation of purgatory by the council of Florence, laid the papal bull on this council at the feet of the emperor. The archbishop of Mentz took it up and handed it to the archbishops of Cologne and Treves, who received it reverently, and passed it to the other princes. The nuncio, having thus accused Luther, now proceeded to the second point, which was to justify Rome.

" At Rome," says Luther, " they promise one thing with the lip and do its opposite with the hand. If this fact is true, must not; the inference be the very reverse of what he draws from it ? If the ministers of a religion live conformably to its precepts it is a proof that it is false. Such was the religion of the ancient Romans . . Such is that of Mahomet, and that of Luther himself ; but such is not the religion which the pontiffs of Rome teach us. Yes, the doctrine which they confess condemns all as faulty, several as culpable, and some even (I say it candidly) as criminal.[2] . . . This doctrine delivers their actions to the censure of men during their life, and to historical infamy after their death.[3] Now what pleasure, what advantage, I ask, could the pontiffs have found in inventing such a religion ?

" The Church, it will be said, was not governed in primitive times by Roman pontiffs—What must the conclusion be ? With such arguments they might persuade men to live on acorns, and princesses to be their own washerwomen.'

But it was against his adversary, the Reformer, that the nuncio chiefly directed his attack. Full of indignation against those who said that he ought to be heard, he exclaimed, " Luther will not allow any one to instruct him. The pope summoned him to Rome, but he did not obey. The pope summoned him to Augsburg before his legate, and he would not appear without a safe-conduct from the emperor, i. e. until the hands of the legate were tied, and nothing left free to him but his tongue.[4] " Ah !" said Aleander, turning towards Charles V, " I supplicate your imperial majesty

[1] " Weil er verbiete jemand mit Todes Strafe zu belegen der nicht ein Todtsünde begangen." (Seckend. p. 333.) [2] " Multos ut quadantenus reos, nonnullos (dicam ingenuè) ut scelestos." (Pallavicini, i, p. 101.) [3] " Linguarum vituperationi dum vivunt, historiarum infaminæ post mortem. (Ibid.) [4] Quod idem erat, ac revincti legati brachiis et lingua solum soluta." (Ibid. p. 109.)

not to do what would issue in disgrace. Interfere not with a matter of which laics have no right to take cognisance. Do your own
work. Let Luther's doctrine be interdicted throughout the empire:
let his writings be everywhere burnt. Fear not: there is enough
in the writings of Luther to burn a hundred thousand heretics.[1]
. . . And what have we to fear? . . . The populace? Before the
battle they seem terrible from their insolence ; in the battle they
are contemptible from their cowardice. Foreign princes? The
king of France has prohibited Luther's doctrine from entering his
kingdom, while the king of Great Britain is preparing a blow for it
with his royal hand. You know what the feelings of Hungary, Italy,
and Spain are, and none of your neighbours, how great soever the
enmity he may bear to yourself, wishes you any thing so bad as
this heresy. If the house of our enemy is adjacent to our own we
may wish him fever, but not pestilence. . . . Who are all these Lutherans? A huddle of insolent grammarians, corrupt priests, disorderly monks, ignorant advocates, degraded nobles, common people
misled and perverted. Is not the Catholic party far more numerous, able, and powerful? A unanimous decree of this assembly
will enlighten the simple, give warning to the imprudent, determine those who are hesitating, and confirm the feeble. . . . But if
the axe is not laid to the root of this poisonous shrub, if the fatal
stroke is not given to it, then . . . . I see it covering the heritage
of Jesus Christ with its branches, changing the vineyard of the
Lord into a howling forest, transforming the kingdom of God into
a den of wild beasts, and throwing Germany into the frightful state
of barbarism and desolation to which Asia has been reduced by
the superstition of Mahomet."

The nuncio ceased. He had spoken for three hours. The torrent of his eloquence had moved the assembly. " The princes
shaken and alarmed," says Cochlœus, " looked at each other; and
murmurs were soon heard from different quarters against Luther
and his partisans.[2] Had the mighty Luther been present,
had he been permitted to answer the discourse, had he, availing
himself of the concession forced from the Roman orator by the
remembrance of his old master, the infamous Borgia, been permitted to show that these arguments, designed to defend Rome,
constituted her condemnation, and that the doctrine which gave
proof of her iniquity was not invented by him, as the orator said,
but was the very religion which Christ had given to the world, and
which the reformation was establishing in its primitive lustre,

---

[1] Dass 100,000 Ketzer ihrenthalben verbrannt werden. (Seckend. p. 332.)
[2] Vehementer exterriti atque commoti, alter alterum intuebantur, atque in Lutherum ejusque fautores murmurare cœperunt. (Cochl., p. 28.)

could he have presented an exact and animated picture of the errors and abuses of the papacy, and shown how it had perverted the religion of Jesus Christ into an instrument of aggrandisement and rapine,—the effect of the nuncio's harangue would have been neutralised at the moment of its delivery ; but nobody rose to speak. The assembly remained under the impression of the address, and, excited and carried away, showed themselves ready violently to eradicate the heresy of Luther from the soil of the empire.[1]

Still the victory was only apparent. It was the will of God that Rome should have an opportunity of displaying her reasons and her strength. The greatest of her orators had addressed the assembled princes, and said all that Rome had to say. But the last effort of the papacy was the very thing which was destined to become, in regard to several of those who witnessed it, the signal of her defeat. If, in order to secure the triumph of truth, it is necessary to proclaim it aloud, so in order to secure the destruction of error, it is sufficient to publish it without reserve. Neither the one nor the other, in order to accomplish its course, should be concealed. The light judges all things.

CHAP. IV.

Sentiments of the Princes—Speech of Duke George—Character of the Reformation —A hundred and one grievances—Charles yields—Tactics of Aleander—The Grandees of Spain—Luther's peace—Death and not Retractation.

A few days sufficed to wear off these first impressions, as always happens when an orator shrouds the emptiness of his arguments in high sounding phrases.

The majority of the princes were ready to sacrifice Luther, but none were disposed to sacrifice the rights of the empire and the redress of German grievances. There was no objection to give up the insolent monk who had dared to speak so loud, but it was wished to make the pope so much the more sensible of the justice of a reform which was demanded by the heads of the kingdom. Accordingly, it was the greatest personal enemy of Luther, Duke George of Saxony, who spoke most energetically against the encroachments of Rome. The grandson of Podiebrad, King of Bohemia, repulsed by the doctrines of grace which the Reformer proclaimed, had not yet abandoned the hope of seeing a

---

[1] Lutheranam hæresin esse funditus evellendam. (Pallavicini, i, p. 101, Roscoe's Life of Leo X, p. 50.)

moral and ecclesiastical reform, and what irritated him so much
against the monk of Wittemberg, was that he had spoiled the
whole affair by his despised doctrines. But now, seeing the nuncio
sought to confound Luther and reform in one common condemnation,
George suddenly stood up among the assembled princes, and, to
the great astonishment of those who knew his hatred to the Reformer, said, "The Diet must not forget the grievances of which it
complains against the Court of Rome. What abuses have crept
into our states! The annats which the emperor granted freely
for the good of Christendom now demanded as a debt—the Roman
courtiers every day inventing new ordinances, in order to absorb,
sell, and farm out ecclesiastical benefices—a multitude of trans-
gressions winked at; rich offenders unworthily tolerated, while
those who have no means of ransom are punished without pity—
the popes incessantly bestowing expectancies and reversions on
the inmates of their palace, to the detriment of those to whom
the benefices belong—the commendams of abbeys and convents of Rome conferred on cardinals, bishops, and prelates, who
appropriate their revenues, so that there is not one monk in convents which ought to have twenty or thirty—stations multiplied
without end, and indulgence shops established in all the streets and
squares of our cities, shops of St. Anthony, shops of the Holy
Spirit, of St. Hubert, of St. Cornelius, of St. Vincent, and many
others besides—societies purchasing from Rome the right of holding such markets, then purchasing from their bishop the right of
exhibiting their wares, and, in order to procure all this money,
draining and emptying the pockets of the poor—the indulgences
which ought to be granted solely for the salvation of souls, and
which ought to be merited only by prayers, fastings, and the salvation of souls, sold at a regular price—the officials of the bishop,.
oppressing those in humble life with penances for blasphemy, adultery, debauchery, the violation of this or that feast day, while, at
the same time, not even censuring ecclesiastics who are guilty
of the same crimes—penances imposed on the penitent, and artfully
arranged, so that he soon falls anew into the same fault, and pays so
much the more money.[1]... Such are some of the crying abuses of
Rome; all sense of shame has been cast off, and one thing only is
pursued... money! money! Hence preachers who ought to teach
the truth, now do nothing more than retail lies—lies, which are
not only tolerated, but recompensed, because the more they lie, the
more they gain. From this polluted well comes forth all this
polluted water. Debauchery goes hand in hand with avarice.

---

[1] Sondern dass er est bald wieder begehe und mehr Geld erlegen musse. (Archives.
of Weimar, Seckend p. 398.)

The officials cause women to come to their houses under divers pretexts, and strive to seduce them, sometimes by menaces, sometimes by presents; or, if they cannot succeed, injure them in their reputation.[1] Ah! the scandals caused by the clergy precipitate multitudes of poor souls into eternal condemnation! There must be a universal reform, and this reform must be accomplished by summoning a general Council. Wherefore, most excellent princes and lords, with submission I implore you to lose no time in the consideration of this matter." Several days after Aleander's address, Duke George produced the list of grievances which he had enumerated. This important document is preserved in the archives of Weimar.

Luther had not spoken more forcibly against the abuses of Rome but he had done something more. The duke pointed out the evil, Luther had, along with the evil, pointed out both the cause and the cure. He had shown that the sinner receives the true indulgence, that which comes from God, solely by faith in the grace and merits of Jesus Christ, and this simple but powerful doctrine had overturned all the markets established by the priests. "How can one become pious?" asked he one day. "A Cordelier will reply Pii on a grey hood, and tie a cord round your waist. A Roman will reply, Hear mass, and fast. But a Christian will say, Faith in Christ alone justifies and saves. Before works we must have eternal life. After we are born anew, and made children of God by the word of grace, then it is we do good works." [2]

The duke spoke the language of a secular prince—Luther. the language of a reformer. The great sore of the Church was that she had devoted herself entirely to externals; had made all her works and her graces to consist of outward and material things. Indulgences had carried this to its extreme point, and pardon, the most spiritual thing in Christianity, had been purchased in shops like meat and drink. The great work of Luther consisted in his availing himself of this extreme point in the degeneracy of Christendom; in order to bring back the individual and the Church to the primitive source of life, and to re-establish the reign of the Holy Spirit within the sanctuary of the heart. Here, as often happens, the cure sprung out of the disease, and the two extremes met. Henceforward the Church, which during so many ages had been developed externally by ceremonies, observances, and human practices, began again to be developed within by faith, hope, and charity.

The duke's address produced the greater effect from his opposition to Luther being well known. Other members of the Diet

[1] Dass sie Weibesbilder unter mancherley schein beschicken, selbige sodann mit Drohungen und Geschenken su fällen suchen, oder in einen bösen verdacht bringen. (Weimar Arch. Seck., p. 330.)   [2] L. Op. (W.) xxii, 743-752.

stated different grievances. The ecclesiastical princes themselves supported these complaints.[1] "We have a pontiff," said they, "who spends his life in hunting and pleasure. The benefices of Germany are given at Rome to huntsmen, domestics, grooms, stable boys, body servants, and other people of that class, ignorant unpolished people, without capacity, and entire strangers to Germany."[2] The Diet appointed a commission to collect all these grievances. Their number was found to be a hundred and one. A deputation, consisting of secular and ecclesiastical princes, presented the list to the emperor, imploring him to give redress, as he had engaged to do at his election. "How many Christian souls are lost?" said they to Charles V. "How many depredations, how much extortion, are caused by the scandals with which the spiritual chief of Christendom is environed? The ruin and dishonour of our people must be prevented. Therefore, we all, in a body, supplicate you most humbly, but also most urgently, to ordain a general reformation, to undertake it, and to accomplish it."[3] There was, at this time, in Christian society, an unseen power influencing princes and their subjects, a wisdom from above dragging forward even the adversaries of the Reformation, and preparing that emancipation whose appointed hour had at length arrived.

Charles could not be insensible to these remonstrances of the empire. Neither himself nor the nuncio had expected them. His confessor had even denounced the vengeance of Heaven against him if he did not reform the Church. The emperor immediately withdrew the edict which ordered Luther's writings to be committed to the flames in every part of the empire, and in its place substituted a provisional order remitting these books to the magistrates.

This did not satisfy the assembly, who were desirous that the Reformer should appear. It is unjust, said his friends, to condemn Luther without having heard him, and without knowing from himself whether he is the author of the books which are proposed to be burnt. His doctrine, said his opponents, has so taken possession of men's hearts, that it is impossible to arrest their progress without hearing him. There need be no discussion with him. If he avows his writings, and refuses to retract them, then all of us, electors, princes, states of the whole empire, true to the faith of our ancestors, will, in a body, aid your majesty, by all the means in our power, in the execution of your decrees.[4]

[1] Seckend. Vorrede von Frick.   [2] Bücksenmeistern, Falknern, Pfistern, Eseltreibern, Stallknechten, Trabanten . . . (Kapp's Nachlese nützl Ref. Urkunden, iii, p. 262.)   [3] Dass eine Besserung und gemeine Reformation geschehe. (Ibid., p. 275.)   [4] L. Op. (L.) xxii, p. 567.

Aleander, alarmed, dreading both the intrepidity of Luther and the ignorance of the princes, immediately set himself to the task of preventing the Reformer's compearance. He went from the ministers of Charles to the princes who were most disposed to favour the pope, and from these princes to the emperor himself.[1] "It is unlawful," said he, "to bring into question what the sovereign pontiff has decided. There will be no discussion with Luther, you say ; but continued he, will not the power of this audacious man, will not the fire of his eye, and the eloquence of his tongue, and the mysterious spirit which animates him, be sufficient to excite some sedition ?[2] Several already venerate him as a saint, and you everywhere meet with his portrait surrounded with a halo of glory, as round the head of the Blessed. If it is determined to cite him, at least let it be without giving him the protection of public faith."[3] These last words were meant to frighten Luther, or prepare his ruin.

The nuncio found easy access to the grandees of Spain. In Spain, as in Germany, the opposition to the Dominican inquisitors was national. The yoke of the inquisition, which had been discontinued for a time, had just been re-established by Charles. A numerous party in the Peninsula sympathised with Luther ; but it was not so with the great, who, on the banks of the Rhine, again met with what they had hated beyond the Pyrenees. Inflamed with the most violent fanaticism, they were bent on annihilating the new heresy. In particular, Frederick, Duke of Alba, was transported with rage whenever the subject of Reformation was mooted.[4] His wish would have been to wade in the blood of all its adherents. Luther had not yet been called to appear, and yet his mere name was already agitating all the grandees of Christendom then assembled at Worms.

The man who was thus agitating the mighty of the earth was the only one who seemed to be at peace. The news from Worms were alarming. Even. Luther's friends were frightened. "Nothing now is left us but our wishes and our prayers," wrote Melancthon to Spalatin. "Oh l if God would deign to ransom the safety of the Christian people by my blood."[5] But Luther was a stranger to fear. Shutting himself up in his peaceful cell, he sat down to meditate, applying to himself the words of Mary, the mother of our Lord, when she exclaimed, "*My soul doth magnify the Lord, and my spirit hath rejoiced in God my Saviour. For he that is mighty has done for me*

<hr>

[1] Quam ob rem sedulo contestatus est apud Cæsaris administ os . . . (Pallavicini, i, p. 113.) [2] Lingua promptus, ardore vultus, et oris spiritu ad concitandam seditionem . . . (Ibid.) [3] Haud certe fidem publicam illi præbendam . . . (Ibid.) [4] Albæ dux videbatur aliquando furentibus modis agitari . . . (Pallavicini, i, p. 362.) [5] Utinam Deus redimat nostro sanguine salutem Christiani populi. (Corp. Ref. i, p. 362.)

great things, and holy is His name. He has shown strength with his arm; he hath put down the mighty from their seats, and exalted them of low degree."[1] The following are some of the thoughts which filled Luther's heart ... " 'He that is mighty,' says Mary. Oh! how great boldness on the part of a young girl! With a single word she strikes all the strong with languor, all the mighty with feebleness, all the wise with folly, and all those whose name is glorious on the earth with ignominy, and lays at the feet of God all strength, all power, all wisdom, all glory.[2] 'His arm,' continues she, and she thus appeals to that power by which he acts of himself, and without the agency of his creatures—a mysterious power operating in secrecy and in silence, until his purpose is accomplished. Hence destruction comes before any one is aware of its approach; hence elevation, when no one is thinking of it. He leaves his children in oppression and feebleness, so that each of them says to himself, ' We are all lost!' Then, however, they are most strong. For it is where the power of man ends that the power of God begins. Only let faith wait upon Him ... And, on the other hand, God permits his adversaries to increase their power and grandeur. He withdraws from them the aid of his strength, and leaves them to be inflated with their own.[3] He leaves them void of his eternal wisdom, and lets them fill themselves with their wisdom of a day. And while they rise up in the greatness of their might, the arm of the Lord keeps back, and their work ... vanishes like a soap bubble when it bursts in the air."

It was on the 10th of March, at the moment when his name was filling the imperial city with alarm, that Luther finished this exposition of the Magnificat.

He was not allowed to remain tranquil in his retreat. Spalatin, in conformity to the orders of the Elector, sent him a note of the articles of which it was proposed to demand a retractation from him. A retractation after the refusal at Augsburg![4] .... "Fear not," he wrote to Spalatin, " that I will retract a single syllable, since their only argument is to insist that my writings are opposed to the rites of what they call the Church. If the Emperor Charles summon me merely for the purpose of retracting, I will answer him that I will remain here ; and it will be just the same thing as if I had been to Worms and come back again. But if, on the contrary, the emperor chooses to summon me in order that I may be put to death, I am ready to repair at his call ; for, with the help of Christ, I will not desert his word on the battle-field. I know it :

[1] Luke, i, 46-55.　　　[2] *Magnificat.* L. Op. Wittemberg, Deutsch. Ausg. iii, p. 11, etc.　　[3] Er zieht seine Krafft heraus und laesst sie von eigener Krafft sich aufblasen. (L. Op. Wittemb. Deutsch. Ausg. iii, pp. 11, etc.)　　　[4] Si ad me occidendum deinceps vocare velit. . . offeram me venturum. (L. Ep. i, p. 574.)

these bloody men will never rest till they have deprived me of life Oh, that none but papists would become guilty of my blood!"

CHAP. V.

Will a Safe-conduct be given ?—Safe-conduct—Will Luther go ?—Holy Thursday at Rome—The Pope and Luther.

At length the emperor decided. The appearance of Luther before the Diet seemed the only thing fitted to bring this affair which occupied the whole empire, to some kind of termination. Charles V resolved to cite him, but without giving him a safe-conduct. Here Frederick again began to act as his protector. Every body saw the danger which threatened the Reformer. Luther's friends, says Cochlœus, were afraid that he would be delivered up to the pope, or that the emperor himself would put him to death as unworthy, on account of his obstinate heresy, that any faith should be kept with him.[1] On this subject there was a long and keen debate among the princes.[2] Struck, at last, with the general agitation then prevailing almost throughout the whole population of Germany, and afraid that, as Luther passed along, some sudden tumult or dangerous sedition might break forth,[3] (doubtless in favour of the Reformer,) the princes deemed it wise to calm men's minds on his account, and not only the emperor, but also the Elector of Saxony, Duke George, and the Landgrave of Hesse, through whose states he had to pass, each gave him a safe-conduct.

On the 6th March, 1521, Charles V signed the following summons addressed to Luther :—

" Charles, by the grace of God, elected Roman Emperor, always Augustus, etc., etc.

" Honourable, dear, and pious! We, and the States of the Holy Empire, having resolved to make an inquest touching the doctrine and the books which you have published for some time past have given you, to come here and return to a place of safety our safe-conduct and that of the empire here subjoined. Our sincere desire is that you immediately prepare for this journey, in order that, in the space of twenty-one days mentioned in our safe-conduct you may be here certainly, and without fail. Have no apprehension of either injustice or violence. We will firmly enforce our safe-conduct under-written, and we expect that you

[1] Tanquam perfido hæretico nulla sit servanda fides. (Cochlœus, p. 28.)
[2] " Longa consultatio difficilisque disceptatio." (Ibid.) · [3] Cum autem grandis -abique per Germaniam fere totam excitata esset . . . animorum commotio." (Ibid.)

will answer to our call. In so doing you will follow our serious advice.

"Given at our imperial city of Worms, the sixth day of March, in the year of our Lord, 1521, and in the second of our reign.

"CHARLES.

"By order of my Lord the Emperor, with his own hand, Albert, Cardinal of Mentz, Arch-chancellor.   *Nicolas Zwyl.*"

The safe-conduct enclosed in this letter bore the following address:—"*To the honourable, our dear and pious doctor Martin Luther, of the order of the Augustins.*"

It began thus:—

"We, Charles, fifth of the name, by the grace of God, elected Roman Emperor, always Augustus, King of Spain, of the Two Sicilies, of Jerusalem, Hungary, Dalmatia, Croatia, etc., Arch-Duke of Austria, Duke of Burgundy, Count of Hapsburg, Flanders, the Tyrol, etc., etc."

Then the king of so many nations giving to wit that he had summoned before him an Augustin monk named Luther, ordered all princes, lords, magistrates, and others, to respect the safe-conduct which he gave him, under pain of punishment by the emperor and the empire.[1]

Thus the emperor gave the title of "dear, honourable, and pious," to a man at whose head the Church had launched her excommunication. It had been wished, in the drawing up of the document, to remove all distrust from the mind of Luther and his friends. Gaspard Sturm was appointed to carry this message to the Reformer, and accompany him to Worms. The Elector, dreading the public indignation, wrote, on the 12th March, to the magistrates of Wittemberg to see to the safety of the emperor's officer, and, if deemed necessary, to provide him with a guard. The herald set out.

Thus the designs of God were accomplished. God was pleased to set upon a hill that light which he had kindled in the world, and emperors, kings, and princes, without knowing it, were forthwith in motion to execute his design. It is easy for him to exalt the lowest to the highest. An act of his power suffices to raise the humble child of Mansfeld from an obscure hut to the palace where kings are assembled. In regard to Him, there is nothing small, nothing great. When he wills it, Charles V and Luther meet face to face.

But will Luther obey this citation? His best friends were in doubt. The Elector on the 25th of March wrote his brother— "Doctor Martin is summoned hither, but I know not if he will

[1] Lucas Cranach's Stammbuch, etc., herausgegeben, v. Chr. v. Mecheln, p. 12.

come. I cannot augur any good of it." Three weeks later (16th April), this excellent prince seeing the danger increase wrote anew to Duke John. " There is a proclamation against Luther. The cardinals and bishops attack him with much severity. May God turn all to good. Would to God I could procure him an equitable reception !" [1]

While these things were passing at Worms and Wittemberg, the Papacy was reiterating its blows. On the 28th March, the Thursday before Easter, Rome resounded with a solemn excommunication. At this season it is usual to publish the dreadful bull *in Cœna Domini*, which is only a long series of imprecations. On that day, the avenues to the church in which the sovereign pontiff was to officiate were occupied at an early hour by the papal guards, and by a crowd of people who had flocked from all parts of Italy to receive the benediction of the holy father. The square in front of the Basilisk was decorated with branches of laurel and myrtle ; wax tapers were burning on the balcony of the church, and the ostensorium was raised upon it. All at once bells make the air re-echo with solemn sounds ; the pope, clothed in his pontifical robes, and carried in a chair, appears on the balcony ; the people kneel, all heads are uncovered, the colours are lowered, the muskets grounded, and a solemn silence reigns. Some moments after, the pope slowly stretches out his hands, raises them towards heaven, then bends them slowly towards the ground, making the sign of the cross. This movement is repeated thrice, and the air echoes anew with the ringing of bells, which intimate the pope's benediction to the surrounding country ; then priests advance with impetuosity, holding lighted torches, which they reverse, brandish, and throw about with violence, to represent the flames of hell ; the people are moved and agitated, and the words of malediction are heard from the height of the temple. [2]

When Luther was informed of this excommunication, he published the tenor of it, with some remarks, written in that caustic style in which he so much excelled. Although this publication did not appear till afterwards, we will here give some idea of it. Let us hear the high priest of Christendom on the balcony of his Basilisk, and the monk of Wittemberg answering him from the bosom of Germany. [3]

There is something characteristic in the contrast of the two voices.

[1] Die Cardinæle und Bischöfe sind ihm hart zuwieder . . . (Seckend, p. 365.)
[2] This ceremony is described in different works, among others—" Tagebuch einer Reise durch Deutschland und Italien." (Berlin, 1817, iv, p. 94.) The principal formalities are of earlier date than the days of Luther. [3] For the papal bull and Luther's commentary, see " Die Bulla vom Abendfressen." . . . . (L. Op. (L.) xviii, p. 1.)

The Pope.—" Leo Bishop."

Luther.—" Bishop . . . as a wolf is a shepherd ; for the bishop ought to exhort according to the doctrine of salvation, not belch out imprecations and maledictions."

The Pope.—". . . Servant of all the servants of God. . . . "

Luther.—" In the evening when we are drunk; but in the morning we call ourselves Leo lord of all the lords."

The Pope.—" The Roman bishops, our predecessors, have been wont, on this festival, to employ the weapons of righteousness." . . .

Luther.—" Which, according to you, are excommunication and anathema, but according to St. Paul, patience, meekness, and charity." (2 Cor. vi, 7.)

The Pope.—" According to the duty of the apostolic office, and to maintain the purity of Christian faith."

Luther—" In other words, the temporal possessions of the pope."

The Pope.—" And its unity, which consists in the union of the members with Christ their head . . . and with his vicar. . . . "

Luther.—" For Christ is not sufficient; one more than he is necessary."

The Pope.—" To guard the holy communion of the faithful, we follow the ancient custom, and excommunicate and anathematise on the part of God Almighty the Father. '

Luther.—" Of whom it is said, ' *God sent not his Son into the world to condemn the world.*' " (John, iii, 17.)

The Pope.—". . . And the Son and the Holy Spirit, and according to the power of the Apostles Peter and Paul . . . and our own. . . . "

Luther.—" And myself! says the ravenous wolf, as if the power of God were too feeble without him."

The Pope.—" We curse all heretics,—the Garasi,[1] the Patarini, the Pauperes of Lyon, the Arnoldists, the Speronists, the Passagians, the Wickliffites, the Hussites, the Fraticelli."

Luther.—" For they wished to possess the Holy Scriptures, and insisted that the pope should be sober and preach the Word God."

The Pope.—" And Martin Luther recently condemned by us for a similar heresy, as well as all his adherents, and all, whosoever they be, that show him any favour."

Luther.—" I thank thee, most gracious Pontiff, for condemning me in common with all these Christians. I count it an honour to have my name proclaimed at Rome during the feast in so glorious a manner, and carried over the world with the names of all those humble confessors of Jesus Christ."   •

The Pope.—" Likewise we excommunicate and curse all pirates and corsairs. . . . "

[1] This name is inaccurate ; read Gazari or Cathari.

Luther.—" Who then is the greatest of pirates and corsairs if it be not he who robs souls, chains them, and puts them to death ? "

The Pope.—" Particularly those who sail upon our sea."

Luther.—" Our SEA ! . . . Saint Peter, *our* predecessor, said, ' *Silver and gold have I none*,' (Acts, iii, 6.) Jesus Christ said, ' *The kings of the Gentiles exercise lordship over them ; but it shall not be so with you.*' (Luke, xxii, 25.) But if a waggon loaded with hay must, on meeting with a drunken man, give way to him, *à fortiori* must St. Peter and Jesus Christ himself give way to the pope."

The Pope.—" Likewise we excommunicate and curse all who falsify our bulls, and our apostolic letters. . . . "

Luther.—" But the letters of God, the Scriptures of God, all the world may condemn and burn."

The Pope.—" Likewise we excommunicate and curse all who detain provisions which are on the way to Rome. . . . "

Luther.—" He barks and bites like a dog threatened to be deprived of his bone." [1]

The Pope.—" Likewise we condemn and curse all who keep back judicial rights, fruits, tithes, revenues, appertaining to the clergy."

Luther.—" For Jesus Christ has said, ' *Whosoever will sue thee at the law and take away thy coat, let him have thy cloak also.*' (Matt. v, 40.) and this is our commentary upon the passage."

The Pope.—" Whatever be their station, dignity, order, power, or rank ; be they even bishops or kings. . . . "

Luther.—" For ' *There will arise false teachers among you who will despise dominion and speak evil of dignities,*' saith the Scripture. (Jude, 8.) "

The Pope.—" Likewise we condemn and curse all those who in any kind of way attack the city Rome, the kingdom of Sicily, the islands of Sardinia and Corsica, the patrimony of St. Peter in Tuscany, the duchy of Spoleto, the margravate of Ancona, the Campagna, the cities of Ferrara and Benevento, or any other city or country appertaining to the Church of Rome."

Luther.—" O, Peter, poor fisherman ! where did you get Rome and all those kingdoms? I salute you, Peter, king of Sicily ! . . . and fisherman at Bethsaida ! "

The Pope.—" We excommunicate and curse all chancellors, counsellors, parliaments, procurators, governors officials, bishops, and others who oppose our letters of exhortation, invitation, prohibition, mediation, execution, etc."

Luther.—" For the holy see seeks only to live in idleness, mag-

---

[1] Gleich wie ein Hund ums Beines willen. (L. Op. (L.) xviii, p. 12.

nificence, and debauchery, to command, storm, deceive, lie, insult, and commit all sorts of wickedness in peace and safety. . . ."

" O Lord, arise! it is not as the papists pretend. Thou hast not forsaken us, nor is thy favour turned away from us."

So spake Leo X at Rome, and Luther at Wittemberg.

The pontiff having finished his anathemas, the parchment on which they were written was torn in pieces, and the fragments thrown to the people. Immediately there was a great rush among the crowd, all pressing forward, and striving to get hold of a morsel of the terrible bull.

Such were the holy relics which the papacy offered to her faithful on the eve of the great day of grace of expiation. The multitude soon dispersed, and the vicinity of the Basilisk resumed its wonted stillness. Let us return to Wittemberg.

CHAP. VI.

Luther's courage—Bugenhagen at Wittemberg—Persecutions in Pomerania—Melancthon wishes to set out with Luther—Amsdorff—Schurff—Suaven—Hütten to Charles V.

It was the 24th of March. The imperial herald, Gaspard Sturm, having at length passed the gates of the town where Luther was, presented himself before the doctor, and put the summons of Charles V into his hands. A grave and solemn moment for the Reformer! All his friends were in consternation. No prince, not even excepting Frederick the Wise, had as yet declared in his favour. Knights, it is true, uttered menaces, but the mighty Charles despised them. Still Luther was not troubled. "The papists," said he, on seeing the anguish of his friends, "have no wish for my arrival at Worms, they only wish my condemnation and death.[1] No matter, pray not for me, but for the Word of God. Before my blood is cold, thousands throughout the world will be called to answer for having shed it. The *most holy* adversary of Christ, the father, master, and generalissimo of homicides, insists on having my life. Amen! Let the will of the Lord be done. Christ will give me his Spirit to vanquish these ministers of error. I despise them during my life, and will triumph over them by my death.[2] They are doing all they can at Worms, to compel me to retract. Here then will be my retractation : I once said, that the pope was the vicar of Christ ; now, I say that

---

[1] Damnatum et perditum. (L. Ep. i, p. 556.)   [2] . . . ut hos Satanæ ministros et contemnam vivens et vincam moriens. (Ibid. p. 579.)

he is the enemy of the Lord, and the apostle of the devil." And when he learned that all the pulpits of the Franciscans were resounding with imprecations and maledictions against him, he exclaimed, "O what wondrous joy it gives me!"[1] He knew that he had done the will of God, and that God was with him ; why then should he not set out boldly ? This purity of intention, this liberty of conscience is a hidden power of incalculable might which never fails the servant of God, and which makes him more invincible than helmets and armied hosts could make him.

At this time arrived at Wittemberg a man who, like Melancthon, was destined to be Luther's friend through life, and to console him at the moment of his departure.[2] It was a priest of thirty-six years of age, named Bugenhagen, who had fled from the severities with which the Bishop of Camin, and Prince Bogislas of Pomerania, persecuted the friends of the gospel of all classes— clergy, citizens, and literati.[3] Of a senatorial family at Wollin in Pomerania, from which he is commonly called 'Pomeranus, Bugenhagen, at twenty years of age, began to teach at Treptow. Youth flocked to hear him, while nobles and learned men vied with each other for his society. He was a diligent student of the Holy Scriptures, and prayed to God to instruct him.[4] One day towards the end of December, 1520, when he was supping with several friends, Luther's treatise on the *Captivity of Babylon* was put into his hands. After turning it over, he exclaimed, " Many heretics have infested the Church since our Saviour died, but never was there one more pestilential than the author of this work." Having taken the book home with him, and read it over and over, his views entirely changed ; new truths presented themselves to his mind, and returning some days afterwards to his companions, he said to them, " The whole world is fallen into Cimmerian darkness. This man and none but he sees the truth."[5] Some priests, a deacon, even the abbot himself, received the pure doctrine of salvation, and preaching it with power, soon," (says a historian,) " turned away their hearers from human superstitions to the sole efficacious merit of Jesus Christ.[6] "Then persecution burst forth. Several were already immured in dungeons, when Bugenhagen escaped from his enemies, and arrived at Wittemberg. " He suffers for the love of the gospel," immediately wrote Melancthon to the Elector's chaplain, " where could he fly if not to our *ασυλον*, (asylum,) to the protection of our prince ?"[7]

[1] Quod mire quam gaudeam! (L. Ep. i, p. 567.)   [2] Venit Vittembergam paullo ante iter Lutheri ad comitia Wormatiæ indicta. (Melch. Adam. Vita Bugenhagii, p. 514.)
[3] Sacerdotes cives et scholasticos in vincula conjecit. (Ibid., p. 313.)
[4] Precesque adjunxit, quibus divinitus se regi ac doceri petivit. (Ibid., p. 312.)
[5] ... In Cimmeriis tenebris versatur; hic vir unus et solus verum videt. (Ibid., p. 313.)
[6] A superstitionibus ad unicum Christi meritum traducere. (Ibid.)
[7] Corp. Refor., i, p. 861.

But none received Bugenhagen with so much delight as Luther. It was arranged between them that, immediately after the Reformer's departure, Bugenhagen should begin to expound the Psalms. Thus divine Providence brought this powerful mind to aid in supplying the place of him whom Wittemberg was going to lose. Placed a year after at the head of the church of this town, Bugenhagen presided over it for thirty-six years. Luther distinguished him by the name of *The Pastor*.

Luther behoved to depart. His alarmed friends thought that unless God miraculously interposed, he was going to death. Melancthon, who had left his native country, had become attached to Luther with all the affection of his soul. " Luther," said he, " is to me in place of all my friends : I feel him to be greater and more admirable than I can express. You know how Alcibiades admired his Socrates;[1] but I admire Luther in a higher sense, for he is a Christian." Then he added the simple but beautiful expression, "Every time I contemplate him, I find him even greater than himself." [2] Melancthon wished to follow Luther in his dangers. But their common friends, and doubtless the doctor himself, were against it. Must not Philip supply the place of his friend? and, should that friend never return, who would direct the cause of the Reformation? " Ah ! would to God," said Melancthon, resigned, but grieved, " would to God I had been allowed to go with him." [3]

The ardent Amsdorff immediately declared that he would accompany the doctor. His strong soul felt a pleasure in exposing itself to danger. His high bearing enabled him to appear fearless before an assembly of kings. The Elector had invited to Wittemberg, as professor of law, Jerome Schurff, the son of a physician of St. Gall, a celebrated man, of great meekness of temper, and a very intimate friend of Luther. " He has not yet summoned up courage," said Luther, "to pronounce sentence of death on a single malefactor.[4] Yet this timid individual volunteered to act as the doctor's counsel on this dangerous journey. A young Danish student named Peter Suaven, who boarded with Melancthon, and afterwards distinguished himself by his labours in Pomerania and Denmark, also declared that he would accompany his master. The youth in schools were entitled to have their representative beside the champion of truth.

Germany was moved at the thought of the dangers which threatened the representative of her people, and found a voice well fitted to express her fears. Ulric von Hütten shuddered at the thought

---

[1] " Alcibiades was persuaded that the demon of Socrates was assistance which the gods sent to instruct and save." (Plutarch's Life of Alcibiades.)   [2] " Quem quoties contemplor, se ipso subinde majorem judico. (Corp. Ref., i, p. 264.)
[3] " Utinam licuisset mihi una proficisci." (Ibid., p. 365)   [4] L. Op. (W.) xxii, p. 2067. 1819.

of the blow about to be struck at his country, and, on the 1st of April wrote directly to Charles V as follows :—"Most excellent emperor, you are on the point of destroying us, and yourself with us. What is intended in this affair of Luther but just to destroy our liberty and abridge your power? There is not throughout the whole breadth of the empire a good man who does not feel the liveliest interest in this business.[1] The priests alone are in arms against Luther because he is opposed to their excessive power, their shameful luxury, their depraved lives, and has pleaded for the doctrine of Christ, his country's freedom, and purity of manners.

" O emperor! dismiss from your presence those orators of. Rome, those bishops and cardinals who would prevent every thing like reform. Did you not observe the sadness of the people on-seeing you on your arrival approach the people surrounded by those wearers of red hats, by a herd of priests and not a band of valiant warriors?

" Do not give up your sovereign majesty to those who would trample it under their feet! Have pity on us! Do not in your, ruin drag the whole nation along with you! Place us amid the greatest perils, under the swords of the enemy and the canon's, mouth ;[2] let all nations conspire against us ; let all armies assail us, so that we may be able openly to manifest our valour, and. not be thus vanquished and enslaved in the dark, like women,. without arms and without a struggle . . . . Ah! our hope was that you would deliver us from the yoke of the Romans and over-throw the pontifical tyranny. God grant that the future may turn out better than the commencement.

" All Germany kneels before you; she supplicates you with tears, implores your aid, your pity, your faith, and, by the holy memory, of those Germans, who, when the whole world was subjugated to Rome, refused to bend their head before that proud city, conjures you to save her, restore her to' herself, deliver her from slavery, and avenge her of her tyrants! . . . ."

So spoke Germany to Charles V through the instrumentality of the knight. The emperor paid no attention to the letter; perhaps threw it disdainfully from him to one of his secretaries. He was a Fleming, and not a German. Personal aggrandisement, not the liberty and glory of the empire, was the object of all his desires.

[1] " Neque enim quam lata est Germania, ulli boni sunt . . . . (L. Op. Lat. ii, p. 182, verso.)   [2] " Duc nos in manifestum potius periculum, duc in ferrum, duo in ignes. . . . (Ibid. p. 183.)   [3] Omnem nunc Germaniam quasi ad genua pro-volutum tibL . . . (ibid., p. 184.)

CHAP. VII.

.Departure for the Diet of Worms—Luther's Adieu—His Condemnation Published—
Cavalcade near Erfurt—Meeting of Jonas and Luther—Luther in his old Convent
Luther Preaches at Erfurt—Incident—Faith and Works—Concourse of People—
Luther's Courage—Luther to Spalatin—Halt at Frankfort—Fears at Worms—
Plan of the Imperialists—Luther's Firmness.

The 2nd of April had arrived, and Luther behoved to take leave
of his friends. After writing a note to Lange to intimate that he
would spend the following Thursday or Friday at Erfurt,[1] he bade
adieu to his colleagues. Turning to Melancthon he said to him, in a
tone which betrayed emotion, "If I do not return, and my enemies
put me to death, O, my brother, cease not to teach, and remain firm
in the truth. Labour in my stead, since I shall not be able to
labour any longer for myself. If you live, it matters little though I
perish." Then, committing himself to the hand of Him who is
faithful and true, Luther took his seat and quitted Wittemberg.
The town council had provided him with a modest carriage with a
cloth covering which might be put on or off at pleasure. The
imperial herald, clad in his insignia, and wearing the imperial
eagle, was on horseback in front, followed by his servant. Next
followed Luther, Schurff, Amsdorff, and Suaven in their carriage.
The friends of the gospel, the citizens of Wittemberg, in deep emotion, were invoking God, and shedding tears. Such was Luther's
departure.

He soon observed that the hearts of those whom he met were
filled with gloomy forebodings. At Leipsic no honour was paid
to him. He only received the usual present of wine. At Naumburg he met a priest, probably J. Langer, a man of stern zeal, who
carefully preserved in his study the portrait of the famous Jerome
Savonarola of Ferrara, who was burnt at Florence in 1498, by
order of pope Alexander VI, as a martyr to liberty and morality,
as well as a confessor of evangelical truth. Having taken the portrait of the Italian martyr, the priest came up to Luther, and held
out the portrait to him without speaking. Luther understood
what the dumb figure intimated, but his intrepid soul remained
firm. "It is Satan," said he, "who, by these terrors, would
fain prevent a confession of the truth from being made in the
assembly of the princes, because he foresees the blow which
this will give to his kingdom."[3] "Adhere firmly to the truth

[1] "Omnem nunc Germaniam quasi ad genua provolutam tibi , . ." (L. Op. Lat. II,
p. 184.)   [2] L. Ep. i, p. 580.   [3] "Terrorem hunc a Sathana sibi dixit
adferri . . . . (Melch. Adam., p. 117.(

, which thou hast perceived," said then the priest to him gravely, " and thy God will also adhere firmly to thee."[1]

Having spent the night at Naumburg, where the burgomaster had hospitably entertained him, Luther arrived next evening at Weimar. He was scarcely a moment there when he heard loud cries in all directions. They were publishing his condemnation. "Look," said the herald to him. He looked, and his astonished eyes beheld imperial messengers traversing the town, and posting up the imperial edict, which ordered his writings to be laid before the magistrates. Luther had no doubt that these harsh measures were exhibited before-hand, to deter him from coming, that he might afterwards be condemned for having refused to appear. "Well, doctor, will you go on?" said the imperial herald to him in alarm. "Yes," replied Luther, "though put under interdict in every town, I will go on : I confide in the emperor's safe-conduct."

At Weimar, Luther had an audience of the Elector's brother, Duke John, who was then residing there. The prince invited him to preach. He consented, and from his heart, now under deep emotion, came forth the words of life. John Voit, the friend of Frederick Myconius, a Franciscan monk, heard him, and being converted to evangelical doctrine, quitted the convent two years after. At a later period, he became professor of theology at Wittemberg. The duke gave Luther the money necessary for his journey.

From Weimar the Reformer proceeded to Erfurt. It was the town of his youth, and he hoped to see his friend Lange, provided, as he had written him, he could enter the town without danger.[2] He was still three or four leagues off, near the village of Nora, when he saw a troop of horsemen appear in the distance. Were they friends, or were they enemies ? Shortly Crotus, the rector of the university, Eobanus Hesse, Melancthon's friend, whom Luther called the king of poets, Euricius Cordus, John Draco, and others, to the number of forty, members of the senate, the university, and the municipality, all on horseback, saluted him with acclamation. A multitude of the inhabitants of Erfurt covered the road, and gave loud expression to their joy. All were eager to see the mighty man who had ventured to declare war against the pope.

A young man of twenty-eight, named Justus Jonas, had got the start of the party.[3] Jonas, after studying law at Erfurt, had been appointed rector of the university in 1519. Illumined by the evan-

[1] Er wolle bey der erkandten Wahrheyt mit breytem Fuss aushalten ... (Mathesius Historien, p. 23—the quotation from the first edition of 1566. [2] " Nisi periculum sit Erfordiam ingredi." (L. Ep. i, p 580.)
[3] Hos inter qui nos prævenerant, ibat Jonas,
  Ille decus nostri, primaque fama Chori.—(Eob. Hessi Elegia secunda.)
2
l

·gelical light which then radiated in all directions, he felt desirous to become a theologian.   " I believe," wrote Erasmus to him, " that God has elected you as an instrument to spread the glory of his Son Jesus." [1]   All Jonas' thoughts were turned to Wittemberg and Luther.   Some years before, when only a student of law, being of an active enterprising spirit, he had set out on foot, accompanied by some friends, and in order to reach Erasmus, then at Brussels, had traversed forests infested by robbers, and towns ravaged by the plague.   Will he not now confront other dangers in order to accompany the Reformer to Worms?   He earnestly begged the favour, and Luther consented.   Thus met these two doctors, who were to labour through life in the renovation of the Church.   Divine Providence gathered around Luther men destined to be the light of Germany : the Melancthons, the Amsdorffs, the Bugenhagens, the Jonases.   On his return from Worms, Jonas was appointed provost of the Church of Wittemberg, and doctor in theology.   " Jonas," said Luther, " is a man whose life would deserve to be purchased at a large price, in order to detain him on the earth." [2]   No preacher ever surpassed him in the gift of captivating his hearers.   " Pomeranus is an expositor," said Melancthon, " and I am a dialectitian,—Jonas is an orator.   The words flow from his lips with surpassing grace, and his eloquence is overpowering.   But Luther is beyond us all." [2]   It seems that nearly about the same time a companion of Luther's childhood, one of his brothers, joined the escort.

The deputation turned their steeds, and horsemen and footmen, surrounding Luther's carriage, entered the town of Erfurt. At the gate, in the squares and streets, where the poor monk had so often begged his bread, the crowd of spectators was immense. Luther dismounted at the Augustin convent, where the gospel had consoled his heart.   Lange received him with joy; Usingen, and some of the more aged fathers, showed great coolness.   There was a general desire to hear him preach, and though he was interdicted from doing it, the herald himself could not resist the desire, and consented.

Sunday after Easter, the Augustin church at Erfurt was crowded. That friar who formerly opened the doors and swept the church, mounted the pulpit, and having opened the Bible, read these words : " *Peace be with you ; and when he had so said, he showed*

. [1] " Velut organum quoddam electum ad illustrandam filii sui Jesu gloriam." (Erasmi Ep. v. 27.)   [3] Vir est quem oportuit multo pretio emptum et servatum in terra. (Weismanni, p. 1436.)   [2] Pomeranus est grammaticus, ego sum dialecticus, Jonas est orator . . . Lutherus vero nobis omnibus antecedit. (Knapp. Narrat. de J. Jona. p. 58L)

them his hands and his side." (John, xx, 19, 20.) " All the philosophers, doctors, and writers," said he, " have exerted themselves
to show how man may obtain eternal life, and have not succeeded.
I will now tell you."

This has, in all ages, been the great question ; accordingly Luther's hearers redoubled their attention.

" There are two kinds of works," continued the Reformer ;
" works foreign to ourselves—these are good works ; and our own
works—these are of little value. One builds a church ; another goes
on a pilgrimage to St. James or St. Peter ; a third fasts, prays, takes
the cowl, walks barefoot; a fourth does something else. All these
works are nothing, and will perish: for our own works have no efficacy
in them. But I am now going to tell you what is the genuine
work. God raised a man again from the dead, even the Lord
Jesus Christ, that he might crush death, destroy sin, and shut the
gates of hell. Such is the work of salvation. The devil thought
that he had the Lord in his power when he saw him between the
two thieves, suffering the most ignominious martyrdom, accursed
of God and men. . . But the Divinity displayed its power, and
annihilated sin, death, and hell. . .

" Christ has vanquished; this is the grand news ; and we are
saved by his work, not by our own. The pope gives a very different
account. But I maintain that the holy Mother of God herself was
saved neither by her virginity nor maternity, neither by her purity
nor her works, but solely by means of faith and by the works of
God. . ."

While Luther was speaking, a sudden noise was heard; one of
the galleries gave a crack, and seemed as if it were going to give
way under the pressure of the crowd. Some rushed out, and others
sat still, terror-struck. The orator stopped for a moment, and then,
stretching out his hand, exclaimed, with a loud voice, " Fear
nothing ; there is no danger ; the devil is seeking, in this way, to
prevent me from proclaiming the gospel, but he shall not succeed."[1]
At these words, those who were running out, stopped astonished and
rivetted to the spot; the assembly calmed, and Luther, without
troubling himself with the attempts of the devil, continued. " You
will perhaps say to me, You tell us a great deal about faith.
Tell us, also, how we can obtain it. Yes ; well, I will tell you.
Our Lord Jesus Christ says, '*Peace be with you ; behold my hands:*'
in other words, 'Behold, O man, it is I, I alone who have taken
away thy sin, and ransomed thee, and now thou hast peace, saith
the Lord.'

[1] Agnosco insidias, hostis acerbe, tuas. (Hessi Eleg. Tertia.) Bitter foe, your
wiles I see.

" I did not eat the fruit of the tree," resumed Luther; " neither did you eat it; but we received the sin which Adam has transmitted to us, and are guilty of it. In like manner. I did not suffer on the cross, nor did you suffer on it; but Christ suffered for us; we are justified by the work of God, and not by our own . . . . ' I am,' saith the Lord, ' thy righteousness and thy redemption.' . . . .

" Let us believe the gospel, let us believe St. Paul, and not the letters and decretals of the popes."

Luther, after having preached faith as the mean of the sinner's justification, preaches works as the consequence and evidence of salvation.

"Since God has saved us," continues he, " let us so order our works that he may take pleasure in them. Art thou rich,—let thy wealth be useful to the poor. Art thou poor,—let thy service be useful to the rich. If thy toil is useful only to thyself, the service which thou pretendest to render to God is mere falsehood."[1]

There is not a word in the sermon on Luther himself; no allusion to the circumstances in which he is placed; nothing on Worms, on Charles, or the nuncios; he preaches Christ, and Christ only; at this moment, when the world has its eyes upon him, he is not in the least occupied with himself; and herein is the mark of a genuine servant of God.

Luther set out from Erfurt, and passed through Gotha, where he again preached. Myconius adds, that at the moment when the people were coming out from the sermon the devil detached from the pediment of the church some stones which had not budged for two centuries. The doctor slept in the convent of the Benedictines, at Rheinhardsbrunn, and thence proceeded to Eisenach, where he felt indisposed. Amsdorff, Jonas, Schurff, and all his friends, were alarmed. He was bled, and the greatest possible attention was paid him. Even the Schulthess of the town, John Oswald, hastened to him with a cordial. Luther, after drinking it, fell asleep, and was thereby so far recovered that he was able to proceed on the following day.

Wherever he passed the people flocked to see him. His journey was a kind of triumphal procession. Deep interest was felt in beholding the intrepid man who was on the way to offer his head to the emperor and the empire. An immense concourse surrounded him. " Ah!" said some of them to him, " there are so many car-

---

[1] L. Op. (L.) xii,'p. 485.

[1] Iter faciente occurrebant populi. (Pallavcini, Hist. C. Tr. i, p. 114.

[2] Quacunque iter faciebant, frequens erat concursus hominum, ridendi Lutheri studio. (Cochlœus, p. 29.)

dinals and so many bishops at Worms, they will burn you; they
will reduce your body to ashes, as was done with that of John
Huss." But nothing terrified the monk. "Were they to make a
fire," said he, "that would extend from Worms to Wittemberg, and
reach even to the sky, I would walk across it in the name of the
Lord; I would appear before them; I would walk into the jaws
of this Behemoth, and break his teeth, and confess the Lord Jesus
Christ."[1]

One day, when just going into an inn, and while the crowd were
as usual pressing around him, an officer came up to him and said,
"Are you the man who undertakes to reform the papacy? How
will you succeed?" "Yes," replied Luther, "I am the man. I
confide in Almighty God, whose word and command I have before
me." The officer, affected, gave him a milder look, and said,
"Dear friend, there is something in what you say; I am the servant of Charles, but your Master is greater than mine. He will
aid you and guard you."[2] Such was the impression which Luther
produced. Even his enemies were struck at the sight of the multitudes that thronged around him, though they have painted the
journey in different colours.[3] At length the doctor arrived at
Frankfort, on Sunday, 14th April.

News of Luther's advance had reached Worms. The friends of
the pope had thought he would not obey the summons of the emperor. Albert, cardinal-archbishop of Mentz, would have given
anything to stop him by the way, and new schemes were set on
foot for this purpose.

Luther, on his arrival at Frankfort, took some repose, and then
announced his approach to Spalatin, who was at Worms with the
Elector. It is the only letter which he wrote during his journey.
"I am getting on," says he, "though Satan has striven to stop
me on the way by sickness. From Eisenach to this I have never
been without a feeling of languor, and am still completely worn
out. I learn that Charles has published an edict to frighten me.
But Christ lives, and we shall enter Worms in spite of all the
barriers of hell and all the powers of the air.[4] Therefore, make
ready my lodging."

---

1 "Ein feuer das bis an den Himmel reichte" . . . (Keil, i, p. 98.)
2 "Nun habt Ihr einen grössern Herrn, denn Ich. (Ibid., p. 99.)
3 "In diversoriis multa propinatio, læta compotatio, musices quoque gaudia; adeo
ut Lutherus ipse alicubi sonora testudine Iudens, omnium in se oculos converteret,
velut Orpheus quidam, sed rasus adhuc et cucullatus, eoque mirabilior." (Cochlœus,
p. 29.) "In the inns there was much quaffing and joyous carousing, nor were the
pleasures of music wanting ; Luther himself, sometimes playing on a sonorous harp,
turned all eyes upon him, as if he had been a kind of Orpheus, shaven and cowled,
no doubt, but on that account the greater wonder.)   4 Intrabimus Wormatiam,
invitis omnibus portis inferni et potentatibus æris. (L. Ep. i, p. 987.)

The next day Luther visited the learned school of William Nesse, a celebrated geographer of that time. "Be diligent," said he to the scholars, "in the reading of the Scriptures, and the investigation of truth." Then placing his right hand on the head of one of the children, and his left on another, he pronounced a blessing on the whole school.

While Luther blessed the young, he was also the hope of the old. Catharine of Holzhausen, a widow advanced in years, and serving God, went to him, and said, "My father and mother told me that God would raise up a man who should oppose the papal vanities, and save the Word of God. I hope you are that man, and I wish you, for your work, the grace and the Holy Spirit of God."[1]

These were by no means the sentiments universally entertained at Frankfort. John Cochlœus, dean of the church of Notre Dame, was one of those most devoted to the Roman Church. On seeing Luther pass through Frankfort on his way to Worms, he could not suppress his fears. He thought the Church was in want of devoted defenders, and scarcely had Luther quitted the town than Cochlœus set out in his track, ready, as he says, to give his life in defence of the honour of the Church.[2]

There was great alarm in the camp of the pope's friends. The heresiarch was at hand—every day, every hour brought him nearer Worms. If he entered, all was perhaps lost. The Archbishop Albert, the confessor Glapio, and all the politicians about the emperor, felt uneasy. How can the arrival of this monk be prevented? It is impossible to carry him off, for he has the emperor's safe-conduct. Stratagem alone can arrest him. These intriguers immediately arranged the following plan. The emperor's confessor, and his high chamberlain, Paul of Armsdorff, quit Worms in great haste, and proceed about ten leagues distant, to the castle of Ebernburg, the residence of Francis de Seckingen, the knight who had offered Luther an asylum. Bucer, a young dominican, chaplain to the Elector-Palatine, and who had been gained to the evangelical doctrine at the Heidelberg discussion, had then taken refuge in "this hôtel of the just." The knight, who had no great knowledge of the affairs of religion, was easily imposed upon, while the disposition of the Palatine chaplain favoured the designs of the confessor. In fact, Bucer was inclined to pacific measures.

Ich hoffe dass du der verherssene . . . Cypr. Hilar. Ev. p. 608.   [2] Lutherum illac transeuntem subsequutus ut pro honore ecclesiæ vitam suam . . . . expoueret, (Cochlœus, p. 36.) This Cochlœus is the writer whom we frequently quote.

[3] Dass der Keyser seinen Beichtvater und Ihrer Majest. Ober-Kammerling, zu Seckingen schickt. (L. Op. xvii, p. 587.)

Distinguishing between fundamental and secondary points, he thought he might sacrifice the latter to unity and peace.[1] The chamberlain and confessor begin their attack. They give Seckingen and Bucer to understand that it is all over with Luther if he goes to Worms. They assure him that the emperor is ready to send certain learned men to Ebernburg there to confer with the doctor. "Under your charge," say they to the knight, "the two parties will be placed." "We are at one with Luther on all essential points," say they to Bucer: "only some secondary points remain; and as to these you will be mediator." The knight and the chaplain are shaken. The confessor and chamberlain continue. "The invitation addressed to Luther must come from you," say they to Seckingen, "and let Bucer be the bearer of it."[2] Every thing was arranged according to their wish. Let Luther only be credulous enough to come to Ebernburg; his safe-conduct will soon expire, and then who will be able to defend him?

Luther had arrived at Oppenheim. His safe-conduct was available only for three days longer. He sees a troop of horsemen approaching, and soon recognises at their head the Bucer with whom he had such intimate conference at Heidelberg.[3] "These horsemen belong to Francis of Seckingen," said Bucer to him after the first expressions of friendship. "He sends me to you to conduct you to his strong castle.[4] The emperor's confessor is desirous of a conference with you. His influence over Charles is unbounded: every thing may be arranged. But beware of Aleander!" Jonas Amsdorff and Schurff knew not what to think; Bucer insisted; but Luther hesitated not. "I continue my journey," was his answer to Bucer; "and if the emperor's confessor has any thing to say to me, he will find me at Worms. I go where I am called."

Meanwhile Spalatin himself began to be troubled and afraid. Surrounded at Worms by the enemies of the Reformation, he heard them saying that no respect should be paid to the safe-conduct of a heretic. He became alarmed for his friend; and at the moment when the latter was approaching the town a messenger presented himself and said to him on the part of the chaplain, "Don't enter Worms!" This from his best friend, the Elector's confidant, Spalatin himself! Luther unmoved, turns his eye on the messenger, and replies, "Go and tell your master, that were there as many devils in Worms as

---

[1] Condoce faciebat τα αναγκαια a probabilibus distinguere, ut scirent quæ retinenda ... (Melch. Adam. Vit. Buceri, p. 223.) He taught that a distinction should be made between the necessary and the probable in order to ascertain what ought to be retained. [2] Dass er sollte der Luther zu sich fodern. (L. Ep. xvii, p. 587.) [3] Da kam Bucer zu, mit et lichen Reutern. (Ibid.) [4] Und wollte mir überreden zu Seckingen gen. Ebernburg zu kommen. (Ibid.)

there are tiles upon the roofs, I would enter."[1] Never, perhaps, was
Luther so grand. The envoy returned to Worms with his extraordinary message. " I was then intrepid," said Luther a few days
before his death, "I feared nothing ; God can give man such boldness ; I know not if at present I would have as much liberty and
joy."—" When the cause is good," adds his disciple Mathesius,
" the heart expands, giving courage and energy to evangelists and
soldiers." [2]

CHAP. VIII.

Entry into Worms—Chant for the Dead—Council held by Charles V—Capito and
the Temporisers—Concourse around Luther—Citation—Hutten to Luther—Proceeds to the Diet—Saying of Freundsberg—Imposing Assembly—The Chancellor's Address—Luther's Reply—His Wisdom—Saying of Charles V—Alarm—
Triumph—Luther's Firmness—Insults from the Spaniards—Council—Luther's
Trouble and Prayer—Might of the Reformation—Luther's Oath to Scripture—The
Court of the Diet—Luther's Address—Three kinds of Writings—He demands
Proof of his Error—Solemn Warnings—He repeats his Address in Latin—Here I
am : I can't do otherwise—The " weakness" of God—New Attempt.

At length, on the morning of the 16th April, Luther perceived
the walls of the ancient city. All were looking for him, and
there was only one thought in Worms. The young noblemen,
Bernard of Hirschfeld and Albert of Lindenau, with six cavaliers,
and other gentlemen in the suite of the princes, to the number of
a hundred, if we may believe Pallavicini, unable to restrain their
impatience, galloped to meet him, and surrounded him in order to
escort him at the moment of his entry. He approached. Before
him pranced the imperial herald decked in all the insignia of his
office. Next came Luther in his humble carriage. Jonas followed
on horseback surrounded by the cavaliers. A large crowd was
waiting in front of the gates. It was near mid-day when he
passed those walls which so many persons had foretold him he
should never leave. It was the dinner hour, but the moment when
the sentinel stationed in the cathedral steeple tolled the signal,
every body ran into the street to see the monk. Thus was Luther
in Worms.

Two thousand persons accompanied him through the streets :
there was a rush to meet him. The crowd was increasing every moment, and was much larger than when the emperor made his entry.

[1] Wenn so viel Teufel zu Worms wären, als Ziegel auf den Dächern, noch wollt Ich
hinein ! (L. Opp. (L.) xvii, p. 587.)   [2] So wächst das Herz im Leibe . . .
(Math. p. 24.)

Suddenly, relates a historian, a man clad in a singular dress, and carrying a large cross before him, as is usual at funerals, breaks off from the crowd, advances towards Luther, and then, in a loud voice, and with the plaintive cadence which is used in saying mass for the repose of the souls of the dead, chants the following stanzas as if he had been determined that the very dead should hear them :—

> Advenisti, O desiderabilis !
> Quem expectabamus in tenebris ![1]

Luther's arrival is celebrated by a *Requiem*. If the story is true, it was the court fool of one of the dukes of Bavaria who gave Luther one of those warnings remarkable at once for wisdom and irony, of which so many instances are furnished by these individuals. But the clamour of the multitude soon drowned the *De Profundis* of the cross-bearer.

The train could scarcely proceed through the moving mass. At length the imperial herald stopped before the hotel of the Knights of Rhodes. Here lodged two of the Elector's counsellors, Frederic of Thun and Philip of Feilitsch, as well as the marshal of the empire, Ulric of Pappenheim. Luther got out of his carriage, and, on alighting, said, "The Lord will be my defence."[1] . . . .

"I entered Worms," said he afterwards, "in a covered car in my frock. Everybody ran into the street to see friar Martin."[2]

The news of his arrival filled the Elector of Saxony and Aleander with alarm. The young and elegant Archbishop Albert, who held a mean between those two parties, was amazed at Luther's boldness. "Had I not had more courage than he," said Luther, "it is true I never should have been seen in Worms."

Charles V immediately assembled his council. The counsellors in the emperor's confidence repaired in haste to the palace for they too were in dismay. "Luther is arrived," said Charles, "what must be done?"

Modo, bishop of Palermo and chancellor of Flanders, if we are to receive Luther's own statement, replied, "We have long consulted on this subject. Let your imperial Majesty speedily get rid of this man. Did not Sigismond cause John Huss to be burnt? There is no obligation either to give or observe a safe-conduct to a heretic."[4] "No," said Charles : "what has been promised must be performed." There was nothing for it, therefore, but to make the Reformer appear.

While the councils of the great were thus agitated on the subject

---

[1] Thou hast arrived—thou whom we longed and waited for in darkness.
[2] Deus stabit pro me. (Pallavicini, i, p. 114.)   [3] L. Op. xvii, p. 587.
[4] . . . Dass Ihre Majestät den Lu her aufs erste beyseit thäte und umbringen liess.. . (Ibid.)

of Luther, there were many men in Worms who rejoiced that they were able at length to behold this illustrious servant of God. In the first rank among them was Capito, chaplain and counsellor to the Archbishop of Mentz. This remarkable man, who a short time before had preached the gospel in Switzerland with great freedom,[1] thought it due to the place which he then occupied to pursue a course which exposed him to a charge of cowardice from the Evangelists, and of dissimulation from the Romans.[2]   He had, however, preached the doctrine of faith clearly at Mentz, and on his departure had succeeded in supplying his place by a young preacher full of zeal, named Hedio. In this town, the ancient see of the primate of the German Church, the word of God was not bound. The gospel was eagerly listened to: in vain did the monks strive to preach the gospel after their own way, and employ all the means in their power in order to arrest the general impulse ; they had no success.[3]   But Capito, even while he preached the new doctrine, laboured to continue in friendship with those who persecuted it. He flattered himself, with others of the same sentiments, that he would thus be of great utility to the Church. To hear them talk it might have been supposed that, if Luther was not burnt, if all the Lutherans were not excommunicated, it was owing entirely to Capito's influence over the Archbishop Albert.[4]   Cochlœus, dean of Frankfort, arriving at Worms almost at the same time with Luther, immediately waited upon Capito, who being, apparently at least, on very good terms with Aleander, introduced Cochlœus to him, thus serving as a connecting link between the two greatest enemies of the Reformer.[5]   Capito doubtless thought that he would do great service to the cause of Christ by all this management; but it cannot be said that any good resulted from it. The event almost always belies these calculations of human wisdom, and proves that a decided course, while it is the most frank, is also the most wise.

Meanwhile the crowd continued around the hotel of Rhodes at which Luther had alighted. Some looked upon him as a prodigy of wisdom, and others as a monster of iniquity. The whole town wished to see him.[6]   The first hours were left him to recover from his fatigue, and converse with his most intimate friends; but as soon as evening came, counts, barons, knights, gentlemen, ecclesiastics, and citizens flocked in upon him. All, even his

---

[1] See Book viii.   [2] Astutia plusquam vulpina vehementer callidum . . . .
Lutherismum versutissime dissimulabat. (Cochlœus, p. 36.)   Exceedingly crafty having more cunning than a fox: he most astutely disguised his Lutheranism.
[3] Evangelium audiunt avidissime, verbum Dei alligatum non est. . . (Caspar Hedi), Zw. Ep., p. 157.)   [4] Lutherus in hoc districtu dudum esset combustus. Lutherani ασοσυναγωγοί nisi Capito aliter persuasisset principi." (Ibid., 148.)   [5] Hic (Capito) illum (Cochlœum) insinuavit Hieronymo Aleandro, nuncio Leonis X. (Cochlœus, p. 36.)
[6] Eadem die tota civitas solicite confluxit . . . (Pallavicini, i, p. 114.)

greatest enemies, were struck with the bold step he had taken, the joy which appeared to animate him, the power of his eloquence, and the lofty elevation and enthusiasm which made the influence of this simple monk almost irresistible. Many attributed this grandeur to something within him partaking of the divine, while the friends of the pope loudly declared that he was possessed with a devil.[1] Call followed call, and the crowd of curious visitors kept Luther standing to a late period of the night.

The next morning, (Friday, 17th April,) Ulric of Pappenheim, hereditary marshal of the empire, summoned him to appear at four o'clock, *p. m.*, in presence of his imperial Majesty and the States of the empire. Luther received the summons with profound respect.

Thus every thing is fixed, and Luther is going to appear for Jesus Christ before the most august assembly in the world. He was not without encouragement. The ardent knight, Ulric von Hütten, was then in the castle of Ebernburg. Not being able to appear at Worms, (for Leo X had asked Charles to send him to Rome bound hand and foot,) he desired to stretch out a friendly hand to Luther, and on the same day (17th April) wrote to him, borrowing the words of a king of Israel:[2] " The Lord hear thee in the day of trouble : the name of the God of Jacob defend thee : send thee help from the sanctuary, and strengthen thee out of Zion : remember all thy offerings, and accept thy burnt sacrifice." O dearly beloved Luther! my respected father, fear not and be strong. The counsel of the wicked has beset you, they have opened their mouths upon you like roaring lions. But the Lord will rise up against the wicked and scatter them. Fight then valiantly for Christ. As for me I also will fight boldly. Would to God I were permitted to see the wrinkling of their brows. But the Lord will cleanse his vine which the wild boar of the forest has laid waste . . . May Christ preserve you! "[3]

Bucer did what Hütten was unable to do: he came from Ebernburg to Worms, and remained the whole time beside his friend.[4]

Four o'clock having struck, the marshal of the empire presented himself. It was necessary to set out, and Luther made ready. He was moved at the thought of the august congress before which he was going to appear. The herald walked first, after him the marshal, and last the Reformer. The multitude thronging the streets was still more numerous than on the previous evening. It was im-

---

[1] Nescio quid divinum suspicabantur: ex adverso alii malo dæmone obsessum existimabant. (Pallavicini, i, p. 114.) [2] David, Psalm xx. [3] Servet te Christus. (L. Op. ii, p. 175.) [4] Bucerus eodem nit. (M. Adam. Vit Buceri. p. 212.)

possible to get on; it was in vain to cry, Give place: the crowd increased. At length, the herald seeing the impossibility of reaching
the town hall caused some private houses to be opened, and conducted Luther through gardens and secret passages to the place of
meeting.[1] The people perceiving this rushed into the houses on the
steps of the monk of Wittemberg, or placed themselves at the windows which looked into the gardens, while great numbers of persons got up on the roofs. The tops of the houses, the pavement,.
every place above and below was covered with spectators.[2]

Arrived at length at the town, Luther and those who all accompanied him were again unable, because of the crowd, to reach
the door. Give way! give way! Not one stirred. At last
the imperial soldiers forced a passage for Luther. The people
rushed forward to get in after him, but the soldiers kept them
back with their halberds. Luther got into the interior of the building, which was completely filled with people. As well in the ante-
chambers as at the windows there were more than five thousand
spectators—German, Italian, Spanish, etc. Luther advanced with
difficulty. As he was at length approaching the door, which was
to bring him in presence of his judges, he met a valiant knight,
the celebrated general, George of Freundsberg, who, four years
afterwards, at the head of the German lansquenets couched his
lance on the field of Pavia, and bearing down upon the left
wing of the French army, drove it into the Tessino, and in a
great measure decided the captivity of the king of France. The
old general, seeing Luther pass, clapped him on the shoulder,.
and shaking his head, whitened in battle, kindly said to him,
"Poor monk, poor monk, you have before you a march, and an
affair, the like to which neither I nor a great many captains
have ever seen in the bloodiest of our battles. But if your cause is
just, and you have full confidence in it, advance in the name of God
and fear nothing. God will not forsake you."[3] A beautiful
homage borne by warlike courage to courage of intellect. It is
the saying of a king,[4] "*He that ruleth his spirit is greater than he
that taketh a city.*"

At length the doors of the hall being opened, Luther entered,
and many persons not belonging to the Diet made their way in
along with him. Never had man appeared before an assembly so
august. The emperor Charles V, whose dominions embraced the old
and the new world; his brother, the Archduke Ferdinand; six.

---

1 Und ward also durch heimliche Gänge geführt. (L. Op. (L.) xvii, p. 574.)
2 Doch lief das Volk häufig zu, und stieg sogar auf Dächer. (Seck. 348.)
3 Münchlein, Münchlein, du gehest jetzt einen Gang, einen solchen Stand zu thun,.
dergleichen Ich und mancher Obrister, auch in unser allerernestesten Schlacht-Ord-
nung nicht gethan haben . . . (Ibid.)   4 Proverbs, xvi, 32.

electors of the empire, whose descendants are now almost all wearing the crown of kings ; twenty-four dukes, the greater part of
them reigning over territories of greater or less extent, and, among
whom are some bearing a name which will afterwards become formidable to the Reformation (the Duke of Alva, and his two sons) ;
eight margraves ; thirty archbishops, bishops, or prelates ; seven
ambassadors, among them those of the kings of France and England ; the deputies of ten free towns ; a great number of princes,
counts, and sovereign barons ; the nuncios of the pope ; in all, two
hundred and four personages. Such was the court before which
Martin Luther appeared.

This appearance was in itself a signal victory gained over the
papacy. The pope had condemned the man ; yet here he stood
before a tribunal which thus far placed itself above the pope. The
pope had put him under his ban, debarring him from all human society, and yet here he was convened in honourable terms, and admitted before the most august assembly in the world. The pope had
ordered that his mouth should be for ever mute, and he was going
to open it before an audience of thousands, assembled from the remotest quarters of Christendom. An immense revolution had thus
been accomplished by the instrumentality of Luther. Rome was
descending from her throne, descending at the bidding of a monk.

Some of the princes seeing the humble son of the miner of Mansfeld disconcerted in presence of the assembly of kings, kindly approached him ; and one of them said, " *Fear not them who can kill
the body, but cannot kill the soul.*" Another added, " *When you
will be brought before kings it is not you that speak but the Spirit of
your Father that speaketh in you* "[1] Thus, the Reformer was consoled in the very words of his Master, by the instrumentality of
the rulers of the world.

During this time, the guards were making way for Luther, who
advanced till he came in front of the throne of Charles V. The
sight of the august assembly seemed for a moment to dazzle and
overawe him. All eyes were fixed upon him. The agitation gradually calmed down into perfect silence. " Don't speak before
you are asked," said the marshal of the empire to him and withdrew.

After a moment of solemn stillness, John of Eck, the chancellor
of the Archbishop of Trèves, a friend of Aleander, and who must
not be confounded with the theologian of the same name, rose up
and said, in a distinct and audible voice, first in Latin and then in

[1] Einige aus denen Reichs-Gliedern sprachen Ihm einen Muth, mit Christi Worten,
in . . . (Matthew, x, 20, 28. Seckend. p. 348.)

German, " Martin Luther, his sacred and invincible imperial Majesty has cited you before his throne, by the advice and counsel of the States of the holy Roman empire, in order to call upon you to answer these two questions : First, Do you admit that these books were composed by you? "—At the same time the imperial orator pointed to about twenty books lying on the table in the middle of the hall in front of Luther—" I did not exactly know how they had procured them," says Luther, in relating the circumstance. It was Aleander who had taken the trouble. " Secondly," continued the chancellor, " do you mean to retract these books and their contents, or do you persist in the things which you have advanced in them ? "

Luther, without hesitation, was going to reply in the affirmative to the former question, when his counsel, Jerôme Schurff, hastily interfering, called out, "Read the titles of the books."[1] The chancellor going up to the table read the titles. The list contained several devotional works not relating to controversy.

After the enumeration, Luther said, first in Latin, and then in German.

" Most gracious Emperor ! Gracious Princes and Lords !

" His imperial Majesty asks me two questions.

" As to the first, I acknowledge that the books which have been named are mine : I cannot deny them.

' As to the second, considering that is a question which concerns faith and the salvation of souls, a question in which the Word of God is interested, in other words, the greatest and most precious treasure either in heaven or on the earth,[2] I should act imprudently were I to answer without reflection. I might say less than the occasion requires, or more than the truth demands, and thus incur the guilt which our Saviour denounced when he said, ' Whoso shall deny me before men, him will I deny before my Father who is in Heaven.' Wherefore, I pray your imperial Majesty, with all submission, to give me time that I may answer without offence to the Word of God."

This reply, far from countenancing the idea that there was any hesitation in Luther, was worthy of the Reformer and the assembly. It became him to show calmness and circumspection in so grave a matter, and to refrain on this solemn moment from every thing that might seem to indicate passion or levity. Moreover, by taking a suitable time, he would thereby the better prove the immovable firmness of his resolution. History shows us many men who,

---

[1] " Legantur tituli librorum." (L. Op. (L.) xvii, p. 583.)   [2] Weil dies eine Frage vom Glauben und der Seelen Seligkeit ist, und Gottes Wort belanget . . . (Ibid.)

by a word uttered too hastily, brought great calamities on themselves, and on the world. Luther curbs his naturally impetuous character; restrains a tongue always ready to give utterance; is silent when all the feelings of his heart are longing to embody themselves in words. This self restraint, this calmness, so extraordinary in such a man, increased his power a hundred-fold, and put him into a position to answer afterwards with a wisdom, power, and dignity which will disappoint the expectation of his enemies, and confound their pride and malice.

Nevertheless, as he had spoken in a respectful and somewhat subdued tone, several thought he was hesitating and even afraid. A ray of hope gleamed into the souls of the partizans of Rome. Charles, impatient to know the man whose words shook the empire, had never taken his eye off him. Now turning towards one of his courtiers, he said with disdain, " Assuredly that is not the man who would ever make me turn heretic."[1] Then rising up, the young emperor withdrew with his ministers to the council' chamber: the electors with the princes were closeted in another, and the deputies of the free towns in a third. The Diet when it again met, agreed to grant Luther's request. It was a great mistake in men under the influence of passion. " Martin Luther," said the chancellor of Trèves, " his imperial Majesty, in accordance with the goodness which is natural to him, is pleased to gran you another day, but on condition that you give your reply verbally and not in writing."

Then the imperial herald advanced and reconducted Luther to his hôtel. Menaces and cheers succeeded each other as he passed along. The most unfavourable reports were circulated among Luther's friends. " The Diet is dissatisfied," said they, " the envoys of the pope triumph, the Reformer will be sacrificed." Men's passions grew hot. Several gentlemen hastened to Luther's lodgings. " Doctor," asked they in deep emotion, " how does the matter stand? It is confidently said that they mean to burn you."[2] " That won't be," continued they, or they shall pay for it with their lives."—" And that would have been the result," said Luther, twenty years later at Eisleben, when quoting these expressions.

On the other hand, Luther's enemies were quite elated. " He has asked time," said they; " he will retract. When at a distance he spoke arrogantly, but now his courage fails him . . . He is vanquished."

Luther, perhaps, was the only tranquil person in Worms. A

---

[1] " Hic certe nunquam efficeret ut hæreticus evaderem." 'Pallavicini. i, p. 115.)
[2] Wie geht's ? man sagt sie wollen euch verbrennen . . . (L. Op. L. xvii, p. 588.)

few moments after his return from the Diet, he wrote to the imperial counsellor Cuspianus. " I write you from the midst of tumult,
(meaning, probably, the noise of the crowd outside his hotel;) I
have, within this hour, appeared before the emperor and his
brother.[1] I have acknowledged the authorship, and declared that
to-morrow I will give my answer concerning retractation. By the
help of Jesus Christ, not one iota of all my works will I retract."[2]

The excitement of the people and of the foreign troops increased
every hour. While parties were proceeding calmly to the business
of the Diet, others were coming to blows in the streets. The Spanish
soldiers, proud and merciless, gave offence by their insolence to the
burghers of the town. One of these satellites of Charles, finding in a
bookseller's shop the papal bull, with a commentary on it by Hütten, took and tore it to pieces, and then trampled the fragments under his feet. Others, having discovered several copies of Luther's
' Captivity of Babylon,' carried them off and tore them. The
people, indignant, rushed upon the soldiers, and obliged them to
take flight. On another occasion, a Spanish horseman, with drawn
sword, was seen in one of the principal streets of Worms in pursuit
of a German who was fleeing before him, while the people durst not
interfere.[3]

Some politicians thought they had discovered a method of saving
Luther. " Recant your errors in doctrine," said they to him;
" but persist in all you have said against the pope and his court,
and you are safe." Aleander shuddered at this advice. But Luther, immovable in his purpose, declared that he set little value
on a political reform, if not founded on faith.

The 18th of April having arrived, Glapio, the Chancellor Eck,
and Aleander, met at an early hour, by order of Charles V, to fix
the course of procedure in regard to Luther

Luther had been for a moment overawed on the evening before
when he had to appear before so august an assembly. His heart
had been agitated at the sight of so many princes before whom great
kingdoms humbly bent the knee. The thought that he was going
to refuse obedience to men whom God had invested with sovereign
power gave him deep concern ; and he felt the necessity of seeking
strength from a higher source. " He who, attacked by the enemy,
holds the shield of faith," said he one day, " is like Perseus holding
the head of the Gorgon, on which whoever looked, that moment died.
So ought we to hold up the Son of God against the snares of the
devil.[4] On this morning of the 18th April, he had moments of

[1] " Hac hora coram Cæsare et fratre Romano constiti." (L. Ep. i, p. 587.)
[2] " Verum ego ne apicem quidem revocabo. (Ibid.)   [3] Kappens Ref.
Urkunden ii, p. 448.   [4] " Also sollen wir den Sohn Gottes als Gorgonis
Haupt...(L. Op. (W.) xxii, p. 1659.)

trouble, when the face of God was hid from him. His faith becomes faint; his enemies seem to multiply before him; his imagination is overpowered . . . His soul is like a ship tossed by a violent tempest, now plunged to the depths of the sea, and again mounting up towards heaven. At this hour of bitter sorrow, when he drinks the cup of Christ, and feels as it were in a garden of Gethsemane, he turns his face to the ground, and sends forth broken cries, cries which we cannot comprehend, unless we figure to ourselves the depth of the agony from which they ascended up to God.[1] "God Almighty! God Eternal! how terrible is the world! how it opens its mouth to swallow me up! and how defective my confidence in thee! How weak the flesh, how powerful Satan! If I must put my hope in that which the world calls powerful, I am undone! . . . The knell is struck,[2] and judgment is pronounced! . . . O God! O God! O thou, my God! assist me against all the wisdom of the world! Do it: Thou must do it . . . Thou alone . . . for it is not my work, but Thine. I have nothing to do here; I have nothing to do contending thus with the mighty of the world! I, too, would like to spend tranquil and happy days. But the cause is Thine: and it is just and everlasting! O Lord! be my help! Faithful God, immutable God! I trust not in any man. That were vain. All that is of man vacillates! All that comes of man gives way. O God, O God, dost thou not hear? . . . My God! art thou dead? . . . No, thou canst not die! Thou only hidest Thyself. Thou hast chosen me for this work. I know it! Act, then, O God! . . . Stand by my side, for the sake of thy well beloved Son Jesus Christ, who is my defence, my buckler, and my fortress."

After a moment of silence and wrestling, he continues thus: "Lord, where standest thou? . . . O, my God, where art thou? . . . Come! come! I am ready! . . . I am ready to give up my life for thy truth . . . . patient as a lamb. For the cause is just, and it is thine! . . . I will not break off from thee either now or through eternity! . . . And though the world should be filled with devils, though my body, which however is the work of thy hands, should bite the dust, be racked on the wheel, cut in pieces . . . ground to powder . . . . my soul is thine.[3] Yes, thy Word is my pledge. My soul belongs to thee, and will be eternally near thee . . . Amen . . . O God, help me . . . Amen."

This prayer explains Luther and the Reformation. History here lifts the veil of the sanctuary, and shows us the secret place whence

---

[1] L. Op. (L.) xvii, p. 589.   [2] "Die Glocke ist schon gegossen." (Ibid.) The affair is decided.   [3] "Die Seele est dien." (Ibid.)

strength and courage were imparted to this humble man, who was
the instrument of God in emancipating the soul and the thoughts
of men, and beginning a new era. Luther and the Reformation
are here seen in actual operation. We perceive their most secret
springs. We discover where their power lay. This meditation,
by one who is sacrificing himself to the cause of truth, is found
among the collection of pieces relating to Luther's appearance at
Worms, under number XVI, among safe-conducts, and other documents of a similar description. Some of his friends doubtless extended it, and so have preserved it to us. In my opinion, it is one
of the finest documents on record.

Luther, after he had thus prayed, found that peace of mind
without which no man can do anything great. He read the Word
of God; he glanced over his writings, and endeavoured to put his reply
into proper shape. The thought that he was going to bear testimony to Jesus Christ and his Word, in presence of the emperor and
the empire, filled his heart with joy. The moment of appearance
was drawing near; he went up with emotion to the sacred volume,
which was lying open on his table, put his left hand upon it, and
lifting his right toward heaven, swore to remain faithful to the
gospel, and to confess his faith freely, should he even seal his confession with his blood. After doing so, he felt still more at peace.

At four o'clock the herald presented himself and conducted him
to the place where the Diet sat. The general curiosity had increased, for the reply behoved to be decisive. The Diet being
engaged, Luther was obliged to wait in the court in the middle of
an immense crowd, who moved to and fro like a troubled sea, and
pressed the Reformer with its waves. The doctor spent two long
hours amid this gazing multitude. " I was not used," says he, " to
all these doings and all this noise." [1] It would have been a sad
preparation for an ordinary man. But Luther was with God. His
eye was serene, his features unruffled; the Eternal had placed him
upon a rock. Night began to fall, and the lamps were lighted in the
hall of the Diet. Their glare passed through the ancient windows
and shone into the court. Every thing assumed a solemn aspect.
At last the doctor was introduced. Many persons entered with
him, for there was an eager desire to hear his answer. All minds
were on the stretch waiting impatiently for the decisive moment
which now approached. This time Luther was free, calm, self-
possessed, and showed not the least appearance of being under
constraint. Prayer had produced its fruits. The princes having
taken their seats, not without difficulty, for their places were almost

---

[1] Des Getümmels und Wesens war Ich gar nicht gewohnt. (L. Op. xvii, p. 535, 588.)

invaded, and the monk of Wittemberg again standing in front of Charles V, the chancellor of the Elector of Trèves rose up, and said —:

"Martin Luther ! you yesterday asked a delay, which is now expired. Assuredly it might have been denied you, since every one ought to be sufficiently instructed in matters of faith to be able always to render an account of it to whosoever asks,—you above all, so great and able a doctor of Holy Scripture . . . . Now, then, reply to the question of his Majesty, who has treated you with so much mildness, Do you mean to defend your books out and out, or do you mean to retract some part of them ?"

These words, which the chancellor had spoken in Latin, he repeated in German.

" Then doctor Martin Luther," say the Acts of Worms, "replied in the most humble and submissive manner. He did not raise his voice; he spoke not with violence, but with candour, meekness, suitableness, and modesty, and yet with great joy and Christian firmness." [1]

" Most serene Emperor! illustrious princes, gracious lords," said Luther, turning his eyes on Charles and the assembly, " I this day appear humbly before you, according to the order which was given me yesterday, and by the mercies of God I implore your Majesty and august Highnesses to listen kindly to the defence of a cause which I am assured is righteous and true. If from ignorance I am wanting in the usages and forms of courts, pardon me ; for I was not brought up in the palaces of kings, but in the obscurity of a cloister.

"Yesterday two questions were asked me on the part of his imperial Majesty : the first, if I was the author of the books whose titles were read; the second, if I was willing to recal or to defend the doctrine which I have taught in them. I answered the first question, and I adhere to my answer.

"As to the second, I have composed books on very different subjects. In some I treat of faith and good works in a manner so pure, simple, and christian, that my enemies even, far from finding any thing to censure, confess that these writings are useful, and worthy of being read by the godly. The papal bull, how severe soever it may be, acknowledges this.· Were I then to retract these what should I do ? . . . . Wretch! I should be alone among men abandoning truths which the unanimous voice of my friends and enemies approves, and opposing what the whole world glories in confessing.

" In the second place, I have composed books against the papacy,

---

[1] " Schreyt nicht sehr noch heftig, sondern redet fein, sittich, züchtig und bescheiden. . . . (L. Op. (L.) xvii, p. 576.)

books in which I have attacked those who, by their false doctrine, their bad life, and scandalous example, desolate the Christian world, and destroy both body and soul. Is not the fact proved by the complaints of all who fear God? Is it not evident that the human laws and doctrines of the popes entangle, torture, martyr the consciences of the faithful, while the clamant and never-ending extortions of Rome engulph the wealth and riches of Christendom, and particularly of this illustrious kingdom?

" Were I to retract what I have written on this subject what should I do? . . . . What but fortify that tyranny, and open a still wider door for these many and great iniquities?[1] Then, breaking forth with more fury than ever, these arrogant men would be seen increasing, usurping, raging more and more. And the yoke which weighs upon the Christian people would by my retractation not ony be rendered more severe, but would become, so to speak, more legitimate ; for by this very retractation it would have received the confirmation of your most serene Majesty and of all the States of the holy empire. Good God! I should thus be as it were an infamous cloak destined to hide and cover all sorts of malice and tyranny.

" Thirdly and lastly, I have written books against private individuals who wished to defend Roman tyranny and to destroy the faith. I confess frankly that I have perhaps attacked them with more violence than became my ecclesiastical profession. I do not regard myself as a saint ; but no more can I retract these books : because, by so doing, I should sanction the impiety of my opponents, and give them occasion to oppress the people of God with still greater cruelty.

" Still I am a mere man and not God ; and I will defend myself as Jesus Christ did. He said, ' If I have spoken evil, bear witness of the evil.' (John, xviii, 23.) How much more should I, who am but dust and ashes and so apt to err, desire every one to state what he can against my doctrine?

" Wherefore, I implore you, by the mercies of God, you, most serene Emperor, and you, most illustrious princes, and all others of high or low degree, to prove to me by the writings of the prophets and the apostles that I am mistaken. As soon as this shall have been proved, I will forthwith retract all my errors, and be the first to seize my writings and cast them into the flames.

" What I have just said shows clearly, I think, that I have well considered and weighed the dangers to which I expose myself; but, far from being alarmed, it gives me great joy to see that

[1] "Nicht allein die Fenster, sondern auch Thür und Thör aufthäte." (L. Op. (L.) xvii, p. 573.)

the gospel is now, as in former times, a cause of trouble and discord. This is the characteristic and the destiny of the Word of God. '*I came not to send peace, but a sword*,' said Jesus Christ. (Matt. x, 34.) God is wonderful and terrible in working: let us beware, while pretending to put a stop to discord, that we do not persecute the holy Word of God, and bring in upon ourselves a frightful deluge of insurmountable dangers, present disasters, and eternal destruction. . . . . Let us beware that the reign of this young and noble prince, the Emperor Charles, on whom, under God, we build such high hopes, do not only begin, but also continue and end under the most fatal auspices. I might cite examples taken from the oracles of God," continues Luther, speaking in presence of the greatest monarch in the world with the noblest courage, "I might remind you of the Pharaohs, the kings of Babylon, and of Israel, who never laboured more effectually for their ruin than when by counsels, apparently very wise, they thought they were establishing their empire. '*God removeth the mountains, and they know not*.' (Job, ix, 5.)

" If I speak thus, it is not because I think such great princes have need of my counsels, but because I wish to restore to Germany what she has a right to expect from her children. Thus, commending myself to your august Majesty and your serene Highnesses, I humbly supplicate you not to allow the hatred of my enemies to bring down upon me an indignation which I have not deserved." [1]

Luther had spoken these words in German, modestly, but also with much warmth and firmness.[2] He was ordered to repeat them in Latin. The emperor had no liking for German. The imposing assembly which surrounded the Reformer, the noise and excitement, had fatigued him. " I was covered with perspiration," says he, "heated by the crowd, standing in the midst of the princes." Frederick de Thun, confidential counsellor of the Elector of Saxony, stationed by his master's order behind the Reformer, to take care that he was not taken by surprise or overborne, seeing the condition of the poor monk, said to him, " If you cannot repeat your address, that will do, doctor." But Luther, having paused a moment to take breath, resumed, and pronounced his address in Latin, with the same vigour as at first [3]

" This pleased the Elector Frederick exceedingly," relates the Reformer.

<hr/>

[1] This address, as well as all the expressions quoted, are taken literally from authentic documents. (See L. Op. (L.) xvi, p. 776-780.)   [2] "Non clamose at modeste, non tamen sine Christianâ animositate et constantiâ. (L. Op. Lat. ii, p. 165.) Not clamorously, but modestly ; yet not without Christian warmth and firmness.
[3] L. Op. Lat. ii, p. 165-167.

As soon as he had ceased, the Chancellor of Trêves, the orator of the Diet, said to him, indignantly, " You have not answered the question which was put to you. You are not here to throw doubt on what has been decided by Councils. You are asked to give a clear and definite reply. Will you, or will you not retract?" Luther then replied, without hesitation, " Since your most serene Majesty, and your high Mightinesses, call upon me for a simple, clear, and definite answer, I will give it; [1] and it is this : I cannot subject my faith either to the pope or to councils, because it is clear as day that they have often fallen into error, and even into great self-contradiction. If, then, I am not disproved by passages of Scripture, or by clear arguments ; if I am not convinced by the very passages which I have quoted, and so bound in conscience to submit to the word of God, *I neither can nor will retract any thing*, for it is not safe for a Christian to speak against his conscience." Then, looking around on the assembly before which he was standing, and which held his life in its hands, " HERE I AM," says he, " I CANNOT DO OTHERWISE: GOD HELP ME. AMEN." [2]

Thus Luther, constrained to obey his faith, led by his conscience to death, impelled by the noblest necessity, the slave of what he believes, but in this slavery supremely free, like to the ship tossed by a fearful tempest, which, in order to save something more precious than itself, is voluntarily allowed to dash itself to pieces against a rock, pronounces these sublime words, which have not lost their thrilling effect after the lapse of three centuries ; thus speaks a monk before the emperor and the magnates of the empire, and this poor and feeble individual standing alone, but leaning on the grace of the Most High, seems greater and stronger than them all. , His word has a power against which all these mighty men can do nothing. The empire and the Church, on the one side, the obscure individual, on the other, have been confronted. God had assembled these kings and prelates that he might publicly bring their wisdom to nought. They have lost the battle, and the consequences of their defeat will be felt in all nations, and during all future ages.

The assembly were amazed. Several princes could scarcely conceal their admiration. The emperor, changing his first impression, exclaimed, " The monk speaks with an intrepid heart and immovable courage." [3]   The Spaniards and Italians alone felt dis-

---

[1] Dabo illud neque dentatum, neque cornutum.   (Ibid., p. 166.)   I will give it without either teeth or horns.   [2] Hier stehe ich : Ich kan nicht anders : Gott helfe mir! Amen.   (L. Op. (L.) xvii, p. 580.)   [3] Der Mönch redet unerschrocken, mit getrostem Muth i   (Seckend. p. 350.)

concerted, and soon began to deride a magnanimity which they could not appreciate.

After the Diet had recovered from the impression produced by the address, the chancellor resumed: " If you do not retract, the emperor and the states of the empire will consider what course they must adopt towards an obstinate heretic." At these words, Luther's friends trembled, but the monk again said, " God help me; for I can retract nothing."[1]

Luther then withdraws, and the princes deliberate. Every one felt that the moment formed a crisis in Christendom. The yea or nay of this monk was destined, perhaps for ages, to determine the condition of the Church and the world. It was wished to frighten him, but the effect had been to place him on a pedestal in presence of the nation. It was meant to give more publicity to his defeat, and all that had been done was to extend his victory. The partisans of Rome could not submit to bear their humiliation. Luther was recalled, and the orator thus addressed him : " Martin, you have not spoken with the modesty which became your office. The distinction you have made between your books was useless, for if you retract those which contain errors, the empire will not allow the others to be burnt. It is extravagant to insist on being refuted from Scripture, when you revive heresies which were condemned by the universal Council of Constance. The emperor, therefore, orders you to say simply, Do you mean to maintain what you have advanced, or do you mean to retract any part of it— yes, or no ? " I have no other answer than that which I have already given," replied Luther calmly. He was now understood. Firm as a rock, all the billows of human power had dashed against him in vain. The vigour of his eloquence, his intrepid countenance, the flashing of his eye, the immovable firmness imprinted in bold lineaments on his German features, had produced the deepest impression on this illustrious assembly. There was no longer any hope. Spaniards, Belgians, and even Romans, were mute. The monk was victorious over earthly grandeur. He had negatived the Church and the empire. Charles rose up, and all the assembly with him. " The Diet will meet to-morrow morning to hear the emperor's decision," said the chancellor, with a loud voice.

L. Op. (W.) xv, 2286.

CHAP. IX.

Victory—Tumult and calm—Duke Erick's Glass of Beer—The Elector and Spalatin —Message from the Emperor—Wish to violate the Safe-conduct—Strong opposition—Enthusiasm for Luther—Voice for Conciliation—The Elector's Fear—Assemblage at Luther's Lodging—Philip of Hesse.

It was night, and each regained his dwelling in the dark. Two imperial officers were ordered to accompany Luther. Some persons imagining that his fate was decided, and that they were conducting him to prison, which he should leave only for the scaffold, an immense tumult arose. Several gentlemen exclaimed, "Are they taking him to prison?" "No," replied Luther, "they are accompanying me to my hotel." At these words the tumult calmed. Then some Spaniards of the emperor's household, following this bold champion, hissed and jeered at him[1] as he passed along the streets, while others howled like wild beasts deprived of their prey. Luther remained firm and peaceful.

Such was the scene at Worms. The intrepid monk, who had hitherto hurled defiance at his enemies, spake, when in the presence of those who had thirsted for his blood, with calmness, dignity, and humility. There was no exaggeration, no human enthusiasm, no anger; he was peaceful amid the strongest excitement; modest, while resisting the powers of the earth; great, in presence of all the princes of the world. In this we have an irrefragable proof that Luther was then obeying God—not following the suggestions of his own pride. In the hall of Worms there was One greater than Luther and Charles. Jesus Christ has said, " *When they deliver you up, take no thought how or what you shall speak. For it is not ye that speak.*"[2] Never, perhaps, was this promise so manifestly fulfilled.

A deep impression had been produced on the heads of the empire. Luther had observed this, and it had increased his courage. The servants of the pope were angry at John Eck for not having oftener interrupted the guilty monk. Several princes and nobles were gained to a cause which was maintained with such conviction. In some, it is true, the impression was evanescent, but, on the other hand, several who till then had concealed their sentiments, henceforth displayed great courage.

Luther had returned to his hotel, and was reposing from the

---

[1] " Subsannatione hominem Dei et longo rugitu prosecuti sunt." (L. Op. Lat. ii, p. 166.) Followed the man of God with jeers and loud bellowing.   [2] Matt. x, 18, 20.

fatigue of the severe service in which he had been engaged. Spalatin and other friends were around him, and all were giving thanks to God. While they were conversing, a valet entered, bearing a silver vase full of Eimbeck beer. "My master," said he, presenting it to Luther, "begs you to refresh yourself with this draught of beer." "What prince is it," asked Luther, "who so graciously remembers me?" It was old Duke Erick of Brunswick. The Reformer was touched by the offering thus made him by so powerful a prince; one, too, belonging to the papal party. "His highness," continued the valet, "was pleased to taste the draught before sending it to you." Luther, being thirsty, poured out the duke's beer, and after drinking it, said, "As Duke Erick has this day remembered me, so may the Lord Jesus Christ remember him in the day of his final combat."[1] The present was in itself of little value, but Luther, wishing to show his gratitude to a prince who had thought of him at such a moment, gave him what he had—a prayer. The valet returned with the message to his master. The old duke, in his last moments, remembered the words, and addressing a young page, Francis de Kramm, who was standing at his bedside, said to him, "Take the gospel and read it to me." The child read the words of Christ, and the soul of the dying man was refreshed. "*Whosoever*," says the Saviour, "*shall give to one of you a cup of cold water in my name, because you are my disciple, verily I say unto you, he shall in no wise lose his reward.*"

The valet of the Duke of Brunswick was no sooner gone than a message from the Elector of Saxony ordered Spalatin to come to him instantly. Frederick had come to the Diet full of disquietude. He thought that, in presence of the emperor, Luther's courage might give way, and he had accordingly been deeply moved by the Reformer's firmness. He was proud of having taken such a man under his protection. When the chaplain arrived, the table was covered, and the Elector was going to sit down to supper with his Court—the valets having already brought in the vase for washing the hands. The Elector seeing Spalatin enter, immediately beckoned him to follow, and when alone with him in his bed-chamber, said to him, with deep emotion, "Oh! how well father Luther spoke before the emperor and all the states of the empire! My only fear was, that he would be too bold."[2] Frederick then formed a resolution to protect the doctor in future with greater courage.

Aleander saw the impression which Luther had produced. There was no time, therefore, to be lost. The young emperor must be

[1] Also gidencke seiner unser Herr Christus in seinem letzten Kampff. (Seck. n. 354.)
[2] O wie schon hat Pater Martinus geredet. (Ibid., p. 355.)

induced to act vigorously. The moment was favourable, for there was immediate prospect of war with France. Leo X, wishing to enlarge his states, and caring little for the peace of Christendom, caused two treaties to be secretly negotiated, at the same time, the one with Charles against Francis, and the other with Francis against Charles.[1] By the former he stipulated with the emperor for Parma, Placenza, and Ferrara; by the latter, he stipulated with the king for a part of the kingdom of Naples, of which Charles was thus to be deprived. Charles felt the importance of gaining over Leo, in order that he might have him as an ally against his rival of France. Luther was an easy price to pay for the friendship of the mighty pontiff.

The day after Luther's appearance, he caused a message to be read to the Diet, which he had written in French, with his own hand.[2] " Sprung," said he, " from the Christian emperors of Germany, from the Catholic kings of Spain, the archdukes of Austria, and the dukes of Burgundy, who are all illustrious as defenders of the Roman faith, it is my firm purpose to follow the example of my ancestors. A single monk, led astray by his own folly, sets himself up in opposition to the faith of Christendom. I will sacrifice my dominions, my power, my friends, my treasure, my body, my blood, my mind, and my life, to stay this impiety.[3] I mean to send back the Augustin, Luther, forbidding him to cause the least tumult among the people ; thereafter I will proceed against him and his adherents as against declared heretics, by excommunication and interdict, and all means proper for their destruction.[4] I call upon the members of the states to conduct themselves like faithful Christians."

This address did not please every body. Charles, young and impassioned, had not observed the ordinary forms ; he ought previously to have asked the opinion of the Diet. Two extreme views were immediately declared. The creatures of the pope, the Elector of Brandenburg, and several ecclesiastical princes, demanded that no regard should be paid to the safe-conduct which had been given to Luther.[5] " The Rhine," said they, " must receive his ashes, as a century ago it received the ashes of John Huss." Charles, if we may believe a historian, afterwards bitterly repented that he had

[1] Guicciardini, p. 175. Dumont Corp. Dipl. t. iv, p. 96. Bicesi del papa Leone, che quando l'aveva fatto lega con alcuno, prima soleva dir che pero non si dovea restar de tratar cum lo altro principe opposto. It is said of Leo X, that after entering into league with any one, he was wont to say there was no occasion to cease treating with princes on the opposite side. (Suriano, Venetian Ambassador at Rome, M.S. Archives of Venice.)
[2] Autographum in linguæ Burgundica, ab ipsomet exaratum. (Cochlœus, 3.'.)
[3] " Regna, thesauros, amicos, corpus, sanguinem, vitam, spiritumque profundere. (Pallavicini, i, p. 118.)   [4] Und andern Wegen sie zu vertilgen. (L. Op. (L.) xvii, p. 581.)   [5] Dass Luthero das sichere Geleit nicht mochte gehalten werden. (Seckend. p. 357.)

not followed this dastardly counsel. "I confess," said he, to-wards the close of his life, "that I committed a great fault in al-lowing Luther to live. That heretic having offended a greater master than I, even God himself, I was not obliged to keep my promise to him. I might, nay, I ought to have forgotten my word, and avenged the insult which he offered to God; because I did not put him to death, the heresy has not ceased to gain strength. His death would have strangled it in the cradle."[1]

This horrible proposition filled the Elector and all Luther's friends with terror. "The execution of John Huss," said the Elector Palatine, "brought too many calamities on Germany to allow such a scaffold to be erected a second time." "The princes of Germany," exclaimed George of Saxony, himself the irre-concilable enemy of Luther, "will not allow a safe-conduct to be violated. This first Diet, held by our new emperor, will not incur the guilt of an act so disgraceful. Such perfidy accords not with old German integrity." The princes of Bavaria, also devoted to the Church of Rome, joined in this protestation. The death scene which Luther's friends had already before their eyes ap-peared to be withdrawn.

The rumour of these debates, which lasted for two days, spread over the town. Parties grew warm. Some gentlemen, partisans of reform, began to speak strongly against the treachery demanded by Aleander. "The emperor," said they, "is a young man whom the papists and bishops lead at pleasure by their flattery."[2] Pallavicini makes mention of four hundred nobles who were ready to maintain Luther's safe-conduct with the sword. On Saturday morning placards were found posted up on the houses and public places, some against Luther and others in his favour. One of them merely contained the energetic words of Ecclesiastes, "Woe to thee, O land, when thy king is a child!" Seckingen, it was said, had assembled at some leagues from Worms, behind the im-pregnable ramparts of his fortress, a large body of knights and soldiers, and only waited the issue of the affair that he might know how to act. The popular enthusiasm, not only in Worms, but also in the most distant towns of the empire,[3] the intrepidity of the knights, the attachment of several princes to the Reformer, all must have made Charles and the Diet comprehend that the step de-

---

[1] Sandoval Hist. de Carlos V, quoted in Llorente, History of the Inquisition, ii, p. 57. According to Llorente, the idea that Charles, toward the close of his life, inclined to evangelical opinions, is a mere invention of Protestants and the enemies of Philip II. This question forms a historical problem which the numerous quotations of Llorente appear unhappily to solve in conformity to his view.   [2] Eum esse puerum, qui nutu et blanditiis Papistarum et Episcoporum trahatur quocunque velint. (Cochlœus, p. 33.)   [3] Verum etiam in longinquis Germaniæ civitatibus, motus et murmura plebium. (Ibid., p. 33.)

manded by the Romans might compromise the supreme authority, excite revolts, and even shake the empire.[1] It was only a simple monk that they proposed to burn ; but the princes and partisans of Rome, taken all together, had neither power nor courage enough to do it. Doubtless, also, Charles V, their young emperor, had still a fear of perjury. This would seem indicated by an expression, which, if some historians speak true, he uttered on this occasion: "Were fidelity and good faith banished from the whole world, they ought to find an asylum in the hearts of princes." It is said he forgot this when on the brink of the grave. But there were other motives which might have had their influence on the emperor. The Florentine Vettori, a friend of Leo X and of Machiaveli, affirms, that Charles spared Luther only that he might keep the pope in check.[2]

On the Saturday's sitting, the violent counsels of Aleander were negatived. There was a feeling in favour of Luther, and a wish to save the simple-hearted man whose confidence in God was so affecting ; but there was a wish also to save the Church. The Diet shuddered equally at the consequences which would result from the triumph and from the destruction of the Reformer. Proposals of conciliation were heard, and it was suggested that a new attempt should be made with the doctor of Wittemberg. The archbishop-elector of Mentz himself, the young and extravagant Albert, more devout than courageous, says Pallavicini,[3] had taken alarm on seeing the interest which the people and the nobility showed in the Saxon monk. His chaplain, Capito, who, during his residence at Bâle, had been intimate with the evangelical priest of Zurich, named Zuinglius, the intrepid defender of the truth, of whom we have already had occasion to speak, had also, doubtless, represented to Albert the righteousness of the Reformer's cause. The worldly archbishop had one of those returns to Christian sentiment which his life occasionally exhibits, and agreed to go to the emperor and ask him to allow one last attempt. But Charles flatly refused. On Monday (22nd April) the princes met in a body to renew the solicitations of Albert. " I will not depart from what I have decreed," replied the emperor. I will not commission any person to go officially to Luther. " But," added he, to the great scandal of Aleander, "I give this man three days to reflect ; during this time any one

---

[1] Es wäre ein Aufruhr dauraus worden, says Luther.   [2] Carlo si excusò di non poter procedere piu oltre, rispetto al salvocondotto, ma la verità fu che conoscendo che il Papa temeva molto di questa doctrina di Luthero, lo volle tenere con questo freno." Charles pretended that he could not go farther from regard to the safe-conduct ; but the truth was that. knowing the pope was much afraid of this doctrine, he wished to hold him with this bridle. (Vettori, Istoria d'italia M.S. Biblioth. Corsini at Rome, extracted by Ranke.)   [3] Qui pio magis animo erat quam forti. (Pallavicini, p. 113.) Who was more of a devout than of a strong mind.

may, as an individual, give him suitable advice."[1] This was all that was asked.' The Reformer, thought they, elevated by the solemnity of his public appearance, will yield in a more friendly conference, and perhaps be saved from the abyss into which he is ready to fall.

The Elector of Saxony knew the contrary; accordingly he was in great fear. "If it were in my power," wrote he next day to his brother, Duke John, "I would be ready to support Luther. You could not believe to what a degree I am attacked by the partisans of Rome. If I could tell you all, you would hear very strange things.[2] They are bent on his ruin, and however slight interest any one shows for his person, he is immediately decried as a heretic. May God, who forsakes not the righteous cause, bring all to a good end!" Frederick, without showing the strong affection which he felt for the Reformer, contented himself with not losing sight of any of his movements.

It was not so with men of all ranks then in Worms. Many fearlessly gave full vent to their sympathy. From the Friday, a crowd of princes, counts, barons, knights, gentlemen, ecclesiastics, laics, and common people surrounded the hotel where the Reformer lodged; they came in and went out, and could not see enough of him.[3] He was become *the man* in Germany. Even those who doubted not that he was in error were touched by the nobleness of soul which had led him to sacrifice his life at the bidding of his conscience. With several of the personages present at Worms, and forming the flower of the nation, Luther had occasionally conversations full of that salt with which his sayings were always seasoned. None left him without feeling animated with a generous enthusiasm for the truth. George Vogler, the private secretary of the margrave Casimir of Brandenburg, writing to a friend, says, "What things I should have to tell you! What conversations full of piety and kindness Luther has had with myself and others! How winning that man is!

One day a young prince of seventeen came prancing into the court of the hotel: it was Philip, who had been reigning for two years in Hesse. The young landgrave was of an active and enterprising character, of a wisdom beyond his years, a martial spirit, and an impetuous temper, seldom allowing himself to be guided by any ideas but his own. Struck with Luther's addresses he wished to have a nearer view of him. "As yet, however," says Luther, in relating his visit, "he was not for me."[4] He dismounted, and

---

[1] Quibus privatim exhortari hominem possent. (Pallav. i, p. 119.) [2] Wunde. hören werden. (Seckend. 365.) [3] Und konnten nicht satt werden ihn zu sehen (L. Op. xvii, p. 581.) [4] Wie eine holdselige Person er ist. (Menzel Magaz, i, p. 297.)
[5] War noch nicht auf meiner Seite. (L. Op. xvii, p. 589.)

without any other formality, came up into the Reformer's room. and addressing him, said, " Well, dear doctor, how goés it ? " " Gracious lord," replied Luther, " I hope it will go well." "From what I learn," resumed the landgrave laughing, "you teach, doctor, that a wife may quit her husband, and take another, when the former is found to be too old ! " The people of the imperial court had told this story to the landgrave. The enemies of the truth never fail to circulate fabulous accounts of the lessons of Christian teachers— " No, my lord," replied Luther gravely, " let your highness not speak so, if you please." Thereupon the prince briskly held out his hand to the doctor, shook his cordially, and said, " Dear doctor, if you are in the right, may God assist you." On this he left the room, again mounted his horse and rode off. This was the first interview between these two men, who were afterwards to stand at the head of the Reformation, and to defend it, the one with the sword of the word, and the other with the sword of kings.

It was the Archbishop of Trêves, Richard de Greifenklau, who, with permission of Charles V, had undertaken the office of mediator. Richard, who was on an intimate footing with the Elector of Saxony, and a good Roman Catholic, was desirous to arrange this difficult affair, and thereby at once do a service to his friend and to the Church. On Monday evening, (22nd April,) just as Luther was going to sit down to table, a messenger of the archbishop came to say, that the prelate wished to see him the day after to-morrow (Wednesday), at six o'clock in the morning.

CHAP. X.

Conference with the Archbishop of Trêves—Wehe's advice to Luther—Luther's Replies—Private Conversation—Visit of Cochlœus—Supper at the Archbishop's— Attempt on the Hôtel of Rhodes—A Council proposed—Last interview between Luther and the Archbishop—Visit to a sick friend—Luther ordered to quit Worms.

That day the chaplain and the imperial herald, Sturm, were both at Luther's before six o'clock in the morning. Aleander had caused Cochlœus to be called at four. The nuncio had not been slow in discovering in the man who had been presented to him by Capito, a devoted servant of Rome, on whom he could calculate as on himself. Not being able to be present at this interview, Aleander wished to have a substitute at it. " Be present at the Archbishop's of Trêves," said he to the Dean of Frankfort. " Do not enter into discussion with Luther, but content yourself with paying the closest attention to every thing that is said, so as to be able to bring me back a faithful report."[1] The Reformer on arriving with some friends at the house of the archbishop, found him surrounded by the margrave, Joachim of Brandenburg and Augsburg, several nobles, deputies from free towns, lawyers, and theologians, among whom were Cochlœus and Jerome Wehe, chancellor of Baden. The latter, an able lawyer, wished a reformation in manners and discipline. He went even further. " The Word of God," said he, " which has so long been hid under the bushel, must reappear in all its lustre."[2] This conciliatory individual was entrusted with the conference. Turning kindly towards Luther, he said to him, " We did not make you come in order to dispute with you, but in order to give you brotherly advice. You know how carefully the Scripture requireth us to guard against the flying arrow, and the devil that walketh at noon-day. This enemy of the human race has instigated you to publish things contrary to religion. Think of your own safety, and that of the empire. Take care that those whom Jesus Christ has ransomed by his own death, from death eternal, be not seduced by you and perish for ever. . . . Do not set yourself up against holy councils. If we do not maintain the decrees of our fathers, there will be nothing but confusion in the Church. The distinguished princes now listening to me take a particular interest in your safety. But if you persist, the emperor will banish you from the empire,[3] and no place in the world will be able to offer you an asylum . . . Reflect on the fate which awaits you."

" Most Serene Princes 1 " replied Luther, " I give you thanks for your solicitude, for I am only a poor man, and am too humble to be exhorted by such high lords."[4] Then he continued, " I have not blamed all the councils, but only that of Constance ; because, in condemning this doctrine of John Huss, viz.—*that the Christian Church is the assembly of those who are predestinated to salvation*[5]—it condemned this article of our creed, *I believe in the holy Catholic Church;* and the Word of God itself. My lessons, it is said, give offence," added he. " I answer that the gospel of Christ cannot be preached without offence. How then should this fear or apprehension of danger detach me from the Lord, and from this divine Word, which is the only truth? No, rather give my body, my blood, and my life ! l . . .

The princes and doctors having deliberated, Luther was recalled,

---

[1] Aleander, mane hora quarta vocaverit ad se Cochlœum, jubens ut . . . audiret solum . . . (Cochlœus, p. 36.)   [2] Dass das Wort Gottes, Welches so lange unter dem Scheffel verborgen gesteckt, heller scheine . . . (Seckend. 364.)   [3] Und aus- dem Reich verstossen. (L. Op. (L) xvii, 582. Sleidan, i, p. 97.)   [4] Agnosco enim me homuncionem, longe viliorem esse, quam ut a tantis principibus . . . (L. Op. (L.) p. 167.)   [5] Ecclesia Christi est universitas prædestinatorum. (Ibid.)

and Wehe mildly resumed, "It is necessary to honour princes, even when they are mistaken, and to make great sacrifices to charity." Then he said, in a more urgent tone, " Cast yourself upon the judgment of the emperor, and have no fear."

Luther.—" I consent, with all my heart, that the emperor, the princes, and even the humblest Christian, shall examine and judge my books; but on one condition, and it is, that they take the Word of God for their standard. Men have nothing else to do but to obey. My conscience is dependent upon it, and I am captive under its authority.[1]

The Elector of Brandenburg.—" I understand you perfectly, doctor. You will not acknowledge any judge but the Holy Scripture?"

Luther.—" Yes, my lord , exactly. That is my last word."[2]

Then the princes and doctors withdrew, but the worthy Archbishop of Trèves could not resolve to abandon his undertaking. "Come," said he to Luther, as he passed into his private room, and, at the same time, ordered John Eck and Cochlœus, on the one side, and Schurff and Amsdorff, on the other, to follow them. " Why appeal incessantly to the Holy Scriptures?" said Eck keenly; " out of it all heresies have sprung." But Luther, says his friend Mathesius, remained immovable, like a rock resting on the true rock, the Word of the Lord. " The pope," replied he, " is no judge in things pertaining to the Word of God. Every Christian must see and understand for himself how he ought to live and die."[3] The parties separated. The partisans of the papacy felt Luther's superiority, and attributed it to there being nobody present who could answer him. " If the emperor," says Cochlœus, " had acted wisely in calling Luther to Worms, he would also have called theologians who might have refuted his errors."

The Archbishop of Trèves repaired to the Diet, and announced the ill success of his mediation. The surprise of the young emperor equalled his indignation. " It is time," said he, " to put an end to this affair." The archbishop asked two days more, and the whole Diet seconded him. Charles V yielded. Aleander, transported with rage, uttered the bitterest invectives.[4]

While these things were passing at the Diet, Cochlœus was burning with eagerness to gain a victory denied to prelates and kings. Though he had, from time to time, thrown in a few words at the archbishop's, the order which he had received from Alean-

[1] Sie wollten sein Gewissen das mit Gottes Wort und heiliger Schrifft gebunden und gefangen ware nicht dringen. (Math. p. 27)   [2] Ja darauf stehe Ich. (L. Op. (L.) xvii, p. 604)   [3] Ein Christenmensch muss zuschen und richten . . . (L. Ep. i, p. 604.)   [4] De iis Aleander acerrime conquestus est. (Pallavicini, l, p. 120.)

·der had laid him under restraint. He resolved to compensate him-self, and had no sooner given an account of his mission to the papal nuncio, than he presented himself at Luther's lodging. He accosted him as a friend, and expressed the grief which he felt .at the emperor's resolution. After dinner, the conversation grew .animated.[1] Cochlœus pressed Luther to retract. He declined by a nod. Several nobles, who were at table, had difficulty in restrain-ing themselves. They were indignant that the partisans of Rome ·should wish not to convince the Reformer by Scripture, but constrain him by force. Cochlœus, impatient under these reproaches, says to Luther, "Very well, I offer to dispute publicly with you, if you ·renounce the safe-conduct."[2] All that Luther demanded was a public debate. What ought he to do? To renounce the safe-·conduct was to be his own destroyer; to refuse the challenge of Cochlœus was to appear doubtful of his cause. The guests ·regarded the offer as a perfidious scheme of Aleander, whom the Dean of Frankfort had just left. Vollrat of Watzdorff, one of the ·number, freed Luther from the embarrassment of this puzzling ·alternative. This baron, who was of a boiling temperament, in-·dignant at a snare which aimed at nothing less than to give up Luther ·into the hands of the executioner,[3] started up, seized the terri-fied priest, and pushed him to the door. There would even ʹhave been bloodshed had not the other guests risen up from the ·table, and interposed their mediation between the furious baron and the trembling Cochlœus,[4] who withdrew in confusion from the ·hotel of the Knights of Rhodes.

The expression had no doubt escaped the dean in the heat of discussion, and was not a premeditated scheme between him .and Aleander to make Luther fall into a perfidious snare. Coch-·lœus denies that it was, and we have pleasure in giving credit :to his testimony, though it is true he had come to Luther's from .a conference with the nuncio.

In the evening, the Archbishop of Trêves entertained those who had ʹbeen present at the morning conference. He thought it might be a means of calming down their minds, and bringing them nearer each other. Luther, who was so intrepid and immovable before arbiters or judges, had, in private society, a good humour and gayety which seemed to promise anything that might be asked of him. The arch-·bishop's chancellor, who had shown so much sternness in his official ·capacity, joined in the attempt, and, towards the end of the repast, ·drank Luther's health. He was preparing to return the honour,

---

[1] Peracto prandio. (Cochlœus) [2] Und wollte mit mir disputiren, ich sollte :allein das Geleit aufsagen. (L. Op. (L.) xvii, p. 589.) [3] Atque ita traderet eum ·carnificinæ. (Cochlœus, p. 36.) [4] Dass Ihm das Blut über den Kopff gelaufen ·wäre wo man nicht gewehret hätte. (L. Op. (L.) xvii, p. 589.)

the wine was poured out, and he was, according to his custom, making the sign of the cross on his glass, when suddenly the glass burst in his hands, and the wine was spilt upon the table. The guests were in consternation. " There must be poison in it,"[1] said some of Luther's friends, quite loud. But the doctor, without being moved, replied, with a smile, " Dear friends, either this wine was not destined for me, or it would have been hurtful to me." Then he calmly added, "The glass burst, no doubt, because in washing it had been too soon plunged in cold water." These simple words, in the circumstances in which they were uttered, have some degree of grandeur, and bespeak unalterable peace. We cannot suppose that the Roman Catholics could have wished to poison Luther, es- pecially at the house of the Archbishop of Trèves. This repast neither estranged nor approximated the parties. The Reformer's resolution came from a higher source, and could not be influenced either by the hatred or the favour of men.

On Thursday morning (25th April) Chancellor Wehe and doc- tor Peutinger of Augsburg, imperial counsellor, who had shown great affection for Luther ever since his interview with de Vio, repaired to the hotel of the Knights of Rhodes. The Elector of Saxony sent Frederick De Thun, and another of his counsellors, to be present at the conference. " Put yourself in our hands," ear- nestly said Wehe and Peutinger, who would willingly have sacri- ficed every thing to prevent the division which was about to rend the Church. " This affair will be terminated in a Christian manner ; we give you our word for it." " In two words," said Luther to them, " here is my answer : I renounce the safe-conduct.[2] I place in the hands of the emperor my person and my life ; but the Word of God . . . . never!" Frederick de Thun affected rose and said to the deputies, "Is it not enough? Is not the sacrifice great enough ?" Then declaring that he would hear nothing more, he took his leave. Wehe and Peutinger, hoping to have better suc- cess with the doctor, came and sat down on each side of him. "Throw yourself upon the Diet," said they to him. " No," replied Luther, for *cursed be the man that trusteth in man*." (Jeremiah, xvii, 5.) Wehe and Peutinger redoubled their counsels and attacks, press- ing more closely on the Reformer. Luther worn out, rose up and put an end to the interview, saying, "I will not allow any man to set himself above the word of God."[3] "Reflect once more," said they to him on retiring, " we will return after mid-day."

---

[1] "Es müsse Gift darinnen gewesen seyn.—Luther does not mention the circum- stance, but Ratzeburg, a friend of Luther, and physician to the Elector John Frederick, relates it in a manuscript history which is extant in the library of Gotha, and says he had it from an eye-witness.   [2] Er wollte ehe das Geleit aufsagen . . . . (L. Op. (L.) xvii, 589.)   [3] Er wollte kurtzrum Menschen über Gottes Wort nicht erkennen. (Ibid., p. 583.)

They, in fact, did return; but convinced that Luther would not yield, they brought a new proposal. Luther had refused to be judged first by the pope, then by the emperor, then by the Diet. There remained one judge to whom he himself had once appealed—a general council. No doubt such a proposal would have been scouted by Rome; but it was the last plank for escape. The delegates offered Luther a Council; and he had it in his power to accept it unfettered by any precise definition. Years might have elapsed before the difficulties which the calling of a Council would have encountered on the part of the pope could have been obviated. To the Reformation and the Reformer a gain of years would have gained every thing. God and time would then have done the rest. But Luther preferred the straight course to every other: he would not save himself at the expense of truth though all that might have been necessary was to disguise it by keeping silence. "I consent," replied he, " but (this was equivalent to a refusal of the Council) on condition that the Council will judge only according to the Holy Scriptures." [1]

Peutinger and Wehe, thinking that a Council could not judge otherwise, hastened overjoyed to the archbishop. "Dr. Martin," said they, "submits his books to a Council." The archbishop was going to carry the good news to the emperor, when some doubt occurring to him, he sent for Luther

Richard of Grieffenklau was alone when the doctor arrived. "Dear doctor," said the archbishop, with much cordiality and kindness,[2] "my doctors assure me that you consent without reservation to submit your cause to a Council." "My Lord," replied Luther, "I can bear every thing, but cannot abandon the Holy Scriptures." The archbishop then perceived that Wehe and Peutinger had not explained themselves properly. Never could Rome consent to a Council bound to decide according to Scripture. " It was just," says Pallavicini, "to insist that a weak eye should read very small writing, and at the same time deny the use of spectacles." [3] The good archbishop sighed. "It was well," said he, "I made you come. What would have become of me had I immediately gone to the emperor with the news?"

The immovable firmness, the stern rectitude of Luther, are, no doubt, astonishing, but they will be comprehended and respected by all who know the claims of God. Seldom has a nobler homage been paid to the immutable word of Heaven, and that at the risk of life and liberty by the man who paid it.

---

[1] Das daruber aus der heiligen Schrifft gesprochen. (L. Op. (L.) xvii, p. 584.)
[2] Ganz gut und mehr denn gnædig. (L. Ep. i, p. 604.)   [3] Simulque conspi-ciliorum omnium usum negare. (Ibid., p. 110.)

" Well," said the venerable prelate to Luther, " do you yourself then point out a remedy."

Luther, (after a moment's silence).—"My Lord, I know no other than that of Gamaliel: ' *If this counsel or this work be of men it will come to nought, but if it be of God ye cannot overthrow it, lest haply ye be found even to fight against God.*' Let the emperor, the electors, the princes, and the states of the empire, deliver this answer to the pope."

Archbishop.—" At least retract some articles."

Luther.—" Provided it be not those which the Council of Constance condemned."

Archbishop.—" Ah, I fear they are the very ones which will be asked."

Luther.—" Then sooner sacrifice my body and my life—better allow my legs and arms to be cut off than abandon the clear and genuine word of God." [1]

The archbishop at length understood Luther. " You may withdraw," said he to him, always with the same gentleness. " Your Lordship," resumed Luther, " will be so good as to see that his Majesty cause the safe-conduct necessary for my return to be expedited." " I will see to it," replied the good archbishop, and they parted.

So ended these negotiations. The whole empire had assailed this man with the most urgent entreaties and the most fearful menaces,[2] and this man had never flinched. His refusal to bend under the iron arm of the pope emancipated the Church, and commenced a new era. The intervention of Providence was evident, and the whole presents one of those grand historical scenes in which the majestic form of the Divinity appears conspicuously displayed.

Luther withdrew in company with Spalatin who had arrived at the archbishop's during the course of the visit. John von Minkwitz, one of the Elector of Saxony's counsellors, had fallen sick at Worms. The two friends repaired to his lodging, and Luther administered the tenderest consolation to the sick man. " Adieu," said he to him on leaving, " to-morrow I shall quit Worms."

Luther was not mistaken. He had not been three hours returned to the hotel of the Knights of Rhodes when chancellor Eck and the chancellor of the emperor, with a notary, made their appearance.

The chancellor said to him, " Martin Luther, his imperial Majesty, the Electors, Princes, and States of the empire, having exhorted you to submission again and again, and in various manners,

---

[1] Ehe Stumpf und Stiel fahren lassen . . . . (L. Op. (L.) xvii, p. 584.)
[2] Totum imperium ad se conversum spectabat. (Pallavicini, i, p. 120.)

but always in vain, the emperor, in his quality of advocate and defender of the Catholic faith, sees himself obliged to take other steps. He therefore orders you to return to your home in the space of twenty-one days, and prohibits you from disturbing the public peace by the way, either by preaching or writing.

Luther was well aware that this message was the first step in his condemnation. " It has happened as Jehovah pleased," said he meekly. " Blessed be the name of Jehovah !" Then he added, "Before all things, very humbly and from the bottom of my heart, I thank his Majesty, the Electors, Princes, and other States of the empire, for having listened to me with so much kindness. I have desired, and do desire one thing only—a reformation of the Church agreeably to Holy Scripture. I am ready to do every thing and suffer every thing in humble submission to the will of the emperor. Life and death, honour and disgrace, are all alike to me : I make only one reservation—the preaching of the gospel; for, says St. Paul, 'The word of God cannot be bound.'" The deputies withdrew.

On the morning of Friday (26th April) the Reformer's friends and several nobles met at his lodgings.[1] They were gratified at seeing the Christian constancy which he had opposed to Charles and the empire, and to recognise in him the features of the ancient portrait :

> " Justum ac tenacem propositi virum,
> Non civium ardor prava jubentium,
> Non vultus instantis tyranni,
> Mente quatit solida . . . ."[2]

They wished once more, perhaps for ever, to bid adieu to this intrepid monk. Luther took a frugal meal. Now he must take leave of his friends, and flee far from them under a sky surcharged with storms. He wished to pass this solemn moment in the presence of God. He lifted up his soul and blessed those who were around him.[3] Ten in the morning having struck, Luther quitted the hotel with the friends who had accompanied him to Worms. Twenty gentlemen on horseback surrounded his carriage. A great crowd accompanied him beyond the walls. The imperial herald, Sturm, rejoined him some time after at Oppenheim, and the following day they reached Frankfort.

[1] Salutatis patronis et amicis qui eum frequentissimi convenerunt . . . . (L. Op. t at. ii, p. 168.) Having saluted his patrons and friends, who called upon him in great numbers. [2] Horat. Od. lib. iii, 3. , [3] Seine Freunde gesegnet. (Mathesius, p. 27.)

CHAP. XI.

Luther's Departure—Journey from Worms—Luther to Cranach—Luther to Charles V—Luther with the Abbot of Hirschfeld—The Curate of Eisenach—Several Princes leave the Diet—Charles signs Luther's Condemnation—The Edict of Worms—Luther with his parents—Luther attacked and carried off—The ways of God—Wartburg—Luther a Prisoner.

Luther having thus escaped from these walls of Worms, which threatened to become his tomb, his whole heart gave glory to God. " The devil himself," said he, " guarded the citadel of the pope. But Christ has made a large breach in it; and Satan has been forced to confess that the Lord is mightier than he."[1]

" The day of the Diet of Worms," says the pious Mathesius, the disciple and friend of Luther,"is one of the greatest and most glorious days given to the world before its final close."[2]   The battle fought at Worms re-echoed far and wide, and while the sound travelled over Christendom, from the regions of the North to the mountains of Switzerland, and the cities of England, France, and Italy, many ardently took up the mighty weapon of the Word of God.

Luther, having arrived at Frankfort, on the evening of Saturday, (27th April,) took advantage next day of a moment of leisure, the first he had had for a long time, to write a note, in a style at once playful and energetic, to his friend, Lucas Cranach, the celebrated painter, at Wittemberg.   " Your servant, dear compeer Lucas," said he to him, " I thought his majesty would assemble at Worms some fifty doctors to confute the monk off hand.   But not at all. Are these books yours?   Yes.   Will you retract them?   No. Ah well! get you gone!   Such was the whole story.   O blind Germans, how like children we act in allowing ourselves to be played upon and duped by Rome! . . . The Jews must for once have their chant, Yo! Yo! Yo!   But our passover also will come, and then we will sing Hallelujah![3] . . . There must be silence and suffering for a short time.   Jesus Christ says, '*A little while and ye shall not see me, and again a little while and ye shall see me.*' (John, xvi, 16.)   I hope it will be so with me.   I commend you altogether to the Eternal.   May He through Christ protect us against the attacks of the wolves and dragons of Rome.   Amen."

[1] Aber Christus macht ein Loch dei..in.   (L. Op. (L.) xvii, p. 589.)   [2] Diss ist der herrlichen grossen Tag einer vorm Ende der Welt.   (p. 28.)   [3] " Es müssen die Juden einmal singen, Io, Io, Io! . . . (L. Ep. i, p. 589.)   These cries of joy by the Jews at the time of the crucifixion represent the songs of triumph by the partisans of the papacy on occasion of the catastrophe which is going to befall Luther; but the Reformer discovers in the distance hallelujahs of deliverance.

After writing this somewhat enigmatical letter, Luther, as time was pressing, set out immediately for Friedberg, which is six leagues from Frankfort. The next day Luther again communed with himself. He was desirous to write once more to Charles V, being unwilling to confound him with guilty rebels. In his letter to the emperor he clearly expounded the nature of the obedience which is due to man, and that which is due to God, and the limit where the former must stop and give place to the latter. In reading Luther, we involuntarily call to mind the saying of the greatest autocrat of modern times : " My rule ends where that of conscience begins." [1] " God, who is the searcher of hearts, is my witness," says Luther, " that I am ready with all diligence to obey your majesty, whether in honour or disgrace, whether by life or by death, and with absolutely no exception but the word of God, from which man derives life. ' In all the affairs of the present life my fidelity will be immutable, for as to these loss or gain cannot at all affect salvation. But in regard to eternal blessings, it is not the will of God that man should submit to man. Subjection in the spiritual world constitutes worship, and should be paid only to the Creator.[2]

Luther also addressed a letter, but in German, to the States of the empire. It was nearly the same in substance as that to the emperor. It contained an account of all that had taken place at Worms. This letter was repeatedly printed and circulated all over Germany ; " Every where," says Cochlœus, · " it excited the popular indignation against the emperor and the dignified clergy." [3]

Early next day, Luther wrote a note to Spalatin, enclosing in it the two letters which he had written the evening before, and sent back the herald Sturm, who had been won to the gospel. Having embraced him he set out in all haste for Grunberg.

On Tuesday, when about two leagues from Hirschfeld, he met the chancellor of the abbot - prince of this town, who had come out to receive him. Shortly after a troop of horsemen appeared with the abbot at their head. The latter leapt from his horse, and Luther having alighted from his carriage, the prince and the Reformer embraced, and then entered Hirschfeld. The senate received them at the gates.[4] The princes of the Church ran to meet a monk anathematised by the pope, and the most distinguished among the laity, bowed the head before an individual whom the emperor had put under the ban.

" At five in the morning we will be at the church," said the prince,

[1] Napoleon to the Protestant deputation after his accession to the empire.
[2] Nam ca fides et submissio proprie est vera illa latria et adoratio Dei . . . (L. Ep. 4, p. 592.) For that faith and submission is, properly speaking, true worship and adoration of God. [3] Per chalcographos multiplicata et in populos dispersa est ea epistola . . . Cæsari autem et clericis odium populare, etc. (Cochlœus, p. 383.)
[4] Senatus intra portas nos excepit. (L. Ep. ii, p. 6.)

on rising in the evening from table, at which the Reformer was a
guest. He even wished Luther to occupy his own bed. Next day,
Luther preached, the abbot-prince accompanying him with his suite.
In the evening, Luther arrived at Eisenach, the abode of his
infancy. All his friends in the town gathered round him, and begged
him to preach. The next day they conducted him to the church.
The curate made his appearance, attended by a notary and witnesses. He came forward in great tremor, divided between the
fear of losing his place, and that of opposing the powerful man before him. At last he said, in a tone of embarrassment, " I protest
against the liberty which you are going to take." Luther mounted
the pulpit, and that voice which, twenty-three years before, sung in
the streets of this town for bread, caused the arches of the ancient
church to ring with accents which had begun to shake the world.
After the sermon, the curate, in confusion, stept softly forward to
Luther. The notary had drawn up his instrument, the witnesses
had signed it, and everything was in regular order to put the
curate's place in safety. " Pardon me," said he humbly to the
doctor ; " I have done it from fear of the tyrants who oppress the
Church."[1]

There was, in fact, some ground to fear them. At Worms,
the aspect of affairs had changed. Aleander seemed to reign
supreme. "Luther has nothing before him but exile," wrote Frederick to his brother, Duke John. Nothing can save him. If God
permits me to return, I will have things almost incredible to
tell you. Not only Annas and Caiaphas, but also Pilate and Herod, have leagued against him." Frederick, having little wish to
remain longer, left Worms. The Elector-Palatine did the same,
as did also the Archbishop-Elector of Cologne. Princes of less
elevated rank imitated them. Deeming it impossible to avert the
blow which was about to be struck, they preferred, perhaps erroneously, to abandon the place. The Spaniards, Italians, and the
most Ultra-Montane of the German princes, alone remained.

The field was free, and Aleander triumphed. He laid before
Charles the draft of an edict, which he intended should serve as the
model of that which the Diet was to issue against the monk. The
nuncio's labour pleased the irritated emperor. He assembled the
remains of the Diet in his chamber, and caused Aleander's edict
to be read to them　All who were present, (so says Pallavicini,)
approved it.

The next day—the day of a great festival—the emperor was in
the church, surrounded by the nobility of his court. The religious
solemnity was finished, and a multitude of people filled the church,

1 Humiliter tamen excusante . . . ob metum tyronnorum suorum. (L. Ep. ii, p. 6.)

Then Aleander, clad in all the insignia of his rank, approached Charles V.[1] He held in his hand two copies of the edict against Luther, the one in Latin, and the other in German, and, kneeling down before his majesty, implored him to append his signature and the seal of the empire. It was at the moment when the host had just been offered, when incense filled the temple, when music was still ringing under its arches, and, as it were, in the presence of the Divinity, that the destruction of the enemy of Rome was to be completed. The emperor, assuming the most gracious manner,[2] took the pen and signed. Aleander went off in triumph, put the decree immediately to press, and sent it over all Christendom.[3] This fruit of the labour of Rome had cost the papacy some pains. Pallavicini himself informs us that this edict, though dated the 8th May, was signed later, but was antedated, to make it be supposed that it was executed during the time when all the members of the Diet were actually assembled.

"We Charles Fifth," said the emperor, (then followed all his titles,) "to all the electors, princes, prelates, and others, whom it may concern,

"The Almighty having entrusted to us, for the defence of his holy faith, more kingdoms and power than he gave to any of our predecessors, we mean to exert ourselves to the utmost to prevent any heresy from arising to pollute our holy empire.

"The Augustin monk, Martin Luther, though exhorted by us, has rushed like a madman against the holy Church, and sought to destroy it by means of books filled with blasphemy. He has, in a shameful manner, insulted the imperishable law of holy wedlock. He has striven to excite the laity to wash their hands in the blood of priests ;[4] and, overturning all obedience, has never ceased to stir up revolt, division, war, murder, theft, and fire, and to labour completely to ruin the faith of Christians. . . . In a word, to pass over all his other iniquities in silence, this creature, who is not a man, but Satan himself under the form of a man, covered with the cowl of a monk,[5] has collected into one stinking pool all the worst heresies of past times, and has added several new ones of his own. . .

"We have, therefore, sent this Luther from before our face, that all pious and sensible men may regard him as a fool, or a man possessed of the devil ; and we expect that, after the expiry of his safe-conduct, effectual means will be taken to arrest his furious rage.

---

[1] " Cum Cæsar in templo adesset ... processit illi obviam Alcander." (Pallavicini, i, p. 22.)   [2] " Festivissimo vultu." (Ibid.)   [3] " Et undique pervulgata." (Ibid.)   [4] " Ihre Hände in der Priester Blut zu waschen." (L. Op. (L.) xvii, p. 598.)   [5] " Nicht ein Mensch, sondern als der böse Feind in Gestalt eines Menschen mit angenommener Mönchshütten." . . . (Ibid.)

" Wherefore, under pain of incurring the punishment due to the crime of treason, we forbid you to lodge the said Luther so soon as the fatal term shall be expired, to conceal him, give him meat or drink, and lend him, by word or deed, publicly or secretly, any kind of assistance. We enjoin you, moreover, to seize him, or cause him to be seized, wherever you find him, and bring him to us without any delay, or to keep him in all safety until you hear from us how you are to act with regard to him, and till you receive the recompence due to your exertions in so holy a work.

" As to his adherents you will seize them, suppress them, and confiscate their goods.

" As to his writings, if the best food becomes the terror of all mankind as soon as a drop of poison is mixed with it, how much more ought these books which contain a deadly poison to the soul to be not only rejected but also annihilated.

" You will therefore burn them, or in some other way destroy them entirely.

" As to authors, poets, printers, painters, sellers or buyers of placards, writings, or paintings, against the pope, or the Church, you will lay hold of their persons and their goods, and treat them according to your good pleasure.

" And if any one, whatever be his dignity, shall dare to act in contradiction to the decree of our imperial Majesty, we ordain that he shall be placed under the ban of the empire.

" Let every one conform hereto."

Such was the edict signed in the Cathedral of Worms. It was more than a Roman bull which, though published in Italy, might not be executed in Germany. The emperor himself had spoken, and the Diet had ratified his decree. All the partisans of Rome sent forth a shout of triumph. " It is the end of the tragedy,'' exclaimed they. " For my part," said Alphonso Valdez, a Span-iard at the emperor's court, " I am persuaded it is not the end but the beginning." [1] Valdez perceived that the movement was in the Church, in the people, in the age, and that though Luther should fall, his cause would not fall with him. But no one disguised to himself the imminent, the inevitable danger to which the Reformer was exposed, while the whole tribe of the superstitious were seized with horror at the thought of the incarnate Satan whom the emperor pointed out to the nation as disguised under a monk's frock.

The man against whom the mighty of the earth were thus forg-ing their thunders had left the Church of Eisenach, and was pre-paring to separate from some of his dearest friends. He did not

---

[1] Non finem sed initium. (P. Martyris Ep. p. 212.)

wish to follow the road of Gotha or Erfurt, but to repair to the village of Mora, his father's birth place, that he might there see his grandmother, who died four months after, his uncle, Henry Luther, and other relations. Schurff, Jonas, and Suaven, set off for Wittemberg; Luther mounted his vehicle with Amsdorff who remained with him, and entered the forest of Thuringia.[1]

The same evening he reached the village of his fathers. The poor old peasant clasped in her arms this grandson who had just been showing front to the emperor Charles and pope Leo. Luther spent the next day with his family, happy in substituting this tranquil scene for the tumult at Worms. On the following day he resumed his journey, accompanied by Amsdorff and his brother James. In these lonely spots the Reformer's lot was to be decided. They were passing along the forest of Thuringia, on the road to Wallershausen. As the carriage was in a hollow part of the road, near the old church of Glisbach, at some distance from the castle of Altenstein, a sudden noise was heard, and at that moment five horsemen, masked and in complete armour, rushed upon the travellers. Luther's brother, as soon as he perceived the assailants, lept from the vehicle, and ran off at full speed without uttering a word. The driver was for defending himself. "Stop!" cried one of the assailants in a stern voice, and rushing upon him threw him to the ground.[2] A second man in a mask seized Amsdorff, and prevented him from coming near. Meanwhile the three other horsemen laid hold of Luther, keeping the most profound silence. They pulled him violently from the carriage, threw a horseman's cloak upon his shoulders, and placed him on a led horse. Then the other two quitted Amsdorff and the driver, and the whole lept into their saddles. The hat of one of them fell off, but they did not even stop to lift it, and in a twinkling disappeared in the dark forest with their prisoner. They at first took the road to Broderode, but they soon retraced their steps by a different road, and without quitting the forest, made turnings and windings in all directions, in order to deceive those who might attempt to follow their track.

Luther, little accustomed to horseback, was soon overcome with fatigue. Being permitted to dismount for a few moments, he rested near a beech tree, and took a draught of fresh water from a spring, which is still called, *Luther's Spring*. His brother James always continuing his flight arrived in the evening at Wallershausen. The driver in great alarm had got up on his vehicle, into which Amsdorff

[1] Ad carnem meam trans sylvam profectus. (L. Ep. i, p. 7.) Proceeding beyond the forest to my kindred. [2] Dejectoque in solum auriga et verberato. (Pallavicini, i, p. 122.) Having thrown the driver to the ground and bound him with cords.
[3] Dejecto in solum auriga et verberato. (Ibid.) [4] Longo itinere, novus eques, fessus. (L. Ep. ii, p. 3.)

also mounted, and urging on his horses, which proceeded at a rapid pace, brought Luther's friend as far as Wittemberg. At Wallershausen, and Wittemberg, and the interjacent country, villages, and towns, all along the road, news of Luther's having been carried off were spread, news which, while it delighted some, filled the greater number with astonishment and indignation. A cry of grief soon resounded throughout Germany—" Luther has fallen into the hands of his enemies ! "

After the violent combat which Luther had been obliged to maintain, God was pleased to conduct him to a peaceful resting place. After placing him on the brilliant theatre of Worms, where all the powers of the Reformer's soul had been so vigorously exerted, He gave him the obscure and humiliating retreat of a prison. From the deepest obscurity He brings forth the feeble instruments by which he proposes to accomplish great things, and then, after allowing them to shine for a short time with great lustre on an elevated stage, sends them back again to deep obscurity. Violent struggles and pompous displays were not the means by which the Reformation was to be accomplished. That is not the way in which the leaven penetrates the mass of the population. The Spirit of God requires more tranquil paths. The man of whom the champions of Rome were always in pitiless pursuit, behoved for a time to disappear from the world. It was necessary that personal achievements should be eclipsed in order that the revolution about to be accomplished might not bear the impress of an individual. It was necessary that man should retire and God alone remain, moving, by his Spirit, over the abyss in which the darkness of the middle age was engulphed, and saying,—"*Let there be light.*"

Nightfall having made it impossible to follow their track, the party carrying off Luther took a new direction, and about an hour before midnight arrived at the foot of a mountain.[1] The horses climbed slowly to its summit on which stood an old fortress surrounded on all sides, except that of the entrance, by the black forests which cover the mountains of Thuringia.

To this elevated and isolated castle, named the Wartburg, where/ the Landgraves of old used to conceal themselves, was Luther conducted. The bolts are drawn, the iron bars fall, the gates open, and the Reformer clearing the threshold, the bars again close behind him. He dismounts in the court. Burkard de Hund, Lord of Allenstein, one of the horsemen, withdraws ; another, John of Berlepsch, Provost of Wartburg, conducts Luther to the chamber which was to be his prison, and where a knight's dress and a sword

---

[1] Hora ferme undecima ad mansionem noctis perveni in tenebris. (L. Ep. i, p. 3.)

were lying. The three other horsemen, dependants of the provost, carry off his ecclesiastical dress, and put on the other which had been prepared for him, enjoining him to allow his hair and beard to grow,[1] in order that none even in the castle might know who he was. The inmates of the Wartburg were only to know the prisoner under the name of Chevalier Georges. Luther scarcely knew himself in the dress which was put upon him.[2] At length he is left alone, and can turn in his thoughts the strange events which had just taken place at Worms, the uncertain prospect which awaits him, and his new and strange abode. From the narrow windows of his keep he discovers the dark, solitary, and boundless forests around. "There," says Mathesius, the biographer and friend of Luther, "the doctor remained like St. Paul in his prison at Rome."

Frederick de Thun, Philip Feilitsch, and Spalatin, had not concealed from Luther, in a confidential interview which they had with him at Worms by order of the Elector, that his liberty behoved to be sacrificed to the wrath of Charles and the pope.[3] Still there was so much mystery in the mode of his being carried off that Frederick was long ignorant of the place of his confinement. The grief of the friends of the Reformation was prolonged. Spring passed away, succeeded by summer, autumn, and winter; the sun finished his annual course, and the walls of the Wartburg still confined their prisoner. The truth is laid under interdict by the Diet; its defender, shut up within the walls of a strong castle, has disappeared from the stage of the world, none knowing what has become of him. Aleander triumphs, and the Reformation seems lost; . . . . but God reigns, and the blow which apparently threatened to annihilate the cause of the gospel will serve only to save its intrepid minister and extend the light of faith.

Let us leave Luther a captive in Germany on the heights of the Wartburg, and let us see what God was then doing in the other countries of Christendom.

---

[1] Exutus vestibus meis et equestribus indutus, comam et barbam nutriens . . . . . (L. Ep. i, p. 7.) [2] Cum ipse me jam dudum non noverim. (Ibid., ii, p. 7.) [3] Seckend., p. 366.

CHAP. I.

Movements in Switzerland—Source of the Reformation—Democratic Character—
Foreign Service—Morality—The Tockenburg—An Alpine Hut—A Pastoral
Family.

At the moment when the decree of the Diet of Worms appeared, a continually increasing movement was beginning to shake the quiet valleys of Switzerland. The voice which was heard in the plains of Upper and Lower Saxony was answered from the bosom of the Helvetic mountains by the energetic voices of its priests, its shepherds, and the citizens of its warlike cities. The partisans of Rome, seized with terror, exclaimed that a vast and dreadful conspiracy was every where formed against the Church. The friends of the gospel filled with joy, said, that as in spring a living breath is felt from the streams which run into the sea up to the mountain tops, so, throughout all Christendom, the Spirit of God was now melting the ices of a long winter, and covering with verdure and flowers the lowest plains as well as the steepest and most barren rocks.

Germany did not communicate the truth to Switzerland, nor Switzerland to France, nor France to England. All these countries received it from God, just as one part of the world does not transmit the light to another part, but the same shining globe communicates it directly to all the earth. Christ, *the day-spring from on high*, infinitely exalted above all mankind, was, at the period of the Reformation as at that of the establishment of Christianity, the divine fire which gave life to the world. In the sixteenth century one and the same doctrine was at once established in the homes and churches of the most distant and diversified nations. The reason is, that the same Spirit was every where at work producing the same faith.

The reformation of Germany and that of Switzerland demon-strate this truth. Zuinglius had no intercourse with Luther. There was, no doubt, a link between these two men; but we must search. for it above the earth. He who from heaven gave the truth to · Luther, gave it to Zuinglius. God was the medium of communica-tion between them. "I began to preach the gospel," says Zuinglius, "in the year of grace, 1516, in other words, at a time when the name of Luther had never been heard of in our country. I did not learn the doctrine of Christ from Luther, but from the word of God. If Luther preaches Christ, he does what I do ; that is- all." [1]

But if the different reformations, which all proceeded from the same Spirit, thereby acquired great unity, they also received cer-tain peculiar features, corresponding to the different characters of. the people among whom they took place.

We have already given a sketch of the state of Switzerland at the period of the Reformation,[2] and will only add a few words to what we have already said. In Germany, the ruling principle was monarchical, in Switzerland it was democratic. In Germany the Reformation had to struggle with the will of princes ; in Swit-zerland, with the will of the people. A multitude are more easily led away than an individual, and are also more prompt in their · decisions. The victory over the papacy on the other side of the · Rhine was the work of years, but on this side of it required only. months or days.

In Germany, Luther's person stands forth imposingly from the ; midst of his Saxon countrymen. He seems to struggle alone in his attack on the Roman Colossus, and wherever the battle is fought, we see his lofty stature on the field of battle. Luther is, as it. were, the monarch of the revolution which is being accomplished.. In Switzerland, several cantons are at once engaged in the contest. We see a confederacy of Reformers, and are astonished at their · numbers. No doubt there is one head which stands elevated above the rest, but no one has the command. It is a republican magis-tracy, where each presents his peculiar physiognomy, and exercises his separate influence. We have Wittemberg, Zuinglius, Capito, Haller, Œcolampadius. Again, we have Oswald Myconius, Leo Juda, Farel, and Calvin, and the Reformation takes place at Glaris, Bâle, Zurich, Berne, Neufchatel, Geneva, Lucerne, Schaf-ausen, Appenzel, St. Gall, and in the Grisons. In the Reforma-

---

[1] ... 1516, eo scilicet tempore, quum Lutheri nomen in nostris regionibus inaudi-.- tum adhuc erat ... doctrinam Christi non a Luthero, sed ex verbo Dei didici. (Zwin. ghi Opera, curant. Schulero et Schulthesio, Turici, 1829, vol. i, p. 273, 276.
[2] First Volume.

tion of Germany, one scene only is seen, and that one level like the country around; but in Switzerland, the Reformation is divided, as Switzerland itself is divided by its thousand mountains. So to speak, each valley has its awakening, and each Alpine height its gleams of light

A lamentable period had commenced in the history of the Swiss after their exploits against the dukes of Burgundy. Europe, which had learned to know the strength of their arm, had brought them forth from their mountains, and robbed them of their independence, by employing them to decide the destiny of states on battle-fields. Swiss brandished the sword against Swiss on the plains of Italy and France; and the intrigues of strangers filled these high valleys of the Alps, so long the abode of simplicity and peace, with envy and discord. Led away by the attraction of gold, sons, labourers, and servants, stole away from the chalets of alpine pastures towards the banks of the Rhine or the Po. Helvetic unity was crushed under the slow step of mules loaded with gold. The object of the Reformation in Switzerland—for there too it had a political aspect—was to re-establish the unity and ancient virtues of the cantons. Its first cry was that the Swiss should tear asunder the perfidious nets of strangers, and embrace each other in strict union at the foot of the cross. But the generous call was not listened to. Rome, accustomed to purchase in these valleys the blood which she shed in order to increase her power, rose up in wrath. She set Swiss against Swiss, and new passions arose which rent the body of the nation in pieces.

Switzerland stood in need of a reformation. It is true there was among the Helvetians a simplicity and good-nature, which the polished Italians thought ridiculous, but, at the same time, it was admitted that by no people were the laws of chastity more habitually transgressed. Astrologers ascribed this to the constellations;[1] philosophers, to the ardent temperament of this indomitable population; and moralists, to the principles of the Swiss, who regarded trick, dishonesty, and slander as much greater sins than uncleanness.[2] The priests were prohibited from marrying, but it would have been difficult to find one of them who lived in true celibacy. The thing required of them was, to conduct themselves not chastely, but prudently. This was one of the first disorders against which the Reformation was directed. It is time to trace the beginnings of this new day in the valleys of the Alps.

Towards the middle of the eleventh century, two hermits set

[1] Wirz, Helvetische Kirchen Geschichte, iii, p. 201.   [2] Sodomitis melius erit in die judicii, quam rerum vel honoris ablatoribus. (Hemmerlin, de anno jubilæo.)

out from Saint Gall, and proceeding towards the mountains at the south of this ancient monastery, arrived in a deserted valley about ten leagues long.[1] Towards the north, the high mountains of Sentis, the Sommerigkopf, and the Old-Man, separate this valley from the canton of Appenzel. On the south, the Kuhfirsten, with its seven heads, rises between it and the Wallenses, Sargans, and the Grisons, while the eastern side of the valley opens to the rays of the rising sun, and discovers the magnificent prospect of the Tyrolese Alps. The two solitaries having arrived near the source of a small river, (the Thur,) built two cells. The valley gradually became inhabited. On the highest portion of it, 2010 feet above the Lake of Zurich, there was formed, around a church, a village named Wildhaus, or the Wild House, with which two hamlets are now connected, viz., Lisighaus, or the House of Elizabeth, and Schœnenboden. The fruits of the earth are unable to grow upon these heights. A green carpet of Alpine freshness covers the whole valley, and rises upon the sides of the mountains, above which masses of enormous rocks lift their wild grandeur towards heaven.

At a quarter of a league from the church near Lisighaus, on the side of a path which leads into the pastures beyond the river, a solitary house is still standing. The tradition is, that the wood used in building it was cut upon the very spot.[3] Everything indicates that it must have been erected at a very remote period. The walls are thin. The windows have little round panes, and the roof is formed of slabs, on which stones are laid to prevent the wind from carrying them away. In front of the house there is a limpid gushing spring.

In this house, towards the end of the fifteenth century, lived a man named Zuinglius, amman or bailiff of the district. The family of the Zwingles, or Zwingli, was ancient, and in high esteem among the inhabitants of these mountains.[3] Bartholomew, brother of the bailiff, at first curate of the parish, and, after 1487, dean of Wesen, was a person of some celebrity in the district.[4] Margaret Meili, the wife of the amman of Wildhaus, and whose brother John was afterwards abbot of the convent of Fischingen in Thurgovia, had already given birth to two sons, Heini and Klaus, when, on the first day of the year 1484, seven weeks after the birth of Luther, a third son, Ulric, was born in this solitary hut.[5] Five other sons, John,

---

[1] The Tokenburg.   [2] Schuler's Zwinglis Bildungs Gesch. p. 290.
[3] Diss Geschlächt der Zwinglinen, wass in guter Achtung diesser Landen, als ein gut alt ehnlich Geschlächt. (II. Bullinger's Histor. Beschreibung der Eidg. Geschichten. This valuable work existed only in manuscript in 1837, and was communicated to me by the kindness of M. J. G. Hess. In the quotations I preserve the orthography of the period and of the manuscript. The friends of history have since caused it to be printed.   [4] Ein verrumbter Mann. (Ibid.)   [5] Quadragesimum octavum agimus, writes Zuinglius to Vadian, 17th September, 1531.

2   O

Wolfgang, Bartholomew, James, Andrew, and a daughter, Anna, were afterwards added to this Alpine family. No person in the country was more venerated than amman Zuinglius.[1] His character, his office, his numerous children, made him the patriarch of these mountains. He and all his sons were shepherds. No sooner did the first days of May open upon these mountains than the father and the children departed with their flocks for the pastures, rising gradually from station to station, and so, towards the end of July, reaching the highest summits of the Alps. Then they began gradually to redescend towards the valley, and in autumn the whole population of Wildhaus returned to their humble huts. Sometimes, during the summer, the young people who had been obliged to remain at home, eager for the mountain breezes, set out in bands for the chalets, uniting their voices to the melody of their rustic instruments. On their arrival on the Alps, the shepherds from a distance saluted them with their horns and their songs, and regaled them with a feast of milk. Afterwards the joyous band, by turnings and windings, descended again into the valley, moving to the sound of their pipes. Ulric in his youth doubtless joined occasionally in this amusement. He grew up at the foot of those rocks which seem eternal, and whose tops reach the heavens. "I have often thought," says one of his friends, " that, being brought near to heaven on these sublime heights, he there contracted something celestial and divine." [2]

There were long winter evenings in the cottages of Wildhaus, and then young Ulric, seated at the paternal hearth, listened to the conversation of the bailiff and the old men of the district. He heard them tell how the inhabitants of the valley had formerly groaned under a heavy yoke. With the old men his heart beat high at the thought of the independence which the Tockenburg had acquired, and which the alliance with the Swiss had secured. A patriotic feeling was kindled in his breast. Switzerland became dear to him; and if any one uttered an unfavourable expression against the confederates, the child instantly stood up and warmly defended their cause.[3] During these long evenings he was often seen quietly seated at the feet of his pious grandmother, with his eyes rivetted upon her, listening to her Bible stories, and devout lessons, as he eagerly received them into his heart.

---

[1] Clarus fuit pater ob spectatam vitæ sanctimoniam. (Oswald Myconius, Vita Zwingli.)   [2] Divinitatis nonnihil cœlo propriorem contraxisse. (Ibid.)
[3] Schulers Zw. Bildung, p. 291.

CHAP. II.

Young Ulric at Wesen—At Bâle—At Berne—The Dominican Convent—Jetzer—
The Apparitions—The Passion of the Lay Brother—The Imposture—Discovery
and Punishment—Zuinglius at Vienna—At Bâle—Music at Bâle—Wittembach
teaches the Gospel—Leon Juda—The Curate of Glaris.

The good amman was delighted with the happy presages in his son.
He perceived that Ulric would be able to do something else than
herd his cows on Mount Sentis, singing the shepherd's song. One
day he took him by the hand and proceeded with him towards
Wesen. He traversed the verdant ridges of the Ammon, avoiding
the wild and precipitous rocks which border the lake of Wallen-
stadt. On arriving at the town, he called upon his brother the
dean, to whom he intrusted the young mountaineer, in order that
he might ascertain what his talents were.[1] The leading feature
in his character was an innate horror at falsehood and a great love
of truth. He himself relates that one day, when he was beginning
to reflect, the thought struck him that falsehood should be punished
more severely than even theft; "for," adds he, "veracity is the
parent of all the virtues." The dean soon loved his nephew as if
he had been his son ; delighted with his sprightliness, he entrusted
his education to a schoolmaster who in a short time taught him
all that he knew himself. Young Ulric, when ten years of age,
having given indications of a high order of intellect,[2] his father
and his uncle resolved on sending him to Bâle.

When the child of the Tockenburg arrived in this celebrated
city, with an integrity and purity of heart which he seemed to have
inhaled from the pure air of his mountains, but which came from
a higher source, a new world opened before him. The celebrity of
the famous council of Bâle ; the university which Pius II had
founded in 1460 ; the printing presses, which revived the master-
pieces of antiquity, and circulated over the world the first fruits of
the revival of letters; the residence of distinguished men ; the
Wessels, the Wittembachs, and, in particular, that prince of scholars
and luminary of the schools, Erasmus, rendered Bâle, at the period
of the Reformation, one of the great foci of light in the west.

Ulric entered the school of St. Theodore, which was taught by
Gregory Binzli, a man of an affectionate and gentle temper, at

---

[1] Tenerrimum ad fratrem sacrificum adduxit, ut ingenii ejus periculum faceret.
(Melch. Ad. Vit. Zw. p. 25.)   [2] Und in ihm erschienen merkliche Zeichen eines
edlen Gemüths. (Manuscript de Bullinger.)

this period rare among teachers. Young Zuinglius made rapid progress. The learned disputes which were then fashionable among the doctors of universities had even descended to the youth in schools. Ulric took part in them. He exercised his growing strength against the children of other schools, and was always victorious in those struggles which formed a kind of prelude to those by which the papacy was to be overthrown in Switzerland.[1] His success excited the jealousy of rivals older than himself. The school of Bâle was soon outstripped by him as that of Wesen had been.

Lupulus, a distinguished scholar, had just opened at Berne the first learned school that was founded in Switzerland. The bailiff of Wildhaus and the curate of Wesen resolved to send their child thither, and Zuinglius, in 1497, quitting the smiling plains of Bâle, again drew near to the high Alps, where he had spent his childhood, and whose snowy tops, gilded with the rays of the sun, he could see from Berne. Lupulus, a distinguished poet, introduced his pupil to the sanctuary of classic literature, a sanctuary then unknown, only a few of the initiated having passed the threshold.[2] The young neophyte ardently breathed an atmosphere rich in the perfumes of antiquity. His intellect was developed and his style formed. He became a poet.

Among the convents of Berne, that of the Dominicans held a distinguished place. These monks were engaged in a serious quarrel with the Franciscans. The latter maintained the immaculate conception of the virgin, while the former denied it. In every step the Dominicans took—before the rich altars which decorated their church, and between the twelve pillars on which its arches were supported—they thought only of humbling their rivals. They had observed the fine voice of Zuinglius, and heard of his precocious intellect, and thinking that he might throw lustre on their order, strove to gain him.[3] With this view they invited him to remain in their convent till he should make his noviciate. The whole prospects of Zuinglius were threatened. The amman of Wildhaus having been informed of the bait to which the Dominicans had had recourse, trembled for the innocence of his son, and ordered him forthwith to quit Berne. Zuinglius thus escaped those monastic enclosures into which Luther rushed voluntarily. What happened afterwards may enable us to comprehend the imminent danger to which Zuinglius had been exposed.

[1] In disputationibus, quæ pro more tum erant inter pueros usitatæ, victoriam semper reportavit. (Osw. Myc. Vit. Zw.)   [2] Ab eo in adyta classicorum scriptorum introductus. (Ibid.)   [3] Und als er wol singen kœndt lœkten Ihn die prediger Mœnchen in dass Kloster. (Bullinger, M.S.)

In 1507 great excitement prevailed in the town of Berne. A young man of Zurzach, named John Jetzer, having one day presented himself at this same Dominican convent, had been repulsed. The poor youth in despair had returned to the charge, holding in his hand fifty-three florins and some pieces of silk. "It is all I possess," said he, "take it, and receive me into your order." He was admitted on the 6th January among the lay brothers. But the very first night a strange noise in his cell filled him with terror. He fled to the Carthusian convent, but was again sent back to that of the Dominicans.

On the following night, being the eve of the feast of St. Matthew, he was awoke by deep sighs, and perceived at his bedside a tall phantom in white. "I am," said a sepulchral voice, "a soul escaped from the fire of purgatory." The lay brother trembling, replied, "God save you; for me, I can do nothing." Then the spirit advanced towards the poor friar and, seizing him by the throat, indignantly upbraided him with his refusal. Jetzer in terror exclaimed, "What then can I do to save you?" "Flagellate yourself for eight days till the blood comes, and lie prostrate on the pavement of the chapel of St. John." So answered the spirit, and disappeared. The lay brother gave information of the apparition to his confessor, a preacher of the convent, and by his advice submitted to the discipline required. The rumour soon spread throughout the town that a soul had applied to the Dominicans to be delivered from purgatory. The Franciscans were deserted, and every one ran to the church to see the holy man lying prostrate on the ground. The soul from purgatory had intimated that he would reappear in eight days. On the night appointed it in fact did appear, accompanied by two other spirits that were tormenting it and howling horribly. "Scotus," said the spirit, "Scotus, the inventor of the Franciscan doctrine of the immaculate conception of the Virgin, is among those who like me are suffering these fierce pains." At this news, which soon spread over Berne, the partisans of the Franciscans were still more alarmed. The spirit on disappearing had announced a visit from the Virgin herself. In fact, on the day appointed, the astonished friar saw Mary herself appear in his cell. He could not believe his eyes. She approached him kindly, gave him three of our Saviour's tears, three drops of his blood, a crucifix, and a letter addressed to Pope Julius II, "who," said she, "was the individual chosen by God to abolish the festival of her pretended immaculate conception." Then coming still closer to the bed on which the friar lay, she announced, in a solemn tone, that a great grace was to be conferred on him, and drove a nail into his hand. The lay brother uttered a loud shriek, but Mary wrapt up his hand in a piece of linen which her Son, she said, had worn after his flight into Egypt. This wound was not sufficient to make the glory of the Dominicans equal to that of the Franciscans. Jetzer must have the five wounds of Christ and of St. Francis in his hands, feet, and side. The four others were inflicted, and then, after giving him a draught, he was placed in a hall hung with pictures representing our Saviour's passion. Here having spent whole days fasting, his imagination soon became heated. The doors of the hall were then thrown open from time to time to the public who came in crowds to contemplate with devout astonishment the friar with his five wounds, stretching out his arms, bending his head, and by his positions and gestures imitating the crucifixion of our Lord. Sometimes, out of his wits, he foamed, and seemed about to breathe his last. The whisper went round, "He is enduring the cross of Christ." The multitude, eager for miracles, continually thronged the convent. Men worthy of high esteem, among others Lupulus himself, the master of Zuinglius, were overawed, and the Dominicans, from the height of the pulpit extolled the glory which God was bestowing on their order.

This order had for some years felt the necessity of humbling the Franciscans, and of augmenting the respect and liberality of the people by means of miracles. Berne, "a simple, rustic, and ignorant town," as the sub-prior of Berne described it to the Chapter held at Wimpfen on the Necker, had been selected as the theatre of their operations. The prior, sub-prior, preacher, and purveyor of the convent, had undertaken to perform the leading characters, but they wanted the talent necessary to perform them to the end. A new apparition of Mary having taken place, Jetzer thought he recognised the voice of his confessor, and having said so aloud, Mary disappeared. She soon made her appearance again, to censure the incredulous friar. "This time it is the prior," exclaimed Jetzer, rushing forward with a knife in his hand. The saintess threw a pewter plate at the poor friar's head, and likewise disappeared.

In consternation at the discovery which Jetzer had thus made, the Dominicans tried to disencumber themselves of him by means of poison. He perceived it; and, having taken flight, disclosed the imposition. They put on a good countenance, and sent deputies to Rome. The pope committed the decision to his legate in Switzerland, and the bishops of Lausanne and Sion. The four Dominicans being convicted, were condemned to be burnt alive ; and on the 1st May, 1509, were consumed by the flames, in presence of more than thirty thousand spectators. The affair made a noise throughout Europe, and by unveiling one of the worst sores of the Church, prepared the Reformation.[1]

Such were the men into whose hands Ulric Zuinglius had nearly fallen. He had studied literature at Berne; he behoved now to devote himself to philosophy, and with this view repaired to Vienna. A youth from St. Gall, named Joachim Vadian, whose genius gave promise to Switzerland of a distinguished scholar and a statesman; Henri Loreti, of the canton of Glaris, commonly called Glarean, and apparently destined to shine among poets; John Heigerlin, son of a forgemaster, and hence surnamed Faber, of a versatile temper, fond of honour and glory, possessing all the qualities indicative of a courtier—such were Ulric's fellow-students and companions in the capital of Austria.

Zuinglius returned to Wildhaus in 1502; but on revisiting his mountains he felt that he had drunk of the cup of science, and could no longer live amid the songs of his brothers and the bleating of their flocks. He was eighteen years of age, and repaired to Bâle,[2] to engage again in literary pursuits, and thus at once master and pupil he taught at the school of St. Martin, and studied at the university; from this time he was able to dispense with assistance from his father. Shortly after, he took the degree of master of arts. An Alsatian, named Capito, nine years older than he, was one of his best friends.

Zuinglius devoted himself to the study of scholastic theology; for, being called one day to combat its sophisms, he behoved to explore its obscure labyrinth. But the light hearted student of the mountains of Sentis was often seen suddenly to shake off the dust of the school, and, substituting amusement for his philosophic toils, seize the lute, or the harp, or the violin, or the flute, or the tympanon, or the cornet, or the hunting horn, extract joyous sounds from these instruments as in the prairies of Lisighaus, and make his lodgings, or the dwellings of his friends, re-echo with the airs of his country, accompanying them with his voice. In regard to music, he was a true child of the Tockenburg, superior to all.[3] In addition to the instruments we have already named, he played several others. An enthusiast in the art he diffused a taste for it in the university, not from any desire of dissipation, but because he loved thus to relax his mind when fatigued by serious study, and fit himself for returning with greater zeal to difficult labours.[4] None had a gayer humour, a

[1] Wirz, Helvetische Kirchen Gesch. vol. iii, p. 387. Anshelms Cronik, iii and iv. No event of the period of the Reformation has given rise to so many writings. See Haller's Biblioth. der Schw. Gesch. iii. [2] Ne diutius ab exercitio literarum cessaret. (Osw. Myc. Vit. Zw.) [3] Ich habe auch nie von Keinem gehört der in der Kunst Musica . . . so erfahren gewesen. (B. Weysen, Füsslin Beyträge zur Ref. Gesch. iv, 35.) [4] Ut ingenium seriis defatigatum recrearetur et paratius ad sollta studia redderetur . . . (Melch. Ad. Vit. Zw.)

more amiable disposition, or more engaging conversation.[1] He was a vigorous Alpine tree which developed itself in all its gracefulness and strength, and which, never having been pruned, threw out strong branches in all directions. The time was coming when these branches would turn vigorously in the direction of heaven.

After he had forced an entrance into scholastic theology he left its arid tracts fatigued and disgusted, having found nothing in it but confused ideas, vain babbling, vain glory, barbarism, and not one sound idea of doctrine. "It is only a loss of time," said he, and waited for something better.

At this time, (November, 1505,) arrived at Bâle Thomas Wittembach, son of a burgomaster of Bienne. Wittembach had till then taught at Tubingen, side by side with Reuchlin. He was in the vigour of life, sincere, pious, skilled in the liberal arts, and mathematics, and well acquainted with the Holy Scriptures. Zuinglius and all the academic youth immediately flocked around him. A spirit hitherto unknown animated his lectures, and prophetic words escaped from his lips : "The time is not distant," said he, "when scholastic theology will be abolished and the ancient doctrine of the Church restored."[2] "The death of Christ," added he, "is the only ransom of our souls."[3] The heart of Zuinglius eagerly received these seeds of life.[4] At this period classical studies began every where to supplant the scholastics of the middle age. Zuinglius, like his preceptors and friends, threw himself into this new course.

Among the students who followed the lessons of the new teacher with the greatest enthusiasm was a young man of twenty-three, of small stature, and a feeble sickly appearance, but whose eye bespoke at once gentleness and intrepidity. This was Leo Juda, son of an Alsatian curate, and whose uncle had fallen at Rhodes, fighting in defence of Christendom, under the standard of the Teutonic knights. Leo and Ulric were on intimate terms. Leo played the tympanon, and had a very fine voice. The joyous melodies of the young friends of the arts were often heard in his lodgings. Leo Juda, at a later period, became the colleague of Zuinglius, and even death could not destroy their sacred friendship.

At this time the office of pastor of Glaris having become vacant, Henry Goldli, a young courtier of the pope, and groom of the stable to his holiness, obtained the appointment from his master, and hastened with it to Glaris. But the Glarian shepherds, proud of

---

[1] Ingenio amœnus, et ore jucundus, supra quam dici possit, erat. (Os. Myc. Vit. Zw.)
[2] Et doctrinam Ecclesiæ veterem . . . instaurari oporteat. (Gualterus, Misc. Tig. iii, 102.)   [3] Der Tod Christi sey die einige Bezahlung fur unsere Sünde. . . . (Füslin Beyr. ii, p. 268.)   [4] Quum a tanto viro semina quædam . . . Zuingliano pectori injecta essent. (Leo Jud. in Præf. ad. Ann. Zw. in N. T.) When the great man had deposited some seeds in the breast of Zuinglius.

the antiquity of their race, and of their battles for freedom, were not disposed to bow implicitly to a piece of parchment from Rome. Wildhaus is not far from Glaris ; and Wesen, where Zuinglius' uncle was curate, is the place where the market of the district is held. The reputation of the young master of arts of Bâle had penetrated even into these mountains ; and the Glarians, wishing to have him for their priest, gave him a call in 1506. Zuinglius having been ordained at Constance by the bishop, preached his first sermon at Rapperswil, read his first mass at Wildhaus on St. Michael's day, in presence of all his relations and the friends of his family, and towards the close of the year arrived at Glaris.

CHAP. III.

Love of War—Schinner—Pension from the Pope—The Labyrinth—Zuinglius in. Italy—Principle of Reform—Zuinglius and Luther—Zuinglius and Erasmus— Zuinglius and the Elders—Paris and Glaris.

Zuinglius immediately engaged in the zealous discharge of the work which his vast parish imposed upon him. Still he was only twenty-two years of age, and often allowed himself to be carried away by the dissipation and lax ideas of his age. A priest of Rome he was like the other priests around him. But even at this period, though the evangelical doctrine had not changed his heart, Zuinglius did not give way to those scandals which frequently afflicted the Church.[1] He always felt the need of subjecting his passions to the holy rule of the gospel.

A love of war at this time inflamed the quiet valleys of Glaris where there were families of heroes—the Tschudis, the Walas, the Æblis, whose blood had flowed on the field of battle. The youth listened with eagerness to the old warriors when they told them of the wars of Burgundy and Suabia, of the battles of St. James and Ragaz. But alas! it was no longer against the enemies of their liberties that these warlike shepherds took up arms. They were seen, at the bidding of the kings of France, of the emperor, the dukes of Milan, or the holy father himself, descending from the Alps like an avalanche, and rushing with the noise of thunder against the troops drawn up in the plain.

A poor boy named Matthew Schinner, who was at the school of Sion in the Valais, (it was toward the middle of the latter half of

[1] Sic reverentia pudoris, imprimis autem officii divini, perpetuo cavit. (Osw. Myc. Vit. Zw.)

the fifteenth century,) singing before the houses, as young Martin Luther shortly after did, heard himself called by an old man, who, being struck with the frankness with which the child answered his questions, said to him with that prophetic spirit with which man is said to be sometimes endowed when on the brink of the grave, "Thou art to be a bishop and a prince." [1] The expression sunk deep into the young mendicant, and from that moment boundless ambition took possession of his heart. At Zurich and Como the progress he made astonished his masters. Having become curate of a small parish in Valais, he rose rapidly, and being sent at a later period to ask from the pope the confirmation of a bishop of Sion, who had just been elected, he obtained the bishopric for himself, and girt his brow with the episcopal mitre. This man, ambitious and crafty, but often noble and generous, always considered any dignity bestowed upon him as only a step destined to raise him to some still higher dignity. Having offered his services to Louis XII, and named his price, "It is too much for one man," said the king. " I will show him," replied the bishop of Sion, offended, " that I am a man worth several men." In fact he turned towards pope Julius II, who gladly received him, and Schinner succeeded in 1510 in linking the whole Swiss confederation to the policy of this ambitious pontiff. The bishop having been rewarded with a cardinal's hat smiled when he saw that there was now only one step between him and the papal throne.

Schinner's eye was continually turned to the cantons of Switzerland, and as soon as he there discerned any man of influence he hastened to attach him to himself. The pastor of Glaris drew his attention, and Zuinglius soon received intimation that the pope had granted him an annual pension of fifty florins, to encourage him in the cultivation of letters. His poverty did not allow him to purchase books; and the money during the short time that Ulric received it was devoted to the purchase of classical or theological works, which he procured from Bâle.[2] Zuinglius was now connected with the cardinal, and accordingly joined the Roman party. Schinner and Julius II at last disclosed the end which they had in view in these intrigues. Eight thousand Swiss mustered by the eloquence of the cardinal-archbishop, passed the Alps; but famine, war, and French gold obliged them to return to their mountains without glory. They brought back the usual results of these foreign wars, —distrust, licentiousness, party spirit, all sorts of violence and disorder. Citizens refused to obey their magistrates, and children their parents; agriculture and the care of their flocks were neglected;

[1] Helvet. Kirch Gesch. von Wirz, iii, p. 314.   [2] Wellches er an die Bücher verwändet. (Bullinger MS.)

luxury and mendicity kept pace with each other ; the most sacred ties were broken, and the confederation seemed on the point of being dissolved.

The eyes of the young curate of Glaris were now opened, and his indignation aroused. He raised his voice aloud to warn them of the abyss into which they were about to fall. In 1510 he published his poem entitled " The Labyrinth." Behind the windings of this mysterious garden, Minos has hidden the Minotaur, that monster, half man half bull, whom he feeds on the flesh of young Athenians. " The Minotaur, . . . in other words," says Zuinglius, " sin, vice, irreligion, and the foreign service of the Swiss,"devour the sons of his countrymen.

Theseus, a man of courage, wishes to deliver his country, but numerous obstacles arrest him ;—first, a lion with one eye ; this is Spain and Arragon ;—then a crowned eagle, whose throat is opened to devour it ; this is the empire ;—then a cock, with his comb up, and calling for battle ; this is France. The hero surmounts all these obstacles, gets up to the monster, stabs it, and saves his country.

" So now," exclaims the poet, " men wander in a labyrinth, but having no thread to guide them they cannot regain the light. No where is there any imitation of Jesus Christ. A little glory makes us hazard our life, torment our neighbour, rush into strife, war, and combat . . . One would say that the furies have escaped from the depths of hell." [1]

A Theseus, a Reformer was required. Zuinglius perceived this, and thenceforth had a presentiment of his mission. Not long after he composed an allegory with a still clearer application.[2]

In April, 1512, the confederates rose anow at the bidding of the cardinal, for the deliverance of the Church. Glaris was in the foremost rank. The whole population was brought into the field, ranged round their banner with their landaman and their pastor. Zuinglius behoved to march. The army passed the Alps, and the cardinal appeared amidst the confederates with the presents given him by the pope,—a ducal hat adorned with pearls and gold, and surmounted by the Holy Spirit, represented under the form of a dove. The Swiss escaladed the fortresses and towns, swam rivers in the presence of the enemy, unclothed, and with halberds in their hands ; the French were every where put to flight ; bells and trumpets resounded, and the population flocked from all quarters ; the nobles

[1] Dass wir die höllschen wütterinn'n
Mögend denken abbrochen syn.
{Zw. Op. ed. Schüler et Schulthess, ii, part ii, p. 249.}
[2] Fabelgedicht vom Ochsen und etlichen Thieren, iez loufender dinge begriffenuch.
{Ibid. p. 257.}

supplied the army with wine and fruits in abundance ; the monks and priests mounted on platforms, and proclaimed, that the confederates were the people of God taking vengeance on the enemies of the Lord's spouse ; and the pope becoming prophet, like Caiaphas of old, gave the confederates the title of " Defenders of the liberty of the Church." [1]

This sojourn of Zuinglius in Italy was not without its effect, in reference to his vocation of Reformer. On his return from this campaign, he began to study Greek, " in order," says he, " to be able to draw the doctrine of Jesus Christ from the very fountain of truth." [2] Writing to Vadian, 23rd February, 1513, he says, " I have resolved so to apply myself to the study of Greek, that none will be able to turn me from it but God. I do it not for fame, but from love to sacred literature." At a later period, a worthy priest, who had been his school companion, having come to pay him a visit, said to him, " Master Ulric, I am assured that you are tainted with the new heresy, that you are a Lutheran." " I am not a Lutheran," said Zuinglius, " for I knew Greek before I heard of the name of Luther." [3] To know Greek, to study the gospel in the original tongue, was, according to Zuinglius, the basis of the Reformation.

Zuinglius did more than recognise, at this early period, the great principle of evangelical Christianity—the infallible authority of the Holy Scriptures. Besides this, he understood how the meaning of the divine Word ought to be ascertained. " Those," said he, " have a very grovelling idea of the Scriptures who regard whatever seems to them at variance with their own reason as frivolous, vain, and unjust.[4] Men have no right to bind the gospel at pleasure to their own sense, and their own interpretation." [5] " Zuinglius raised his eye to heaven," said his dearest friend, " unwilling to have any other interpreter than the Holy Spirit himself." [6]

Such, from the commencement of his career, was the man, whom some have not scrupled to represent as having wished to subject the Bible to human reason. " Philosophy and theology," said he, " ceased not to raise up objections against me. I, at length, arrived at this conclusion, ' We must leave all these things, and seek our knowledge of God only in his Word.' I began," continues he, " earnestly to supplicate the Lord to give me his light,

---

1 De Gestis inter Gallos et Helvetios, relatio II. Zwinglii. 2 Ante decem-annos, operam dedi graecis literis, ut ex fontibus doctrinam Christi haurire possem. (Zw. Op. i, p. 274, in his Explan. Artic. dated 1523.) 3 Ich hab graecae können, ehe ich ni nut von Luther gehot hab. (Salat. Chronik. MS.) 4 Nihil sublimius de evangelio sentiunt, quam quod, quidquid eorum rationi non est consentaneum, hoc iniquum, vanum et frivolum existimant. (Zw. Op. i, p. 262.)
5 Nec posse evangelium ad sensum et interpretationem hominum redigi. (Ibid., p. 215.) 6 In coelum suspexit, doctorem quaerens Spiritum. (Osw. Myc. Vit. Zw.)

and though I read only the text of Scripture, it became far clearer
to me than if I had read a host of commentators." Comparing
the Scriptures with themselves and explaining passages that were
obscure by such as were more clear,[1] he soon had a thorough
knowledge of the Bible, especially the New Testament.[2] When
Zuinglius thus turned toward the Holy Scriptures, Switzerland
took her first step in the Reformation. Accordingly, when he expounded the Scriptures, every one felt that his lessons came from
God, and not from man.[3] "Work all divine!" here exlaims Oswald Myconius; "thus was the knowledge of heavenly truth restored to us!"

Zuinglius did not, however, despise the expositions of the most
celebrated doctors : at a later period, he studied Origen, Ambrose,
Jerome, Augustine, Chrysostom, but not as authorities. "I study
the doctors," says he, "with the same feelings with which one asks
a friend, 'What do you understand by this?'" The Holy Scripture was, according to him, the touch-stone by which the most
holy of the doctors were themselves to be tested.[4]

Zuinglius's step was slow, but progressive. He did not come
to the truth like Luther amid those tempests which compel the soul
to seek a speedy shelter. He arrived at it by the peaceful influence of Scripture, whose power gradually gains upon the heart.
Luther reached the wished-for shore across the billows of the
boundless deep ; Zuinglius, by allowing himself to glide along the
stream. These are the two principal ways by which God leads
men. Zuinglius was not fully converted to God and his gospel
till the first period of his sojourn at Zurich ; yet, in 1514 or 1515,
at the moment when the strong man began to bend the knee to
God, praying for the understanding of his Word, the rays of that
pure light by which he was afterwards illumined, first began to
gleam upon him.

At this period, a poem of Erasmus, in which Jesus Christ was
introduced addressing man as perishing by his own fault, made a
powerful impression on Zuinglius. When alone in his study, he
repeated the passage in which Jesus complains that all grace is
not sought from him, though he is the source of all that is good.
"ALL!" said Zuinglius, "ALL!" And this word was incessantly
present to his mind. "Are there then creatures, saints, from
whom we ought to ask assistance? No! Christ is our only
treasure."[5]

[1] Scripta contulit et obscura claris elucidavit. (Ib.o.)   [2] In summa, er
macht im, die II. Schrifft, Insonders dass N. T. gantz gemein. (Bullinger, MS.)
[3] Ut nemo non videret Spiritum doctorem, non hominem. (Osw. Myc. Vit. Zw.)
[4] Scriptura canonica, seu Lydio lapide probandos. (Ibid.)   [5] Dass Christus
unser armen seelen ein einziger Schatz sey. (Zw. Op. i, p. 398.) Zuinglius says in
1522 that he had read the poem of Erasmus eight or nine years before.

Zuinglius did not confine his reading to Christian writings. One of the distinguishing characteristics of the sixteenth century is the profound study of the Greek and Roman authors. The poetry of Hesiod, Homer, Pindar, enraptured him, and he has left us commentaries, or characteristics, on the two last poets. It seemed to him that Pindar spoke of his gods in such sublime strains that he must have had some presentiment of the true God. He studied Cicero and Demosthenes thoroughly, and learned from them both the art of the orator and the duties of the citizen. He called Seneca a holy man. The Swiss mountaineer loved also to initiate himself in the mysteries of nature, through the writings of Pliny. Thucydides, Sallust, Livy, Cæsar, Suetonius, Plutarch, and Tacitus, taught him to know the world. He has been censured for his enthusiastic admiration of the great men of antiquity, and it is true that some of his observations on this subject cannot be defended. But if he honoured them so much, it was because he thought he saw in them not human virtues, but the influence of the Holy Spirit. The agency of God, far from confining itself to ancient times within the limits of Palestine, extended, according to him, to the whole world.[1] " Plato," said he, "has also drunk at the Divine source. And if the two Catos, if Camillus, if Scipio had not been truly religious, would they have been so magnanimous ?"[2]

Zuinglius diffused around him a love of letters. Several choice youths were trained in his school. " You offered me not only books, but also yourself," wrote Valentine Tschudi, son of one of the heroes of the wars of Burgundy; and this young man, who at that time had already studied at Vienna and Bâle, under the most celebrated teachers, adds, " I have never met with any one who explained the classics with so much precision and profundity as yourself."[3] Tschudi repaired to Paris, and was able to compare the spirit which prevailed in that university, with that which he had found in the narrow Alpine valley, over which impend the gigantic peaks and eternal snows of the Dodi, the Glarnisch, the Viggis, and the Freyberg. " How frivolously," says he, " the French youth are educated! No poison is so bad as the sophistical art in which they are trained—an art which stupifies the senses, destroys the judgment, brutifies the whole man. Man is thenceforth, like the echo,. an empty sound. Ten women could not keep pace with one of these

[1] Spiritus ille cœlestis non solam Palestinam vel creaverat vel fovebat, sed mundum universum . . . . . . (Œcol. et Zw. Ep. p. 9.)   That celestial Spirit had created and continued to cherish not only Palestine, but the whole world.
[2] Nisi religiosi nunquam fuissent magnanimi. (Ibid.)   [3] Nam qui sit acrioris in enodandis autoribus judicii, vidi neminem. (Zw. Ep. p. 13.) For I have never seen any one so acute and judicious in unravelling authors.

rhetoricians.[1] In their prayers even they present their sophisms to God, (I know the fact,) and pretend, by their syllogisms, to constrain the Holy Spirit to hear them." Such, then, were Paris and Glaris; the intellectual metropolis of Christendom, and a village of Alpine shepherds. A ray of the Divine Word gives more light, than all human wisdom.

CHAP. IV.

Zuinglius in regard to Erasmus—Oswald Myconius—The Vagrants—Œcolampadius—Zuinglius at Marignan—Zuinglius and Italy—Method of Zuinglius—Commencement of Reform—Discovery.

A great man of this age, Erasmus, had much influence on Zuinglius, who, as soon as any of his writings appeared, lost no time in procuring it. In 1514, Erasmus had arrived at Bâle, and been received by the bishop with marks of high esteem. All the friends of letters had immediately grouped around him. But the monarch of the schools had no difficulty in singling out him who was to be the glory of Switzerland. "I congratulate the Swiss nation," wrote he to Zuinglius, "that by your studies and your manners, both alike excellent, you labour to polish and elevate them." Zuinglius had a most ardent desire to see him. "Spaniards and Gauls went to Rome to see Titus Livy," said he. He set out, and on arriving at Bâle, found a personage of about forty years of age, of small stature, a frail body, a delicate look, but a remarkably amiable and winning address.[3] It was Erasmus. His affability removed the timidity of Zuinglius, while the power of his intellect overawed him. "Poor," said Ulric to him, "as Eschines, when each of the scholars of Socrates offered a present to his master, I give you what Eschines gave—I give you myself."

Among the literary men who formed the court of Erasmus, the Amerbachs, the Rhenans, the Frobeniuses, the Nessens, the Glareans, Zuinglius observed a youth from Lucerne, of twenty-seven years of age, named Oswald Geisshüsler. Erasmus hellenising his name, had called him Myconius. We will often designate him by his surname, to distinguish the friend of Zuinglius from Frederick Myconius, the disciple of Luther. Oswald, after studying

[1] Ut nec decem mulierculæ . . . . uni sophistæ adæquari queant. (Zw. Ep., p. 13.)
[2] Tu, tuique similes optimis etiam studiis ac moribus et expolietis et nobilitabitis. (Ibid., p. 10.) [3] Et corpusculo hoc tuo minuto, verum minimo inconcinno, urbanissime gestientem videre videar. (Ibid.) Methinks I see you with your diminutive, but by no means inelegant, person, showing the greatest politeness.

first at Rothwyl with Berthold Haller, a young man of his own age, next at Berne, and lastly at Bâle, had in this last town been appointed rector of the school of St. Theodoret, and afterwards of that of St. Peter. The humble schoolmaster had a very limited income ; but, notwithstanding, had married a young girl of a simplicity and purity of soul which won all hearts. We have already seen that Switzerland was then in a troubled state, foreign wars having stirred up violent disorders, and the soldiers having brought back to their country licentiousness and brutality. One dark and cloudy winter day, some of these rude men, in Oswald's absence, attacked his quiet dwelling. They knocked at the door, threw stones, and applied the grossest expressions to his modest spouse. At last they burst open the windows, and having forced their way into the school and broken every thing to pieces, made off. Oswald arrived shortly after. His little boy, Felix, ran out to meet him crying, while his wife, unable to speak, showed signs of the greatest terror. He understood what had happened, and at that moment, hearing a noise in the street, unable to restrain himself, he seized a musket, and pursued the villains as far as the burying ground. They retreated, intending to defend themselves. Three of them rushed upon Myconius and wounded him, and, while his wound was being dressed, these wretches again attacked his house, uttering cries of fury. Oswald says no more of the matter.[1] Such scenes frequently occurred in Switzerland at the beginning of the sixteenth century, before the Reformation had softened and dis-- ciplined manners.

The integrity of Oswald Myconius, his thirst for science and virtue, brought him into connection with Zuinglius. The rector of the school of Bâle was alive to all that was grand in the curate of Glaris. Full of humility, he shunned the praises bestowed upon him by Zuinglius and Erasmus. "You schoolmasters," often said the latter, "I esteem as highly as I do kings." But the modest Myconius did not think so. "I only crawl along the ground," said he. "From infancy I had always a feeling of littleness and humility."[2]

A preacher who had arrived at Bâle about the same time as Zuinglius was attracting attention. Of a mild and pacific disposition, he led a tranquil life; slow and circumspect in conduct, his chief pleasure was to labour in his study, and produce concord among Christians.[3] He was named John Hausschein, in Greek Œcolampadius, that is, "light of the house," and was born of

---

[1] Erasmi, Laus Stultitiæ, cum annot. Myconii.   [2] Equidem humi repere didici hactenus,et est natura nescio quid humile vel a cunabulis in me. (Osw. Myc. Vit Zw.) Hitherto I have learned to creep on the ground; and there is in me naturally, even from the cradle, a feeling of the humble.   [3] Ingenio miti et tranquillo, pacis et concordiæ studiosissimus. (Melch. Ad. Vit. Œc., p. 58.)

wealthy parents in Franconia, a year before Zuinglius. His pious mother longed to consecrate to literature and to God the only child whom He had left her. The father intended him first for a mercantile life, then for law. But as Œcolampadius was returning from Bologna, where he had been studying law, the Lord, who designed to make him a lamp in the Church,[1] called him to the study of theology. He was preaching in his native town when Capito, who had known him at Heidelberg, procured his appointment as preacher at Bâle. There he proclaimed Christ with an eloquence which filled his hearers with admiration.[2] Erasmus admitted him to his intimacy. Œcolampadius was enraptured with the hours which he spent in the society of this great genius. " In the Holy Scriptures," said the prince of literature, " one thing only ought to be sought, viz., Jesus Christ." [3] As a memento of his friendship he gave the young preacher the commencement of John's Gospel. Œcolampadius often kissed this precious pledge of affection, and kept it suspended to his crucifix, " in order," said he, " that I may always remember Erasmus in my prayers."

Zuinglius returned to his mountains, his mind and heart full of all that he had seen and heard at Bâle. " I could not sleep," wrote he to Erasmus, shortly after his return, " if I had not conversed for some time with you. There is nothing of which I boast so much as of having seen Erasmus." Zuinglius had received a new impulse. Such journeys often exercise a great influence over the career of the Christian. The disciples of Zuinglius—Valentin, Jost, Louis, Peter, and Ægidius Tschudi ; his friends, the landäman Æbli, the curate, Binzli of Wesen. Fridolin Brunnen, and the celebrated professor Glarean, saw with admiration how he grew in wisdom and knowledge. The old honoured him as a courageous servant of his country, and faithful pastors honoured him as a faithful servant of the Lord. Nothing was done in the district without taking his advice. All the good hoped that he would one day restore the ancient virtue of the Swiss.[4]

Francis I, having mounted the throne, and being desirous to vindicate the honour of the French name in Italy, the pope in alarm laboured to gain the cantons. Accordingly, in 1515, Ulric revisited the plains of Italy amid the phalanxes of his fellow-citizens. But the division which French intrigues produced in the army stung him to the heart. He was often seen in the middle of the camp

---

[1] Flectente et vocante Deo, qui eo in domo sua pro lampade usurus erat. (Melch. Ad. Vit. Œc. p. 46.) [2] Omnium vere spiritualium et eruditorum admiratione Christum predicavit. (Ibid.) He preached Christ to the admiration of all who were truly learned and spiritually minded. [3] Nihil in sacris literis præter Christum quærendum. (Erasmi, Ep., p. 403.) [4] Justitiam avitam per hunc olim restitutum iri. (Osw. Myc. Vit. Zw.)

energetically, and at the same time wisely, haranguing his hearers
in full armour ready for battle.[1] On the 8th September, five days-
before the battle of Marignan, he preached in the public square of
Monza, where the Swiss soldiers, who remained true to their colours,
had reassembled. "Had the counsels of Zuinglius been followed
then and afterwards," says Werner Steiner of Zug, "what evils
would not our country have been saved!" But all ears were shut
to words of concord, prudence, and submission. The vehement
eloquence of Cardinal Schinner electrified the confederates, and
hurried them impetuously to the fatal field of Marignan. There
fell the flower of the Helvetic youth. Zuinglius, who had been
unable to prevent all these disasters, threw himself, for the cause
of Rome, into the midst of danger. His hand seized the sword.
Sad error of Zuinglius! A minister of Christ, he more than once-
forgot that it was his duty to fight only with spiritual weapons,.
and he was to see in his own person a striking fulfilment of our
Saviour's prophecy, *He who takes the sword shall perish by the
sword.*

Zuinglius and his Swiss had been unable to save Rome. The
ambassador of Venice was the first in the pontifical city who-
received news of the defeat of Marignan. Delighted, he repaired at
an early hour to the Vatican. The pope came out of his apartment-
half dressed to give him an audience. Leo X, on learning the
news, did not disguise his terror. At this moment of alarm he saw
only Francis I, and hoped only in him. "Ambassador," said he
trembling to Zorsi, "we must throw ourselves into the arms of the-
king, and cry for mercy." Luther and Zuinglius in their danger-
knew another arm, and invoked another mercy.[3]

This second sojourn in Italy was not without use to Zuinglius.-
He observed the differences between the Ambrosian ritual used at
Milan and that of Rome. He collected and compared together the-
most ancient canons of the mass. In this way a spirit of enquiry
was developed in him even ·amid the tumult of camps. At the-
same time the sight of his countrymen led away beyond the Alps,
and given up, like cattle, to the slaughter, filled him with indignation. "The flesh of the confederates," it was said, "is cheaper-
than that of their oxen and their calves." The disloyalty and ambition of the pope,[4] the avarice and ignorance of the priests, the-
licentiousness and dissipation of the monks, the pride and luxury of

---

[1] In dem Heerlager hat er Flyssig geprediget. (Bullinger MS.)　　　[2] . . . In den-
Schlachten sich redlich und dapfer gestellt mit Rathen, Worten, und Thaten. (Ibid.)-
[3] Domine orator, vederemo quel fara il re Christmo semetteremo in le so man diman--
dando misericordia. (Zorsi Relatione MS.)　　　[4] Bellissimo parlador ; prometen
assa ma non atendea . . . Most beautiful speechifier ; he (Leo X) promised largely, but-
did not perform. (Relatione MS.- ·E Cradenigo ven. to orator di Roma.)

prelates, the corruption and venality employed on all hands to win the Swiss, being forced on his view more strongly than ever, made him still more alive to the necessity of a reform in the Church.

From this time Zuinglius preached the Word of God more clearly. In explaining the portions of the gospel and epistles selected for public worship, he always compared Scripture with Scripture.[1] He spoke with animation and force,[2] and followed with his hearers the same course which God was following with him. He did not, like Luther, proclaim the sores of the Church ; but as often as the study of the Bible suggested some useful instruction to himself, he communicated it to his hearers. He tried to make them re-- ceive the truth into their hearts, and then trusted to it for the works which it behoved to produce.[3] "If they understand what is true," thought he, " they will discern what is false." This maxim is good at the commencement of a Reformation, but a time comes when error must be boldly stigmatised. This Zuinglius knew very well. ."The spring," said he, " is the season to sow ;" and with him it was now spring.

Zuinglius has marked out this period (1516) as the commencement of the Swiss Reformation. In fact, if four years before he had bent his head over the Word of God, he now raised it, and turned it toward his people, to make them share in the light which he had found. This forms a new and important epoch in the history of the development of the religious revolution of those countries, but it has been erroneously concluded, from these dates, that the Reformation of Zuinglius preceded that of Luther. It may be that Zuinglius preached the gospel a year before Luther's Theses, but Luther himself preached it four years before these famous propositions.[4] Had Luther and Zuinglius confined themselves merely to sermons, the Reformation would not have so quickly gained ground in the Church. Neither Luther nor Zuinglius was the first monk or the first priest who preached a purer doctrine than that of the schoolmen. But Luther was the first who publicly, and with indomitable courage, raised the standard of truth against the empire of error, called general attention to the fundamental doctrine of the gospel—salvation by grace, introduced his age to that new career of knowledge, faith, and life, out of which a new world has arisen ; in a word, began a true and salutary revolution. The great struggle, of which the Theses of 1517 were the signal, was truly the birth-

---

[1] Non hominum commentis, sed sola scripturarum collatione. (Zw. Op. i, p. 273.) Not by the inventions of men, but solely by comparing the Scriptures.
[2] Sondern auch mit predigen, dorrinen er heftig wass. (Bullinger's MS.)
[3] Volebat veritatem cognitam, in cordibus auditorum, agere suum officium. (Osw. Myc. Vit. Zw.) He wished the truth when known to do its work on the hearts of his hearers. [4] First Volume.

throe of the Reformation, giving it at once both a body and a soul. Luther was the first Reformer.

A spirit of enquiry began to breathe on the mountains of Switzerland. One day the curate of Glaris, happening to be in the smiling district of Mollis, with Adam its curate, Bunzli, curate of Wesen, and Varachon, curate of Kerensen, these friends discovered an old liturgy, in which they read these words: " After baptising the child, we give him the sacrament of the Eucharist and the cup of blood."[1] " Then," said Zuinglius, "the supper was at that period dispensed in our churches under the two kinds." The liturgy was about two hundred years old. This was a great discovery for these priests of the Alps.

The defeat of Marignan had important results in the interior of the cantons. The conqueror, Francis I, lavished gold and flattery in order to gain the confederates, while the emperor besought them by their honour, by the tears of widows and orphans, and the blood of their brethren, not to sell themselves to their murderers. The French party gained the ascendancy at Glaris, which, from that time, was an uncomfortable residence to Ulric.

Zuinglius, at Glaris, might perhaps have remained a man of the world. Party intrigues, political questions, the empire, France, or the Duke of Milan, might have absorbed his whole life. Those whom God means to prepare for great services he never leaves amid the turmoil of the world. He leads them apart, and places them in a retreat where they commune with Him and their own consciences, and receive lessons never to be effaced. The Son of God himself, who in this was a type of the training given to his servants, spent forty days in the desert. It was time to remove Zuinglius from political movements, which, continually pressing upon his thoughts, might have banished the Spirit of God from them. It was time to train him for another stage than that on which courtiers, cabinets, and parties move, and where he should have wasted powers worthy of nobler employment. His country, indeed, needed something else. It was necessary that a new life should now come down from heaven, and that he who was to be the instrument in communicating it should unlearn worldly things, in order to learn things above. The two spheres are entirely distinct; a wide space separates these two worlds, and before passing entirely from the one to the other, Zuinglius was to sojourn for a time on neutral ground, in a kind of intermediate and preparatory state, to be there taught of God. God accordingly took him away from the factions of Glaris ; and, with a view to this noviciate, placed him in the solitude of a hermitage

[1] Detur Eucharistiæ sacramentum, similiter poculum sanguinis. (Zw. Op. i, p. 266.) Let the sacrament of the Eucharist be given, likewise the cup of blood.

┌confining within the narrow walls of an abbey this noble germ of the Reformation, which was shortly after to be transplanted to a better soil, and cover the mountains with its shadow.

CHAP. V.

Meinrad of Hohenzollern—Our Lady of Einsidlen—Calling of Zuinglius—The Abbot—Geroldsek—Companionship in Study—The Bible copied—Zuinglius and Superstition—First Opposition to Error—Sensation—Hedio—Zuinglius and the Legates—The Honours of Rome—The Bishop of Constance—Samson and Indulgences—Stapfer—Charity of Zuinglius—His Friends.

Meinrad of Hohenzollern, a German monk, about the middle of the ninth century, wandering on till he came between the lakes of Zurich and Wallstetten, had stopped upon a hill, resting on an amphitheatre of firs, and there built a cell. Banditti imbrued their hands in the blood of the saint. The bloody cell was long deserted, but towards the end of the tenth century, a convent and a church, in honour of the Virgin, were erected on the sacred spot. On the eve of the day of consecration, when the Bishop of Constance and his priests were at prayers in the church, a celestial chant, proceeding from invisible voices, suddenly echoed through the chapel. They prostrated themselves and listened in amaze. The next day, when the bishop was going to consecrate the chapel, a voice repeated thrice, "Stop, brother, stop! God himself has consecrated it!"[1] It was said, that Christ in person had blessed it during the night, that the chant which they had heard proceeded from angels, apostles, and saints, and that the Virgin, standing upon the altar, had blazed forth like a flash of lightning. A bull of Pope-Leo VII forbade the faithful to question the truth of this legend. Thenceforward an immense crowd of pilgrims ceased not to repair to Our Lady of the Eremites to the " consecration of angels." Delphi and Ephesus, in ancient, and Loretto in modern times, alone have equalled the fame of Einsidlen. It was in this strange place that, in 1516, Ulric Zuinglius was called as priest and preacher.

Zuinglius hesitated not. "Neither ambition nor avarice takes me there," said he ; " but the intrigues of the French."[2] Higher motives determined him. On the one hand, having more solitude, more calmness, and a less extensive parish, he could devote more time to study and meditation ; on the other hand, this place of

[1] Cessa, cessa, frater, divinitus capella consecrata est. (Hartm. Annal. Einsidl. p. 51. [2] Locum mutavimus non cupidinis aut cupiditatis moti stimulis, verum Gallorum technis. (Zw. Ep. 24.)

pilgrimage would give him facilities for spreading the knowledge of Jesus Christ to the remotest countries.[1]

The friends of evangelical preaching at Glaris expressed deep grief. " What worse could happen to Glaris," said Peter Tschudi, one of the most distinguished citizens of the canton, " than to be deprived of so great a man."[2]   His parishioners finding him immovable, resolved to leave him the title of pastor of Glaris, with part of the benefice, and the means of returning when he chose.[3]

Conrad of Rechberg, a gentleman of ancient family, grave, candid, intrepid, and occasionally somewhat rude, was one of the most celebrated sportsmen of the district to which Zuinglius was removed. He had established on one of his farms a manége in which he reared a breed of horses which became celebrated in Italy. Such was the abbot of our Lady of the Eremites. Rechberg was equally averse to the pretensions of Rome and the discussions of theologians. One day, during a visitation of the Order, some observations were made to him. " I am master here, not you," said he, somewhat rudely; " get along." One day at table when Leo Juda was discussing some difficult point with the administrator of the convent, the hunting abbot exclaimed, " You, there, leave your disputes to me. I exclaim with David, ' Have pity on me, O God, according to thy goodness, and enter not into judgment with thy servant.' I have no need to know any more."[4]

Baron Theobald of Geroldsek was administrator of the monastery. He was of a meek spirit, sincerely pious, and had a great love of literature. His favourite design was to form a society of well-informed men in his convent; and it was for this reason he had given a call to Zuinglius. Eager for instruction and reading, he begged his new friend to direct him. " Read the Holy Scriptures," replied Zuinglius, " and that you· may the better understand them, study Jerome. However," added he, " the time will come, (and, by God's help, it is not far off,) when Christians will not set a high value either on Jerome or any other doctor, but only on the word of God.[1] The conduct of Geroldsek gave indication of his progress in the faith. He allowed the nuns of a convent dependent on Einsidlen to read the Bible in the vulgar tongue; and, some years after, Geroldsek came to live at Zurich beside Zuinglius, and to die with him on the field of Cappel. The charm which hung about Zuinglius soon united him in tender friendship, not only with Ger-

<hr />

[1] Christum et ejus veritatem in regioni· s et varias et remotas divulgari tam felici opportunitate. (Osw. Myc. Vit. Zw.)   ·' Quid enim Glarcanæ nostræ tristius accidere poterat, tanto videlicet privari viro. (Zw. Ep., p. 16.)   [3] Two years later Zuinglius signs, Pastor Glaronæ, Minister Eremi. (Ibid., p. 30)   [4] Wirz, K. Gesch., iii, 363. Zuinglius Bildung, v. Schüler, p. 174. Misceli. Tigur., iii, 23.
[4] Fore, idque brevi, Deo sic juvante, ut neque Hieronymus neque cæteri, sed sola Scriptura divina apud Christianos in prætio sit futura. (Zw. Op. i, p. 273.)

oldsek, but also the chaplain Zink, the excellent Œxlin, and other inmates of the abbey. These studious men, far from the noise of party, joined together in reading the Scriptures, the Fathers of the Church, the master-pieces of antiquity, and the writings of the restorers of letters. This interesting society was often enlarged by friends from a distance. Among others, Capito one day arrived at Einsidlen. The two old friends of Bâle walked together over the convent and the wild scenery in its neighbourhood, absorbed in conversation, examining the Scriptures, and seeking to know the Divine will. There was a point on which they were agreed, and it was this—"The pope of Rome must fall." At this time Capito was more courageous than he was at a later period.

Repose, leisure, books, friends—all these Zuinglius had in this tranquil retreat—and he accordingly grew in understanding and in faith. At this period (May, 1517) he commenced a work which was of great utility to him. As in old time the kings of Israel wrote the law of God with their own hand, so Zuinglius with his copied the Epistles of St. Paul. The only editions of the New Testament then in existence were of large size, and Zuinglius wished to have one which he could carry about with him.[1] These Epistles he learned by heart, as he did afterwards the other books of the New, and a part of the Old Testament. Thus his heart became always more attached to the sovereign authority of the Word of God. He was not satisfied with merely acknowledging this; he was, moreover, desirous to bring his life into true subjection to it. His views gradually became more decidedly Christian. The end for which he had been brought into this desert was accomplished. It is no doubt true that Zurich is the place where his whole soul became thoroughly pervaded with Christian principle; but even now at Einsidlen he made decided progress in the work of sanctification. At Glaris he had taken part in the amusements of the world; at Einsidlen he was more anxious for a life unsullied by any taint of worldliness. Beginning to have a better idea of the great spiritual interests of the people, he gradually learned what God designed to teach him.

Providence had also other views in bringing him to Einsidlen. Here he obtained a nearer view of the superstitions and abuses which had invaded the Church. An image of the Virgin which was carefully preserved in this monastery, had, it was said, the power of working miracles. Above the gate of the Abbey appeared this presumptuous inscription:—"Here is obtained a plenary remission of all sins." A multitude of pilgrims flocked to Einsidlen from all parts of Christendom, to merit this grace by their pilgri-

[1] This manuscript is extánt in the library of the town of Zurich.

mage. The church, the abbey, and the whole valley were crowded with devout worshippers on the festivals of the Virgin. But it was especially at the grand festival of " the consecration of the angels," that the hermitage was crowded to overflowing. Thousands of individuals of both sexes climbed the acclivity of the hill leading to the oratory, singing hymns and counting their beads. These devout pilgrims crowded into the Church, thinking they were there nearer God than any where else.

The residence of Zuinglius at Einsidlen was, in regard to the exposure of papal abuses, similar in effect to Luther's visit to Rome. Zuinglius' education for reformer was completed at Einsidlen. God alone is the source of salvation, and he is so every where, —these were the two truths which he learned at Einsidlen, and they became fundamental articles in his creed. The serious impression produced on his soul soon manifested itself externally. Struck with the many prevailing evils, he resolved to oppose them boldly. Not hesitating between his conscience and his interest, he stood up openly, and, in plain and energetic terms, attacked the superstition of the surrounding crowds: " Think not," said he from the pulpit, " that God is in this temple more than in any other part of his creation. Whatever be the country in which you dwell, God encompasses you, and hears you as well as in our Lady of Einsidlen. Can useless works, long pilgrimages, offerings, images, the invocation of the Virgin, or the saints, obtain the grace of God ? . . . . What avails the multitude of words in which we embody our prayers? What avails a glossy hood— a head well shaven—a long robe with its neat folds, and mules caparisoned with gold? God looks to the heart, but our heart is alienated from God." [1]

But Zuinglius wished to do more than lift his voice against superstition. He wished to satisfy that eager longing for reconciliation with God, felt by many of the pilgrims who had flocked to the chapel of our Lady of Einsidlen. " Christ," cried he, like a John Baptist in this new wilderness of Judea, " Christ, who was once offered on the cross, is the expiatory victim, who, even through eternity, makes satisfaction for the sins of all believers." [2] Thus Zuinglius advanced. The day when this bold sermon was heard in the most venerated sanctuary of Switzerland, the standard prepared against Rome began to be more distinctly displayed on its mountain heights, and there was, so to speak, a heaving of reform reaching even to their deepest foundations.

---

[1] Vestes oblonga et plicis plena, muli auro ornati . . . Cor vero interim procul a Deo est. (Zw. Op. i, p. 236.)   [2] Christus qui sese semel in cruce obtulit, hostia est et victima satisfaciens in æternum, pro peccatis omnium fidelium. (Ibid. p. 236.

In fact, universal astonishment seized the multitude on hearing the discourse of the eloquent priest. Some walked off in horror; others hesitated between the faith of their fathers and the doctrine fitted to secure their peace, while several came to Jesus Christ who was thus preached to them, and finding rest to their souls, took 'back the tapers which they had intended to present to the Virgin. A crowd of pilgrims returned to their homes, announcing every where what they had heard at Einsidlen. "Christ ALONE saves, and saves EVERYWHERE." Bands, astonished at what they heard, stopped short without finishing their pilgrimage. The worshippers of Mary diminished from day to day. Their offerings formed almost the whole income of Zuinglius and Geroldsek; but the intrepid witness of the truth felt happy to be impoverished in order that souls might be spiritually enriched.

During the feast of Pentecost, in the year 1518, among the numerous hearers of Zuinglius, was a learned man of meek temper and active charity, named Gaspard Hedio, doctor of theology at Bâle. Zuinglius preached on the cure of the paralytic, (Luke, v,) where our Saviour declares, "The Son of Man hath power upon earth to forgive sins," words well fitted to strike the crowd assembled in the Church of the Virgin. The preacher roused, enraptured, and inflamed his audience, especially the doctor from Bâle.[1] A long time after, Hedio expressed his high admiration; "How beautiful," said he, "this discourse, how profound, weighty, complete, penetrating, and evangelical; how much it reminds one of the ενεργεια (energy) of the ancient doctors.[2] From that moment Hedio admired and loved Zuinglius.[3] He would fain have gone to him, and opened his heart; he wandered around the abbey but durst not approach, kept back, as he expresses it, by a superstitious timidity. He again mounted his horse and slowly retired from our Lady, ever and again turning his head to the spot which contained so great a treasure, and feeling in his heart the keenest regret.[4]

Thus Zuinglius preached; less forcibly, no doubt, than Luther, but with more moderation, and not less success. He did nothing precipitately, and did not come so violently into collision with men's minds as the Saxon Reformer; he expected every thing from the power of truth. He displayed the same wisdom in his relations with the heads of the Church. Far from immediately declaring himself their enemy, he long remained their friend. They were

---

[1] Is sermo ita me inflammavit. . . (Zw. Ep. p. 90.) copiosus, penetrans, et evangelicus . . . (Ibid., 89.) apatissime complecti, suscipere et admirari. (Ibid.) sine tamen molestia, quam tamen ipse mihi pepereram. (Ibid., p. 90.) And so rode away, not without vexation, of which, however, I was myself the cause.
[2] Elegans ille, doctus, gravis,
[3] Ut inciperem Zwinglium.
[4] Sicque abequitavi, non sine tamen molestia,

·exceedingly indulgent to him, not only because of his learning and
·talents, (Luther had the same claims to the regard of the bishops
·of Mentz and Brandenburg,) but especially because of his attach-
·ment to the pope's political party, and the influence possessed by
·such a man as Zuinglius in a republican state.

In fact, several cantons, disgusted with the service of the pope,
·were disposed to break with him   But the legates flattered them-
·selves they might retain several of them by gaining Zuinglius, as
they gained Erasmus, with pensions and honours.   At this time
the legates, Ennius and Pucci, went frequently to Einsidlen,
where from its proximity to the democratic cantons, it was
more easy to carry on negotiations with them.   But Zuinglius, far
from sacrificing the truth to the demands and offers of Rome,
·omitted no opportunity of defending the gospel.   The famous
Schinner, who had then some disturbance in his diocese, passed
some time at Einsidlen.   "The whole papacy," said Zuinglius one
·day, "rests on a bad foundation.[1]   Put your hand to the work,
·remove errors and abuses, or you will see the whole edifice crumble
·to pieces with fearful uproar"[2]

He spoke with the same frankness to legate Pucci.   Four times
did he return to the charge.   "With the help of God," said he to
·him, "I will continue to preach the gospel, and this preaching will
·shake Rome."   Then he pointed out to him what was necessary to
·save the Church.   Pucci promised every thing, but did nothing.
Zuinglius declared that he renounced the pension from the pope.
The legate entreated him to retain it ; and Zuinglius, who at that
·time had no thought of placing himself in open hostility to the
head of the Church, consented for three years to receive it.   "But
·think not," added he, "that for the love of money I retrench a
·single syllable of the truth."[3]   Pucci, alarmed, made the Reformer
·be appointed chaplain acolyte to the pope.   It was an avenue to
new honours.   Rome thought to frighten Luther by sentences of
·condemnation, and to win Zuinglius by favours—darting her ex-
·communications at the one, and displaying her gold and magnificence to the other.   She thus endeavoured, by two different meth-
·ods, to attain the same end, and silence the bold lips which dared,
·in spite of the pope, to proclaim the Word of God in Germany and
·Switzerland.   The latter method was the more skilful, but neither
·of them succeeded.   The enfranchised souls of the preachers of
·truth were equally inaccessible to menace and favour.

Another Swiss prelate, Hugo of Landenberg, bishop of Con-

---

[1] Dass das ganz papstum einen schlechten grund habe.   (Zw. Op. ii, part i, p. 7.)
[2] Oder aber sy werdind mit grosser unrüw selbs umfalien.   (Ibid.)   [3] Frustra
·sperari me vel verbulum de veritate diminiturum esse, pecuniæ gratia.   (Zw. Op. i,
p. 365.)   It was vain to hope that I would keep back one iota of the truth for the
·sake of money.

stance, at this time gave some hopes to Zuinglius. He ordered a general visitation of the churches. But Landenberg, a man of no character, allowed himself to be led alternately by Faber, his vicar, and by an abandoned female, from whose sway he was unable to escape. He occasionally appeared to honour the gospel, and yet any one who preached it boldly was in his eyes only a disturber. He was one of those men too common in the Church, who, though loving truth better than error, have more indulgence for error than for truth, and often end by turning against those with whom they ought to make common cause. Zuinglius applied to him, but in vain. He was to have the same experience which Luther had; to be convinced that it was useless to invoke the heads of the Church, and that the only method of restoring Christianity was to act as a faithful teacher of the Word of God. An opportunity of doing so soon occurred.

In August, 1518, a Franciscan monk was seen travelling on the heights of St. Gothard, in those lofty passes which have been laboriously cut across the steep rocks separating Switzerland from Italy. Having come forth from an Italian convent, he was the bearer of papal indulgences which he was commissioned to sell to the good Christians of the Helvetic league. Brilliant success, obtained under two preceding popes, had signalised his exertions in this shameful traffic. Companions, intended to puff off the merchandise which he was going to sell, were accompanying him across mountains of snow and ice coeval with the world. This avaricious band, in appearance miserable enough, and not unlike a band of adventurers roaming for plunder, walked in silence, amid the noise of the foaming torrents which give rise to the Rhine, the Reuss, the Aar, the Rhone, the Tessino, and other rivers, meditating how they were to plunder the simple population of Helvetia. Samson (this was the Franciscan's name) and his company first arrived in Uri, and there commenced their traffic. They had soon done with these poor peasants, and passed into the canton of Schwitz. Here Zuinglius was, and here the combat between these two servants of two very different masters was to take place. " I can pardon all sins," said the Italian monk, the Tezel of Switzerland. " Heaven and hell are subject to my power, and I sell the merits of Jesus Christ to whoever will purchase them, by paying in cash for an indulgence."

Zuinglius heard of these discourses, and his zeal was inflamed. He preached powerfully against them. " Jesus Christ, the Son of God," said he, " thus speaks, ' *Come unto* ME, *all ye that labour and are heavy laden, and I will gve you rest.*' Is it not then audacious folly and insensate temerity to say on the contrary, Purchase letters of indulgence ! run to Rome ! give to the monks!

sacrifice to the priests! If you do these things I will absolve you from your sins! [1] Jesus Christ is the only offering; Jesus Christ is the only sacrifice; Jesus Christ is the only way." [2]

Every body at Schwitz began to call Samson rogue and cheat. He took the road to Zug, and for this time the two champions failed to meet.

Scarcely had Samson left Schwitz when a citizen of this canton, named Stapfer, a man of distinguished talent, and afterward secretary of state, was with his family reduced to great distress. "Alas," said he, when applying in agony to Zuinglius, "I know not how to satisfy my own hunger and the hunger of my poor children." [3] Zuinglius knew to give where Rome knew to take; he was as ready to practise good works, as to combat those who taught that they were the means of obtaining salvation. He daily gave liberally to Stapfer. [4] "It is God," said he, anxious not to take any glory to himself, "It is God who begets charity in the believer, and gives him at once the thought, the resolution, and the work itself. Whatever good a righteous man does it is God who does it by his own power." [5] Stapfer remained attached to him through life; and, four years after, when he had become secretary of state, and felt wants of a higher kind, he turned towards Zuinglius, and said to him with noble candour, "Since you provided for my temporal wants, how much more may I now expect from you wherewith to appease the hunger of my soul!"

The friends of Zuinglius increased. Not only at Glaris, Bâle, and Schwitz, did he find men of like spirit with himself; in Uri there was the secretary of state, Schmidt; at Zug, Colin Muller and Werner Steiner, his old companions in arms at Marignan: at Lucerne, Xylotect and Kilchmeyer; Wittembach at Berne, and many others in many other places. But the curate of Einsidlen had no more devoted friend than Oswald Myconius. Oswald had quitted Bâle in 1516, to take charge of the cathedral school at Zurich. In this town there were no learned men, and no schools of learning. Oswald laboured along with some well-disposed individuals, among others, Utinger, notary to the pope, to raise the Zurich population out of ignorance and initiate them in ancient literature. At the same time he defended the immutable truth of the Holy Scriptures, and declared that if the pope or emperor gave commands contrary to the gospel, obedience was due to God alone, who is above both emperor and pope.

---

[1] Romam curre! redime literas indulgentiarum! da tantundem monachis! offer sacerdotibus, etc. (Zw. Op., i, p. 222.)　[2] Christus una est oblatio, unum sacrificium, una via. (Ibid., p. 201.)　[3] Ut meae, meorumque liberorum inediae corporali subveniretis. (Zw. Ep. 234.)　[4] Largas mihi quotidie suppetias tulisti. (Ibid.)
[5] Caritatem ingenerat Deus, consilium, propositum et opus. Quidquid boni praestat justus, hoc Deus sua virtute praestat. (Zw. Op., i, p. 226.)

CHAP. VI.

Zurich—The College of Canons—Election to the Cathedral—Fable—Accusations—
Confession of Zuinglius—The Designs of God Unfolded—Farewell to Einsidlen—
Arrival at Zurich—Courageous Declaration of Zuinglius—First Sermons—Effects
—Opposition—Character of Zuinglius—Taste for Music—Arrangement of the Day
—Circulation by Hawkers.

Seven centuries had elapsed since Charlemagne had attached a college of canons to this cathedral, over whose school Oswald Myconius then presided. These canons having degenerated from their first institution, and desiring in their benefices to enjoy the sweets of indolence, elected a priest to preach and take the cure of souls. This situation having become vacant some time after Oswald's arrival, he immediately thought of his friend. What a prize it would be for Zurich ! Zuinglius' appearance was prepossessing. He was a handsome man,[1] of graceful address, and pleasing manners. His eloquence had already given him celebrity, while the lustre of his genius made him conspicuous among all the confederates. Myconius spoke of him to the provost of the chapter, Felix Frey, (who from the appearance and talents of Zuinglius was already prepossessed in his favour,)[2] to Utinger, an old man who was held in high respect, and to canon Hoffman, a man of an upright open disposition, who, having long preached against foreign service, was favourably inclined to Ulric. Other Zurichers had, on different occasions, heard Zuinglius at Einsidlen, and had returned full of admiration. The election of preacher to the cathedral soon set all the inhabitants of Zurich in motion. Different parties were formed. Several laboured night and day for the election of the eloquent preacher of Our Lady of the Eremites.[3] Myconius having informed his friend—" Wednesday next," replied Zuinglius, " I will come and dine at Zurich, and talk over matters." He accordingly arrived. A canon to whom he was paying a visit said to him, " Could you come among us to preach the word of God?" " I could," replied he ; "but will not come unless I am called." He then returned to his abbey.

This visit spread alarm in the camp of his enemies. Several priests were urged to apply for the vacancy. A Suabian, named Laurent Fable, even preached as a candidate, and the rumour went

---

[1] Dan Zwingii vom lyb ein hubscher man wass. (Bullinger MS.)   [3] Und als Imme sein e gestalt und geschiklichkeit wol gefiel, gab er Im syn stimm. (Ibid.)
[2] Qui dies et noctes laborarent ut vir ille subrogaretur. (Osw. Myc. Vit. Zw.)

that he was elected. " It is then quite true," said Zuinglius, on-learning it, " that a prophet has no honour in his own country, since a Suabian is preferred to a Swiss. I know what value to set. on popular applause."[1] Zuinglius immediately after received a letter from the secretary of Cardinal Schinner, informing him, that. the election had not taken place. But the false news which he had at first received nettled the curate of Einsidlen. Knowing that a person so unworthy as this Fable aspired to the place, he was more desirous to obtain it for himself, and wrote about it to Myconius, who next day replied, " Fable will always continue fable : my masters have learned that he is already the father of six boys, and possesses I know not how many benefices."[2]

The enemies of Zuinglius did not abandon their opposition. All, it is true, agreed in extolling his learning to the skies ;[3] but said some, " He is too fond of music ; " others, " He loves the world and pleasure;" others again, " In early life he was too closely connected with giddy companions." There was even one individual who charged him with an instance of seduction. Zuinglius was not without blemish. Though superior to the ecclesiastics of his time he more than once, in the first years of his ministry, gave way to youthful propensities. It is difficult to estimate the influence of an impure atmosphere on those who live in it. There were in the papacy certain established irregularities, allowed and sanctioned as conformable to the laws of nature. A saying of Æneas Sylvius, afterwards pope under the name of Pius II, gives an idea of the sad state of public morals at this period. We give it in a note.[4] Disorder had become the rule, order the exception.

Oswald displayed the greatest activity in favour of his friend. He exerted all his powers in defending him, and happily succeeded.[5] He went to burgomaster Roust, to Hofman, Frey, and Utinger. He praised Zuinglius for his probity, honesty, and purity, and confirmed the Zurichers in the favourable opinion which they had of the curate of Einsidlen. Little credit was given to the speeches of his adversaries. The most influential persons said, that Zuinglius should be preacher at Zurich. The canons said so also, but in a whisper. " Hope," wrote Oswald to him with a full heart, " for I hope." At the same time he told him of the accusations of his enemies. Although Zuinglius was not yet become altogether a new man, he belonged to the class of those whose conscience is awak-

---

[1] Scio vulgi acclamationes et illud blandum Euge! Euge! (Zw. Ep. p. 53.) I know the acclamations of the vulgar, and their flattering Bravo! Bravo!
[2] Fabula manebit fabula ; quem domini mei acceperunt sex pueris esse patrem . . . (Ibid.)   [3] Neminem tamen, qui tuam doctrinam non ad cœlum ferat . . . (Ibid.)   [4] Non esse qui vigesimum annum excessit, nec virginem tetigerit. (Ibid. p. 57.)   [5] Reprimo hæc pro viribus, imo et repressi. (Ibid., p. 54.)

ened, and who may fall into sin, but never without a struggle, or without remorse. It had often been his resolution to stand alone in the midst of the world, and maintain a life of holiness. But when he saw himself accused, he did not pretend to boast that he was without sin. Writing to canon Utinger, he said, " Having nobody to go along with me in the resolutions which I had formed, several even of those about me, being offended at them, alas! I fell, and like the dog of whom St. Peter speaks, (2 Ep. ii, 22,) returned to my vomit.[1] Ah! God knows with what shame and anguish I have torn up these faults from the depths of my heart, and laid them before Almighty God, to whom, however, I would be less afraid to confess my misery than to mortal man."[2] But while Zuinglius confessed himself to be a sinner, he, at the same time vindicated himself from the most offensive charges which were brought against him. He declared that he had ever abhorred the idea of invading the sanctity of married life, or seducing innocence,[3]— vices at that time but too common. " or the truth of this," says he, " I appeal to all with whom I have lived."[4]

The election took place on the 11th December, and out of the twenty-four votes which were given, Zuinglius had seventeen. It was time that the Reformation should begin in Switzerland. The chosen instrument which Divine Providence had been preparing during three years in the retreat of Einsidlen, was ready and must now be translated elsewhere. God, who had chosen the new university of Wittemberg, situated in the heart of Germany, and under the protection of the wisest of princes, to call Luther thither, made choice in Switzerland of the city of Zurich, regarded as the head of the confederation, there to station Zuinglius, and to bring him into contact not only with one of the most intelligent, simple, resolute, and intrepid communities of Switzerland, but also with all the cantons which are grouped around this ancient and powerful state. The hand which had taken hold of a young shepherd of Sentis, and led him to the school of Wesen, now brought him forward, powerful in word and in deed, in the face of all, to regenerate his countrymen. Zurich was about to become a focus of light to Switzerland.

The day which announced the election of Zuinglius was to Einsidlen a day at once of joy and grief. The circle which had been formed there was about to be broken up by the withdrawal of its

---

[1] Quippe neminem habens, comitem hujus instituti, scandalisantes vero non paucos heu! cecidi et factus sum canis ad vomitum. (Zw. Ep. p. 55.)   [2] En, cum verecundia (Deus novit!) magna, hæc ex pectoris specubus depromsi, apud eum scilicet, cum quo etiam coram minus quam cum ullo ferme mortalium confiteri vererer. (Zw. Ep.)   [3] Ea ratio nobis perpetuo fuit, nec alienum thorum conscendere nec virginem vitiare. (Ibid.)   [4] Testes invoco cunctos, quibuscum vixi. (Ibid.)

most valuable member, and who could say whether superstition
was not going again to take possession of this ancient place of pilgrimage? .... The council of state in Schwitz conveyed the expression of its sentiments to Ulric by designating him as " reverend,
learned, most gracious master, and good friend."[1] " At least do
you yourself give us a successor worthy of you," said Geroldsek in
despair to Zuinglius. " I have got for you," replied he, " a little
lion, simple and wise ; a man initiated in the mysteries of sacred
science." " Let me have him," immediately rejoined the administrator. It was Leo Juda, at once the gentle and intrepid friend
with whom Zuinglius had been so intimate at Bâle. Leo accepted
the call which brought him near his dear Ulric. Ulric took farewell of his friends, quitted the solitude of Einsidlen, and arrived
at that delightful spot where, smiling and instinct with life, rises
the town of Zurich, surrounded by its amphitheatre of vine-
clad hills, enamelled with meadows and orchards, crowned with
forests, and overtopped by the lofty peaks of the Albis.

Zurich, the centre of the political interests of Switzerland, where
the most influential persons in the nation frequently assembled, was
the place best fitted to act upon the whole country, and shed the
seeds of truth over all its cantons. Accordingly, the friends of
letters and the Bible hailed the appointment of Zuinglius with
acclamation. At Paris, in particular, the Swiss students, who
were there in great numbers, were enraptured with the news.[2]
But if Zuinglius had the prospect of a great victory at Zurich, he
had also the prospect of a severe contest. Glarean wrote him
from Paris, " I foresee that your learning will stir up great enmity;[3] but be of good courage, and you will, like Hercules, subdue monsters."

On the 27th December, 1518, Zuinglius arrived at Zurich, and
took up his quarters at the hotel of Einsidlen. He received a
cordial and honourable welcome. The chapter immediately met
to receive him, and invited him to take his seat in the midst of
them. Felix Frey presided; the canons, friendly or hostile to
Zuinglius, sat indiscriminately around their provost. There was
considerable excitement in the meeting; every one felt, perhaps
without distinctly acknowledging it to himself, how serious the
commencement of this ministry was likely to prove. Some apprehension being entertained of the innovating spirit of the young
priest, it was agreed to set before him the most important duties of his office. " You will use your utmost endeavour," he

---

[1] Reverende, perdocte, admodum gratiose domine ac bone amice. (Zw. Ep. p. 66.)
[2] Omnes adeo quotquot et Helvetiis adsunt juvenes fremere et gaudere. (Ibid., p.
63.) [3] Quantum invidiæ tibi inter istos eruditio tua conflabit. (Ibid., p. 64.)
[4] De er ehrlich und wol empfangen ward. (Bullinger, MS.)

was gravely told, " to secure payment of the revenues of the chapter, without neglecting the least of them. You will exhort the faithful both from the pulpit and in the confessional, to pay the first fruits and tithes, and to show by their offerings that they love the Church. You will make it your business to increase the revenues which are derived from the sick, from sacrifices, and generally from every ecclesiastical act." The chapter added, " As to the administration of the sacraments, preaching, and personal presence, amid the flock, these too are duties of the priest. However, in these different respects, and particularly in regard to preaching, you may supply your place by a vicar. You should administer the sacraments only to persons of distinction, and after being requested. You are expressly forbidden to do it to all persons indiscriminately." [1]

Strange rule to be given to Zuinglius! Money, money, still money! . . . . Was it then for this that Christ established his ministry? Still prudence tempers his zeal; he knows that we cannot all at once deposit the seed in the ground, see the growth of the tree, and gather its fruit. Zuinglius, therefore, without explaining his views on what was enjoined him, humbly expressed his gratitude for the honourable appointment which he had received, and stated what he calculated on being able to do. " The life of Jesus," said he, " has been too long hidden from the people. I will preach on the whole gospel of St. Matthew, chapter by chapter, following the mind of the Holy Spirit, drawing only at the wellsprings of Scripture, [2] digging deep into it, and seeking the understanding of it by persevering fervent prayer. [3] I will consecrate my ministry to the glory of God; the praise of His only Son; the real salvation of souls, and their instruction in the true faith." [4] This new language made a deep impression on the chapter. Some expressed joy, but the majority openly disapproved. [5] " This mode of preaching is an innovation," exclaimed they, " this innovation will soon lead to others, and where is it to stop?" Canon Hoffman in particular thought it his duty to prevent the fatal effects of a choice which he had himself patronised. " This exposition of Scripture," said he, " will be more hurtful than useful to the people." " It is not a new method," replied Zuinglius, " it is the ancient method. Recollect the homilies of St. Chrysostom on St.

---

[1] Schuler's, Zwinglis Bildung, p. 227.   [2] Absque humanis commentationibus, ex solis fontibus Scripturæ sacræ. (Zw. Op. i, p. 273.)   Without human comments, solely from the fountains of sacred Scripture.   [3] Sed mente spiritus quam diligenti Scripturarum collectione, precibusque ex corde fusis, se nacturum. (Osw. Myc. Vit. Zw.)   [4] Alles Gott und seinen einigen Sohn zu Lob und Ehren und zu rechten Heil der Seelen, zur Underrichtung im rechten Glauben. (Bullinger, MS.)
[5] Quibus auditis, mœror simul et lætitia. (Osw. Myc.)

Matthew, and of St. Augustine on St. John. Besides, I will use moderation, and give none any reason to complain."

Thus Zuinglius abandoned the exclusive use of fragments of the gospel as practised since the days of Charlemagne; re-establishing the Scripture in its ancient rights, he, from the commencement of his ministry, united the Reformation to the primitive ages of Christianity, and prepared a more profound study of the Word of God for ages to come. But he did more. The strong and independent position which he took up in the face of the Church showed that the work in which he had engaged was new. The figure of the Reformer stood out in bold relief to the public eye, and the Reformation advanced.

Hoffman, having failed in the chapter, addressed a written request to the provost to prohibit Zuinglius from shaking the popular belief. The provost sent for the new preacher, and spoke to him with great kindness. But no human power could close his lips. On the 31st December, he wrote to the council of Glaris, that he entirely resigned the cure of souls which had hitherto been reserved for him, and gave himself wholly to Zurich, and to the work which God was preparing for him in this town.

On Saturday, being new-year's-day, and also the birthday of Zuinglius, who had completed his thirty-fifth year, he mounted the pulpit of the cathedral. A great crowd, eager to see a man who had already acquired so much celebrity, and to hear this new gospel, of which every one began to speak, filled the church. " It is to Christ," said Zuinglius, " that I wish to conduct you ; to Christ, the true source of salvation. His divine word is the only nourishment which I would give to your heart and life." Then he announced that to-morrow, the first Sunday of the year, he would begin to expound the gospel according to St. Matthew. Accordingly, the preacher, and a still larger audience than the day before, were at their posts. Zuinglius opened the gospel—the gospel which had so long been a sealed book—and read the first page, going over the history of the patriarchs and prophets mentioned in the first chapter of St. Matthew, and expounding it in such a way that all were astonished and delighted, and exclaimed, "We never heard anything like this."[1]

He continued thus to expound St. Matthew, according to the original Greek. He showed how the whole Bible found at once its exposition and its application in the very nature of man. Delivering the loftiest truths of the gospel in simple language, his preaching reached all classes, the learned and the wise, as well as

[1] Dessgleichen wie jederman redt, nie gehört worden war. (B. Weise, a contemporary of Zuinglius. Füsslin Beyträge, iv, 36.)

the ignorant and simple.[1] He extolled the infinite mercies of God the Father, and implored all his hearers to put their confidence m Jesus Christ alone as the only Saviour.[2] At the same time, he earnestly called them to repentance; forcibly attacked the errors which prevailed among the people; fearlessly rebuked luxury, intemperance, extravagance in dress, the oppression of the poor, idleness, foreign service, and foreign pensions. "In the pulpit," says one of his companions, "he spared no one, pope, emperor, kings, dukes, princes, lords, not even the confederates. All his energy, and all the joy of his heart were in God: accordingly he exhorted all the inhabitants of Zurich to put their confidence in Him only."[3] "Never was man heard to speak with so much authority," says Oswald Myconius, who with joy and high hopes watched the labours of his friend.

The gospel could not be preached in vain in Zurich. A continually increasing multitude of men of all classes, and more especially of the common people, flocked to hear him.[4] Several Zurichers had ceased to attend on public worship. "I derive no benefit from the discourses of these priests," often exclaimed Füsslin, a poet, historian, and counsellor of state; " they do not preach the things of salvation; for they do not comprehend them. I see nothing in them but covetousness and voluptuousness. Henry Räuschlin, treasurer of state, one who diligently read the Scriptures, was of the same opinion: "The priests," said he, met in thousands at the Council of Constance . . . to burn the best man among them." These distinguished men, led by curiosity, went to hear Zuinglius' first sermon. Their countenances bespoke the emotion with which they followed the orator. "Glory to God!" said they, on coming out; "this is a preacher of the truth. He will be our Moses to deliver us from Egyptian darkness."[5] From this moment they became the Reformer's intimate friends. "Powers of the world," said Füsslin, "cease to proscribe the doctrine of Christ! After Christ the Son of God was put to death, sinners were raised up. And now, should you destroy the preachers of truth, you will see their places supplied by glaziers, carpenters, potters, founders, shoemakers, and tailors, who will teach with power."[6]

[1] Nam ita simplices æqualiter cum prudentissimis et acutissimis quibusque, proficiebant. (Osw. Myc. Vit. Zw.) [2] In welchem er Gott den Vater prysset und alle Menschen allein uff Issum Christum, als den einigen Heiland verthrauwen Iehrte. (Bullinger, MS.) [3] All sein Trost stuhnd allein mit frölichem Gemüth zu Gott . . . (B. Weise Füsslin Betr. iv, 36.) [4] Do ward bald ein gross gelauff von allerley menschen, Innsonders von dem gemeinen Mann . . . (Bullinger, MS.) [5] Und unser Moses seyn der uns aus Egypten führt. (Ibid.) [6] Werden die Gläser, Müller, Hafner, Giesser, Schuhmacher, und Schneider lehren. (Muller's Reliq. iii, p. 155.)

In Zurich, at the outset, there was only one shout of admiration, but when the first moment of enthusiasm was. over, the adversary resumed courage. Worthy persons alarmed at the idea of a Reformation, gradually drew off from Zuinglius. The violence of the monks which had been veiled for an instant, reappeared, and the college of canons resounded with complaints. Zuinglius stood immovable. His friends beholding his courage, felt in his presence as if a man of apostolic times had reappeared.[1] Among his enemies, some scoffed and jeered; others uttered insulting menaces, but he endured all with Christian patience.[2] " Whoso," he was wont to say, " would gain the wicked to Jesus Christ must wink at many things,"[3]—an admirable saying which ought not to be lost sight of.

His character and general bearing towards all contributed as much as his discourses to win their hearts. He was at once a true Christian and a true republican. The equality of mankind was not with him a mere watchword; it was written on his heart and manifested in his life. He had neither that pharisaical pride, nor that monastic gruffness, which are equally offensive to the simple and the wise of the world. Men were drawn towards him, and felt at ease when conversing with him. Strong and mighty in the pulpit, he was affable to all whom he met in the streets, or in the public squares. At the places where the merchants or incorporations met he was often seen among the citizens expounding the leading points of Christian doctrine, or conversing familiarly with them. He gave the same cordial reception to peasant and patrician. " He invited country folks to dine with him," says one of his bitterest enemies, " walked with them, spoke to them of God, made the devil enter into their hearts and his writings into their pockets., He even went so far that the leading persons in Zurich visited those peasants, entertained them, and walked over the town with them, showing them all sorts of attention."[4]

He continued to cultivate music " with moderation," says Bullinger: nevertheless the enemies of the gospel took advantage of it, and called him " The evangelical flute and lute player."[5] Faber having one day reproached him with his fondness for music, Zuinglius, with noble candour, replied, " My dear Faber, you know not what music is. I have, it is true, learned to play on the lute, the violin, and other instruments, and am able by these means to pa-

---

[1] Nobis apostolici illius sæculi virum repræsentas. (Zw. Ep. p. 74.) [2] Obgar. niunt quidam, rident, minantur, petulanter incessunt . . . at tu vere, Christianâ patientiâ, suffers omnia. (Ibid. 7th May, 1519.) Some jeer. laugh, menace, and petulantly assail, . . . but you with truly Christian patience submit to all. [3] Connivendum ad multa, ei qui velit malos Christo lucri facere . . . (Ibid.) [4] Dass der Rath gemeldete Bauern besucht . . . (Salat's Chronik. p. 155.) [5] Der Lautherschlager und Evangelischer pfyffer. (Bullinger, MS.)

cify little children;[1] but you of course are too holy for music. Do you not know that David was a skilful player on the harp, and in this way drove the evil spirit out of Saul? . . . Ah! if you knew the sound of the heavenly lute, the evil spirit of ambition and avarice by which you are possessed would come out of you also." Perhaps this was Zuinglius' foible, though it was in a spirit of cheerfulness and Christian liberty that he cultivated this art, which religion has always associated with her sublimest flights. He set some of his Christian poems to music, and did not scruple sometimes to amuse the youngest of his flock with his lute. He showed the same good nature to the poor. " He ate and drank," says one of his contemporaries, " with all who invited him,—he despised no one; he was most compassionate to the poor; always firm and always joyful in bad as in good fortune. No evil made him afraid; his words were at all times full of energy, and his heart full of consolation."[2] Thus Zuinglius increased in popularity —after the example of his Master, seated alternately at the table of the common people and the banquet of the great, but still constantly intent on the work to which God had called him.

At the same time he was an indefatigable student. In the morning, till ten, he read, wrote, and translated: Hebrew in particular engaged his attention. After dinner he attended to those who had any thing to tell him, or any advice to ask of him: took a walk with his friends and visited his hearers. At two he resumed his studies. He took a short walk after supper, and afterwards wrote letters which often occupied him till midnight. He always stood when he studied, and did not allow himself to be interrupted unless on important business.[3]

But the labours of a single individual were not sufficient. A person, named Lucian, one day came to him with the writings of the German Reformer. He had been sent by Rhenan, a learned man, then resident at Bâle, and indefatigable in circulating the Reformer's writings throughout Switzerland. Rhenan had become aware that the hawking of books was an important means of diffusing evangelical doctrine. Lucian had travelled almost over the whole of Switzerland, and knew everybody. " See." said Rhenan to Zuinglius, " whether this Lucian has the necessary prudence and ability; if he has, let him go from town to town, burgh to burgh, village to village, and even from house to house, among the Swiss, with Luther's writings, especially his exposition on the Lord's Prayer, written for the laity.[4] The more he is known the

---

[1] Dass kombt mir Ja wol die kind zu geschweigen. (Bullinger MS.)
[2] War allwegen trostlichen Gemüths und tapferer Red. B. Weisse Füssl. Beytr.iv, p. 36.) [3] Certas studiis vindicans horas, quas etiam non omisit, nisi seriis coactus. (Osw. Myc Vit. Zw.) [4] . . . Oppidatim, municipatim, vicatim, imo domesticatim per Helvetios circumferat. . . . (Zw. Ep. p. 81)

more purchasers will he find. But care must be taken not to let him hawk other books. If he has none but Luther's, his sale of them will be the greater." Thus the humble roof of many a Swiss family was penetrated with some rays of light. There was one other book, however, which Zuinglius should have caused to be hawked with those of Luther—the Gospel of Jesus Christ.

CHAP. VII

Indulgences—Samson at Berne—Samson at Baden—The Dean of Bremgarten—Young Henry Bullinger—Samson and the Dean—Internal struggles of Zuinglius—Zuinglius against Indulgences—Samson dismissed.

Zuinglius had not long to wait for an opportunity of displaying his zeal in a new vocation. Samson, the famous indulgence merchant, was slowly approaching Zurich. This miserable trafficker had come from Schwitz to Zug, 20th September, 1518, and had remained there three days. An immense crowd had gathered round him. The poorest were the most eager, so that they prevented the rich from coming forward. This did not suit the monk; accordingly, one of his attendants began to bawl out to the populace, " Good people, do not throng so ! Let those come who have money. We will afterwards try to content those who have none." From Zug Samson and his band repaired to Lucerne ; from Lucerne to Underwald; then crossing the fertile Alps with their rich valleys, passing beneath the eternal ice of Oberland, and in these spots, the grandest in Switzerland, exposing their Roman merchandise, they arrived near Berne. The monk was at first prohibited to enter the town, but succeeded at last in obtaining an introduction by means of persons whom he had in his pay. Exhibiting his wares. in the church of St. Vincent he began to cry louder than ever. " Here," said he to the rich, " are indulgences on parchment for a crown." " There," said he to the poor, " are indulgences on ordinary paper for two farthings !" One day, a celebrated knight, James de Stein, came up prancing on a dapple grey horse ; the monk greatly admired the horse. " Give me," says the knight, " an indulgence for myself, for my troop of five hundred strong, for all my vassals of Belp, and all my ancestors ; I will give you my dapple grey horse in exchange." It was a high price for the horse, but the courser pleased the Franciscan, and the bargain was struck. The horse went to the monk's stable. and all these souls were declared for ever exempted from hell.[1] Another day, he give a burgher, for thirteen florins, an indulgence, in virtue of which his confessor was authorised to absolve him from any species of perjury.[2] So much was Samson in repute, that Counsellor May, an enlightened old man, having said something against him, was obliged to go down on his knees, and ask pardon of the arrogant monk.

This was the monk's last day, and a loud ringing of bells announced his immediate departure from Berne. Samson was in the church standing on the steps of the high altar. Canon Henry Lupulus, formerly Zuinglius's master, was acting as his interpreter. "When the wolf and the fox rendezvous together in the field," said canon Anselm, turning to the Schulthess of Walleville, "the best thing for you, worthy Sir, is to put your sheep and geese in safety." But the monk cared little for these sarcasms, which, besides, did not reach his ear. "Kneel," said he to the superstitious crowd, "repeat three *Paters*, three *Ave Marias*, and your souls will forthwith be as pure as at the moment of baptism." Then all the people fell upon their knees. Samson wishing even to outdo himself, exclaimed, "I deliver from the torments of purgatory and hell all the spirits of the departed Bernese, whatever may have been the manner and place of their death." These jugglers, like those at fairs, kept their finest feat for the last.

Samson set out with a heavy purse towards Zurich, crossing Argovia and Baden. The farther on he got, the monk, whose appearance on passing the Alps was so shabby, proceeded with more pride and splendour. The Bishop of Constance, irritated that Samson had not employed him to legalise his bulls, had forbidden all the curates of his diocese to open their churches to him. At Baden, nevertheless, the curate durst not long oppose his traffic. This redoubled the monk's effrontery. Making the round of the burying ground at the head of a procession, he seemed to fix his eyes on some object in the air, while his acolytes sung the hymn for the dead, and pretending to see souls flying from the burying ground to heaven, he exclaimed—"*Ecce volant!* See how they fly." One day, an inhabitant of the place getting up into the church steeple, a great number of feathers were soon seen in the air falling down on the astonished procession; "See how they fly," exclaimed the wag of Baden, shaking a feather cushion from the steeple. Many began to laugh.[3] Samson fell into a rage, and could not be appeased till he learned that the individual was subject to fits of derangement: he left Baden in a huff.

[1] Um einen Kuttgrowen Hengst. (Anshelm, v, 335, J. J. Hotting. Helv. K. Gesch. 4,29.)   [2] A quovis parjurio. (Muller's Relig. iv, 403.)   [3] Dessen viel Luth gnug lachten. (Bullinger MS.)

Continuing his journey, he arrived, towards the end of February, 1519, at Bremgarten, at the solicitation of the Schulthess and second curate, who had seen him at Baden. No individual in that district had a higher reputation than dean Bullinger of Bremgarten. Though far from enlightened as to the errors of the Church and the Word of God, being open, zealous, eloquent, kind to the poor, and ready to do a service to the humblest, he was loved by every body. He had in his youth formed a connection with the daughter of a counsellor of the place. This was the usual expedient of such of the priests as were unwilling to live in general licentiousness. Anna had borne him five sons, but this had in no way lessened the respect which the dean enjoyed. There was not in Switzerland a more hospitable house than his. A great lover of the chace, he was seen surrounded with ten or twelve dogs, and accompanied by the barons of Hallwyll, the abbot Mury, and the gentry of Zurich, scouring the fields and forests around. He kept open table, and none of his guests was more jovial than himself. When the deputies to the Diet were on their way to Baden, on passing through Bremgarten they failed not to take their seats at the dean's table. "Bullinger," said they, "keeps court like the most powerful baron."

In this house strangers remarked a child of an intelligent countenance. Henry, one of the dean's sons, from his earliest years, had many narrow escapes. Having been seized with the plague, preparations were making for his funeral when he showed some signs of life, and was restored to his delighted parents. On another occasion, a wandering beggar, having won him by caresses, was carrying him off from his family, when some persons in passing recognised and rescued him. At three years of age he could repeat the Lord's prayer and the apostles' creed. One day having slipt into the church, he got into his father's pulpit, stood up gravely, and at the full stretch of his voice, cried out, " I believe in God the Father," and so on. At twelve, he was sent to the Latin school of Emmeric, his heart overwhelmed with fear; for those times were dangerous for a young boy without experience. When the students of an university thought its discipline too severe, they not unfrequently left it in troops, carrying the children with them, and encamped in the woods, from which they sent the youngest of their number to beg, or sometimes with arms in their hands they rushed forth on the passing traveller, robbed him, and then consumed their booty in debauchery. Henry was happily kept from evil in this distant abode. Like Luther, he gained his livelihood by singing before the houses, for his father wished to teach him to live by his own shifts. He was sixteen when he opened a New Testament.

" I found in it," says he, " every thing necessary for man's salvation; and thenceforth I laid it down as a principle to follow the Holy Scriptures alone, and reject all human additions. I believe neither the fathers nor myself, but explain Scripture by Scripture, without adding any thing or taking any thing away."[1] God was thus preparing this young man who was one day to succeed Zuinglius. He is the author of the manuscript journal which we often quote.

About this time Samson arrived at Bremgarten with all his train. The bold dean undismayed by this petty Italian army, prohibited the monk from vending his wares in his neighbourhood. The Schulthess, town clerk, and second pastor, Samson's friends, had met in a room of the inn at which he had alighted, and were standing quite disconcerted around the impatient monk. The dean arrived—" Here are the papal bulls," said the monk to him, " open your church."

The Dean.—" I will not allow the purses of my parishioners to be emptied by means of letters not authenticated, for the bishop has not legalised them ; "

The Monk (in a solemn tone).—" The pope is above the bishop. I enjoin you not to deprive your flock of this distinguished grace."

The Dean.—" Should it cost me my life, I wont open my church."

The Monk (with indignation).—" Rebellious priest! in the name of our most holy lord the pope, I pronounce against you the greater excommunication, and will not absolve you till you ransom your unheard-of audacity at the price of three hundred ducats." . . .

The Dean (turning on his heel and retiring).—" I will know how to answer before my lawful judges: as for you and your excommunication I have nothing to do with them."

The Monk (transported with rage).—" Impudent brute! I am on my way to Zurich, and will there lay my complaint before the deputies of the Confederation."[2]

The Dean.—" I can appear there as well as you, and this instant I set out."

While these things were taking place at Bremgarten, Zuinglius, who saw the enemy gradually approaching, kept preaching vigorously against indulgences.[3] Vicar Faber of Constance encouraged him, promising him the bishop's support.[4] " I know," said Samson, while proceeding towards Zurich, " that Zuinglius will attack me, but I will stop his mouth." Zuinglius was in truth too

---

[1] Bulling. Ep. Franz's Merkw. Zuge, p. 19.   [2] Du freche Bestie . . . etc. (Bullinger MS.)   [3] Ich prengete streng wider des Pabsts Ablass . . . (Zw. Op. ii, 1st part, p. 7.)   [4] Und hat mich darm gestärkt: er welle mir mit aller traw byston. (Ibid.)

much alive to the value of pardon by Christ not to attack the
paper indulgences of these men.   Often, like Luther, he trembled
because of sin ; but in the Saviour found deliverance from his fears.
This modest but brave man was advancing in the knowledge of
God.   " When Satan frightens me," said he, " by crying to me :
You do not this, and you do not that, and yet God commands
them !—immediately the soft voice of the gospel consoles me, saying : What thou canst not do (and assuredly thou canst do nothing,) Christ does for thee."   " Yes," continues the pious evangelist, " when my heart is agonised because of my powerlessness,
and the feebleness of my flesh, my spirit revives at the sound of
this glad news : Christ is thy innocence ! Christ is thy righteousness ! Christ is thy salvation ! Thou art nothing, thou canst do
nothing ! Christ is the Alpha and the Omèga ! Christ is all, and
can do all.[1]   All created things will forsake and deceive thee, but
Christ, the Holy and Righteous One, will receive and justify thee
. . . " Yes," exclaims Zuinglius, " He is our righteousness, and
the righteousness of all who shall ever appear as righteous before
the judgment seat of God ! . . . "

Indulgences could not stand a moment when confronted with
such truths ; and hence Zuinglius never hesitated to attack them.
" No man," said he, " is able to forgive sins.   Christ alone, very
God and very man, is able to do it.[2]   Go, buy indulgences . . . but
rest assured you are not at all forgiven. Those who vend forgiveness
of sins for money are the companions of Simon Magus, the friends
of Balaam and the ambassadors of Satan."

Dean Bullinger, still warm from his conference with the monk,
arrived at Zurich before him.   He came to complain to the Diet
against this shameless dealer and his traffic.   Envoys from the
bishop had arrived for the same purpose.   They made common
cause, and promised to support each other.   The spirit which animated Zuinglius breathed upon this town, and the council of State
resolved to oppose the monk's entry into Zurich.

Samson had arrived in the suburbs, and alighted at an inn.
One foot was already on the stirrup preparatory to his entry, when
deputies from the council arrived, and while making the customary
offer of wine to him as a papal envoy, intimated to him that he
might dispense with appearing in Zurich.   " I have something to
communicate to the Diet in the name of his holiness," replied the
monk.   It was a trick.   However, it was resolved to admit him ;

---

[1] Christus est innocentia tua ; Christus est justitia et puritas tua ; Christus est
salus tua ; tu nihil es, tu nihil potes ; Christus est A et Ω ; Christus est prora et pup-
pis ; Christus est omnia . . . (Zw. Op. i, p. 207.)   [2] Nisi Christus Jesus, verus
Deus et verus homo . . . (Ibid. p. 412.)

but as he spoke only of his bulls he was dismissed, after being compelled to retract the excommunication which he had pronounced against the dean of Bremgarton. He went off in a rage, and the pope shortly after recalled him to Italy. A car drawn by three horses, and loaded with the money of which his lies had robbed the poor, preceded him on the steep tracts of St. Gothard, which eight months before he had crossed in poverty, without style, merely the bearer of a few papers.[1]

On this occasion the Helvetic showed more firmness than the Germanic Diet. The reason was, because no cardinals and bishops sat in it. Hence the pope deprived of these supports dealt more gently with Switzerland than Germany. In other respects, the affair of indulgences, which played so important a part in the Reformation of Germany, is only an episode in that of Switzerland.

CHAP. VIII.

The Labours of Zuinglius—The Baths of Pfeffers—God's time—The Great Death—Zuinglius seized with the Plague—His Enemies—His Friends—Convalescence—General Joy—Effect of the Plague—Myconius at Lucerne—Oswald encourages Zuinglius—Zuinglius at Bâle—Capito called to Mentz—Hedio at Bâle—An Unnatural Son—Preparation for Battle.

Zuinglius did not spare himself. His many labours called for some relaxation, and he was ordered to the baths of Pfeffers. "Ah!" said Herus, one of the pupils who lodged with him, and who thus expressed the feeling of all who knew Zuinglius, " had I a hundred tongues, a hundred mouths, a brazen throat, as Virgil expresses it ; or rather had I the eloquence of Cicero, how could I express all I owe you, and all that I feel at this separation."[2] Zuinglius, however, set out and reached Pfeffers through the astonishing gorge formed by the impetuous torrent of the Jamina. He descended into that infernal abyss, as the hermit David called it, and arrived at the baths, which are perpetually agitated by the dashing of the torrent, and bedewed by the spray of its foaming water. Where Zuinglius lodged it was so dark that candles were burnt at mid-day. He was even assured by the inmates, that frightful phantoms sometimes appeared in the darkness.

Even here Zuinglius found opportunity to serve his Master. His affability won the heart of several of the patients, among others

---

[1] Und führt mit Ihm ein threspendiger Schatz an gelt, den er armen lüthen abgelogen hat. (Bullinger, MS.)　　[2] Etiamsi mihi sint linguæ centum, sint oraque centum, ferrea vox, ut Virgilius ait, aut potius Ciceroniana eloquentia. (Zw. Ep. p. 84.)

a celebrated poet, Philip Ingentinus, professor at Friburg, in Bri-gau,[1] who thenceforward became a zealous supporter of the Refor-mation.

God watched over his own work, and was pleased to hasten it. Zuinglius' defect lay in his strength. Strong in body, strong in character, strong in talents, he was to see all these varieties of strength broken, that he might thereby become such an instrument as God loves to employ. He stood in need of a baptism, that of adversity, infirmity, feebleness, and pain. Such a baptism Luther had received at that period of agony when the cell and long pas-sages of the convent of Erfurt resounded with his cries. Zuinglius was to receive it by being brought into contact with sickness and death. The heroes of this world—the Charles Twelfths and Na-poleons—have a moment which is decisive of their career and their glory, and it is when they all at once become conscious of their strength. There is an analogous moment in the life of God's heroes, but it is in a contrary direction; it is when they recognise their impotence and nothingness; thenceforth they receive strength from on high. Such a work as that of which Zuinglius was to be the instrument is never accomplished by man's natural strength; it would immediately wither away like a tree transplanted after its full growth, and when in full leaf. A plant must be feeble in order to take root, and a grain of corn must die in the ground be-fore it can yield a full return. God led Zuinglius, and with him the work of which he was the stay, to the gates of the grave. It is from among bones and darkness, and the dust of the dead, that God is pleased to take the instruments, by means of which he illumines, regenerates, and revives the earth.

Zuinglius was hidden among the immense rocks which hem in the furious torrent of the Jamina, when he unexpectedly learned that the plague, or as it was termed " *the great death*," [2] was at Zurich. This dreadful scourge broke out in August, on St. Law-rence day, lasted till Candlemas, and carried off two thousand five hundred persons. The young people who lodged with Zuinglius had immediately left, conformably to directions which he had given. His house was empty, but it was to him the very moment to return. He hurriedly quitted Pfeffers, and reappearing in the bosom of his flock, now decimated by the plague, he immediately sent to Wildhaus for his young brother Andrew, who wished to attend him. From that moment he devoted himself entirely to the victims of this dreadful scourge. Every day he preached Christ and his consolations to the sick.[3] His friends delighted to·

<hr/>

[1] Illic tum comitatem tuam e sinu uberrimo profluentem, non injucunde sum ex-pertus. (Zw. Ep. p. 119.) Then I had the pleasure of experiencing your affability, the offspring of an exhuberant heart.   [2] Der Grosse Tod. (Bullinger, MS.)   [3] Ut in· majori periculo sis, quod in dies te novo exponas, dum invisis ægrotos. (Ibid., MS. 87·

see him safe and sound in the midst of so many fatal darts,[1] still felt a secret alarm. Conrad Brunner, who himself died of the plague a few months after, writing him from Bâle said; " Do good, but at the same time remember to take care of your life." It was too late: Zuinglius was seized with the plague. The great preacher of Switzerland was stretched on a bed from which, perhaps, he was never again to rise. He communed with himself, and turned his eye heavenward. He knew that Christ had given him a sure inheritance, and disclosing the feelings of his heart in a hymn remarkable for unction and simplicity, of which, not being able to give the antique and expressive phraseology, we have endeavoured to preserve the rhythm and literal meaning, he exclaimed:—

> My door has opened . . .
> Death appears.
> My God! my strength!
> Dispel all fears!
>
> Oh, Jesus! raise
> Thy pierced arm,
> And break the sword
> That caused alarm
>
> But if my soul
> In life's mid-day
> Thy voice recalls,[3]
> Then I obey.
>
> Ah! let me die,
> For I am thine;
> Thy mansions wait
> Such faith as mine.

Meanwhile the disease gains ground, and this man, the hope of the Church and of Switzerland, is beheld by his despairing friends as about to become the prey of the tomb. His senses and strength forsake him. His heart becomes alarmed, but he is still able to turn towards God, and exclaims:—

> My ills increase;
> Haste to console;
> Terrors overwhelm
> My heart and soul.

Chateaubriand had forgotten this fact, and thousands similar to it, when he said, " the protestant pastor abandons the poor man on his death-bed, and rushes not into the midst of the plague." (Essai sur la Literature Anglaise.)   [1] Plurimum gaudeo te inter tot jactus telorum versantem, illæsum, hactenus evassisse. (Ibid.)

[2] Ich mein der Tod,
  Sig an der Thür. (Zw. Op. ii, 2nd part, p. 270.)

[3] Willit du dann glych
  Tod haben mich
  In mitts der Tagen min
  So soll's willig sin. (Ibid.)

Death is at hand,
My senses fail,
My voice is choked,
Now, Christ! prevail.[1]

Lo ! Satan strains
To snatch his prey;
I feel his hand,
Must I give way ?

He harms me not,
I fear no loss,
For here I lie
Before thy cross.

Canon Hoffman, sincere in his own belief, could not bear the idea of allowing Zuinglius to die in the errors which he had preached. Accordingly he waited on the provost of the Chapter, and said to him, "Think of the danger of his soul. Does he not give the name of fantastical innovators to all the doctors who have appeared for the last three hundred and eighty years and more—to Alexander Hales, St. Bonaventura, Albert the Great, Thomas Aquinas, and all the canonists? Does he not maintain that their doctrines are the dreams which they dreamed in their cowls within the walls of their cloisters? Better had it been for the town of Zurich that Zuinglius had, for a series of years, destroyed our vintage and harvest! There he lies at the brink of death! Do, I beseech you, save his poor soul!" It would seem that the provost was more enlightened than the canon, and deemed it unnecessary to convert Zuinglius to St. Bonaventura and Albert the Great. He was left at peace.

The whole town was in mourning. All the faithful cried to God night and day, beseeching him to restore their faithful pastor.[2] Terror had passed from Zurich to the mountains of the Tockenburg, where also the plague had appeared. Seven or eight persons had perished in the village, among them a servant of Nicolas, a brother of Zuinglius.[3] No letter was received from the Reformer, and his young brother Andrew wrote, " Tell me, my dear brother, in what state you are. The abbot and all our brothers desire to be remembered." As the parents of Zuinglius are not mentioned it would seem that they were now dead.

The news of Zuinglius' illness, and even a rumour of his death,

[1] Nun ist est um
Min Zung ist stumm
. . . .
Darum ist Zyt
Das du min stryt. (Zw. Op. ii, part ii, p. 271.)
[2] Alle glaubige rufften Gott treuwillich an, dass er Ihren getreuwen Ihirten wieder ufrichte. (Bullinger, MS.) [3] Nicolao verò Germano nostro, etiam obiit servus suus, attamen non in redibus suia. (Zw. Ep. 80.;

spread in Switzerland and Germany. Aias i" exclaimed Hedio in tears, " the safety of the country, the gospel trumpet, the magnanimous herald of truth is smitten with death in the flower of his life, and, so to speak, in the spring tide of his days."[1] When the news reached Bâle the whole town was filled with lamentation and mourning.[2]

The spark of life which remained in Zuinglius was, however, rekindled. Though his body was still feeble, his soul was impressed with the unaltered conviction that God had called him to replace the torch of his Word on the candlestick of the Church. The plague had abandoned its victim, and Zuinglius exclaims with emotion —:

> My God! my Father!
> Healed by thee
> On earth again
> I bend my knee.
>
> Now sin no more
> Shall mark my days
> My mouth, henceforth,
> Shall sing thy praise.
>
> The uncertain hour,
> Come when it may,
> Perchance may bring
> Still worse dismay.[3]
>
> But, let it come,
> With joy I'll rise,
> And bear my yoke
> Straight to the skies.[4]

Zuinglius was no sooner able to hold the pen (this was in the beginning of November) than he wrote to his family. This gave inexpressible delight to them all,[5] especially to his young brother Andrew, who himself died of the plague the following year, and at

---

[1] Quis non enim doleat, publicam patriæ salutem, tubam Evangelii, magnanimum veritatis buccinatorem languere, intercidere . . . (Zw. Ep. p. 90.)   [2] Hen quantum luctus, fatis Zuinglium concecisse importunus ille rumor, suo vehementi impetu divulgavit. (Ibid. p. 91.)   [3] Words which were strikingly fulfilled twelve years after on the bloody plains of Cappel.

[4] So will Ich doch
   Den trutz und poch,
   In diser welt
   Tragen frölich
   Um widergelt.

Although these three poetical fragments are dated " the beginning, middle, and end of the malady," and express the feelings which Zuinglius truly experienced at these different moments, it is probable that they were not put into their present form till afterwards. (See Bullinger MS.)

[5] Inspectis tuis litteris incredibilis quidam æstus lœtitiæ pectus meum subiit. (Zw. Ep. p. 88.) On seeing your letter an incredible burst of joy swelled my breast.

whose death Ulric, to use his own words, wept and cried like a
woman.[1] At Bâle Conrad Brunner, a friend of Zuinglius, and
Bruno Amerbach, a famous printer, both young men, were cut off
after three days' illness. The rumour having spread in this town
that Fuinglius also had fallen, the whole university was in mourning.
" He whom God loves is perfected in the flower of his life," said
they.[2] How great was their joy when Collinus, a student of
Lucerne, and afterwards a merchant in Zurich, brought word that
Zuinglius had escaped the jaws of death.[3] John Faber, vicar to
the bishop of Constance, long the friend and afterwards the most
violent adversary of Zuinglius, wrote to him. " O my dear Ulric,
how delighted I am to learn that you have escaped the jaws of cruel
death. When you are in danger, the Christian commonwealth
is threatened. The design of the Lord in these trials is to urge
you forward in the pursuit of eternal life."

This was, indeed, the design, and it was accomplished, though
in a different way from what Faber anticipated. The plague of
1519, which made such fearful ravages in the north of Switzerland,
was, in the hand of God, a powerful means of converting a great
number of persons.[4] But on none had it a greater influence than
on Zuinglius. Hitherto he had been too much disposed to regard
the gospel as mere doctrine ; but now it became a great reality.
He returned from the gates of the grave with a new heart. His
zeal was more active, his life more holy, his word more free, Christian,
and powerful. This was the period of Zuinglius' complete emancipation. He from this time devoted himself to God. The new
life thus given to the Reformer was communicated at the same
time to the Swiss Reformation. The Divine rod, *the great death*,
in passing over all their mountains and descending into all their
valleys, added to the sacredness of the movement which was then
taking place. The Reformation being plunged, like Zuinglius, into
the waters of affliction and of grace, came forth purer and more
animated. In regard to the regeneration of Switzerland, the gospel
sun was now at its height.

Zuinglius, who still strongly felt the want of new strength,
received it in intercourse with his friends. His closest intimacy was
with Myconius. They walked hand in hand, like Luther and
Melancthon. Oswald was happy at Zurich. It is true, his position

---

[1] Ejulatum et luctum plasquam fœmineum. (Zw. Ep. p. 155.)   [2] Ὃν τι θεοὶ
φιλίουσι, νεανίσκος τελευτᾷ. (Ibid., p. 90.) He whom the gods love, dies young.
[3] E diris te mortis fancibus feliciter ereptum negotiator quidam Tigurinus . . . .
(Ibid., p. 91.) A trader from Zurich informed me that you had been happily rescued
from the dire Jaws of death.   [4] Als die Pestilenz in Jahre, 1519, in dieser
Gegend grassirte, viele neigten sich zu einem bessern Leben. (Georg. Vögelin. Ref.
Hist. Füsslin. Beytr., iv, 174.)

was cramped; but every thing was softened by the virtues of his modest spouse. It was of her that Glarean said, "Were I to meet a young girl resembling her, I would prefer her to the daughter of a king." But a faithful voice was often heard disturbing the sweet friendship of Zuinglius and Myconius. It was that of canon Xylotect, who, calling to Oswald from Lucerne, summoned him to return to his country. "Lucerne," said he to him, "not Zurich, is your country. You say that the Zurichers are your friends: granted; but do you know what the evening star will bring you? Serve your country.[1] This I advise; I implore; and, if I am able, command." Xylotect, not confining himself to words, procured the appointment of Myconius to the college school of Lucerne. After this Oswald no longer hesitated. He saw the finger of God in the appointment, and determined to make the sacrifice, how great soever it might be. Who could say whether he might not be an instrument in the hand of the Lord to diffuse the doctrine of peace in warlike Lucerne? But how painful the separation between Zuinglius and Myconius! They parted in tears. Ulric shortly after wrote to Oswald, "Your departure has been as serious a loss to the cause which I defend, as that which is sustained by an army in battle array when one of its wings is destroyed.[2] Ah! I now am aware of all that my Myconius was able to do, and how often, without my knowing it, he maintained the cause of Christ."

Zuinglius felt the loss of his friend the more, because the plague had left him in a state of great feebleness. Writing on the 30th November, 1519, he says, "It has weakened my memory and wasted my intellect." When scarcely convalescent, he had resumed all his labours. "But," said he, "in preaching I often lose the thread of my discourse. I feel languid in all my members, and somewhat as if I were dead." Moreover, Zuinglius, by his opposition to indulgences, had excited the wrath of their partisans. Oswald strengthened his friend by letters which he wrote him from Lucerne. And did he not also receive pledges of assistance from the Lord in the protection which He gave to the Saxon champion who was gaining such important victories over Rome? "What think you," said Myconius to Zuinglius, "of the cause of Luther? For my part I have no fear either for the gospel or for him. If God does not protect his truth, who will protect it? All that I ask of the Lord is, not to withdraw his aid from those who hold nothing dearer than his gospel. Continue as you have begun, and an abundant recompence awaits you in heaven."

---

[1] Patriam cole, suadeo et obscero, et si hoc possum jubeo. (Xylotect. Myconio.)

[2] Nam res meæ, te absente, non sunt minus accisæ quam si exercitui in procinctu stanti altera alarum abstergatur. (Zw. Ep. p. 98.)

The visit of an old friend helped to console Zuinglius for the loss of Myconius. Bunzli, who had been his teacher at Bâle, and had succeeded the dean of Wesen, the Reformer's uncle, arrived at Zurich, in the first week of the year 1520, and Zuinglius and he thereafter resolved to set out together to Bâle to see their common friends.[1] This visit of Zuinglius bore fruit. " Oh, my dear Zuinglius !" wrote John Glother to him at a later period, " never will I forget you. The thing which binds me to you is the goodness with which, during your stay at Bâle, you came to see me, me, a petty schoolmaster, living in obscurity without learning or merit, and of humble station ! What wins me is the elegance of your manners, and that indescribable meekness with which you subdue all hearts, even stones, if I may so speak." [2] But Zuinglius' visit was still more useful to his old friends. Capito, Hedio, and others, were electrified by the power of his eloquence. The former commencing in Bâle the work which Zuinglius was doing at Zurich, began to expound the gospel of St. Matthew before an auditory which continued to increase. The doctrine of Christ penetrated and inflamed all hearts. The people received it joyfully, and with acclamation hailed the revival of Christianity.[3] It was the aurora of the Reformation. Accordingly a conspiracy of monks and priests was soon formed against Capito. It was at this time that Albert, the young cardinal-archbishop of Mentz, who felt desirous of attaching a man of so much learning to his person, called him to his court.[4] Capito, seeing the difficulties which were thrown in his way, accepted the invitation. The people were moved, and, turning with indignation against the priests, raised a tumult in the town.[5] Hedio was proposed as his successor, but some objected to his youth, while others said, " He is his pupil." " Truth bites," said Hedio : it is not advantageous to offend too delicate ears by telling it. [6] No matter, nothing will turn me from the straight path." The monks redoubled their efforts. " Believe not those," exclaimed they from the pulpit, " who say that the sum of Christian doctrine is found in the Gospel and in St. Paul. Scotus has done more for Christianity than St. Paul himself. All the learning that has ever been spoken or printed has been stolen from Scotus. All that has been done since by men eager for fame has been to throw in some Greek and Hebrew terms, which have only darkened the matter.[7]

---

[1] Zw. Ep. p. 103 and 111.   [2] Morum tuorum elegantia suavitasque incredibilis qua omnes tibi devincis, etiam lapides, ut sic dixerim. (ibid., p. 133.)
[3] Renascenti Christianismo mirum quam faveant. (ibid., p. 120.)   [4] Cardinalis illic invitavit amplissimis conditionibus. (Ibid.) The cardinal invited him thither on the most liberal terms.   [5] Tumultus exoritur et maxima indignatio vulgi erga *ἱερεῖς*. (Ibid.)   [6] Auriculas teneras mordaci radere vero, non usque adeo tutum est. (Ibid.)   [7] Scotum plus profuisse rei Christianæ quam ipsum Paulum . . . quicquid eruditum, furatum ex Scoto. (ibid.)

The tumult increased; and there was reason to fear that, on Capito's departure, it would become still more serious. "I will be almost alone," thought Hedio, "poor I, to struggle with these formidable monsters."[1] Accordingly, he invoked the assistance of God, and wrote to Zuinglius. "Inflame my courage by writing often. Learning and Christianity are now placed between the hammer and the anvil. Luther has just been condemned by the universities of Louvain and Cologne. If ever the Church was in imminent danger, it is at this hour."[2]

Capito left Bâle for Mentz, 28th April, and Hedio succeeded him. Not content with the public assemblies in the church at which he continued his exposition of St. Matthew, he proposed, in the month of June, as he wrote Luther, to have private meetings in his own house, to give more thorough evangelical instruction to those who might feel the want of it. This powerful method of communicating the truth, and exciting in the faithful an interest and zeal in divine things, could not fail then, as it never does, to awaken opposition in the men of the world and in domineering priests, both of whom, though from different motives, are equally desirous that God should be worshipped only within the precincts of a particular building. But Hedio was invincible.

At the same period when he formed this good resolution at Bâle, there arrived at Zurich one of those characters who often emerge, like impure froth, from the vortex of revolutions.

Senator Grebel, a man of great influence in Zurich, had a son named Conrad, a youth of remarkable talents, and a relentless enemy of ignorance and superstition, which he attacked with cutting satire. He was boisterous, violent, sarcastic, and bitter in his expression, without natural affection, given to debauchery, always talking loudly of his own innocence, while he could see nothing but what was wrong in others. We speak of him here because he is afterwards to play a melancholy part. At this period, Vadian married a sister of Conrad, and Conrad, who was studying at Paris where his misconduct had deprived him of the use of his limbs, desiring to be present at the marriage, appeared suddenly about the beginning of June amidst his family. The poor father received the prodigal son with a gentle smile, his fond mother with tears. The tenderness of his parents made no change on his unnatural heart. His kind and unhappy mother having some time after been brought to the gates of death, Conrad wrote his brother-in-law Vadain:—
"My mother is recovered; she again rules the house, sleeps, awakes, grumbles, breakfasts, scolds, dines, makes a racket, sups,

1 Cum pestilentissimis monstris. (Zw. Ep. p. 121.)   2 Si unquam imminebat periculum, jam imminet. (Ibid, 17th March, 1520)

and is perpetually a burden to us.   She runs, cooks, re-cooks, sweeps the house, toils, kills herself with fatigue, and will shortly bring on a relapse."[1]

Such was the man who, at a later period, pretended to lord it over Zuinglius, and who took the lead among fanatical anabaptists. Divine Providence perhaps allowed such characters to appear at the period of the Reformation that their disorders might the better bring out the wise, Christian, and orderly spirit of the Reformers.

Everything announced that the battle between the gospel and the papacy was about to commence. " Let us stir up the temporisers," wrote Hedio to Zurich ; " the peace is broken, let us arm our hearts : the enemies we shall have to combat are most fierce."[2] Myconius wrote in the same strain to Ulric, who, however, answered their warlike appeals with admirable meekness.   " I should like," said he, " to gain these obstinate men by kindness and good offices, rather than overcome them by violence and disputation.[3] That they call our doctrine, (which however is not ours,) a doctrine of the devil, is nothing more than natural.   It proves to me that we are indeed the ambassadors of Christ.   The devils cannot be silent in his presence."

CHAP. IX.

The Two Reformers—The Fall of Man—Expiation of the God-Man—No merit in Works—Objections refuted—Power of Love to Christ—Election—Christ alone Master—Effects of this Preaching—Despondency and Courage—First Act of the Magistrate—Church and State—Attacks—Galster.

Though desirous to follow the path of meekness, Zuinglius was not idle. Since his illness his preaching had become more profound and enlivening. More than two thousand persons in Zurich had received the word of God into their heart, made profession of the evangelical doctrine, and were themselves able to announce it.[4]

Zuinglius' faith was the same as Luther's, but more the result of reasoning. Luther advances with a bound. Zuinglius owes

---

[1] Sic regiert das Hans, schlüft, steht auf, zaukt, fruhstucht, keift ..... (Simml. Samml. iv, Wirz, i, 76.)   [2] Armemus pectora nostra! pugnandum erit contra teterrimos , ostes. (Zw: Ep. p. 10.)   [3] Benevolentia honestoque obsequio potius allici quam animosa oppugnatione trahi. (Ibid., p. 103.)   [4] Non enim soli sumus Tiguri plus duobus millibus permultorum est rationalium qui lac jam Spirituali sugentes .... (Ibid., p. 104.)—For we are not alone : at Zurich are more than two thousand of very rational beings, who now seek spiritual food.

more to clearness of perception. Luther's writings are pervaded with a thorough personal conviction of the benefits which the cross of Christ confers upon himself, and this conviction, glowing with heat and life, is the soul of all he says. The same thing doubtless exists in Zuinglius, but in an inferior degree. He had looked more to the Christian system as a whole, and admired it particularly for its beauty, for the light which it sheds into the human mind, and the eternal life which it brings to the world. The one is more the man of heart, the other more the man of intellect; and hence it is that those who do not experimentally know the faith which animated these two great disciples of the Lord, fall into the grossest error, making the one a mystic and the other a rationalist. The one is more pathetic, perhaps, in the exposition of his faith, and the other more philosophical, but both believe the the same truths. They do not, however, look at all secondary questions from the same point of view, but that faith which is one, that faith which quickens and justifies its possessor, that faith which no confession, no article of doctrine can express, is in the one as in the other. The doctrine of Zuinglius has often been so much misrepresented, that it seems proper here to give an account of what he preached at this time to the increasing crowds who flocked to the cathedral of Zurich.

The fall of Adam, Zuinglius regarded as the key to man's history. ".Before the fall," said he one day, "man had been created with a free will, so that he was able, if he chose, to keep the law; his nature was pure, being as yet untainted by the malady of sin; his life was in his own hand. But wishing to be equal to God, he died . . . and not he only, but every one of his descendants. All men being dead in Adam none can be recalled to life until the Spirit, who is God himself, raise them from death."[1]

The people of Zurich who listened eagerly to this powerful orator were saddened when he set before them the sinful state into which human nature has fallen, but soon after heard words of joy, and learned to know the remedy which is able to recall man to life. ." Christ very man and very God,"[2] said the eloquent voice of this shepherd—son of the Tockenburg, "has purchased for us a redemption which will never terminate. The eternal God died for us : His

---

[1] Quum ergo omnes homines in Adamo mortui sunt . . . . . donec per Spiritum et gratiam Dei ad vitam quæ Deus est excitentur. (Zw. Op. i, p. 203.) Seeing, then, that all men are dead in Adam . . . until they are awakened by the Spirit and grace of God to the life of God. These words, and others which we have quoted, or will quote, are taken from a work which Zuinglius published in 1523, and in which he gave a summary of the doctrine which he had preached for several years. " Ilic recensere cœpi quæ ex verbo Dei prædicavi. (Ibid., p. 223.) These are his own words.   [2] Christus verus homo et verus Deus . . . . . (Zw. Op. i, p. 204.)

passion then is eternal : it brings salvation for ever and ever:[1] it appeases divine justice for ever in favour of all those who lean upon this sacrifice with firm and immovable faith." " Wherever sin ex-ists," exclaimed the Reformer, "death must necessarily supervene. Christ had no sin, there was no guile in his mouth, and yet he died! Ah! it was because he died in our stead. He was pleased to die in order to restore us to life, and as he had no sins of his own, the Father, who is full of mercy, laid the burden of our sins upon him.[2]" The Christian orator continued, " Since the will of man rebelled against the supreme God, it was necessary, if eternal order was to be re-established and man saved, that the human will should be made subject in Christ to the divine will."[3] He often repeated that it was for the faithful people of God, that the expiatory death of Jesus Christ had been endured.[4]

Those in the city of Zurich who were eager for salvation, found rest on hearing these good news. But old errors still remained, and these it was necessary to destroy. Setting out from this great truth of a salvation which is the gift of God, Zuinglius forcibly dis-coursed against the pretended merit of human works. " Since eternal salvation," said he, " proceeds solely from the merits and death of Jesus Christ, the merit of our works is nothing better than folly, not to say rash impiety.[5] Could we have been saved by our works it had not been necessary for Jesus Christ to die. All who have ever come to God came to him by the death of Jesus Christ.[6]

Zuinglius perceived the objections which some of his hearers felt against these doctrines. Some of them called upon him and stated them. He mounted the pulpit and said—" People, more curious perhaps than pious, object that this doctrine makes men giddy and dissolute. But of what consequence are the objections or fears which human curiosity may suggest? Whosoever believes in Jesus Christ is certain that every thing which comes from God is necessarily good. If, then, the gospel is of God it is good.[7] And what other power would be capable of implanting among men in-nocence, truth, and love? O God! most compassionate, most just,

---

[1] Deus enim æternus quum sit qui pro nobis moritur, passionem ejus æternam et perpetuò salutarum esse oportet. (Zw. Op. i, p. 206.) Since he who dies for us is the eternal God, his passion must be eternal and for ever saving. [2] Mori voluit ut nos vitæ restitueret . . . (Ibid., p. 204.) [3] Necesse fuit ut voluntas humana in Christo se divinæ submitteret. (Ibid.) [4] Hostia est et victima satisfaciens in æternum pro peccatis omnium fidelium. (Ibid., p. 253.) 'Expurgata peccata mul-titudinis, hoc est, fidelis populi. (Ibid., p. 264.) [5] Sequitur meritum nostrorum operum nihil esse quam vanitatem et stultitiam, ne dicam impietatem et ignorantem impudentiam. (Ibid., p. 290.) It follows that the merit of our works is nothing but vanity and folly, not to say impiety and ignorant impudence. [6] Quotquot ad Deum venerunt unquam, per mortem Christi ad Deum venisse. (Ibid.)
[7] Certus est quod quidquid ex Deo est bonum sit. Si ergo Evangelium ex Deo num est. (Ibid., p. 209.)

Father of mercies," exclaimed he in the overflowing of his piety,
" with what love hast thou embraced us, us thy enemies ! [1]   With
what great and certain hopes hast thou inspired us, us who should
have known nothing but despair : and to what glory hast thou in
thy Son called our littleness and nothingness! Thy purpose in this
ineffable love is to constrain us to yield thee love for love! . . . "

Then dwelling on this idea, he showed that love to the Redeemer
is a more powerful law than the commandments.   " The Christian," said he, " delivered from the law depends entirely on Christ.
Christ is his reason, his counsel, his righteousness, and whole
salvation.   Christ lives in him and acts in him.   Christ alone
guides him, and he needs no other guide." [2]   And making use of a
comparison adapted to his hearers, he added, " If a government
prohibits its citizens, under pain of death, from receiving pensions
and presents at the hands of princes, how gentle and easy this law
is to those who, from love to their country and to liberty, would,
of their own accord, refrain from so culpable a proceeding ; but
on the contrary, how tormenting and oppressive it feels to those
who think only of their own interest.   Thus the righteous man
lives joyful in the love of righteousness, whereas the unrighteous
walks groaning under the heavy weight of the law which oppres-
ses him." [3]

In the cathedral of Zurich was a considerable number of veteran
soldiers who felt the truth of these words.   Is not love the mightiest of legislators?   Is not every thing that it commands instantly
accomplished?   Does not he whom we love dwell in our heart, and
does it not of itself perform what he enjoins?   Accordingly, Zuinglius, waxing bold, declared to the people of Zurich that love to
the Redeemer was alone capable of making man do things agreeable to God.   " Works done out of Jesus Christ are not useful,"
said the Christian orator ; " since every thing is done of him, in
him, and by him, what do we pretend to arrogate to ourselves?
Wherever faith in God is, there God is, and wherever God is,
there is a zeal which presses and urges men to good works. [4]   Only
take care that Christ be in thee and thou in Christ, and then doubt
not but he will work.   The life of the Christian is just one continued work by which God begins, continues, and perfects in man
every thing that is good." [5]

Struck with the grandeur of this divine love which existed from

[1] Quanta caritate nos fures et perduelles. (Zw. Op. i, p. 207.   [2] Tum enim totus
a Christo pendet.   Christus est ei ratio, consilium, justitia, innocentia et tota salus.
Christus in eo vivit, in eo agit.   (Ibid., p. 233.)   [3] Bonus vir in amore justitiæ
liber et lætus vivit.   (Ibid., p. 234.)   [4] Ubi Deus, illic cura est et studium ad opera
bona urgens et impellens. . . . (Ibid., p. 212.)   [5] Vita ergo pii hominis nihil aliud
est nisi perpetua quædam et indefessa boni operatio, quam Deus incipit, ducit et ab.
solvit.. . . (Ibid., p. 295.)

eternity, the herald of grace raised his voice to all the timid or irresolute. "Can you fear," said he, "to approach the tender Father who has chosen you? Why has he chosen us in his grace? Why has he called us? Why has he drawn us? Was it that we might not dare to go to him?" . . . [1]

Such was the doctrine of Zuinglius. It was the doctrine of Christ himself. "If Luther preaches Christ he does what I do," said the preacher of wurich; "those who have been brought to Christ by him are more numerous than those who have been brought by me. But no matter! I am unwilling to bear any other name than that of Christ, whose soldier I am, and who alone is my head. Never was a single scrap written by me to Luther, or by Luther to me. And why? In order to show to all how well the spirit of God accords with himself, since, without having heard each other, we so harmoniously teach the doctrine of Jesus Christ." [2]

Thus Zuinglius preached with energy and might.[3] The large cathedral could not contain the crowds of hearers. All thanked God that a new life was beginning to animate the lifeless body of the Church. Swiss from all the cantons, brought to Zurich either by the Diet or by other causes, being touched by this new preaching, carried its precious seeds into all the Helvetic valleys. One acclamation arose from mountains and cities. Nicolas Hageus, writing from Lucerne to Zurich, says, "Switzerland has hitherto given birth to Scipios, Cæsars, and Brutuses, but has scarcely produced two men who had the knowledge of Jesus Christ, and could nourish men's hearts, not with vain disputes, but with the Word of God. Now that Divine Providence gives Switzerland Zuinglius for its orator, and Oswald Myconius for its teacher, virtue and sacred literature revive among us. O happy Helvetia! could you but resolve at length to rest from all your wars, and, already so celebrated, become still more celebrated for righteousness and peace." [4] "It was said," wrote Myconius to Zuinglius, "that your voice could not be heard three yards off. But I now see it was a falsehood; for all Switzerland hears you." [5] "You possess intrepid courage," wrote Hedio to him from Bâle, "I will follow you as far as I am able." [6] "I have heard you," said Sebastian Hofmeister of Schaffausen, writing to him from Constance." Ah, would to God that Zurich, which is at the head of our happy con-

[1] Quum ergo Deus pater nos elegit ex gratia sua, traxitque et vocavit, cur ad eum accedere non auderemus ? (Zw. Op. i, p. 287.)   [2] Quam concors sit Spiritus Dei, dum nos tam procul dissiti, nihil colludentes, tam concorditer Christi doctrinam docemus. (Ibid., p. 276.) How well the Spirit of God accords, since we, who are placed at such a distance from each other, with no collusion, so harmoniously teach the doctrine of Christ.   [3] Quam fortis sis in Christo prædicando. (Zw. Ep. p. 160.)
[4] O Helvetiam longe feliciorem, si tandem liceat te a bellis conquiescere! (Ibid. p. 128.)
[5] At video mendacium esse, cum audiaris per totam Helvetiam. (Ibid., p. 135.)
[6] Sequar te quoad potero. (Ibid., p. 134.)

federation was delivered from the disease, and health thus restored to the whole body." [1]

But Zuinglius met with opponents as well as admirers. "To what end," said some, "does he intermeddle with the affairs of Switzerland?" "Why," said others, "does he, in his religious instructions, constantly repeat the same things?" Amid all these combats the soul of Zuinglius was often filled with sadness. All seemed to be in confusion, as if society were turned upside down. [2] He thought it impossible that any thing new should appear without something of an opposite nature being immediately displayed. [3] When a hope sprang up in his heart, a fear immediately sprang up beside it. Still he soon raised his head. "The life of man here below," said he, "is a war; he who desires to obtain glory must attack the world in front, and, like David, make this haughty Goliath, who seems so proud of his stature, to bite the dust. The Church," said he, like Luther, "has been acquired by blood, and must be renewed by blood. [4] The more numerous the defilements in it, the more must we arm ourselves, like Hercules, in order to clean out these Augean stables. [5] I have little fear for Luther," added he, "even should he be thundered against by the bolts of this Jupiter." [6]

Zuinglius stood in need of repose, and repaired to the waters of Baden. The curate of the place, an old papal guard, a man of good temper, but completely ignorant, had obtained his benefice by carrying a halberd. True to his soldier habits, he spent the day and part of the night in jovial company, while Stäheli, his vicar, was indefatigable in fulfilling the duties of his office. [7] Zuinglius invited the young minister to his house. "I have need of Swiss help," said he to him, and from this moment Stäheli was his fellow-labourer. Zuinglius, Stäheli, and Luti, afterwards pastor of Winterthur, lived under the same roof.

The devotedness of Zuinglius was not to pass unrewarded. The Word of God, preached with so much energy, could not fail to produce fruit. Several magistrates were gained, experiencing the Word to be their consolation and their strength. The Council, grieved at seeing the priests, and especially the monks, shamelessly delivering from the pulpit whatever came into their heads, passed a resolution, ordering them not to advance anything in their discourses "that they did not draw from the sacred sources of the Old

---

[1] Ut capite felicis patriæ nostro a morbo erepto, sanitas tandem in reliqua membra reciperetur. (Zw. Ep. p. 147.) [2] Omnia sursum deorsumque moventur. Ibid., p. 142.) [3] Ut nihil proferre caput queat, cujus non contrarium e regione emergat. (Ibid., p. 142.) [4] Ecclesiam puto, ut sanguine parta est, ita sanguine instaurari. (Ibid., p. 143.) [5] Eo plures armabis Hercules qui fimum tot hactenus bonum efferant. (Ibid., p. 144.) [6] Etiamsi fulmine Jovis istius fulminetur. (Ibid.) [7] Misc. Tig., ii, 579-696. Wirz., i, 79, 78.

and New Testament."[1] It was in 1520 that the civil power thus interposed for the first time in the work of the Reformation; acting as a Christian magistrate, say some—since the first duty of the magistrate is to maintain the Word of God and defend the best interests of the citizens; depriving the Church of its liberty, say others,—by subjecting it to secular power, and giving the signal for the series of evils which have since been engendered by the connection between Church and State. We will not give any opinion here on this great controversy which in our day is carried on with so much warmth in several countries. It is sufficient for us to point out its commencement at the period of the Reformation. But there is another thing also to be pointed out—the act of these magistrates was itself one of the effects produced by the preaching of the Word of God. At this period the Reformation in Switzerland ceased to be the work of private individuals, and began to be included within the national domain. Born in the heart of a few priests and literary men, it extended, rose, and took up elevated ground. Like the waters of the ocean, it gradually increased till it had overflowed an immense extent.

The monks were confounded: they were ordered to preach nothing but the Word of God, and the greater part of them had never read it. Opposition provokes opposition. The resolution of the council became the signal of more violent attacks on the Reformation. Plots began to be formed against the curate of Zurich. His life was in danger. One evening, when Zuinglius and his vicars were quietly conversing in their house, some citizens arrived in great haste, and asked, " Are your doors well bolted? Be this night on your guard." " Such alarms were frequent," adds Stäheli; but we were well armed,[2] and a guard was stationed for us in the street."

In other places, means still more violent were resorted to. An old man of Shaffausen, named Galster, a man of piety, and of an ardour rare at his period of life, happy in the light which he had found in the gospel, laboured to communicate it to his wife and children. His zeal, perhaps indiscreet, openly attacked the relics, priests, and superstitions with which this canton abounded. He soon became an object of hatred and terror even to his own family. The old man, penetrating their fatal designs, left his home broken-hearted, and fled to the neighbouring forest. There he lived several days subsisting on whatever he could find, when suddenly, on the last night of the year 1520, torches blazed in all directions through

[1] Vetuit eos Senatus quicquam prædicare quod non ex sacrarum literarum utriusque Testamenti fontibus hausissent. (Zw. Op. iii, 28.)   [2] Wir waren aber gut gerüstet. (Misc. Tig., ii, 681. Wirz., i, 334.)

·the forest, and the cries of men and the barking of dogs re-echoed
·under its dark shades. The council had ordered a hunt in the
·woods to discover him: The dogs scented him out, and the unhappy old man was dragged before the magistrate. He was ordered
·to abjure his faith, but remained immovable, and was beheaded.[1]

CHAP. X.

A new Combatant—The Reformer of Berne—Zuinglius encourages Haller—The
Gospel at Lucerne—Oswald Persecuted—Preaching of Zuinglius—Henry Bullinger and Gerold of Knonau—Rubli at Bâle—The Chaplain of the Hospital—War
in Italy—Zuinglius against Foreign Service.

The year, the first day of which was signalised by this bloody
·execution, had scarcely commenced when Zuinglius was waited on
in his house at Zurich by a young man, of about twenty-eight years
·of age, tall in stature, and with an exterior which bespoke candour,
simplicity, and diffidence.[2] He said his name was Berthold Haller.
Zuinglius, on hearing the name, embraced the celebrated preacher
of Berne, with that affability which made him so engaging.
Haller, born at Aldingen in Wurtemberg,[3] had first studied at
Rotweil under Rubellus, and afterwards at Pforzheim, where
Simler was his teacher, and Melancthon his fellow-student. The
Bernese, who had already distinguished themselves by arms, at
this time resolved to invite literature into the bosom of their re-
·public. Rubellus, and Berthold, not twenty-one years of age,
·repaired thither. Sometime after, the latter was appointed canon,
·and ultimately preacher of the cathedral. The gospel which Zuinglius preached had extended to Berne; Haller believed, and
·thenceforth longed to see the distinguished man, whom he now
looked up to as his father. He went to Zurich after Myconius
·had announced his intended visit. Thus met Haller and Zuinglius.
The former, a man of great meekness, unbosomed his griefs; and
·the latter, a man of might, inspired him with courage. One day,
Berthold said to Zuinglius, " My spirit is overwhelmed . . . I am
·not able to bear all this injustice. I mean to give up the pulpit and
·retire to Bâle beside Wittembach, and there occupy myself exclusively with sacred literature." "Ah !" replied Zuinglius, "I too have
my feelings of despondency, when unjust attacks are made upon

---

[1] Wirz, i, 510. Sebast. Wagner, von Kirchhofer, p. 18.   [2] Animi tui can-
dorem simplicem et simplicitatem candidissimam, hac tua pusilla quidem epistola ...
(w. Ep. p. 186)   [3] Ita ipse in literis MS. (J. J. Hott. iii, 54.)

me; but Christ awakens my conscience, and urges me on by his terrors and his promises. He alarms me when he says, ' *Whoso shall be ashamed of me before men, of him will I be ashamed before my Father ;*' and he sets my mind at ease when he adds, ' *Whoso shall confess me before men, him will I confess before my Father.*' My dear Berthold, rejoice! Our name is written in indelible characters in the register of citizenship on high.[1] I am ready to die for Christ.[2] Let your wild cubs," added he, " hear the doctrine of Jesus Christ, and you will see them become tame.[3] But this task must be performed with great gentleness, lest they turn again and rend you." Haller's courage revived. "My soul," said he to Zuinglius, " is awakened out of its sleep. I must preach the gospel. Jesus Christ must again be established in this city, from which he has been so long exiled."[4] Thus the torch of Berthold was kindled at the torch of Zuinglius, and the timid Haller threw himself into the midst of the ferocious bears, who, as Zuinglius expresses it, " were gnashing their teeth, and seeking to devour him."

In was in another part of Switzerland, however, that persecution was to begin. Warlike Lucerne came forward, like a foe in full armour couching his lance. In this canton, which was favourable to foreign service, a martial spirit predominated, and the leading men knit their brows when they heard words of peace fitted to curb their warlike temper. Meanwhile the writings of Luther having found their way into the town, some of the inhabitants began to examine them, and were horrified. It seemed to them that an infernal hand had traced the lines; their imagination was excited, their senses became bewildered, and their rooms seemed as if filled with demons, flocking around them, and glaring upon them with a sarcastic smile.[5] They hastily closed the book, and dashed it from them in dismay. Oswald, who had heard of these singular visions, did not speak of Luther to any but his most intimate friends, and contented himself with simply preaching the gospel of Christ. Nevertheless, the cry which rung through the town was, " Luther and the schoolmaster (Myconius) must be burnt."[6] " I am driven by my adversaries like a ship by the raging billows,"[7] said Oswald to one of his friends. One day, in-

---

[1] Scripta tamen habeatur in fastis supernorum civium. (Zw. Ep. p. 186.)

[2] Ut mori pro Christo non usque adeo detrectem apud me. (Ibid., p. 187.)

[3] Ut ursi tui ferociusculi, audita Christi doctrina, mansuescere incipiant. (Ibid.) There is a bear in the arms of the town of Berne. [4] Donec Christ__ *ocul*tatis nugis longe a nobis exulem .... pro virili restituerim ... (Ibid., p. 187.) Until I have done my utmost to restore Christ, who has long been exiled from us by monkish trifles. [5] Dum Lutherum semel legerint ut putarent stubellam suam plenam ___ dæmonibus. (Ibid., p. 37.) [6] Clamatur hic per totam civitatem: Lutherum comburendum et ludi magistrum. (Ibid., p. 183.) [7] Non aliter me

the beginning of the year 1520, he was unexpectedly summoned to appear before the council, and told, " Your orders are, not to read the writings of Luther to your pupils, not to name him in their presence, and not even to think of him."[1] The lords of Lucerne pretended, it seems, to have a very extensive jurisdiction. Shortly after, a preacher delivered a sermon against heresy. The whole audience was moved, and every eye was turned on Myconius; for whom but he could the preacher have in his eye ? Oswald kept quietly in his seat, as if the matter had not concerned him. But on leaving the church, as he was walking with his friend, Canon Xylotect, one of the counsellors, still under great excitement, passed close to them, and passionately exclaimed, " Well, disciples of Luther, why don't you defend your master ?" They made no answer. " I live," said Myconius, " among fierce wolves ; but I have this consolation, that the most of them are without teeth. They would bite if they could, but not being able, they bark."

The senate assembled : for the people began to be tumultuous. " He is a Lutheran," said one of the counsellors : " he is a propagator of new doctrines," said another : " he is a seducer of youth," said a third. " Let him appear, let him appear." The poor schoolmaster appeared and again listened to prohibitions and menaces. His unsophisticated soul was torn and overwhelmed. His gentle spouse could only console him by shedding tears. " Every one is rising up against me," exclaimed he in his agony. " Assailed by so many tempests, whither shall I turn, how shall I escape ? . . . Were it not for Christ I would long ago have fallen under these assaults."[2] " What matters it," wrote Doctor Sebastian Hofmeister of Constance to him, " whether Lucerne chooses to keep you or not ? The whole earth is the Lord's. Every land is a home to the brave. Though we should be the most wicked of men our enterprise is just, for we teach the Word of Christ."

While the truth encountered so many obstacles at Lucerne it was victorious at Zurich. Zuinglius was incessant in his labours. Wishing to examine the whole sacred volume in the original tongues, he zealously engaged in the study of Hebrew, under the direction of John Boschenstein, a pupil of Reuchlin. But if he studied Scripture, it was to preach it. The peasants who flocked to the market on Friday to dispose of their goods, showed an eagerness to receive the Word of God. To satisfy their longings, Zuinglius had begun, in December 1520, to expound the Psalms every Friday after studying the original. The Reformers always combined learned with practical labours—the latter forming

---

[1] Imò ne in mentem eum admitterem. (Zw. Ep. p. 159.) [2] Si Christus non esset, jam olim defecissem. (Ibid., p. 160.)

the end, the former only the means.   They were at once students and popular teachers.   This union of learning and charity is characteristic of the period.   In regard to his services on Sunday, Zuinglius, after lecturing from St. Matthew on the life of our Saviour, proceeded afterwards to show from the Acts of the Apostles how the gospel was propagated.   Thereafter he laid down the rules of the Christian life according to the Epistles to Timothy, employed the Epistle to the Galatians in combating doctrinal errors, combined with it the two Epistles of St. Peter, in order to show to the despisers of St. Paul that both apostles were animated by the same spirit, and concluded with the Epistle to the Hebrews, in order to give a full display of the benefits which Christians derive from Jesus Christ their sovereign priest.

But Zuinglius did not confine his attention to adults; he sought also to inspire youth with the sacred flame by which his own breast was animated.   One day in 1521, while he was sitting in his study reading the Fathers of the Church, taking extracts of the most striking passages, and carefully arranging them into a large volume, his door opened, and a young man entered whose appearance interested him exceedingly.[1]   It was Henry Bullinger, who was returning from Germany, and impatient to become acquainted with the teacher of his country, whose name was already famous in Christendom.   The handsome youth fixed his eye first on Zuinglius, and then on the books, and felt his vocation to do what Zuinglius was doing.   Zuinglius received him with his usual cordiality which won all hearts.   This first visit had great influence on the future life of the student, who was on his return to the paternal hearth.   Another youth had also won Zuinglius' heart: this was Gerold Meyer of Knonau.   His mother, Anna Reinhardt, who afterwards occupied an important place in the Reformer's life, had been a great beauty, and was still distinguished for her virtues.   John Meyer of Knonau, a youth of a noble family, who had been brought up at the court of the bishop of Constance, had conceived a strong passion for Anna, who, however, belonged to a plebeian family.   Old Meyer of Knonau had refused his consent to their marriage, and after it took place disinherited his son.   In 1513 Anna was left a widow with a son and two daughters, and devoted herself entirely to the education of her poor orphans.   The grandfather was inexorable.   One day, however, the widow's maid-servant having in her arms young Gerold, then a beautiful sprightly child of three years of age, stopped at the fish market, when old Meyer, who was looking out

---

[1] Ich hab by Ihm ein gross Buch geschen, *Locorum communium*, als ich by Ihm wass, an. 1521, dorinnen er *Sententias* und *dogmata Patrum*, flyssig jedes an seinem ort verzeichnet. (Bullinger, MS.)

at a window,[1] observed him, and, continuing to gaze after him,. asked to whom that beautiful lively child belonged. " It is your son's child," was the answer. The heart of the old man was moved—the ice immediately melted—all was forgotten, and he clasped in his arms the widow and children of his son. Zuinglius loved, as if he had been his own son, the noble and intrepid youth. Gerold, who was to die in the flower of his age side by side with the Reformer, with his sword in his hand, and surrounded alas! with the dead bodies of his enemies. Thinking that Gerold would not be able to prosecute his studies at Zurich, Zuinglius, in 1521, sent him to Bâle.

Young Knonau did not find Hedio the friend of Zuinglius there. Capito being obliged to accompany the archbishop Albert to the coronation of Charles V, had procured Hedio to supply his place. Bâle having thus, one after another, lost her most faithful preachers, the church there seemed forsaken; but other men appeared. Four thousand hearers squeezed into the church of William Roubli, curate of St. Alban. He attacked the mass, purgatory, and the invocation of saints; but this turbulent man who was eager to draw the public attention upon himself, declaimed more against error than in support of truth. On Corpus Christi day he joined the public procession, but in place of the customary relics, caused the Holy Scriptures to be carried before him, splendidly bound, and bearing this inscription:—" THE BIBLE; this is the true relic, the others are only dead bones." Courage adorns the servant of God ; affectation disgraces him. The work of an evangelist is to preach the Bible, and not to make a presumptuous display of it. The enraged priests accused Roubli before the council. A mob immediately gathered in Cordelier Square. " Protect our preacher," said the citizens to the council. Fifty Ladies of distinction interceded in his behalf ; but Roubli was obliged to quit Bâle. At a later period he took part like Grebel in Anabaptist disorders. The Reformation, in the course of its development, every where threw off the chaff which mingled with the good grain.

At this period a modest voice was heard from the humblest of the chapels, clearly proclaiming the evangelical doctrine. It was that of young Wolfgang Wissemberger, son of a counsellor of state and chaplain of the hospital. All in Bâle who felt new religious wants attached themselves to the gentle chaplain, preferring him to the presumptuous Roubli. Wolfgang began to read the

---

[1] Lüget des Kindts grossvater zum fauster uss, und ersach das kind in der fischer bränter (Kufe) so fräch (frisch) und frölich sitzen . . . (Archives of Meyer de Knonau. quoted in a notice on *Anna Rheinardt*, Erlanger, 1835, by M. Gerold Meyer de Knonau.) I am indebted to my friend for some elucidations of obscure points in the life of Zuinglius.

mass in German. The monks renewed their clamour, but this time they failed, and Wissemberger continued to preach the gospel; "for," says an old chronicler, "he was a burgess and his father a counsellor." [1] This first success of the Reformation in Bâle, while it was the prelude of still greater success, at the same time tended greatly to promote the progress of the work throughout the Confederation. Zurich no longer stood alone. Learned Bâle began to be charmed with the new doctrine. The foundations of the new temple were enlarged. The Reformation in Switzerland obtained a fuller development.

The centre of the movement was, however, at Zurich. But, to the deep grief of Zuinglius, important political events occurred in 1521, and in some measure distracted men's minds from the preaching of the gospel. Leo X, who had offered his alliance at once to Charles V and Francis I, had at last declared for the emperor. War between the two rivals was on the point of breaking out in Italy. The French general Lautrec had said, "There will be nothing left of the pope but his ears." [2] This bad jest increased the pontiff's anger. The king of France claimed the aid of the Swiss cantons, all of which, with the exception of Zurich, had formed an alliance with him; he obtained it. The pope flattered himself he would gain Zurich, and the cardinal of Sion, ever given to intrigue, and confident in his ability and his finesse, hastened thither to obtain soldiers for his master. But from his old friend Zuinglius he encountered a vigorous opposition. He was indignant that the Swiss should sell their blood to strangers, and his imagination figured to itself the swords of the Zurichers under the standard of the pope and the emperor in the plains of Italy crossing the swords of the confederates united under the colours of France. At such scenes of fratricide his patriotic and Christian soul shuddered with horror. Thundering from the pulpit he exclaimed, "Would you rend and overthrow the confederation? [3] . . . . We attack the wolves which devour our flocks, but offer no resistance to those who prowl around seeking to devour men. . . . . Ah! it is not without cause that these hats and mantles are of scarlet. Shake their robes and ducats and crowns will tumble out of them, twist them and you will see the blood of your brother, your father, your son, and your dearest friend trickling down from them." [4] The energetic voice of Zuinglius was heard in vain. The cardinal with

---

[1] Dieweil er ein Burger war und sein Vater des Raths. (Fridolin Ryff's Chronik.)

[2] Disse che M. di Lutrech et M. de l' Escu havia ditto che'l voleva che le recchia del papa fusse la major parte retaste di la so persona. (Gradenigo, the Venitian ambassador at Rome, MS., 1523.)   [3] Sagt wie es ein fromme Eidtgnosschafft zertrennan und umblkehren wurde. (Bullinger MS.)   [4] Sie tragen billig rothe hüt und mäntel, dan schute man sie, so fallen Cronen und Duggaten heraus, winde man sie, so rünt deines Bruders, Vaters, Sohns und guten freunds Blut herens. (Ibid.)

the red hat succeeded, and two thousand seven hundred Zurichers set out under the command of George Berguer. Zuinglius was heart-broken. Still, however, his influence was not lost. For a long time the banners of Zurich were not again to be unfurled, and pass the gates of the town in the cause of foreign powers.

* * *

CHAP. XI.

Zuinglius against the Precepts of Man—Fermentation during Lent—Truth advances during Combat—The Deputies of the Bishops—Accusation before the Clergy and Council—Appeal to the Great Council—The Coadjutor and Zuinglius—Decree of the Grand Council—State of Matters—Attack by Hoffman.

Torn in his feelings as a citizen, Zuinglius devoted himself with new zeal to the preaching of the gospel, urging it with growing energy. "I will not cease," said he, "to labour to restore the ancient unity of the Church of Christ."[1] He began the year 1522 by showing what difference there is between the precepts of the gospel and the precepts of men. The season of Lent having arrived, he raised his voice still more loudly. After laying the foundation of the new edifice, he wished to clear away the rubbish of the old. "For four years," said he to the multitude assembled in the cathedral, "you with ardent thirst received the holy doctrine of the gospel. Enkindled by the flames of charity, fed with the sweets of heavenly manna, it is impossible to have still any relish for the sad element of human traditions."[2] Then attacking compulsory abstinence from flesh for a certain time, he exclaimed in his bold eloquence, "There are some who pretend that it is an evil, and even a great sin, to eat flesh, although God never forbade it; and yet do not consider it a crime to sell human flesh to the foreigner, and drag it to slaughter."[3] The friends of foreign service who were present were filled with indignation and rage at these bold words, and vowed not to forget them.

While preaching thus forcibly, Zuinglius still continued to say mass: he observed the usages established by the Church, and even abstained from meat on the forbidden days. He was persuaded that the first thing necessary was to enlighten the people. But certain

[1] Ego veterem Christi ecclesiæ unitatem instaurare non desinam. (Zw. Op. iii, 47.)
[2] Gustum non aliquis humanarum traditionum cibus vobis arridere potuerit. (Ibid., i, 2.)   [3] Aber menschenfleisch verkoufen un ze Tod schlahen . . . . (Ibid., ii, 2nd part, p. 301.)

2   o

turbulent spirits did not act with so much wisdom. Roubli, who had become a refugee at Zurich, allowed himself to be carried away by the impulse of an extravagant zeal. The old curate of St. Alban, a Bernese captain, and Conrad Huber, a member of the great Council, often met at the house of the last to eat meat on Friday and Saturday, and made a boast of it. The question of abstinence was the engrossing topic. An inhabitant of Lucerne, who had come to Zurich, said to one of his friends there, "You do wrong in eating flesh during Lent." The friend answered, "You Lucerne folks also take the liberty of eating it on the forbidden days." The inhabitant of Lucerne rejoined, "We have purchased it from the pope." The friend—"And we from the butcher. If it is a question of money, the one is surely as good as the other."[1] The council, a complaint having been lodged against the transgressors of the ecclesiastical ordinances, asked the advice of the curates. Zuinglius answered that the act of eating meat every day was not blameable in itself; but that it ought to be abstained from so long as competent authority had not given any decision on the point. The other members of the clergy concurred in this opinion.

The enemies of the truth took advantage of this favourable circumstance. Their influence was on the wane. Victory was on the side of Zuinglius. It was necessary, therefore, to make haste and strike a decisive blow. They importuned the Bishop of Constance. "Zuinglius," exclaimed they, "is the destroyer of the flock, and not its shepherd."[2]

Ambitious Faber, the old friend of Zuinglius, had returned full of zeal for the papacy from a visit which he had just paid to Rome. From the inspiration of this proud city the first troubles of Switzerland were to proceed. It was necessary that there should be a decisive struggle between evangelical truth and the representatives of the pontiff. It is especially when attacked that the truth manifests its whole power. Under the shade of opposition and persecution, Christianity at first acquired the power which overthrew her enemies. God was pleased, in like manner, to conduct his truth through difficult paths at the period of revival which we now describe. The priests then, as in the days of the apostles, assailed the new doctrine. But for their attacks it might, perhaps, have remained obscurely hid in some faithful souls. But God watched over it to manifest it to the world. Opposition struck out new paths for it, launched it on a new career, and fixed the eyes of the nation upon it. It was like a breath of wind scattering far and wide seeds which might otherwise have remained inert in the spots

---

[1] So haben wirz von dem Metzger erkaufft . . . (Bullinger, MS.)   [2] Ovilis dominici populator esse, non custos aut pastor. (Zw. Op. iii, p. 28.)

on which they fell. The tree destined to shelter the Helvetic population was indeed planted in the bosom of their valleys, but storms were necessary to strengthen the roots and give full development to the branches. The partisans of the papacy, seeing the fire which was slowly burning in Zurich, threw themselves upon it to extinguish it, and thereby only caused its flames to spread.

On the afternoon of the 7th April, 1522, three ecclesiastic deputies from the Bishop of Constance were seen entering the town of Zurich. Two of them had a stern and angry, the third, a gentle expression of countenance. It was the coadjutor of the Bishop Melchior Battli, Doctor Brendi, and John Vanner, preacher of the cathedral, an evangelical man who, during the whole affair, remained silent.[1] It was night when Luti called in haste on Zuinglius, and said, " Officers from the bishop have arrived ; a great blow is preparing : all the partisans of ancient customs are in motion. A notary has called a meeting of all the priests at an early hour to morrow morning, in the hall of the Chapter."

The assembly of the clergy having accordingly met next day, the coadjutor rose and delivered a speech, which seemed to his opponents full of violence and pride.[2] He affected, however, not to mention Zuinglius by name. Some priests, who had been recently gained to the gospel, and were still irresolute, were terrified ; their pale cheeks, their silence, and their sighs, showed that they had lost all courage.[3] Zuinglius rose and delivered a speech, which closed the mouths of his adversaries. At Zurich, as in the other cantons, the most violent enemies of the new doctrine were in the Lesser Council. The deputation, defeated before the clergy, carried their complaints before the magistrates. Zuinglius was absent, and there was no reply to be dreaded. The result appeared decisive. The gospel and its defenders were on the point of being condemned without a hearing. Never was the Reformation of Switzerland in greater danger. It was going to be stifled in the cradle. The counsellors in favour of Zuinglius appealed to the Great Council. It was the only remaining plank for escape, and God employed it to save the cause of the gospel. The two hundred were convened. The partisans of the papacy used every mean to exclude Zuinglius, who, on the other hand, did all he could to gain admission. As he himself expresses it, he knocked at

---

1 Zw. Op. iii, p. 8.—J. J. Hottinger (iii, 77.) Ruchat (i, 134, 2d edit.) and others say that Faber was at the head of the deputation. Zuinglius mentions the three deputies and does not speak of Faber. These authors have doubtless confounded two different officers of the Roman hierarchy—that of coadjutor and that of vicar-general.

2 Erat tota oratio vehemens et stomachi superciliique plena. (Zw. Op. iii, p. 8.)

3 Infirmos quosdam nuper Christo lucrifactos sacerdotes offensos ea sentirem ex tacitis palloribus ac suspiriis. (Ibid., p. 9.) I could see, by the silent paleness and sighs of certain priests lately gained to Christ, and not well confirmed, that they were overpowered.

every door, and left not a stone unturned,[1] but all in vain! "The
thing is impossible," said the burgomasters;" "the Council has
decreed the contrary." "Then," relates Zuinglius, "I remained
quiet, and with deep sighs carried the matter before Him who
hears the groaning of the prisoner, supplicating him to defend
His own gospel."[2] The patient, resigned waiting of the servants
of God is never disappointed.

On the 9th April, the Two Hundred assembled. "We wish to
have our pastors here," immediately exclaimed the members who
were in favour of the Reformation. The Lesser Council resisted,
but the Great Council decided that the pastors should be present to
hear the charge, and answer it, if they thought fit. The deputies
from Constance were introduced, and then the three curates of
Zurich, Zuinglius, Engelhard, and old Röschli.

After the parties thus brought face to face had for some time
eyed each other, the coadjutor rose. "Had his heart and his head
been equal to his voice," says Zuinglius, "he would, in sweetness,
have surpassed Apollo and Orpheus, and in force the Gracchi and
Demosthenes."

"The civil constitution," said the champion of the papacy,
"and Christianity itself, are threatened. Men have appeared
teaching new, offensive and seditious doctrines." Then, after
speaking at great length, he fixed his eye on the assembled senate,
and said, "Remain with the Church, remain in the Church. Out
of it none can be saved. Ceremonies alone can bring the simple
to the knowledge of salvation,[3] and the pastors of the flocks have
nothing else to do than to explain their meaning to the people."

As soon as the coadjutor had finished his speech, he and his
party were preparing to leave the council-hall, when Zuinglius
said to him, warmly, "Mr. Coadjutor, and you who accompany
him, remain, I pray you, till I have defended myself."

The Coadjutor.—"We are not employed to dispute with any
man whatever."

Zuinglius.—"I mean not to dispute, but to explain to you,
without fear, what I have taught up to this hour."

Burgomaster Roust to the Deputies of Constance.—"I pray
you listen to the curate's reply."

The Coadjutor —"I too well know the man with whom I would
have to do. Ulric Zuinglius is too violent for any man to dispute
with!"

---

[1] Frustra diu movi omnem lapidem. (Zw. Op. iii, p. 9.)   [2] Ibi ego quiescere ac suspiriis rem agere cœpi apud eum qui audit gemitum compeditorum (ibid.)
Then I began to be quiet, and to plead the cause with sighs before Him who hears
the groaning of the prisoners.   [3] Unieas esse per quas simplices Christiani ad
agnitionem salutis inducerentur (Ibid., p. 10.)

Zuinglius.—" When did it become the practice to attack an innocent man so strongly, and afterwards refuse to hear him? In
the name of our common faith—in the name of the baptism which
both of us have received—in the name of Christ, the author of salvation and life, listen to me.[1] If you cannot as deputies, at least
do it as Christians."

After firing a volley into the air, Rome retired with hasty steps
from the field of battle. The Reformer only asked to speak, and
the agent of the papacy thought only of flight. A cause thus
pleaded was already gained on the one side and lost on the other.
The two hundred could not contain their indignation; a murmur
burst forth in the assembly.[2] The burgomaster again pressed the
deputies. They felt ashamed, and silently resumed their seats.
Then Zuinglius said:

· "The Coadjutor speaks of seditious doctrines subversive of civil
laws. Let him know that Zurich is quieter, and more obedient to
the laws than any other town in Switzerland, and this all good
citizens attribute to the gospel. Is not Christianity the most
powerful safeguard of justice among a people?[3] What are ceremonies good for, unless it be to sully the face of Christ and Christians?[4] Yes, there is another method than these vain observances
to bring simple people to the knowledge of the truth—a method
which Christ and the Apostles followed in the gospel itself! Have
no dread of its not being comprehended by the people! Whoever
believes comprehends. The people can believe, and therefore can
comprehend. This is a work of the Divine Spirit, and not of
human reason.[5] For the rest, he who does not find forty days
sufficient may, for me, if he likes, fast every day in the year! All
I ask is, that nobody be compelled to do so, and that, for neglect
of the minutest observance, the Zurichers be not accused of separating from the communion of Christians . . ."

" I did not say so," exclaimed the Coadjutor. " No," said his
colleague, Dr. Brendi, " he did not say it." But the whole senate
confirmed the assertion of Zuinglius, who continued:

" Worthy citizens, let not this accusation move you! The
foundation of the Church is that rock, that Christ, who gave Peter
his name, because he confessed him faithfully. In every nation
whosoever believeth with the heart in the Lord Jesus Christ is
saved. This is the Church out of which no man can be saved.[6]

· 1 Ob communem fidem, ob communem baptismum, ob Christum vitæ salutisque
auctorem. (Zw. Op. iii, 11.)   2 Cœpit murmur audiri civium indignantium.
(Ibid.)   3 Imo Christianismum ad communem justitiam servandum esse po-
tentissimum. (Ibid., p. 13.)   4 Ceremonias haud quicquam aliud agere quam
et Christo et ejus fidelibus os oblinere. (Ibid.)   5 Quidquid hic agitur divino
fit afflatu, non humano ratiocino. (Ibid.)   6 Extra illam neminem salvari.
(Ibid., p. 15.)

As to us ministers of Christ, to explain the gospel and follow it is the whole of our duty. Let those who live by ceremonies make it their business to explain them." This was to touch the sore part.

The Coadjutor blushed and said nothing. The two hundred adjourned, and afterwards, the same day, decided that the pope and cardinals should be requested to explain the controverted point, and that in the meantime flesh should not be eaten during Lent. This was to leave matters on the old footing, and answer the bishop in such a way as to gain time.

This struggle had advanced the work of the Reformation. The champions of Rome and of the Reformation had been in presence of each other, and before the eyes of the whole community, and the advantage had not been on the side of the pope. This was the first engagement in what was to be a long and severe campaign, and to exhibit many alternations of grief and joy. But a first victory at the outset gives courage to the whole army, and fills the enemy with dismay. The Reformation had obtained possession of a territory of which it was not again to be deprived. If the Council deemed it necessary to proceed with some degree of caution, the people loudly proclaimed the defeat of Rome. " Never," said they in the exultation of the moment, " never will they be able to reassemble their beaten and scattered troops." [1] " You," said they to Zuinglius, " have with the spirit of St. Paul attacked these false apostles and their Ananias, their whited walls . . . The utmost the satellites of antichrist can now do is to gnash their teeth against you!" Voices were heard from the centre of Germany joyfully proclaiming " the glory of reviving theology." [2]

At the same time, however, the enemies of the gospel mustered their forces. If they were to strike there was no time to be lost, for it would soon be beyond the reach of their blows. Hoffman laid before the chapter a long accusation against the Reformer. " Were the curate even able," said he, " to prove by witnesses what sins, what irregularities have been committed by ecclesiastics in such a convent, such a street, such a tavern, it would still be his duty not to give any names. Why does he give out (it is true I have scarcely ever heard him myself) that he alone draws his doctrine at the fountain-head, and that others search for it only in sinks and puddles? [3] Is it not impossible, seeing the diversity of spirits, for all to preach the same thing? "

Zuinglius defended himself at a full meeting of the Chapter, scat-

---

[1] Ut, vulgo jactatum sit, nunquam ultra copias sarturos. (Zw. Ep. 203.)

[2] Vale renascentis Theologiæ decus. (Letter of Urban Regius. Ibid., 225.)

[3] Die andern aber aus Rinnen und Plutzen. (Simml. Samml. Wirz i, p. 244.)

tering the accusations of his opponent " as a bull with his horns tosses straw into the air." [1] The affair which had appeared so serious ended in laughter at the canon's expence. But Zuinglius did not stop here; on the 16th April, he published a treatise *On the free use of food.* [2]

CHAP. XII.

Grief and Joy in Germany—Ambush against Zuinglius—Mandate of the Bishop— Archeteles—The Bishop addresses the Diet—Prohibition to attack the Monks— Declaration of Zuinglius—The Nuns of Œtenbach—Zuinglius' address to Schwitz

The Reformer's immovable firmness delighted the friends of truth, and particularly the Evangelical Christians of Germany, so long deprived by the captivity of the Wartburg, of the mighty apostle who had first raised his head in the bosom of the Church. Pastors and faithful people, now exiled by the inexorable decree which the papacy had obtained at Worms from Charles V, found an asylum in Zurich. Nesse, the professor of Frankfort, whom Luther visited when on his way to Worms, in a letter to Zuinglius says—" Oh, how I am delighted to learn with what authority you preach Christ. Speak words of encouragement to those who, by the cruelty of wicked bishops, are obliged to flee far from our churches in sorrow." [3]

But the adversaries of the Reformation did not confine their cruel plots against its friends to Germany. Scarcely an hour passed at Zurich in which the means of getting rid of Zuinglius were not under consideration. [4] One day he received an anonymous letter, which he immediately communicated to his two vicars. It said, " Snares environ you on every side, mortal poison is ready to deprive you of life. [5] Eat only in your own house, and of bread baked by your own cook. The walls of Zurich contain men who are plotting your ruin. The oracle which revealed this to me is truer than that of Delphi. I am on your side, you will yet know me." [6]

The day following that on which Zuinglius received this mysterious letter, at the moment when Staheli was going to enter the church of Eau, a chaplain stopped him and said, " Make all haste

---

[1] Ut cornu vehemens taurus aristas. (Zw. Ep. p. 203.)   [2] De delectu et libero ciborum usu. (Zw. Op. i, p. 1.)   [3] Et ut iis, qui ob malorum episcoporum sœvitiam a nobis submoventur, prodesse velis. (Zw. Ep. p. 208.)   [4] Nulla prætereat hora, in qua non fierent . . . consultationes insidiosissimæ. (Osw. Myc. Vit. Zw.)

[5] Ἕτοιμα φαρμακα λυγρὰ. (Zw. Ep. 199.) Poisoned draughts are ready.

[6] Σος εἰμι ; agnosces me postea. (Ibid.)

and quit the house of Zuinglius; a catastrophe is preparing. Fanatics in despair of being able to arrest the Reformation by word, armed themselves with the poniard. When mighty revolutions are accomplished in society, assassins are often thrown up from the impure dregs of the agitated population. God guarded Zuinglius.

While murderers saw their plots defeated, the legitimate organs of the papacy again began to agitate. The bishop and his coun-sellors were determined to renew the war. From every quarter information to this effect reached Zuinglius, who, leaning on the divine promise, exclaimed with noble confidence, " I fear them . . . as a lofty shore fears the threatening waves . . . . συν τω Θεω with God," added he.[1] On the 2nd May, the Bishop of Constance pub-lished an order in which, without naming either Zurich or Zuing-lius, he complained of the attempts of artful persons to renew the condemned doctrines, and of discussions by the learned and the ignorant, in all places on the most solemn mysteries. John Wan-ner, the preacher of the cathedral of Constance, was the first that was attacked. " I would rather," said he, " be a Christian with the hatred of many, than abandon Christ for the friendship of the world." [2]

But it was at Zurich that the growing heresy required to be crushed. Faber and the bishop knew that Zuinglius had several enemies among the canons, and they were desirous to turn this hatred to account. Toward the end of May, a letter from the bis-hop arrived at Zurich addressed to the provost and his chapter. " Sons of the church," said the prelate, " let them perish that will perish, but let no one sever you from the church." [3] At the same time the bishop urged the canons to prevent the false doctrines engendered by pernicious sects from being preached and discussed, whether in private or in public. When this letter was read in the chapter, all eyes were turned upon Zuinglius, who, understanding what was meant, said, " I see you think that this letter concerns me; have the goodness to put it into my hand, and by the help of God I will answer it."

Zuinglius did reply in his " *Archételés*," a word which signifies *the beginning and end*, " for I hope," said he, " that this first answer will also be the last." He spoke in it in very respectful terms of the bishop, and attributed all the attacks of his enemies to some intriguers. " What then have I done?" said he, " I have called all men to the knowledge of their maladies, I have laboured to bring them to the true God and to his Son Jesus Christ. With

---

[1] Quos ita metuo ut littus altum fluctuum undas minacium. (Zw. Ep. 203.)
[2] Malo esse Christianus cum multorum invidia quam relinquere Christum propter mundanorum amicitiam. (Ibid., 200, 22nd May.)   [3] Nemo vos filios ecclesiae ab ecclesia tollat.

that view I have employed not captious exhortations, but words simple and true, such as the sons of Switzerland can comprehend." Then passing from the defensive and becoming the assailant, he finely adds, "Julius Cæsar, feeling himself mortally wounded, endeavoured to draw up the folds of his robe that he might fall in a becoming manner. The fall of your ceremonies is at hand; act so at least that they may fall decently, and that in every place light may be quickly substituted for darkness." [1]

This was all that the bishop gained by his letter to the chapter of Zurich. Now, therefore, that friendly remonstrances were vain, it was necessary to strike more decisive blows. Faber and Landenberg turned in another direction—towards the Diet, the national council.[2] There deputies from the bishop arrived to state that their master had issued an order, prohibiting all the priests of his diocese from innovating in matters of doctrine, but that his authority being disregarded he now wished the aid of the heads of the confederation to assist him in bringing the rebellious to obedience, and defending the true and ancient faith.[3] The enemies of the Reformation were in a majority in this first assembly of the nation, which a short time before had issued a decree prohibiting the preaching of all priests whose discourses, as it was expressed, produced discord among the people. This decree of the Diet, which thus, for the first time, took up the question of the Reformation, had no result, but now having determined on vigorous measures, this body summoned before it Urban Weiss, pastor of Feilispach, near Baden, whom public rumour charged with preaching the new faith and rejecting the old. Weiss was respited for some time on the intercession of several individuals, and on bail for a hundred florins offered by his parishioners.

But the Diet had taken its part, and having just given proof of it, the priests and monks began every where to resume courage. At Zurich, even after the first decree, they had begun to behave more imperiously. Several members of council were in the practice, morning and evening, of visiting the three convents, and even taking their victuals there. The monks laboured to indoctrinate their kind table companions, and urged them to procure a decree of the government in their favour. "If Zuinglius won't be silent," said they, "we will cry louder still!" The Diet had taken part with the oppressors. The council of Zurich knew not what to do. On the 7th of June, it issued an order forbidding any one to preach against the monks, "but scarcely was the order resolved upon,

---

[1] In umbrarum locum, lux quam ocissime inducatur. (Zw. Op. iii, 69.)
[2] Nam er ein anderen weg an die Hand; schike seine Boten . . . etc. (Bullinger MS.) [3] Und den Wahren alten Glauben erhallten. (Ibid.)

'than," says the chronicle of Bullinger, " a sudden noise was heard
in the council chamber, and made every one look at his neigh-
'bour." [1] Peace was not re-established. The war waged from the
pulpit waxed hotter and hotter. The council named a deputation
who called the pastors of Zurich and the readers and preachers of
the convents to meet them in the provost's house; after a keen
discussion, the burgomaster enjoined the two parties not to preach
any thing which might interrupt concord. "I cannot accept this
injunction," said Zuinglius; "I mean to preach the gospel freely
and unconditionally in conformity to the resolution previously
adopted. I am bishop and pastor of Zurich; it is to me that the
care of souls has been entrusted. It was I that took the oath, not
the monks. They ought to yield, not I. If they preach lies I will
contradict them, and that even in the pulpit of their own convent.
If I myself preach a doctrine contrary to the Holy Gospel, then I
ask to be rebuked, not only by the chapter, but by any citizen whatever, and moreover, to be punished by the Council." [2] "We," said
the monks, " we demand to be permitted to preach the doctrines of
St. Thomas." The committee of the Council having deliberated,
ordered that Thomas, Scotus, and the other doctors, should be let
alone, and nothing preached but the Holy Gospel. Thus the truth
had once more gained the victory. But the wrath of the partisans
of the papacy increased. The Ultra-Montane canons could not
conceal their anger. They impertinently eyed Zuinglius in the
chapter, and by their looks seemed to demand his life. [3]

Zuinglius was not deterred by their menaces. There was one
place in Zurich where, thanks to the Dominicans, the light had
not yet penetrated; this was the nunnery of Œtenbach. The
daughters of the first families of Zurich there took the veil. It
seemed unjust that these poor females, confined within the walls
of their monastery, should alone be excluded from hearing the
Word of God. The Great Council ordered Zuinglius to repair to
it, and the Reformer having mounted a pulpit which had hitherto
been given up to the Dominicans, preached " on the clearness and
certainty of the Word of God." [2] He at a later period published
this remarkable discourse, which was not without fruit, and irritated
the monks still more.

A circumstance occurred to augment this hatred, and give it a
place in many other hearts. The Swiss, headed by Stein and
Winkelried, had just experienced a bloody defeat at Bicoque. They
had rushed impetuously on the enemy, but the artillery of Pescaire

---

[1] Liess die Rathstuben einen grossen Knall. (Bullinger MS.)   [2] Sondern von
einem jedem Bürger wyssen. (ibid.)   [3] Oculos in me procacius torquent, ut
cujus caput peti gauderent. (Zw. Op. iii, 29.)   [4] De claritate et certitudine Verbi
Dei. (Ibid., i, 66.)

and the lancers of that Freundsberg, whom Luther had met at the door of the hall of Worms, had thrown down both leaders and colours, whole companies falling and disappearing at once. Winkelried and Stein, Mulinen, Diesbachs, Bonstettens, Tschudis, and Pfyffers, were left on the battle-field. Schwitz, especially, had been mown down. The bloody wrecks of this dreadful conflict had returned to Switzerland, spreading mourning at every step. A wail of grief had resounded from the Alps to the Jura, and from the Rhone to the Rhine.

But none had felt a deeper pang than Zuinglius. He immediately sent an address to Schwitz dissuading its citizens from foreign service. "Your ancestors," said he to them, with all the warmth of a Swiss heart, "forgot their enemies in defence of their liberties, but they never put Christians to death in order to gain money. These foreign wars bring innumerable calamities on our country. The scourges of God chastise our confederacy, and Helvotic freedom is on the eve of being lost between the selfish caresses and the mortal hatred of foreign princes.[1] Zuinglius went hand in hand with Nicolas Flue, and renewed the entreaties of that man of peace. This exhortation having been presented to the assembly of the people of Schwitz had such an effect that a resolution was passed to desist prospectively for twenty-five years from capitulation. But the French party soon succeeded in getting the generous resolution rescinded, and Schwitz was thenceforth the canton most decidedly opposed to Zuinglius and his works. The very disasters which the partisans of foreign capitulation brought upon their country only increased the hatred of those men against the bold minister, who endeavoured to rescue his country from all this misfortune and all this disgrace. Thus throughout the confederation a party which daily grew more and more violent was formed against Zurich and Zuinglius. The customs of the Church and the practices of the recruiters being at once attacked, they made common cause in resisting the impetus of Reform by which their existence was threatened. At the same time external enemies multiplied. Not merely the pope but other foreign princes also vowed inextinguishable hatred to the Reformation, because it was aiming to deprive them of those Helvetic halberds, to which their ambition and their pride owed so many triumphs? But the cause of the gospel had still God on its side and the best among the people : this was sufficient. Besides, individuals from different countries exiled for their faith were led by the hand of Providence to give Switzerland their aid.

[1] Ein göttlich Vermanung an die cersamen, etc. eidgnossen zu Schwyz.   (Zw. Op. part ii, p. 206.)

CHAP. XIII.

'A French monk—He teaches in Switzerland—Dispute between the Monk and'
Zuinglius—Discourse of the Leader of the Johannites—The Carnival at Berne—
The Eaters of the Dead—The Skull of St. Anne—Appenzel—The Grisons—Mur-
der and Adultery—Marriage of Zuinglius.

On Saturday the 12th July there was seen entering the streets
of Zurich a monk, tall, thin, stiff, gaunt, clad in a grey cordelier
frock, and mounted upon an ass. He had the look of a foreigner,
and his bare feet almost touched the ground.[1] He arrived thus by
the road from Avignon. He did not know one word of German, but
by means of Latin succeeded in making himself understood.
Francis Lambert (this was his name) asked for Zuinglius and delivered him a letter from Berthold Haller. " The Franciscan
father," wrote the Bernese curate, " who is no less than the apostolic preacher of the general convent of Avignon, has, for nearly
five years, been teaching Christian truth : he has preached in Latin
to our priests at Geneva, at Lausanne in presence of the bishop,
at Friburg, and finally at Berne. His subjects were, the Church,
the priesthood, the sacrifice of the mass, the traditions of the Roman bishops, and the superstitions of the religious orders. It
seemed to me wonderful to hear such things from a cordelier and a
Frenchman—circumstances, both of which, as you know, imply a
host of superstitions."[2] The Frenchman himself related to Zuinglius how the writings of Luther having been discovered in his cell,
he had been obliged to take a hasty leave of Avignon ; how he
had first preached the gospel at Geneva, and thereafter at Lausanne. Zuinglius, overjoyed, gave the monk access to the church of
Notre Dame, assigning him a seat in the choir near the high altar.
Lambert here delivered four sermons, in which he forcibly attacked
the errors of Rome, but in the fourth he defended the invocation of
the saints and the Virgin.

" Brother, you are in error,"[3] immediately exclaimed an animated voice. It was the voice of Zuinglius. Canons and chaplains thrilled with joy when they saw a quarrel rising between the
Frenchman and the heretical curate. " He has attacked you,"
said they all to Lambert: " demand a public discussion." The

---

[1] ... Kam ein langer, gerader, barfüsser Mönch ... ritte auf einer Eselin. (Füsslin Beyträge, iv, 39.)   [2] A tali Franciscano, Gallo, quæ omnia mare superstitionem confluere faciunt, inaudita. (Zw. Ep. 207.)   [3] Bruder da irrest du.
(Füsslin Beytr. iv, p. 40.)

man of Avignon did so, and at ten o'clock on the morning of the 12th of July, the two chaplains met in the hall of the canons. Zuinglius opened the Old and New Testament in Greek and Latin : he discussed and lectured till two. Then the French monk, clasping his hands, and raising them towards heaven, exclaimed,[1] " I thank thee, O God, that thou hast by this illustrious instrument given me such a clear knowledge of the truth ! Henceforth," added he, turning towards the assembly, " in all my distresses I will invoke God only and leave off my beads. To-morrow I resume my journey. I go to Bâle to see Erasmus of Rotterdam, and thence to Wittemberg to see the monk Martin Luther." He accordingly remounted his ass and set out. We will again meet with him. He was the first exile from France, for the cause of the gospel, who appeared in Switzerland and Germany—a modest fore-runner of many thousands of refugees and confessors.

Myconius had no such consolation. On the contrary he saw Sebastian Hofmeister, who had come from Constance to Lucerne, and there boldly preached the gospel, obliged to quit the city. Then Oswald's grief increased. The moist climate of Lucerne disagreed with him. He was wasted by fever ; and the physicians declared that if he did not change his residence he would die. Writing to Zuinglius, he says, " There is no place I should like better to be than beside yourself, and no place worse than at Lucerne. Men torture, and the climate consumes me. My disease, some say, is the punishment of my iniquity. Ah, it is vain to speak, vain to act : every thing is poison to them. There is One in heaven on whom alone my hope depends."[2]

This hope was not vain. It was towards the end of March, and the feast of the Annunciation was at hand. The evening before there was a great solemnity in commemoration of a fire which in 1540 had reduced the greater part of the town to ashes. Multitudes from the surrounding districts had flocked into Lucerne, and several hundreds of priests were then assembled. Some distinguished orator was usually employed to preach on this great occasion. Conrad Schmid, commander of the Johannites, arrived to discharge the duty. An immense crowd thronged the church. What was the general astonishment on hearing the commander lay aside the pompous Latin to which they had been accustomed, and speak in good German,[3] so that all could comprehend him, enforce with authority and holy fervour the love of God in sending his Son, eloquently prove that external works cannot save, and

[1] Dass er beyde Hände zusammen hob. (Füsslin Beytr., iv, p. 50.)   [2] Quicquid facio venenum est illis. Sed est in quem omnis spes mea reclinat. (Zw. Ep. 192.)
[3] Wolt er keine pracht tryben mit latein schwätzen, sondern gut teutsch reden. (Bullinger MS.)

that the promises of God are truly the power of the gospel. "God forbid," said the commander to his astonished audience, "that we should receive a chief so full of lies as the Bishop of Rome. and reject Jesus Christ.[1] If the Bishop of Rome dispenses the bread of the gospel, let us receive him as pastor, but not as head ; and if he does not dispense it, let us not receive him in any way whatever." Oswald was unable to restrain his joy. "What a man !" exclaimed he: "what a discourse! what majesty! what authority! what overflowing of the Spirit of Christ!" The impression was general. To the agitation which filled the town succeeded a solemn silence ; but all this was transient. When nations shut their ears against the calls of God, these calls are diminished from day to day, and soon cease. Thus it was at Lucerne.

At Berne, while the truth was preached from the pulpit, the papacy was attacked at the merry-makings of the people. Nicolas Manuel, a distinguished layman, celebrated for his poetical talents, and advanced to the first offices in the state, indignant at seeing his countrymen pillaged by Samson, composed carnival dramas, in which, with the keen weapon of satire, he attacked the avarice, pride, and luxury of the pope and the clergy. On the Shrove Tuesday " of the Lords," (the clergy were at this time the lords, and began Lent eight days before the common people,) all Berne was engrossed with a drama or mystery entitled, "The Eaters of the Dead," which young boys were going to perform in the street of La Croix. The people flocked to it in crowds. In regard to the progress of art, these dramatic sketches of the beginning of the sixteenth century are of some interest ; but we give them here with a very different view. We would have been better pleased not to have had to quote squibs of this description on the part of the Reformation, for truth triumphs by other arms. But the historian does not make his facts. He must give them as he finds them.

At length, to the delight of the eager crowds assembled in the street of La Croix, the representation began. The pope is seen clad in gorgeous robes, and seated on a throne. Around him stand his courtiers, his body guards, and a promiscuous band of priests of high and low degree ; behind are nobles, laymen, and mendicants. A funeral train shortly appears : it is a rich farmer on the way to his last home. Two of his relatives walk slowly in front of the coffin with napkins in their hand. The train having arrived in front of the pope, the bier is laid down at his feet, and the drama begins :

[1] Absit a grege Christiano, ut caput tam lutulentium et peccatis plenum accertans Christum abjiciat. (Zw. Ep. 195.)

FIRST RELATIVE IN A TONE OF DEEP GRIEF.

O noble army of the sainted host,
   Take pity on our doleful plight;
Our cousin, our illustrious boast,
   From life, alas, has taken flight.

Expence we grudge not; cheerfully we'll pay
For priests, monks, and nuns, in costly array:
Yea, one hundred crowns we'll freely devote
If thereby exemption may surely be bought
   From purgatory, that dread scourge,
   With which our frightened souls they urge.[1]

The SACRISTAN, breaking off from the band surrounding the pope, and running hastily to CURATE ROBERT EVER-MORE—

Something to drink, Master Curate, I crave;
A farmer of note now goes to his grave.

THE CURATE.

One!—nay you must tell me of ten:
My thirst will ne'er be quenched till then.
Life flourishes when mortals die,[2]
For death to me brings jollity.

THE SACRISTAN.

Ah! could it shorten mankind's breath!
I'd ring a merry peal for death!
No other trade succeeds so well
As tolling out life's parting knell.

THE CURATE.

But does the bell of death the portals draw
Of heaven's wide gate? I cannot, may not say;
What boots it? to my house it brings
Both fish and flesh, and all good things.

THE CURATE'S NIECE.[3]

'Tis well: I, too, anon will claim my share.
This day this soul must pay to me my fare—
A robe, white, red, and green, a flowered damas,
A pretty kerchief likewise for my eyes at mass.

---

[1] Kein kosten soll uns dauern dran,
   Wo wir Mönch und Priester mögen ha'n,
   Und sollt'es kosten hundert kronen . . . .
            (Bern. Mausol., iv, Wirz, K. Gesch., i, p. 383.)
[2] Je mehr, je besser! Kämen doch noch Zehn! (Ibid.)   [3] The German
is Pfaffenmetze—a term more expressive, but not so becoming.

Cardinal HIGH-PRIDE adorned with a red hat, and close by the pope :—

> If death brought us no heritage,
> Would we cause die in flower of age,
> On battle-plain,
> Such heaps of slain,
> Roused by intrigue, by envy fired ? [1]
> Yes, Rome with Christian blood grows fat !
> Therefore I hoist this scarlet hat,
> To tell the trophies thus acquired

BISHOP WOLF-BELLY.

> In papal rites I'll live and die,
> And clothe me in silk embroidery ;
> In foray or chace I'll take my pleasure,
> And eat and drink in ample measure ;
> Had I been priest in days of yore,
> A peasant's dress I then had wore. [2]

We once were shepherds, but now we reign kings,
For a shepherd I'll pass 'mong the lambkins poor things . . .

A VOICE.

> When ?   When shall this be ?

BISHOP.

> When the wool of the flock shall be gathered by me.
> We truly are wolves, yet we're shepherds of sheep,
> They must feed us, or death is the best they shall reap.
> His Holiness forbids to marry :
> This yoke the wisest ne'er could carry—
> But then ! when priests do cross the score,
> The scandal only swells my store,
> And makes my train extend the more.
> Nought I refuse, e'en farthings tell,
> A monied priest may have a belle.
> Four florins a-year will wipe it away ;
> Does an infant appear ?—again he must pay.
> On two thousand florins I reckon each year,
> Were they chaste, I should starve on a pittance I fear. [3]
> Then hail to the pope ; on my knees I adore
> And swear in his faith to live evermore ;
> His church I'll defend, and till death I avow,
> He alone is the god before whom I will bow.

THE POPE.

> The people now at length believe
> That priests can all their sins reprieve

---

[1] Wenn mir nicht wär' mit Todten wohl,
So läg nicht mancher Acker, voll, &c.
(Bern. Mausol. iv, Wirz, K. Gesch. i.

[2] Wenn es stünd, wie im Anfang der Kilchen,
Ich trüge vielleicht grobes Tuch und Zwilchen. (Ibid.)

[3] The German is very strong.
So bin Ich auf gut Deutsch ein Hurenwirth, etc. (Ibid.)

At pleasure—that to them is given
Full power to shut or open heaven.
Preach loudly, every high decree,
Of him, the conclave's majesty.
Then, we are kings, the laity slaves :
But if the gospel standard waves
We're lost ; for no where does it say,
Make sacrifice, let priests have pay.
The gospel course for us would be,
To live and die in poverty.
Instead of steeds to mark my state,
And chariots on my sons to wait,
A paltry ass must needs supply ₁
A seat for sacred majesty.
No, I cannot take such legacy,
I'll thunder at such temerity ;
Let us but will—the world will nod,
And nations adore us as God.
Slighting their rights I mount my throne,
And partition the world among my own ;
Vile laity must keep far aloof,
Nor dare to enter our blest roof,
To touch our tribute, or our gold.
Holy water e'en let them hold.

We will not continue this literal translation of Manuel's drama. The agony of the clergy on learning the efforts of the Reformers, and their rage against those who threaten to interfere with their irregularities, are painted in lively colours. The dissolute manners of which this piece gave so vivid a representation were too common not to strike the spectator with the truth of the picture. The people were excited. Many jibes were heard as they retired from the play in the street of La Croix ; but some who took the matter more seriously, spoke of Christian liberty and papal despotism, and contrasted the simplicity of the gospel with the pomp of Rome. The contempt of the people was soon displayed in the public streets. On Ash Wednesday, the indulgences were promenaded through the town amid satirical songs. In Berne, and throughout Switzerland a severe blow had been given to the ancient edifice of the papacy.

Sometime after this representation, another comedy was acted at Berne, but there was no fiction in it. The clergy, council, and corporation had assembled in front of the Upper Gate, waiting for the skull of St. Anne, which the famous knight, Albert of Stein, had gone to fetch from Lyons. At length Stein appeared, holding

---

² Wir möchten fast kaum Eselein ha'n. (Bern Mausol. iv, Wirz, K. Gesch. 1, 383.)

2   *t*

the holy relic wrapt in a covering of silk.   As it passed, the Bishop of Lausanne knelt down before it.   This precious skull, the skull of the Virgin's mother, is carried in procession to the church of the Dominicans, and, amid the ringing of bells, enters the church, where it is placed with great solemnity on the altar consecrated to it, behind a splendid grating.   But amid all this joy, a letter arrives from the abbot of the convent of Lyon, where the relics of the saint were deposited, intimating that what the monks had sold to the knight was a profane bone taken at random from the burying ground.   The trick thus played off on the illustrious city of Berne filled its citizens with deep indignation.

The Reformation was making progress in other parts of Switzerland.   In 1521, Walter Klarer, a young man of Appenzel, returned to his native canton from the university of Paris.   Luther's writings fell into his hands, and, in 1522, he preached the evangelical doctrine with all the ardour of a young convert.   An innkeeper, named Rausberg, a wealthy and pious man, and a member of the council of Appenzel, opened his house to all the friends of truth. Bartholomew Berweger, a famous captain, who had fought for Julius II and for Leo X, having at this time returned from Rome, began forthwith to persecute the evangelical ministers.   One day, however, remembering how much vice he had seen at Rome, he began to read the Bible, and to attend the sermons of the new preachers ; his eyes were opened, and he embraced the gospel. Seeing that the crowds could not be contained in the churches, he proposed that they should preach in the fields and the public squares, and, notwithstanding of keen opposition, the hills, meadows, and mountains of Appenzel, thenceforward often echoed with the glad tidings of salvation.

The reformed doctrine, ascending the Rhine, made its way as far as ancient Rhætia.   One day, a stranger from Zurich crossed the river, and waited on the saddler of Flasch, the frontier village of the Grisons.   Christian Anhorn, the saddler, listened in astonishment to the language of his visitor.   " Preach," said the whole village to the stranger, who was called James Burkli.   He accordingly took his station in front of the altar.   A number of persons arrived, with Anhorn at their head, and stood round to defend him from a sudden attack while he preached the gospel.   The rumour of this preaching spread far and wide ; and, on the following Sunday, an immense crowd assembled.   Shortly after, a great proportion of the inhabitants of the district desired to have the Lord's Supper dispensed to them according to its original institution.

But one day the tocsin suddenly sounded in Mayenfield ; the people ran in alarm ; and the priests, after pointing out the danger which threatened the Church, hastened at the head of the fanatical population to Flasch. Anhorn, who was working in the field, astonished at hearing the sound of bells at so unusual an hour, hastened home and concealed Burkli in a deep hole dug in his cellar. The house was by this time surrounded ; the door was forced open, and the heretical preacher everywhere searched for in vain. At length the persecutors withdrew.[1]

The Word of God spread over the extent of the ten jurisdictions. The curate of Mayenfield, on returning from Rome, to which he had fled infuriated at the success of the gospel, exclaimed, " Rome has made me evangelical," and became a zealous reformer. The Reformation soon extended to the league of " the House of God." " Oh !" exclaimed Salandronius to Vadian, " if you but saw how the inhabitants of the mountains of Rhætia cast far from them the yoke of the Babylonish captivity ! "

Shocking disorders hastened the day when Zurich and the neighbouring districts were to shake off the yoke. A married schoolmaster wishing to become a priest, obtained his wife's consent, and they separated. The new curate was unable to keep his vow of celibacy, but not to outrage his wife's feelings quitted the place where she lived, and, having taken up his residence in the diocese of Constance, formed a licentious connection. His wife hastened to the place. The poor priest took compassion on her, and dismissing the person who had usurped her rights, took back his lawful spouse. The procurator-fiscal forthwith drew up a charge against him : the vicar-general began to move; the council of the consistory deliberated. . . . and the curate was ordered to abandon his wife or his benefice. The poor wife left the house weeping bitterly, and her rival returned in triumph. The Church declared itself satisfied, and thenceforth let the adulterous priest alone.[2]

Shortly after a curate of Lucerne eloped with a married woman, and lived with her. The husband went to Lucerne and taking advantage of the priest's absence brought away his wife. While returning they were met by the seducer, who immediately attacked the injured husband, and gave him a wound of which he died.[3] All good men felt the necessity of re-establishing the divine law, which declares *marriage honorable in all*.[4] The evangelical ministers had taught that the law of celibacy was of merely human origin, imposed by Roman pontiffs in opposition to the Word of

---

[1] Anhorn, Wiedergeburt der Ev. Kirchen in den 3 Bündten. Chur, 1680. Wirz. i, 457.
[2] Simml. Samml. vi.—Wirz, K. Gesch. i. 275. [3] Hinc cum scorto redeuntem in itinere deprehendit, adgreditur, lethiferoque vulnere cædit et tandem moritur. (Zw. Ep. p. 206.) [4] Hebrews, xiii, 4.

God, which, when describing a true bishop, represents him as a
husband and father. (1 Tim. iii, 2 and 4.) They saw at the
same time, that of all the abuses which had crept into the Church
none had caused more numerous vices and scandals. They considered it not only as a thing lawful but as a duty in the sight of
God to withdraw from its authority. Several of them at this time
returned to the ancient practice of apostolic times. Xylotect was
married. Zuinglius also married at this period. No lady was
more respected in Zurich than Anna Reinhard, widow of Meyer
of Knonau, the mother of Gerold. From the arrival of Zuinglius she
had been one of his most attentive hearers : she lived in his neighbourhood, and he observed her piety, modesty, and fondness for
her children. Young Gerold, who had become as it were his
adopted son, brought him into closer connection with his mother.
The trials already endured by this Christian woman, who was one day
to be the most cruelly tried of all the women whose history is on
record, had given her a gravity which made her evangelical virtues
still more prominent.[1] She was now about thirty-five years of
age, and her own fortune amounted only to four hundred florins.
It was on her that Zuinglius, on looking out for a companion for life,
turned his eye. He felt how sacred and intimate the conjugal
union is. He termed it " a most holy alliance."[2] " As Christ,"
said he, " died for his people, and gave himself to them entirely,
so ought husband and wife to do and suffer every thing for each
other." But Zuinglius, when he took Anna Reinhard to wife, did
not immediately publish his marriage. This was undoubtedly a culpable weakness in a man otherwise so resolute. The light which
he and his friends had acquired on the subject of celibacy was not
generally diffused. The weak might have been offended. He
feared that his usefulness in the Church might be paralysed if his
marriage were made public.[3] He sacrificed part of his happiness
to these fears—fears to which, though respectable perhaps, he
should have been superior. [4]

---

[1] Anna Reinhard, von Gerold Meyer von Knonau, p. 25.   [2] Ein hochheiliges
Bündniss. (Ibid.)   [3] Qui veritus sis, te marito non tam feliciter usurum
Christum in negotio verbi sui. (Zw. Ep. p. 335.) Who feared that Christ would not
use you as a husband so advantageously in the ministry of his Word.
    [4] Biographers, most respectable historians, and all the authors who have
copied them, place Zuinglius' marriage two years later, viz., in April 1524. Without
going at length into the reasons which satisfy me that this is a mistake, I will merely
indicate the most decisive proofs. A letter from Zuinglius' friend Myconius, 22nd
July, 1522, says, " Vale cum uxore quam felicissime." "All happiness to you and your
wife." Another letter from the same friend, written towards the close of this year,
has the words, " Vale cum uxore." The contents of the letters prove that they are
correctly dated. But what is still stronger is, a letter of Bucer, from Strasburg, at
the time when the marriage was made public, 14th April, 1524, (the date of the
year is wanting, but it is clearly 1524.) This letter contains several passages which
show that Zuinglius had been for some time married. In addition to the one
given in the previous note, we quote the following :—" Professum palam te maritum

CHAP. XIV.

How Truth triumphs—Society at Einsidlen—Request to the Bishops—to the Confederates—The Men of Einsidlen separate—A Scene in a Convent—A Dinner by Myconius—The Strength of the Reformers—Effect of the Petitions to Lucerne—The Council of the Diet—Haller at the Town-House—Friburg—Destitution of Oswald—Zuinglius comforts him—Oswald quits Lucerne—First severity of the Diet—Consternation of the Brothers of Zuinglius—His Resolution—The Future —The Prayer of Zuinglius.

Meanwhile still higher interests occupied the friends of truth. The Diet, as we have seen, urged by the enemies of the Reformation, had ordered the evangelical preachers to desist from preaching the doctrines which troubled the people. Zuinglius felt that the moment for action had arrived, and with the energy which characterised him, called a meeting of the ministers of the Lord, the friends of the gospel, at Einsidlen. The strength of Christians is neither in carnal weapons, nor the flames of martyrdom—it is in a simple but unanimous and intrepid profession of these great truths to which the world must one day be subjugated. In particular, God calls upon those who serve him to hold these heavenly doctrines prominently forth in presence of the whole people without being dismayed by the clamour of adversaries. Those truths are able of themselves to secure their triumph, and as of old with the ark of God, idols cannot stand in their presence. The time had come when God willed that the great doctrine of salvation should be confessed in Switzerland. It was necessary that the gospel standard should be planted on some eminence. Providence was going to draw humble but intrepid men out of unknown retreats that they might bear a striking testimony in presence of the nation.

legi. Unum hoc desiderabam in te." I read that you *openly* professed to be a husband. This was the only thing in you I regretted the want of. "Quæ multum facilius quam *connubii tui confessionem* Antichristus posset ferre." These things Antichrist could bear more easily than *the confession of your marriage.*—" Αγαμον ab eo, quod cum fratribus .... episcopo Constantiensi congressus es, nullus credidi." That you were unmarried I did not believe from your disputes with the friars ... the Bishop of Constance. "Qua ratione id *tam diu celares* ..... non dubitarim, rationibus huc adductum, quæ apud virum evangelicum non queant omnino repudiari" ... etc. On what account you concealed it so long ... I doubt not you were influenced by reasons which ought not to be entirely rejected by a Christian man. (Zw. Ep. p. 335.) In 1524, then, Zuinglius did not marry, but publish his marriage contracted two years before. The learned editors of the letters of Zuinglius ask, "Num forte jam Zuinglius Annam Reinhardam, clandestino in matrimonio habebat ?" May not Zuinglius have already been secretly married to Anna Reinhard ? p. 210. This seems to me not a matter of doubt, but a well ascertained historical fact.

Towards the end of June and the beginning of July, 1522, pious ministers were seen proceeding in all directions towards the celebrated chapel of Einsidlen on a new pilgrimage.[1] From Art, in the canton of Schwitz, came its curate, Balthasar Traschel; from Weiningen near Baden, curate Staheli; from Zug, Werner Steiner; from Lucerne, canon Kilchmeyer; from Uster, curate Pfister; from Hongg, near Zurich, curate Stumpff; from Zurich itself, canon Fabricius, chaplain Schmid, the preacher of the hospital, Grosmann, and Zuinglius. Leo Juda, curate of Einsidlen, most cordially welcomed all these ministers of Jesus Christ to the ancient abbey. Since the time when Zuinglius took up his residence in it, this place had been a citadel of truth, and a hotel of the just.[2] In like manner had thirty-three bold patriots, resolved to break the yoke of Austria, met two hundred years before in the solitary plain of Grutli. The object of the meeting at Einsidlen was to break the yoke of human authority in the things of God. Zuinglius proposed to his friends to present earnest addresses to the cantons, and to the bishop, praying for the free preaching of the gospel, and at the same time for the abolition of compulsory celibacy, the source of so many irregularities. The proposal was unanimously adopted.[3] Ulric had himself prepared the addresses. That to the bishop was first read. It was dated 2nd July, 1522, and signed by all the evangelists we have mentioned. The preachers of the truth in Switzerland were united in cordial affection. Many others besides sympathised with the party at Einsidlen: such were Haller, Myconius, Hedio, Capito, Œcolampadius, Sebastian Meyer, Hoffmeister, and Waimer. This harmony is one of the finest traits in the Swiss Reformation. These excellent persons always acted as one man, and remained friends till death.

The men of Einsidlen were aware that it was only by the power of faith that the members of the Confederation, divided by foreign enlistments, could become one body. But their views were carried higher. "The celestial doctrine," said they to their ecclesiastical head, in the address of 2nd July, " that truth which God the Creator has manifested by his Son to the human race now plunged in evil, has been long veiled from our eyes by the ignorance, not to say the malice of certain men. But God Almighty has resolved to re-establish it in its primitive condition. Join yourself to those who demand that the multitude of the faithful return to their head, who is Christ.[4] For our part we have resolved to promulgate his

---

[1] Thaten sich zusammen etliche priester. (Bullinger MS.)   [2] Zu Einsidlen hätten sie alle Sicherheit dahin zu gehen und dort zu wohnen . (J. J. Hottinger, Helv. K. Gesch., iii, 86.)   [3] Und wurden eins an den Bischoff zu Constantz und gmein Eidtgnossen ein Supplication zu stellen. (Bullinger MS.)
[4] Et universa Christianorum multitudo ad caput suum quod Christus est redeat. (Supplicatio quorundam apud Helvetios Evangelistarum. Zw. Op. iii, 18.)

gospel, with indefatigable perseverance, and at same time with such
wisdom that none can complain.[1] Favour this enterprise ; astonishing, perhaps, but not rash. Be like Moses on the march at the
head of the people coming out of Egypt, and overthrow the obstacles
which oppose the triumphant progress of truth."

After this warm appeal, the evangelists met at Einsidlen came to
celibacy. Zuinglius had no longer any demand to make on this
head for himself, having already one answering the description
given by Paul of what a minister's wife ought to be, *grave, sober,
faithful in all things.* (1 Tim. iii, 2.) But he thought of his brethren,
whose consciences were not yet like his, emancipated from human
ordinances. He sighed moreover for the time when all the servants
of God might live openly and without fear in the bosom of their
own family, *keeping their children*, says the apostle, *in subjection, with
all gravity* (1 Tim. iii, 4.) " You are not ignorant," said the men
of Einsidlen, that hitherto chastity has been deplorably violated by
the priests. When on the consecration of the servants of the Lord
he who speaks for all is asked, 'Are those whom you present
righteous ? He answers—They are righteous. Are they learned?
They are learned. But when he is asked—Are they chaste ? he
answers : As far as human weakness permits.[2] Everything in the
New Testament condemns licentiousness : every thing in it sanc-
tions marriage." Then follows the quotation of a great number of
passages. " Wherefore," they continued, " we implore you by the
love of Christ, by the liberty which he has purchased for us, by the
misery of so many weak and wavering souls, by the wounds of so
many ulcerated consciences, by every thing human and divine ;
. . . . allow that which was rashly done to be wisely repealed,
lest the majestic edifice of the Church fall with fearful uproar,
and drag boundless ruin after it.[3] See with what storms the
world is threatened. If wisdom interpose not it is all over with
the priesthood."

The petition to the Confederation was of greater length. The
band of Einsidlen, addressing the Confederates, thus conclude:
" Honoured Sirs,—we are all Swiss, and you are our fathers.
There are some among us who have shown themselves faithful in combat, in plague, and other calamities.[4] It is in the
name of true chastity that we speak to you. Who knows not
that we could satisfy sensual appetite far better by not sub-

---

[1] Evangelium irremisso tenore promulgare statuimus . . . . (Ibid.)
[2] Suntne casti ? reddidit : Quatenus humana imbecillitas permittit. (Ibid., iii, 18.)
[3] Ne quando moles ista non ex patris cœlestis sententia constructa, cum fragore
longe perniciosiore corruat. (Ibid., 24.) Lest one day that edifice, not built according
to the view of the heavenly parent, fall with a much more dreadful crash.
[4] Amica et piu paraenesis ad communem Helvetiorum civitatem scripta, ne evangelicæ doctrinæ cursum impediant, etc. (Zw. Op. i, 39.)

mitting to the laws of a legitimate union? But it is necessary to put an end to the scandals which afflict the church of Christ. If the tyranny of the Roman pontiff would oppress us, fear nothing, brave heroes! The authority of the Word of God, the rights of Christian liberty, and the sovereign power of grace, guard around us.[1] We have the same country, we have the same faith, we are Swiss, and the valour of our illustrious ancestors always manifested its power by an indomitable defence of those oppressed by injustice."

Thus in Einsidlen itself, in this old rampart of superstition, which is still, in our day, one of the most famous sanctuaries of Roman superstition, Zuinglius and his friends boldly raised the standard of truth and freedom. They appealed to the heads of the State and the Church. They fixed their thesis, like Luther, both on the gate of the episcopal palace and on that of the national council. The friends met at Einsidlen parted calm, joyful, full of hope in that God to whom they had committed their cause. Some passing near the battle-field of Morgarten, others over the chain of the Albis, and others again by different valleys or mountains, all returned to their posts. "There was truly something grand in these times,"[2] says Henry Bullinger, "in men thus daring to put themselves forward, rallying around the gospel, and exposing themselves to all dangers. But God defended them so, that no evil reached them: for God preserves his people at all times." It was indeed something grand, it was a great step in the progress of the Reformation, one of the brightest days of religious revival in Switzerland. A holy confederation was formed at Einsidlen. Humble and courageous men had seized the sword of the Spirit, which is the Word of God, and the shield of faith. The gauntlet was thrown down, and the challenge given, not by a single man, but by men of different cantons, ready to sacrifice their lives. It only remained to await the battle.

Everything announced that it was to be fierce. Five days after (7th July), the magistracy of Zurich, wishing to give some satisfaction to the Roman party, summoned before them Conrad Grebel and Claus Hottinger, two of those extreme men who seemed desirous to go beyond the bounds of a wise Reformation. "We forbid you," said Burgomaster Roust, "to speak against the monks or on controverted points." At these words, a loud noise was heard in the chamber, says an ancient chronicle. God was so manifestly in favour of the work, that people were everywhere anticipating signs of his interposition. All present looked around in

---

[1] Divini enim verbi auctoritatem, libertatis Christianæ et divinæ gratiæ præsidium nobis adesse conspicietis. (Zw. Op. i, 63.) [2] Es wass zwahren gros zu denen Zyten. (Bullinger MS.)

astonishment, without being able to discover the cause of this mysterious circumstance.[1]

But indignation was carried to its greatest height in convents. Every meeting held in them, whether for discipline or festivity, witnessed some new attack. One day, when a great festival was celebrated in the convent of Fraubrunn, the wine having got into the heads of the guests, they began to shoot the most envenomed arrows at the gospel.[2] What especially excited the rage of these priests and monks was the evangelical doctrine—that in the Christian Church there ought to be no sacerdotal caste above believers. Only one friend of the Reformation, a simple layman, Macrin, schoolmaster at Soleure, was present. He at first shunned the contest by changing his seat to another table. But at last, no longer able to endure the furious invectives of the guests, he stood up boldly, and exclaimed, "Yes, all true Christians are priests, and offer sacrifice according to the words of St. Peter, ' *You are a royal priesthood.*'" At these words, one of the most intrepid bawlers, the dean of Burgdorff, a tall, stout man, with a stentorian voice, uttered a loud laugh. "You little Greeks and school rats! You a royal priesthood! . . . Beautiful priesthood! . . . Mendicant kings! . . . priests without prebends and benefices!"[3] And instantly all the priests and monks fell with one accord on the impudent laic.

But it was in Lucerne that the bold step of the men of Einsidlen was to produce the strongest sensation. The Diet had met in this town, and complaints arrived from all quarters against the rash preachers who were preventing Helvetia from quietly selling the blood of her sons to the stranger. On the 22nd July, as Oswald Myconius was entertaining canon Kilchmeyer, and several other friends of the gospel, at dinner, a boy, sent by Zuinglius, knocked at the door.[4] He was the bearer of the two famous petitions from Einsidlen, and of a letter from Zuinglius, which requested Oswald to circulate them in Lucerne. "My advice is, that the thing be done quietly, by degrees, rather than all at once; but, for the love of Christ, it is necessary to forsake everything, even wife."

Thus the crisis approached in Lucerne: the shell had fallen, and could not but burst. The guests read the petitions. "May God bless this beginning,"[5] said Oswald, looking up to heaven, and then added, "This prayer must, from this moment, be the constant

[1] Da liess die Stube einen grossen Knall. (Fusslin Beytr. iv, 39.)   [2] Cum invalescente Baccho, disputationes, imo verius jurgia ... (Zw. Ep. i, 230.) With the progress of the wine disputes, nay, rather brawls, began.   [3] Estote ergo Græculi ac Donatistæ regale sacerdotium. (Ibid., p. 230.)   [4] Venit puer, quam misisti, inter prandendum. ·. . . . (Ibid., p. 209.)   [5] Deus cœpta fortunet! (Ibid., p. 210.)

occupation of our hearts." The petitions were forthwith circulated, perhaps with more ardour than Zuinglius had requested. But the moment was singular. Eleven individuals, the flower of the clergy, had placed themselves in the breach : it was necessary to enlighten men's minds, to fix the irresolute, and gain over the most influential members of the Diet.

Oswald, in the midst of this labour, did not forget his friend. The young messenger had told him of the attacks which Zuinglius had to endure from the monks at Zurich. Writing him the same day, he says, "The truth of the Holy Spirit is invincible. Armed with the shield of the Holy Scriptures you have remained conqueror, not in one combat only, nor in two, but in three, and the fourth is now commencing. . . . . Seize those powerful weapons which are harder than diamond! Christ, in order to protect his people, has need only of his Word. Your struggles give indomitable courage to all who have devoted themselves to Jesus Christ."[1]

At Lucerne, the petitions did not produce the result anticipated. Some pious men approved of them, but these were few in number. Several, fearing to compromise themselves, were unwilling either to praise or blame.[2] "These folks," said others, "will never bring this affair to a good end!" All the priests murmured, grumbled, and muttered between their teeth. As to the people, they were loud against the gospel. A rage for war was awakened in Lucerne after the bloody defeat of Bicoque, and engrossed all thoughts.[3] Oswald, who was an attentive observer of these different impressions, felt his courage shaken. The evangelical future which he had anticipated for Lucerne and Switzerland seemed to vanish. "Our people," said he, uttering a deep sigh, "are blind to the things of heaven. In regard to the glory of Christ, there is no hope of the Swiss."[4]

Wrath prevailed, especially in the Council and the Diet. The pope, France, England, and the empire, all around Switzerland, was in agitation after the defeat of Bicoque, and the evacuation of Lombardy by the French under Lautrec. Were not political interests at that moment complicated enough before these eleven men came with their petitions to mingle religious questions with them? The deputies of Zurich alone were favourably disposed to the gospel. Canon Xylotect, afraid for his own life and that of his wife, (he had married into one of the first families in the country,) had refused, with tears of regret, to repair to Einsidlen and sign the addresses. Canon Kilchmeyer had shown greater courage. He, too,

---

[1] Is permaneas, qui es, in Christo Jesu . . . . (Zw. Ep. p. 210.)   [2] Boni qui pauci sunt, commendant libellos vestros ; alii non laudant nec vituperant. (Ibid., p. 210.)   [3] Belli furor occupat omnia. (Ibid.)   [4] Nihil ob id apud Helvetios agendum de iis rebus quæ Christi gloriam possunt augere. (Ibid.)

had everything to fear. "Condemnation threatens me," he writes to Zuinglius', on the 13th August; "I await it without fear . . ." As he was writing these words, an officer of the council entered the room, and cited him to appear next day."[1] "If they put me in irons," said he, continuing his letter, "I claim your help; but it will be easier to transport a rock from our Alps than to move me a finger's breadth from the word of Jesus Christ." The regard which was deemed due to his family, and the resolution which they had taken to let the storm fall upon Oswald, saved the canon.

Berthold Haller, probably because he was not a Swiss, had not signed the petitions. But full of courage, he, like Zuinglius, expounded the gospel according to Matthew. A vast crowd filled the cathedral of Berne. The word of God operated more powerfully on the people than Manuel's dramas. Haller was summoned to the Town House; the people accompanied their good-natured pastor, and remained around the spot. The council was divided. " This concerns the bishop," said the leading men. "The preacher must be handed over to my lord of Lausanne." The friends of Haller trembled at these words, and told him to withdraw as quickly as possible. The people flocked round, and accompanied him to his house, where a great number of burghers remained in arms prepared to make a rampart of their bodies in defence of their humble pastor. The bishop and council were overawed by this energetic demonstration, and Haller was saved. Haller was not the only combatant at Berne. Sebastian Meyer at this time refuted the pastoral letter of the Bishop of Constance, and in particular the formidable charge, "that the gospellers teach a new doctrine, but that the old doctrine is the true." "To be wrong for two thousand years," said Meyer, "is not to be right for a single hour; otherwise the heathen ought to have adhered to their belief. If the most ancient doctrines must carry the day, fifteen hundred years are more than five hundred years, and the gospel is more ancient than the ordinances of the pope."[2]

At this period the magistrates of Friburg intercepted letters addressed to Haller and Meyer by a canon of Friburg, named John Hollard, a native of Orb. They imprisoned, then deposed, and at last banished him. John Vannius, a chorister in the cathedral, shortly after embraced the evangelical doctrine; for in the Christian warfare one soldier no sooner falls than another takes his place. "How could the muddy water of the Tiber," said Vannius, "sub-

---

[1] Tu vero audi. Hæc dum scriberem, irruit præco, a Senatoribus missus . . . (Zw. Ep. 213.) [2] Simml. Samml. vi.

sist beside the pure water which Luther has drawn from the spring
of St. Paul." But the chorister's mouth was also closed. Myconius wrote to Zuinglius, " Scarcely will you find in Switzerland
men more averse to the gospel than the Friburghers." [1]

Lucerne ought to have been stated as an exception. This Myconius knew. He had not signed the famous petitions, but his
friends had if he had not, and a victim was required. The ancient
literature of Greece and Rome began, thanks to him, to shed some
light in Lucerne; numbers arrived from different quarters to attend
the learned professor, and the friends of peace were charmed with
sounds sweeter than those of halberds, swords, and cuirasses, which
alone had hitherto resounded in the warlike city. Oswald had
sacrificed everything for his country. He had quitted Zurich and
Zuinglius; he had lost his health; his wife was pining; [2] his son was
in childhood; if even Lucerne rejected him he could nowhere hope
for an asylum. But no matter; factions have no pity, and the
thing which ought to excite their compassion stimulates their rage.
Herbenstein, burgomaster of Lucerne, an old and valiant warrior
who had gained a distinguished name in the wars of Suabia and
Burgundy, followed up the deposition of the teacher, and wished
to banish, from the canton, with himself, his Greek, his Latin, and
his gospel. He succeeded. On coming out of the Council, after the
sederunt at which Myconius had been deposed, Herbenstein met
the Zurich deputy, Bergner. "We are sending you back your
schoolmaster," said he to him ironically, " get a good lodging for
him." " We wont let him sleep in the open air," [3] immediately
replied the courageous deputy. But Bergner promised more than
he could perform.

The news given by the burgomaster were but too true, and were
soon intimated to the unhappy Myconius. He is deposed and
banished, and the only crime laid to his charge is that of being a
disciple of Luther. [4] He looks all around but nowhere finds a
shelter. He sees his wife, his son, and himself, all three feeble and
sickly, exiled from their country, and Switzerland, all around
agitated by a whirlwind, which breaks and destroys every thing
that stands in its way. " Here," said he then to Zuinglius, " is
poor Myconius banished by the council of Lucerne. [5] . . . Whither
shall I go? I know not . . . Assailed yourself by these furious
storms how could you shelter me? I cry then in my distress to
that God who is the first in whom I hope, who is ever bountiful, ever

---

[1] Hoc audio vix alios esse per Helvetiam, qui pejus velint sanæ doctrinæ. (Zw. Ep.
p. 226.)   [2] Conjux infirma. (Ibid. p. 192.)   [3] Veniat! efficiemus enim ne dor-
miendum sit ei sub dio. (Ibid. p. 216.) Let him come, we will see to it that he do not
sleep in the open air.   [4] Nil exprobrarunt nisi quod sim Lutheranus. (Ibid.)
[5] Expellitur ecce miser Myconius a Senatu Lucernano. (Ibid., p. 215.)

kind, and who never calls upon any to seek his face in vain. May He supply my wants!"

Thus spoke Oswald, and he was not obliged to wait long for a word of consolation. There was one in Switzerland inured to the battles of the faith. Zuinglius drew near to his friend, and comforting him, thus expressed himself, "The blows by which men attempt to overthrow the house of God are so violent, and the assaults which they make upon it so frequent that not only do the wind and rain beat upon it, as our Saviour predicted, (Matt. vii, 27,) but the hail and the thunder.[1] Had I not perceived the Lord guiding the ship I should, long ere now, have cast the helm into the sea, but I see him amid the tempest, strengthening the tackling, arranging the yards, stretching the sails, what do I say? commanding the very winds . . . Should I not then be a coward unworthy of the name of a man if I abandoned my post and fled to a shameful death? I confide entirely in his sovereign goodness. Let him govern, transport, hasten, retard, precipitate, arrest, break down, let him even plunge us to the bottom of the abyss, we fear nothing.[2] We are vessels which belong to him. He can use us as he pleases, for honour or disgrace." After words thus full of faith Zuinglius continues. "As to your case this is my opinion. Present yourself before the council, and there deliver an address worthy of Christ and of yourself, that is to say, proper to touch and not to irritate men's hearts. Deny that you are a disciple of Luther, declare that you are a disciple of Jesus Christ. Let your pupils surround you, and let them speak, and if all this does not succeed, come to your friend, come to Zuinglius, and consider our home as your own fireside."

Oswald, strengthened by these words, followed the noble counsel of the Reformer, but all his efforts were useless. The witness to the truth behoved to quit his country. His enemies in Lucerne were so loud against him, that the magistrates would not allow any one to give him an asylum. Broken-hearted at the sight of so much enmity, the confessor of Jesus Christ exclaimed, "All that now remains for me is to beg from door to door to sustain my miserable life."[3] Shortly after, the friend and most powerful assistant of Zuinglius, the first man in Switzerland who had united literary instruction with the love of the gospel, the reformer of Lucerne, and at a later period one of the leaders of the Helvetic church, was obliged, with his sickly wife and little boy, to quit this ungrateful city, where, out of all his family, the only one who had

---

[1] Nec ventos esse, nec imbres, sed grandines et fulmina. (Zw. Ep. p. 217.)
[2] Regat, vehat, festinet, maneat, acceleret, moretur, mergat! . . . Ibid.
[3] Ostiatim quærere quod edam. (Ibid., p. 245.)

received the gospel was a sister. He crossed its ancient bridges, and bade adieu to those mountains which seem to rise from the bosom of the lake of Waldstetten up to the clouds. Canons Xylotect and Kilchmeyer, the only friends whom the Reformation yet numbered among his countrymen, followed shortly after. And, at the moment when this poor man, with two feeble companions, whose existence depended on him, with his eye turned towards its lake, and shedding tears for his deluded country, took leave of those sublime scenes which had surrounded his cradle, the gospel itself took leave of Lucerne, and Rome reigns in it to this day.

Shortly after the Diet itself, which was assembled at Baden, stung by the petitions of Einsidlen, (which, being printed, produced a great sensation,) and urged by the Bishop of Constance to strike a blow at innovations, had recourse to measures of persecution, ordered the authorities of the villages to bring before it all priests and laymen who should speak against the faith, seized, in its impatience, on the evangelist, who happened to be nearest at hand, Urban Weiss, pastor of Filispach, who had been previously released on caution, made him be brought to Constance, and then gave him up to the bishop, by whom he was long kept in prison. "Thus," says the Chronicle of Bullinger, "the persecution of the gospel by the confederates commenced, and that at the instigation of the clergy, who have at all times delivered Jesus Christ to Herod and Pilate."[1]

Zuinglius was not to escape his share of trial. Blows to which he was most sensible were then struck at him. The rumour of his doctrines and his contests had passed Santis, penetrated the Tockenburg, and reached the heights of Wildhaus. The pastoral family from whom the Reformer had sprung were moved. Of the four brothers of Zuinglius, some had continued peacefully to occupy themselves with their mountain toils, whilst others, to the great grief of their brother, had quitted their flocks and served foreign princes. All were alarmed at the news which rumour brought as far as their chalets. They already saw their brother seized, dragged perhaps to Constance to his bishop, and a pile erected for him at the same place which had consumed the body of John Huss. These proud shepherds could not bear the idea of being called the brother of a heretic. They wrote to Ulric, describing their sorrow and their fears. Zuinglius replied, " So long as God permits, I will perform the task which he has entrusted to me, without fearing the world and its proud tyrants. I know the

---

[1] **Uss anstifften der geistlecten, Die zu allen Zyten Christum Pilato und Herodi vür-stellen. (MS.)**

worst that can happen to me. There is no danger, no misfortune which I have not long carefully weighed. My own strength is mere nothingness, and I know the power of my enemies, but I know also that I can do everything through Christ strengthening me. Were I silent, some other would be constrained to do what God now does by me, and I would be punished by God. Cast far from you all your anxiety, my dear brothers. If I have a fear, it is that I have been gentler and more easily persuaded than is suitable for this age.[1] What shame, you say, will be cast on all our family if you are burnt, or put to death in some other way![2] O, dearly beloved brethren! the gospel derives from the blood of Christ this wondrous nature, that the most violent persecutions far from arresting, only hasten its progress. Those only are true soldiers of Christ who fear not to bear in their body the wounds of their Master. All my labours have no other end than to make men know the treasures of happiness which Christ has acquired for us, in order that all may flee to the Father through the death of his Son. If his doctrine offends you, your anger cannot stop me. You are my brothers, yes, my own brothers, the sons of my father, and the offspring of the same mother . . . . but if you were not my brethren in Christ, and in the work of faith, my grief would be so extreme that nothing could equal it. Adieu. I will never cease to be your true brother, provided you do not yourselves cease to be the brethren of Jesus Christ."[3] .

The confederates seemed to rise against the gospel as one man. The petitions of Einsidlen had been the signal. Zuinglius, concerned for the lot of his dear Myconius, saw in this misfortune only the beginning of calamity. Enemies in Zurich: enemies abroad— a man's own relatives becoming his enemies,—a furious opposition on the part of monks and priests,—violent measures of the Diet and the councils,—rude, perhaps bloody, assaults on the part of the partisans of foreign service,—the highest valleys of Switzerland, the cradle of the confederation, sending forth phalanxes of invincible soldiers to save Rome, and, at the sacrifice of life, annihilating the growing faith of the sons of the Reformation—such was the prospect at which the penetrating mind of the Reformer shuddered when he beheld it in the distance. What a prospect! Was not the work, scarcely well begun, on the point of being destroyed? Zuinglius, thoughtful and agitated, spread all his anguish before his God. " O Jesus," said he, " you see how wicked men and

[1] Plus enim metuo ne forte lenior, mitiorque fuerim. De semper casta Virgine Maria. (Zw. Op. i. p. 104.)　　[2] Si vel igni vel alio quodam supplicii genere tollaris e medio. (ibid.)　　[3] Frater vester germanus nunquam desinam, &c. modo vos fratres Christi esse perrexeritis. (Ibid., p. 107.)

blasphemers stun the ears of thy people with their cries.[1] Thou knowest that from my infancy I have hated disputes, and yet in spite of myself thou hast ceased not to urge me on to the combat . . . Wherefore, I confidently call upon thee, as thou hast begun so to finish. If in any thing I have built up improperly, beat it down with thy mighty hand. If I have laid some other foundation beside thine let thy powerful arm overthrow it.[2] O most beloved vine, of which the Father is the vine-dresser, and of which we are the branches, forsake not thy offsping.[3] For thou hast promised to be with us, even to the end of the world ! "

It was on the 22nd of August, 1522, that Ulrich Zuinglius, the Reformer of Switzerland, when he saw violent storms descending from the mountains on the frail bark of faith, thus expressed the troubles and hopes of his soul in the presence of his God.

[1] Vides enim, piissime Jesu, aures eorum septas esse nequissimis susurronibus, sycophantis, lucrionibus . . . (Zw. Op. iii, p. 74.) For thou seest, O most beloved Jesus how these ears are beset with whisperers, sycophants, and lovers of lucre.

[2] Si fundamentum aliud præter te jecero, demoliaris. (Ibid.) [3] O suavissima vitis, cujus vinitor, Pater, palmites vero nos sumus ; stationem tuam ne deseras. (Ibid.)

 END OF THE SECOND VOLUME.

GLASGOW : JAMES KAY, PRINTER.